CRIME FILMS

This book surveys the entire range of crime films, including important subgenres such as the gangster film, the private-eye film, film noir, as well as the victim film, the erotic thriller, and the crime comedy. Focusing on ten films that span the range of the twentieth century, from *Fury* (1936) to *Fargo* (1996), Thomas Leitch traces the transformation of the three leading figures that are common to all crime films: the criminal, the victim, and the avenger. Analyzing how each of the subgenres establishes oppositions among its ritual antagonists, he shows how the distinctions among them become blurred throughout the course of the century. This blurring, Leitch maintains, reflects and fosters a deep social ambivalence toward crime and criminals, while the criminal, victim, and avenger characters effectively map the shifting relations between subgenres, such as the erotic thriller and the police film, within the larger genre of crime film that informs them all.

Thomas Leitch is Professor of English and Director of Film Studies at the University of Delaware. A contributing editor of *Literature/Film Quarterly,* he is the author of *What Stories Are: Narrative Theory and Interpretation* and *The Encyclopedia of Alfred Hitchcock.*

GENRES IN AMERICAN CINEMA

General Editor
Barry Keith Grant, *Brock University, Ontario, Canada*

Genres in American Cinema examines the significance of American films in a series of single-authored volumes, each dedicated to a different genre. Each volume will provide a comprehensive account of its genre, from enduring classics to contemporary revisions, from marginal appropriations to international inflections, emphasizing its distinctive qualities as well as its cultural, historical, and critical contexts. Their approach will be methodologically broad, balancing theoretical and historical discussion with close readings of representative films. Designed for use as classroom texts, the books will be intellectually rigorous, yet written in a style that is lively and accessible to students and general audiences alike.

CRIME FILMS

Thomas Leitch
University of Delaware

CAMBRIDGE
UNIVERSITY PRESS

PUBLISHED BY THE PRESS SYNDICATE OF THE UNIVERSITY OF CAMBRIDGE
The Pitt Building, Trumpington Street, Cambridge, United Kingdom

CAMBRIDGE UNIVERSITY PRESS
The Edinburgh Building, Cambridge CB2 2RU, UK
40 West 20th Street, New York, NY 10011–4211, USA
477 Williamstown Road, Port Melbourne, VIC 3207, Australia
Ruiz de Alarcón 13, 28014 Madrid, Spain
Dock House, The Waterfront, Cape Town 8001, South Africa
http://www.cambridge.org

First published 2002

Printed in the United Kingdom at the University Press, Cambridge

Typefaces Cheltenham 10/13 pt. and Clearface   *System* Quark XPress™   [MG]

A catalog record for this book is available from the British Library

Library of Congress Cataloging-in-Publication Data
Leitch, Thomas M.
Crime films / Thomas Leitch.
    p.   cm. – (Genres in American cinema)
Filmography: p.
Includes bibliographical references and index.
ISBN 0-521-64106-3 (hb) – ISBN 0-521-64671-5 (pb)
1. Detective and mystery films – United States – History and criticism.
2. Gangster films – United States – History and criticism.   3. Police films – United
States – History and criticism.   I. Title.   II. Series.
PN1995.9.D4 L45 2002

                                                                    2001052965

ISBN 0 521 64106 3 hardback
ISBN 0 521 64671 5 paperback

To Gloria A. Leitch

Thanks, Mom

Contents

Illustrations

Acknowledgments

Both Barry Grant, my series editor, and Michael Gnat, my production editor, have been so helpful and generous with suggestions for improving this book that if it were a Hollywood movie, either one of them could have delayed its release for months by claiming a coauthorship credit, and I humbly acknowledge both their help and their forbearance. The stills illustrating this volume came from Jerry Ohlinger's Movie Materials Store and the archives of *Literature/Film Quarterly*, which Jim and Anne Welsh graciously allowed me to plunder. I am grateful to Judith Leitch and Beatrice Rehl for timely technical advice, and to Lisa Elliott for everything else. Finally, I offer my heartfelt appreciation to the University of Delaware undergraduates who for ten years have helped provoke my thinking about crime films by their willingness not only to engage in endless discussions of films noirs and gangster movies, but to sign up for courses with such unlikely titles as Victim Films and Comedies of Crime. Here's looking at you, kids.

1

The Problem of the Crime Film

The crime film is the most enduringly popular of all Hollywood genres, the only kind of film that has never once been out of fashion since the dawn of the sound era seventy years ago. It is therefore surprising to discover that, at least as far as academic criticism is concerned, no such genre exists. Carlos Clarens's magisterial study *Crime Movies* (1980) begins by criticizing Robert Warshow's seminal essay "The Gangster as Tragic Hero" (1948) for its narrow definition of the gangster film, based on liberal social assumptions that "limited genres to one dimension apiece." Yet Clarens's definition of the crime film is equally delimited by its pointed exclusion of "psychological thriller[s]" like *Shadow of a Doubt* (1943), *Laura* (1944), and *Kiss Me Deadly* (1955) from its purview on the grounds that their characters are insufficiently emblematic of "the Criminal, the Law, and Society."[1] Larry Langman and Daniel Finn place themselves outside the debate over whether or not crime films include psychological thrillers by announcing in the Preface to their encyclopedic reference, *A Guide to American Crime Films of the Forties and Fifties:* "The American crime film does not belong to any genre. . . . Instead, it embodies many genres."[2] But their attempt to rise above the problem of classification merely indicates how deeply entrenched that problem is.

None of this academic quibbling has prevented crime films from retaining their popularity, or even from entering universities as the object of closer scrutiny. But subgenres of the crime film, like the gangster film of the 1930s and the film noir of the 1940s, have been more often, and more successfully, theorized than the forbiddingly broad genre of the crime film itself – this genre that is not a genre, even though an enormous audience recognizes and enjoys it, and a substantial following is interested in analyzing it critically. The unabated popularity of mystery and detective fiction, the burgeoning of such recent literary subgenres as the serial-killer novel and the novel of legal intrigue, the efflorescence of true-crime books, and the well-publicized criminal trials that keep Court TV in business all attest to the American public's fascination with narratives of crime. The crime film therefore represents an enormously promising, but hitherto neglected, focus for a genre approach to cultural studies.

To the question of whether the crime film is a genre or an umbrella term for a collection of diverse genres like the gangster film, the detective film, and the police film must be added another question: What does it matter? After all, what difference does it make whether the film noir is a genre or a subheading of a broader genre? To anyone but a few scholars of genre studies, these questions might seem inconsequential to the widespread understanding and enjoyment of crime films.

It is exactly this understanding and enjoyment, though, that are at issue in the definition of any genre. Raymond Bellour has pointed out that viewers for Hollywood musicals like *Gigi* (1958) are able to put aside their general expectation that each scene will advance the plot because of their familiarity with the more specific convention of musicals that successive scenes often present lyrical, tonal, or meditative "rhymes" instead, so that a scene of Gigi explaining how she feels troubled and baffled by love is logically followed by a scene in which Gaston professes similar feelings, even if there is no causal link between the two.[3] On a more practical level, it is viewers' familiarity with the conventions of the musical that prevents them from cringing in bewilderment or distaste when the story stops dead so that Fred Astaire can dance or Elvis Presley can sing. Learning the generic rules of musicals does not necessarily allow viewers to enjoy them more, but it does allow them to predict more accurately whether they are likely to enjoy them at all. It is therefore a matter of some importance to many viewers whether or not films like *The Wizard of Oz* (1939) and *Aladdin* (1992) are categorized as musicals, for their feelings about musicals are likely to influence how much they will enjoy such films, or whether they are likely to watch them in the first place. This is not to say that only viewers who like musicals will like *The Wizard of Oz* and *Aladdin*. Both films, in fact, are well-known for appealing to many viewers who do not ordinarily watch musicals; but appreciative viewers who recognize either film as a musical are more likely to be receptive to other films that resemble them, confirming the importance of genre in accurately predicting their enjoyment.

In the same way, asking whether films like *Bonnie and Clyde* (1967) and *The Wild Bunch* (1969) are westerns, even if different viewers answer the question differently, acknowledges the ways each film's affinities to the western – its similarities in mise-en-scène, action, and moral problems to those of the western – places them in a context that helps to sharpen and illuminate them. A familiarity with John Wayne's outsized heroic persona in westerns like *Stagecoach* (1939) and *Fort Apache* (1948) deepens viewers' understanding of the more problematic but equally outsized heroes he plays in later westerns like *Red River* (1948), *The Searchers* (1956), and *The Shootist* (1976). In each case, the conventions of the western provide a context that may make Wayne's actions more ironic, tragic, or elegiac – certainly more richly nuanced and comprehensible.

Viewers use many contexts, smaller or larger than established genres like the western, to interpret conventions of action and performance. Most viewers watching *Stagecoach,* for example, assume that Wayne's character, the Ringo Kid, will survive his climactic shootout with the Plummer family, even though he is outmanned and outgunned, because the survival of characters played by John Wayne is statistically an excellent bet and because the conventions of classical Hollywood narrative films[4] like *Stagecoach* make it more likely that Ringo will proceed to a rousingly heroic climax rather than survive a hazardous attack by Geronimo's braves only to be shot down on his arrival in Lordsburg. Even more fundamentally, most viewers assume that a climactic shootout will take place in the streets of Lordsburg because the conventions of classical Hollywood narrative predicate the resolution of the leading announced conflicts and an economy of representation that requires each person traveling in the stagecoach to fulfill the promise of his character and reveal his true nature. But all these expectations are generic, based as they are on a knowledge of the wider, though by no means universal, genre of classical Hollywood narrative within which the western occupies a place that gives its own conventions their special potency.

Because viewers understand and enjoy movies largely through their knowledge of the generic conventions, the question of whether gangster films have enough in common with whodunits and erotic thrillers to constitute a single genre of crime films is important to many more

people than just film scholars. Even viewers who think they are inter-
preting Brian De Palma's remake of *Scarface* (1983) exclusively in light
of the conventions of the gangster genre – or, more narrowly, in light
of its departures from Howard Hawks's 1932 film of the same title –
may well be seeing it in the context of the broader genre of the crime
film. The example of *Stagecoach* suggests that genres characteristi-
cally nest in one another, the most sharply focused (the John Wayne
western, for instance) drawing their powers from their specific transformations and adaptations of the conventions of broader genres like
the western or still broader genres like the classical Hollywood narrative. Although viewers are most likely to be consciously aware of the
narrowest genres, the broader genres that are operating simultaneously are equally, though less visibly, influential in directing their responses. Because every genre is a subgenre of a wider genre from
whose contexts its own conventions take their meaning, it makes
sense to think of the gangster film as both a genre on its own terms
and a subgenre of the crime film.

If a genre can be as specific as the John Wayne western or as general as the well-made Hollywood narrative, then it is clearly possible
to defend the crime film as a genre simply by installing it at a level of
generality somewhere between the gangster film and the classical
Hollywood narrative. But such a solution would prove nothing at all;
it would merely introduce still another category to a field already
crisscrossed with genre markers. The aim of this book is therefore not
simply to introduce a new generic category of the crime film but to
explain how such a category has already been operating to inform
viewers' understanding and enjoyment of such apparently diverse
genres as the gangster film, the film noir, and the crime comedy.

Establishing the crime film as a genre as rich as those of the western
or the horror film – or, for that matter, the gangster film or the film noir
– raises the problems involved in defining any genre. Genre theorists
have long recognized this as a chicken-and-egg problem. If a genre like
the western can be defined only in terms of its members, but the members can be recognized as such only by viewers who are already familiar with the genre, how can viewers recognize any genre without
already having seen every film arguably within its boundaries?[5] The
short answer to this question is that they can't; hence the disagree-
ments that inevitably arise over whether *The Wizard of Oz* is to count
as a musical by viewers who have different ideas about what a musical is. A contrary answer is that they can, despite the lack of theoret-

ical justification. Even if theorists were to demonstrate that the western was a logically indefensible category, nonspecialist viewers would go on referring to it because it is so useful and, except at its boundaries, so easily recognized. Most people can recognize their friends more easily than they can describe them because different skills are involved in recognition and description, so that even Supreme Court Justice Potter Stewart's oft-ridiculed pronouncement that he couldn't define pornography, but "I know it when I see it," makes sense.[6]

Recognizing genre conventions is clearly a developmental process. Few children understand the conventions of Hollywood westerns, but most adults do. Adults have gradually picked up the conventions through exposure to particular examples of the genre, because their understanding of the genre and of particular examples of it have been mutually reinforcing. When revisionist westerns like *Duel in the Sun* (1946) or *Unforgiven* (1992) appear, they are either dismissed as nonwesterns or antiwesterns, sharpening the genre's definition through their exclusion, or they succeed in redefining the whole notion of the western by exploring new possibilities implicit in the genre. The mutability of generic conventions makes it clear that genres are best thought of as contexts that evolve in both personal and social history, the contingent results of ongoing transactions between viewers and movies, rather than eternally fixed and mutually exclusive categories.[7]

Even given this transactional, evolutionary concept of genres, there will always be debates about films on the margins of any particular genre, since many viewers believe, for example, that *Singin' in the Rain* (1952) feels more like a musical than *Fun in Acapulco* (1963). Some fifteen years ago, Rick Altman proposed a distinction between syntactic and semantic definitions of genre to account for the phenomenon of musicals that have many of the generic markers of musicals (a recognized musical star like Elvis Presley sings several numbers) but not others (*Fun in Acapulco* does not explore the thematic relationships between performance and sincerity, public and private life, that are central to musicals like *Singin' in the Rain*).[8] More recently, Altman has suggested "a semantic/syntactic/pragmatic approach to genre" to incorporate into his grammar of textual markers a more systematic awareness of the multiple users and uses even the simplest films find.[9]

It is no wonder that Altman has expanded his earlier theory in the light of the many films marked by conflicting, often shifting generic allegiances. Most westerns from *The Great Train Robbery* (1903) to *Unforgiven* are organized around stories of crime and punishment;

1. *Something Wild:* a crime film, or a screwball comedy gone wrong? (Ray Liotta, Melanie Griffith)

yet few viewers have called them crime films. If *Sunset Blvd.* (1950) is to be counted as film noir because of its confining mise-en-scène, its trapped hero, and its use of a fatalistic flashback, should *Citizen Kane* (1941) be counted as noir too? Is *Something Wild* (1986) [Fig. 1] a crime film or a screwball comedy gone wrong? Critics have often coined nonce terms like "superwestern" and "neo-noir" to describe films that transform or combine elements from different genres, but these terms raise as many problems as they solve. If *Outland* (1981) is an outer-space western – *High Noon* (1952) in space – is *Assault on Precinct 13* (1976), John Carpenter's homage to *Rio Bravo* (1959), an inner-city western?

This problem of cross-generic allegiances persists even within the crime film.[10] Is *The Thin Man* (1934) a private-eye story or a crime comedy? Is *The Maltese Falcon* (1941) a hard-boiled detective story or a film noir? *The Usual Suspects* (1995) combines elements of the gangster film and the whodunit; how is it to be classified? What to make of police films that are also studies of criminals, like *The Untouchables* (1987) and *The Silence of the Lambs* (1991) [Fig. 2]? And what about

2. *The Silence of the Lambs:* A police film that is also a study of a monstrous criminal. (Anthony Hopkins)

White Heat (1949), which combines a gangster hero, a film-noir heroine, an undercover cop, and an extended prison sequence that borrows the conventions of many another prison film? These problems
are not solved by using the genre of the crime film to dissolve all distinctions among its long-recognized subgenres; nor are they solved by
declaring one subgenre the categorical victor and ignoring the claims
of others. It makes sense, in such a work of classification as the bibli-
ography to Barry Grant's *Film Genre: Theory and Criticism*, to exclude
gangster films from the crime-film genre on the grounds that "that
group of films is clearly defined to the extent that it can be understood
as comprising a distinct and separate genre."[11] But the distinctiveness
of the gangster film's conventions cannot support an argument for any
essential distinction between gangster films and crime films, because
there is no reason to assume that distinctive genres are parallel and
mutually exclusive. The caper film, for example, has its own distinctive generic rules, but those rules do not prevent it from being widely
recognized as a subgenre of an even more well-established genre, the
gangster film, whose gangsters have been assembled in caper films on
an ad hoc basis for a particular job.

Instead of attempting to construct genres that are mutually exclusive, it would be more judicious to agree with Janet Staiger that "Hollywood films have never been pure instances of genres,"[12] from D. W.
Griffith's combination of historical epic, war movie, domestic melodrama, and racial propaganda in *The Birth of a Nation* (1915) to George
Lucas's revitalization of science fiction in *Star Wars* (1977) by recycling
the story of Akira Kurosawa's samurai comedy-drama *The Hidden For-
tress* (*Kakushi toride no san akunin,* 1958), itself based largely on the
conventions of the Hollywood western.

The multiple generic allegiances of most films, however, are obscured by the fact that some such allegiances have historically overridden others. Any story presented in animated form, from the musical romance *Beauty and the Beast* (1991) to the epic *Lord of the Rings*
(1978), will automatically be classified as a cartoon because the animated cartoon is a stronger genre than the genres of romance and
epic. Virtually any story with a setting in nineteenth-century western
America will be classified as a western, because the claims of the western override the claims of competing genres. Films like *Harlan County,
U.S.A.* (1976) and *Hoop Dreams* (1994) are commonly classified together as documentaries rather than distinguished in terms of their subject matter. In the same way, films like *Blazing Saddles* (1974) and *The*

Naked Gun: From the Files of Police Squad! (1988) are classified as parodies rather than as members of the various genres whose conventions they mock, because their parodic intent trumps their affinities with the specific genres they are sending up.

What makes a genre strong? The example of the cartoon, the strongest of all popular genres, suggests that the most powerful generic claims are based on mise-en-scène. Crime-and-punishment tales like *Winchester 73* (1950) and *Rancho Notorious* (1952) are classified as westerns rather than crime films because their setting takes precedence over their story. Any movie set in outer space, from *Buck Rogers* (1939) to *Alien* (1979), becomes a science-fiction movie. The reason that film noir is such a strong genre, or subgenre, despite the lack of any clear consensus about what sort of stories it tells, is the powerfully homogeneous sense of visual style that unites such diverse noirs as *The Killers* (1946), *Force of Evil* (1948), and *The Big Combo* (1955).

Almost equally powerful as a generic marker is intent.[13] Any movie whose stated aim is to entertain children will be classified as a children's film or a family film, whatever its plot or characters or setting – unless, of course, it is animated, in which case it will be classified as a cartoon. Comedy, which seeks to make viewers laugh; horror, which seeks to make them scream; documentary, which seeks to inform them about some real-life situation; and parody, which seeks to make fun of other genres – all these are such strong genres that critics have long categorized *Arsenic and Old Lace* (1944) and *Married to the Mob* (1988), for example, as comedies about crime, rather than crime films with some laughs; and reviewers who saw *Mars Attacks!* (1996) as more imitation than parody unanimously dismissed the film as a failed parody rather than a successful imitation because they agreed that a parody's first duty is to be funny rather than faithful to its sources.

Weaker genres are based on typological situations (boy meets girl, ordinary characters get into ridiculous scrapes), characters (zombies, monsters, oversexed high-school students, attorneys), or presentational features (the story is periodically interrupted or advanced by dance numbers). Such genres are most likely to be overridden by stronger genres whose claims conflict with theirs. Thus *Abbott and Costello Meet Frankenstein* (1948) is a comedy rather than a monster movie, and the transsexual science-fiction horror parody *The Rocky Horror Picture Show* (1975), however it is categorized, is rarely described as a musical. When Brian Henderson argued that *The Searchers*'s story of rescuers attempting to save a victim who did not want

to be saved actually crossed the boundaries of the western to constitute "an American dilemma," in films as different as *Taxi Driver* (1976)
and *Hardcore* (1979), his premise did not have the effect of establishing a new genre of unwelcome-rescue films because the common story he described did not have the power to override the conflicting generic allegiances of the examples he cited.[14] The disaster genre that
flourished early in the 1970s (*Airport*, 1970; *The Poseidon Adventure*,
1972; *Earthquake*, 1974; *The Towering Inferno*, 1974) shows that small
numbers do not necessarily make a genre weak; but the disaster genre
is easily overridden by the conventions of the parody, as in *Airplane!*
(1980), or the action blockbuster, as in *Jaws* (1975), originally marketed as a disaster movie until it was recognized as inaugurating a far
more profitable, hence stronger, genre.

Lacking the box-office potential of such recent blockbusters as *Independence Day* (1996) and *Titanic* (1997), most genres can best display their strength by articulating the central problems that endow
their stock characters and situations and spectacles with power and
meaning. Even apparently unproblematic genres like the musical and
the cartoon can be seen as organized around problems based on their
distinctive presentational features. Musical performers like Fred Astaire, Gene Kelly, and Judy Garland typically act out rituals dramatizing the complex relationship between realism and artifice, sincerity
and performance, both while they are performing their song-and-
dance numbers and in their characters' more private moments. Their
films use production numbers to raise questions about public and
private identities and the dynamics of self-presentation, particularly
within the ritualistic context of romantic courtship. Similarly, just as
cartoons are defined pictorially by a tension between the highly stylized two-dimensional space in which they are drawn and the more
realistic third dimension they imply, they are defined thematically by
the tension between the requirements of realism (empathetic coming-
of-age rituals for Disney heroes from Pinocchio to Simba) and magic
(from the constant transformations of shapes and animated objects
typical of all Disney cartoons to the playful self-reflexiveness of Warner Bros.' *Duck Amuck,* 1953).

No matter how it is defined, the crime film will never be as strong a
genre as the cartoon, the horror film, or the parody. It lacks both the
instantly recognizable mise-en-scène of the animated film (or even the
compellingly stylized visuals of the film noir) and the singleness of intent of the horror film or the parody. But the crime film is a stronger

3. *Pulp Fiction:* A noir world of criminals like Jules Winnfield (Samuel L. Jackson) without the noir visual style.

genre than theorists of subgenres like the gangster film and the film noir have acknowledged. In fact, it is a stronger genre than the criminal subgenres that have commanded more attention, not only because its scope is by definition broader than theirs, but because the problem it addresses as a genre, the problem that defines it as a genre, places the film noir and the gangster film in a more sharply illuminating context by showing that each of those is part of a coherent larger project.

The defining problem of the crime film is best approached through the specific problems involved in establishing it as a genre. Should the crime film be defined in terms of its subject, its effect, or its visual style? Many crime films adopt the visual conventions of film noir (low-key, high-contrast lighting, unbalanced compositions, night-for-night exterior shooting), but others do not. If the noir visual style is a defining feature of the crime film, how are color films like *Leave Her to Heaven* (1945), *Chinatown* (1974), and *Pulp Fiction* (1994) [Fig. 3] to be categorized?

If the noir visual style seems to produce too narrow a definition of the crime film, its characteristic subject, crime, and its frequently

sought effect, suspense,[15] are impossibly broad. Both crime and suspense have an important role in a very great number of movies. *The
English Patient* (1996) presents several important crimes, from robbery to murder, and a detective figure in David Caravaggio (Willem
Dafoe); do those elements make it a crime film? Every classical Hollywood narrative depends on some disruption of the social order for its
conflict, and an enormous number of social disruptions (e.g., the fire
in *The Towering Inferno*, which is started by the illegal installation
of substandard wiring) are rooted in crimes. It would surely be im-
practical to call every film in which a crime produces the central dramatic situation a crime film. The touchstone of suspense is even more
hopelessly vague, since suspense might be called a defining feature
of the well-made Hollywood narrative. Even Jane Austen adaptations
from *Pride and Prejudice* (1940) to *Emma* (1996) depend on the suspense generated by the questions of who will marry whom, and how
the anticipated happy ending can be compassed. How can the crime
film be distinguished from the broader category of the classical Hollywood narrative, and how useful is such a vaguely defined genre likely
to be?

The problem of defining the crime film is exacerbated by three problems implicit in its subject. John G. Cawelti has noted that popular narrative genres almost by definition package "the ultimate excitements
of love and death" within the most reassuring generic formulas in order to appeal to both viewers' flight from ennui and their love of security.[16] In crime film, this paradox is linked to the question of crime's normalcy. By definition crime is an aberration, a disruption to the normal
workings of society; yet crime films invariably treat crime as normal
even as they observe the ways it undermines the social order. Gangsters do nothing all day long but smuggle or steal. Police officers pursue criminals for a living. Every single case a private eye like Philip
Marlowe takes on turns criminal; every adaptation of a John Grisham
novel of legal intrigue, even if the initial proceeding is a civil one, ex-
plodes in violence sooner or later. Crime films all profess to solve the
criminal problems they present by means of a happy ending; yet the
frequency of crime in such films suggests that the more general problems posed by crime will never be solved. Is criminal behavior in these
films abnormal or all too normal?

The second problem cuts even deeper. In distinguishing between
the heroes of thrillers, who "almost exclusively represent themselves,"
and the heroes of crime films, who "represent the Criminal, the Law,

and Society," Carlos Clarens implies a distinction between crime as an isolated event (the province of the thriller) and crime as a metaphor for social unrest (the province of the crime film).[17] But how solid is this distinction? In Clarens's terms, the work of Alfred Hitchcock, the filmmaker most closely identified with crime, includes only thrillers rather than crime films; yet critics from Eric Rohmer and Claude Chabrol to Robert Corber have recognized that the criminal plots of all Hitchcock's films, from *The Lodger* (1926) to *Psycho* (1960), have obvious moral and social implications that range far beyond the plight of the characters themselves.[18] When is a cinematic crime a metaphor for an enduring moral dilemma or social upheaval or ideological critique, and when is a crime just a crime?

The third problem concerns what may seem like the most straightforward components of the crime film: its stock characters. Every crime story predicates three leading roles: the criminal who commits the crime, the victim who suffers it, and the avenger or detective who investigates it in the hope of bringing the criminal to justice and reestablishing the social order the crime has disrupted. The three roles could hardly be more clear-cut, yet they everywhere overlap and melt into each other. Gangsters like Vito Corleone are devoted family men concerned only to protect and provide for their loved ones. Victims like Paul Kersey, the bereaved hero of the *Death Wish* franchise (1974–94), turn vigilante in order to avenge their loved ones. Maverick cops like Harry Callahan, in *Dirty Harry* (1971) and its sequels *Magnum Force* (1973), *The Enforcer* (1976), *Sudden Impact* (1983), and *The Dead Pool* (1988), break the law in order to catch criminals they know are guilty. A critique of the justice system is obligatory in Hollywood movies about lawyers, police officers, or private eyes. When the hero is a good cop, he is set against an entire corrupt department, as in *Serpico* (1973), or ends up battling vigilante demons inside himself, as in *The Untouchables*. And Hollywood movies about victims who merely suffer, as opposed to taking arms against their oppressors, are virtually unheard of. Evidently crime films both believe and do not believe in the stock characters at their center; they seem determined to undermine and blur the boundaries of the typological figures that might otherwise stake their surest claim to the status of a single genre.

Although these problems might seem to present insuperable obstacles to the definition of the crime film, they are in fact at the heart of such a definition: for the crime film does not simply *embody* these problems; it is *about* them. Crime films present as their defining subject a crime culture that depends on normalizing the unspeakable, a place where crime is both shockingly disruptive and completely normal. Crime may have different metaphorical valences in different criminal subgenres – it can demonstrate the fragility of the social contract in thrillers about innocent men on the run, attack the economic principles of the establishment in gangster films, express philosophical despair in films noirs, test masculine professionalism in private-eye films – but it is always metaphorical. Every crime in every crime film represents a larger critique of the social or institutional order – either the film's critique or some character's. Finally, crime films dramatize not only the distinctive roles of criminal, victim, and avenger but also their interdependence and their interpenetration.

The problem at the heart of crime films, then, is their attempt to mediate between two logically contradictory projects. Like all popular genres, crime films work primarily by invoking and reinforcing a cherished, but not entirely convincing, series of social bromides: The road to hell is paved with good intentions, the law is above individuals, crime does not pay. Crime films need to reinforce these beliefs, just as viewers want to have them reinforced, in order to confirm the distinctiveness of the moral and legal categories that allow viewers to maintain their sense of social decorum and their own secure place in the social order as law-abiding citizens who know right from wrong, identify with the innocent, and wish to see the guilty punished. It is no surprise that the Hollywood film industry is eager to endorse these bromides, since the industry's continued success depends on the health of the capitalist economy. The moral certitudes on which the industry and its audience agree depend on a series of categorical distinctions among the roles of victim, who ought, according to Hollywood's official morality, to be their natural identification figure; the criminal, who ought by the same token to be the target of their fear and hatred; and the avenging detective, who ought to express the law in its purest yet most personal form.

Viewers for crime films know that these three figures – the innocent victim, the menacing criminal, the detective who incarnates the law – never exist in such pure incarnations, not only because of the requirements of realism and narrative complexity but because they would be utterly uninteresting. The ritual triumph of avenging heroes over criminals is compelling only as ritual; to succeed as narrative, it requires complications and surprises in the conception of the leading roles and their relationships. The fascination of crime films arises precisely from the ways they test the limits of their moral categories, engaging and revealing contradictions in the audience's fantasies of identification by mixing elements from these three different positions, the primary colors of crime films that never occur in isolation. Although crime films typically move toward endings that confirm the moral absolutes incarnated in each of their three primary figures, an equally important function crime films share is to call these primary figures, and the moral absolutes that inspire them, into question by making a case for the heroic or pathetic status of the criminal, questioning the moral authority of the justice system, or presenting innocent characters who seem guilty or guilty characters who seem innocent. Even when the endings of crime films endorse a reassuringly absolutist view of crime and punishment, the middle of such films puts absolutist categories like *hero, authority, innocent, guilty, victim, criminal,* and *avenger* into play, engaging the doubts and reservations about these labels that make them fit subjects for mass entertainment as well as moral debate, and so raising questions that the most emphatically absolutist endings can never entirely resolve.

Crime films always depend on their audience's ambivalence about crime. The master criminal is immoral but glamorous, the maverick police officer is breaking the law in order to catch the criminals, the victim is helpless to take any action except capturing or killing the criminal. It is therefore inevitable that they both insist on the distinctions among criminals, crime solvers, and victims, and that their obsessive focus is on the fluid and troubling boundaries among these categories. Crime films are about the continual breakdown and reestablishment of the borders among criminals, crime solvers, and victims. This paradox is at the heart of all crime films.

Crime films operate by mediating between two powerful but blankly contradictory articles of faith: that the social order that every crime challenges is ultimately well-defined, stable, and justified in consigning different people to the mutually exclusive roles of lawbreakers, law enforcers, and the victims who are the audience's natural identification figures; and that every audience member is not only a potential victim but a potential avenger and a potential criminal under the skin. The audience's ambivalence toward both these premises, and the shifting identifications crime films therefore urge among the fictional roles of lawbreaker, law enforcer, and victim, are the defining feature of the genre, and the feature that indicates the place each variety of crime film has within the larger genre.

Hence the genre of crime films includes all films that focus on any of the three parties to a crime – criminal, victim, avenger – while exploring that party's links to the other two. What defines the genre, however, is not these three typological figures any more than a distinctive plot or visual style, but a pair of contradictory narrative projects: to valorize the distinctions among these three roles in order to affirm the social, moral, or institutional order threatened by crime, and to explore the relations among the three roles in order to mount a critique that challenges that order. This contradictory double project, which has often been obscured by the predominance of subgenres like the gangster film and the film noir over the crime film, underlies the ambivalence of all the crime film's subgenres, including several this book will not consider in detail. White-collar crime films like *Wall Street* (1987) explore the paranoid hypothesis that American capitalism is at its heart criminal; caper films like *The Asphalt Jungle* (1950) present a criminal culture more admirable in its honor and professionalism than the official culture it subverts; prison films from *Brute Force* (1947) to *The Shawshank Redemption* (1994) explore the nature of legal and moral guilt in order to consider how individual humanity can survive the dehumanizing rituals of the prison system.

One final apparent omission deserves fuller mention because, as Carlos Clarens has acknowledged, it goes to the heart of the crime film's definition: the thriller. The crime film has much in common with the thriller; but following Charles Derry's brief definition of the thriller as "films in the shadow of Alfred Hitchcock"[19] reveals that the thriller is not, as Clarens argues, a parallel alternative to the crime film but a subset of it. Although every crime film postulates the same three pivotal figures, different figures predominate in different criminal subgenres. The criminal is most prominent in gangster films and films noirs; the avenging crime solver in detective films, police films, and lawyer films; and the victim in the man-on-the-run films of which Hitchcock made such a specialty. In a larger sense, however, all of Hitchcock's films are about victims. The types of crime films Hitchcock never essayed – films about professional criminals, about ordinary people sucked into committing crimes, about heroic agents of the justice system – make up a virtual catalog of the types of films about criminals and avengers. Despite Hitchcock's bromide, "The more successful the villain, the more successful the picture,"[20] he never makes a criminal the hero of a film without recasting that criminal, from Alice White in *Blackmail* (1929) to Marnie Edgar in *Marnie* (1964), as a victim. Hitchcock's distaste for the police is even more well-known; he regards legal authorities of any sort with suspicion and fear. His abiding interest therefore remains with innocent people who are unjustly suspected of crimes (*North by Northwest,* 1959), or who must confront criminals without any help from the authorities (*Shadow of a Doubt*), or who turn detective in order to clear themselves or save their country (*The 39 Steps,* 1935). Hitchcock's thrillers, indeed thrillers generally, are essentially crime films that focus on the victims of crimes, or of the criminal-justice system.

Including in the definition of crime films all films whose primary subject is criminal culture, whether they focus on criminals, victims, or avengers, may seem to make the genre too broad to be truly useful or distinctive. But the test of this definition, like that of any genre, is neither its narrowness nor its inclusiveness; it is its ability to raise questions that illuminate its members in ways existing modes of thinking about crime films do not. If all genres, as Staiger and Altman suggest, are contingent, evolving, and transactional,[21] the question they raise is not whether or not a particular film is a member of a given genre, but how rewarding it is to discuss it as if it were. Nearly any film, from *The Wizard of Oz* to *The English Patient*, might be considered a crime film. The model of ambivalence toward the categories represented by the criminal, the victim, and legal avenger is not meant to distinguish crime films from non–crime films once and for all, but to suggest a new way of illuminating the whole range of films in which crimes are committed.

2

Historical and Cultural Overview

The roots of the crime film go back far beyond the invention of the movies. Criminals have exercised a particular fascination for the literary imagination whenever social orders have been in flux. Shakespeare's great villains – Aaron the Moor, Richard III, King John, Iago, Edmund, Macbeth – are self-made men who seize opportunities for advancement that would never have arisen in a medieval world whose divinely ordained sense of social order seems to reign, for example, at the beginning of *Richard II*.[1] Criminals, even if they end up as kings, are precisely those people who overstep the bounds appointed by their status at birth, striving each "to rise above the station to which he was born."[2] With the waning of the notion that the social and economic status of kings and peasants alike reflect an eternal, God-given order comes the suspicion that some people may be occupying social places they have no right to – a suspicion that produces the rise of the criminal in literature.

Criminals in American literature are as old as American literature itself. The first important novel to appear in the United States, Charles Brockden Brown's *Wieland; or, The Transformation* (1798), is a supernaturally tinged tale of crime that goes far to anticipate the anxieties of film noir in its sense of gathering doom. Half a century later Herman Melville produced an even more memorable portrait of a protean riverboat swindler in *The Confidence-Man: His Masquerade* (1857). The early American writer most immutably associated with crime, however, is Edgar Allan Poe. Only a few years after Sir Robert Peel began England's Bow Street Runners as the world's first official police force, Poe presented the ideally cerebral detective in three short stories:

"The Murders in the Rue Morgue" (1841), "The Mystery of Marie Rô-
get" (1842), and "The Purloined Letter" (1844). These stories, all featuring the reclusive Chevalier Auguste Dupin, have made Poe universally hailed as the father of the detective story.

Dupin, though the only recurring character in Poe's fiction, nevertheless plays a minor role in that fiction as a whole. The Poe of the
popular imagination (and the Poe of innumerable Hollywood horror
extravaganzas) is the high priest of Gothic horror. Although horror in
Poe has many sources – the fear of being watched by a malign presence, communication with the dead, states of consciousness between
life and death (dream, hypnosis, suspended animation, possession by
the dead), the possibility of burial alive, the horror of maiming or dis-
memberment – none of them is richer than the psychopathology of
the criminal mind. Poe is the first writer to explore systematically the
proposition that the ability to imagine an action acts as a powerful in-
ducement to complete it, regardless of the disastrous consequences.
Hence his criminals, from Egaeus, who breaks into his fiancée's tomb
to extract her teeth in "Berenice" (1835), to the anonymous killers of
"The Black Cat" (1843) and "The Tell-Tale Heart" (1843), are typically
driven to crimes they neither understand nor assent to; when these
crimes succeed, they are driven, equally irrationally, to confess, as in
"William Wilson" (1839), "The Imp of the Perverse" (1845), and "The
Cask of Amontillado" (1846). It is no coincidence that Poe is noted
both as the inventor of the detective hero and as the preeminent
American literary explorer of criminal psychology. In Poe's nightmare
world, Dupin, who is given many of the characteristics of Poe's criminals (misogynistic reclusiveness, a love of night and mystery, an ability to identify with the criminals he is seeking), represents a uniquely
successful attempt to impose through a strenuous effort of will what
his author calls "ratiocination" on an imaginative world that is generally irrational in its cosmology and criminal in its morality.

One reason Dupin, unlike his successor Sherlock Holmes, spawned
no imitators and no immediate legacy is that his import is so abstract-
ly philosophical, so little rooted in a particular time and place that Poe
can substitute a minutely detailed Paris, in "The Mystery of Marie Rô-
get," to stand in, street by street and newspaper by newspaper, for the
scene of the actual crime on which the story is based: Hoboken, New
Jersey. But crime films have from their very beginning attempted to
link criminal behavior to specific social settings both in fulfillment of
Hollywood's general tendency toward sensationalizing abstract con-

flicts and as part of its generic project of casting a metaphoric light on the workings of the social order crime challenges. Broadly speaking, the history of the crime film before 1940 follows changing social attitudes toward crime and criminals; the 1940s mark a crisis of ambivalence toward the criminal hero; by 1950, it was following changing attitudes toward the law and the social order that criminals metaphorically reflect.

The Romance of the Silent Criminal

Given the vanishing of so many silent shorts and features, perhaps forever, the power and extent of the crime film in the years before synchronized sound may never be fully understood. To the handful of silent crime films scholars have discussed, Langman and Finn add some three thousand more in their catalog of the period 1903–28.[3] There may seem little point in speculating about the patterns of silent crime films when so much of the evidence has disappeared, but a few generalizations seem safe. From the time of Edwin S. Porter's Edison film *The Great Train Robbery* (1903), one of the earliest of all narrative films, criminals were more prominent on silent screens than enforcers of the law. If the robbers in Porter's seven-minute film are unremarkable, the posse of citizens that ends up shooting them down is even more nondescript, and has much less screen time. As its title indicates, the film is far more interested in the mechanics of crime than in the necessities of punishment.[4]

The work most often cited as the exemplary silent crime film is D. W. Griffith's two-reeler *The Musketeers of Pig Alley* (1912), which is equally memorable for its realistically grubby urban exteriors and its pioneering use of enormous close-ups of gang members as they loom surrealistically before the camera while sneaking out of an alley en route to a shootout with a rival gang. It is easy to forget not only that Griffith, for all the fascination of his lead criminal, the Kid, ends the film with a flourish of his usual sentimentality – in return for the unexpected chivalry he has shown her, the heroine covers up the Kid's culpability by lying to the police – but that crime features prominently in any number of Griffith's contemporaneous films, from *The Lonely Villa* (1909) and *The Lonedale Operator* (1911), which focus on heroines menaced by threatening robbers as stalwart heroes ride to their rescue, to *The Narrow Road* (1912), whose heroine, Mary Pickford, rescues her husband, Elmer Booth (the Kid in *The Musketeers of Pig*

Alley), from temptation by a counterfeiter and pursuit by a relentless police officer. The most elaborate story in Griffith's four-story epic *Intolerance* (1916), later recut and released separately as *The Mother and the Law* (1919), dramatizes the struggles of an innocent man (Robert Harron) when he is unjustly accused of murder and is rescued from the gallows by the last-minute detective work of his faithful wife (Mae Marsh). In all these films, Griffith's interest is less in the charisma or brutality of the criminals than in the dangers they pose the innocent victims, who remain closest to Griffith's heart. *Intolerance* is less an indictment of its sympathetic, distracted murderer, whom the film calls The Friendless One (Miriam Cooper), than of the ruthless industrialism and social hypocrisy that have made its hapless hero and heroine so vulnerable in the first place. Griffith's criminals are more fearsome for what they threaten than for who they are; their romance lies in their function of bringing to a head the social forces that menace Griffith's innocents. Smirking Mack Sennett, who plays the lead villain in *The Lonely Villa,* might just as well be the eagle who menaces the child in what seems to have occasioned Griffith's first lead role as a film actor, *Rescued from an Eagle's Nest* (1908);[5] and the dangers that brought every chapter of the contemporaneous Pearl White serials (*The Perils of Pauline*, 1914; *The Exploits of Elaine*, 1914–15; *The Iron Claw*, 1916) to an end were divided without prejudice between human and natural agency.

Several silent films go much further in exploring the mystique of the criminal. Following the success in France of Louis Feuillade's five multiepisode salutes to the dashing master criminal Fantômas (1913–14), Maurice Tourneur, whose son Jacques would make the important film noir *Out of the Past* (1947), directed *Alias Jimmy Valentine* (1915). Expanding on Paul Armstrong's 1909 play and its basis in the O. Henry short story "A Retrieved Reformation" (1903), the film follows the adventures of Lee Randall, alias gentleman safecracker Jimmy Valentine (Robert Warwick), in what the credits call "his double life" as a member and an enemy of society. In the film's most extraordinary sequence, a high-angle long take shows the interior of a bank shorn of its ceilings as Jimmy and his confederates, often unaware of dangers the audience can see clearly one or two rooms away, go about an expertly planned robbery. When the gang is captured anyway, Jimmy goes to prison, but he eventually wins a pardon, goes straight, and, as trusted cashier Lee Randall, wins the heart of the Lieutenant Governor's daughter. When a toddler is accidentally locked in a bank vault,

Randall's expertise in opening the lock threatens to reveal his double life. But the police detective who, convinced Jimmy never deserved pardon, has been waiting for him to slip, takes a cue from *The Narrow Road* and *The Musketeers of Pig Alley* and passes the incident off with a knowing wink. This frees Jimmy to revert to Lee Randall, the better half of his split identity, which the film had privileged from the beginning.

It is no wonder that *Alias Jimmy Valentine* was torn between romanticizing its safecracker and suggesting from the beginning that he would be redeemed in the end. The lower-class audiences who packed moviehouses in the first two decades of the century would have shrunk from any contact with real-life criminals, who were identified in the popular imagination with the recent waves of European immigrants who had made America's cities so unsavory. But with immigration running at record levels after World War I, it was only a matter of time before a large portion of the audience was drawn from the ranks of those very immigrants. In the meantime, Prohibition, which had become the law of the land in 1920, made it necessary for any law-abiding citizen who wanted a drink to get liquor from criminals. Finally, as the average budget for a Hollywood feature shot from $20,000 in 1914 to $300,000 in 1924[6] and production companies responded to the challenge of higher budgets by merging into bigger and bigger corporations and looking to Wall Street for investment capital, the financial structure of the few surviving studios began to resemble more and more closely that of the gangs who would ultimately finance Harry Cohn's 1932 buyout of his brother Jack at Columbia Pictures and William Fox's unsuccessful attempt to keep control of the company that ended with its 1935 merger with Darryl F. Zanuck's Twentieth Century Productions – the same gangs who would infiltrate the rank and file of the industry through labor racketeering in the early 1930s.[7]

Higher budgets to lure bigger audiences, the rapid rise of largely immigrant audiences, the criminalization of drinking through Prohibition, and the alliance of Hollywood studios with organized crime all combined to shift the romance of criminals from the menace they posed to innocent victims to their own personal mystique. Josef von Sternberg's *Underworld* (1927) retains the redemptive structure of *Alias Jimmy Valentine* while granting its lead criminal, Bull Weed (George Bancroft), a much more glamorous life from which to be redeemed.[8] *Underworld* gives Bull the best of all worlds by making him both a legendary professional criminal whose life-style is an endless round of robberies, parties, and shootouts, and also one of nature's noblemen who knows when it is time to give himself up to the police in order to clear the way for his moll Feathers (Evelyn Brent) and her lover Rolls Royce (Clive Brook), the lawyer he mistakenly thought had betrayed him. So successful was the film that all the major studios rushed to copy it; Sternberg's own copy for Paramount, *Thunderbolt* (1929), also starring Bancroft, was a virtual remake.

Amid the worldwide fascination with larger-than-life criminals, from Feuillade's Fantômas to Fritz Lang's megalomaniacal Dr. Mabuse (1922, 1933), only one fictional detective, Sherlock Holmes, held anything like the same sway onscreen, and for many of the same reasons. Although Arthur Conan Doyle's novels *A Study in Scarlet* (1887) and *The Valley of Fear* (1915) had been adapted for the British screen in 1914 and 1916, audiences responded to Holmes's exotic eccentricities in many other contexts, from the camera trickery of American Mutoscope's short *Sherlock Holmes Baffled* (1903) to the stage play *Sherlock Holmes* (1899), American actor-playwright William Gillette's fantasia on Holmesian themes, twice filmed in Hollywood – first with Gillette in the starring role (1916), then with John Barrymore (1922). Although Conan Doyle had made Holmes resolutely unromantic, Gillette ended by marrying him off to the heroine he had rescued from the clutches of Professor Moriarty, providing audiences with some of the same pleasures as the redemption of Jimmy Valentine or the unselfish romantic posturing of Bull Weed.

Tough Guys

The gangster cycle of the 1930s wasted no time in turning the big-hearted crook silent films had considered ripe for redemption into a remorseless killer. *Little Caesar* (1930), *The Public Enemy* (1931), and *Scarface* (1932) were only the most notorious of a new cycle of tough gangster movies that included *The Racket* (1928), *Alibi* (1929), *Doorway to Hell* (1930), and *Quick Millions* (1931). The groundwork for this new brutality went back to the early 1920s, when high-speed presses and cheap wood-pulp paper stocks led to an explosion in mass-market publishing. At the same time newspapers battling for circulation made folk heroes of bootleggers like Al Capone, pulp magazines like *Black Mask,* founded in 1920 by H. L. Mencken and George Jean Nathan to help support their highbrow magazine *Smart Set,* were chronicling the exploits of hard-edged detectives like Carroll John Daly's Race Williams and Dashiell Hammett's nameless operative of the Continental Detective Agency.[9]

The collapse of the stock market in 1929 lit the match to the tough-guy fuse by sparking a national depression marked by soaring unemployment and widespread despair over the value of public policy and the institutions of government, finance, and the law. When police officers appeared increasingly as enforcers of rich men's law, banks either foreclosed on delinquent mortgages or failed their depositors, and Washington seemed powerless to alleviate the nation's sufferings, audiences turned toward strong heroes who offered them the hope of taking charge of their own future: self-made entrepreneurs in direct sales (albeit the illegal sale of liquor) like Tom Powers in *The Public Enemy* and Tony Camonte in *Scarface*. At the same time, the arrival of synchronized sound, as Jonathan Munby has noted, turned the suddenly speaking gangster from a deracinated outlaw to a member of a specific marginal ethnic group whose "accent frames his desire for success within a history of struggle over national identity."[10] Hence the gangster's inevitable death at the end of each film was not simply the necessary price for the hour and a half of upwardly mobile fantasy that preceded it but a site of the audience's sharp ambivalence toward the immigrant gangster hero [Fig. 4]. The pattern of the new gangster films, tracing the hero's gradual rise to fabulous power and his inevitable meteoric fall – which now substituted for the earlier romantic intrigues of *Alias Jimmy Valentine* and *Underworld* – allowed audiences to indulge both sides of their ambivalence toward an establishment that seemed less and less responsive to their needs: their fantasies of personal empowerment and their fears of defying institutional authority, their despair over the possibility of social justice and their belief in the rough justice of the movies.

In retrospect, it is remarkable how brief this vogue of the tough movie gangster, perhaps the most striking figure in the history of Hollywood crime, actually was. Studio heads were under such constant pressure from public-interest groups to tone down their portrayal of professional criminals that as early as 1931, at the height of the new cycle, Jack L. Warner announced that Warner Bros., whose preference for low-budget urban location shooting and proletarian milieus had made it the major studio most active in the gangster film, would stop producing such films, and that he had not allowed his fifteen-year-old son to watch any of them.[11] In addition, the release of *Scar-*

4. *Scarface* (1932): The Depression-era audience's ambivalence toward an up-wardly mobile fantasy. (Vince Barnett, Paul Muni, Karen Morley)

face, the most violent of the new movies, was delayed for over a year while producer Howard Hughes dickered with the Motion Picture Producers and Distributors of America's Production Code Office (or Hays Office, as it was popularly called for its first leader, former Postmaster General Will Hays) over the film's bloodletting and overtones of incest.

Eventually it was shorn of several repellent or suggestive shots; buttressed by a new sequence shot by Hughes in which a stolid newspaper editor, faced by a citizens' board, denounced the glorification of gangsters in the mass media and urged action on the part of the federal government and the American Legion; and given a new title for its 1932 release: *Scarface: Shame of a Nation.*

The promethean gangster was shackled by the election of Franklin Roosevelt as president in 1932 and the stricter enforcement of the Hays Office's 1930 Production Code, provoked in large measure by the founding of the Catholic Church's Legion of Decency in 1934. Roosevelt, an activist president who assiduously manipulated the newly dominant technology of radio to transform his public image from a New York patrician crippled by polio to a paternal man of the people in whom ordinary Americans could believe, launched a series of high-profile initiatives immediately on his inauguration in 1933: insuring deposits in Federal Reserve banks, mandating increased prices for farm products, and launching the largest public-works programs in American history to start putting the unemployed back to work. That same year, Joseph I. Breen of the Hays Office finally succeeded, with the inadvertent help of the outrageous Mae West and the gangster cycle, in pressing the major studios to abide by the provisions of the 1930 Production Code, which forbade, among other things, nudity, profanity, justified violent revenge, the defeat of the law, seduction or rape, and the ridicule of organized religion or the flag.[12]

Within a year the Hollywood crime film had undergone a seismic shift. Gone was the unquenchable ambition of *Little Caesar,* the cold-hearted brutality of *The Public Enemy,* the sexual explicitness of *Scarface.* But although Roosevelt and the Hays Office could provide new models and regulations for Hollywood, they could do nothing to regulate audiences' desires to see onscreen violence or digs at the justice system. The new wave of crime films that began in 1934 simply channeled their toughness in subtler ways.

The most obvious of these ways was to make law enforcers as glamorous and charismatic as criminals. Since real-life enforcers were by definition organization men and women, the challenge of bringing them to melodramatic life was considerable, and it is not surprising that the first police hero to achieve widespread popularity emerged from the funny pages. Chester Gould's *Dick Tracy,* the comic strip that debuted in 1931, worked by setting its hero – whose creator had originally planned to emphasize his anonymity by calling him Plainclothes

Tracy[13] – against a galaxy of such criminal gargoyles as Flattop, B. B. Eyes, Pruneface, Mumbles, the Brow, and the Mole. Although Tracy, with his trademark square jaw and yellow raincoat, was invariably upstaged by the grotesque villain in each story, he developed a loyal following as the continuing hero of case after case.[14]

As Dick Tracy's readership was expanding among a Depression audience hungry for heroes, a new publicity campaign for real-life detective heroes was under way. Inspired by the activist example of Roosevelt, J. Edgar Hoover, director since 1924 of the Bureau of Investigation (renamed the Federal Bureau of Investigation in 1935), promoted bigger budgets and wider press for his organization and himself through a well-publicized crusade against such gangsters as Machine Gun Kelly, Pretty Boy Floyd, Baby Face Nelson, and John Dillinger – the last pulling off a brilliantly reciprocal publicity coup when he was shot to death by FBI agents as he emerged from a Chicago screening of the gangster film *Manhattan Melodrama* (1934). Hoover's fictionalized exploits were glorified in *"G" Men* (1935) through the sublimely simple tactic of recasting James Cagney, famous as the gangster Tom Powers of *Public Enemy,* as the equally violent and mercurial, but now officially sanctioned, FBI hero. Although the film was as brutal and fast-paced as the gangster films from which it borrowed everything but its moral loyalties, it had no trouble earning a seal of approval from the Hays Office and the semiofficial blessing of Hoover in a prologue for its re-release in 1949.

The other key crime film of the period, which could not have been more different from *"G" Men*, took a completely different approach to the challenge of Hollywood self-censorship. *The Thin Man,* shot in sixteen days in 1934, was a knockabout comedy of crime whose detective hero Nick Charles (William Powell) and his improbable socialite wife Nora (Myrna Loy) were persuaded by Dorothy Wynant (Maureen O'Sullivan) to investigate a series of murders implicating her father, a vanished inventor. Nick and Nora, aided by their terrier Asta, were the model of Hays Office primness. Despite Nick's amusingly extensive underworld connections, they consorted with criminals only reluctantly and fastidiously; their bickering was marked by elaborate courtesy; and each night, after a full day of detecting, they retired to their chaste twin beds. At the same time, their nonstop drinking, sanctioned by the repeal of Prohibition in 1933, and their frankly carnal interest in each other despite the bonds of holy matrimony, proved, like Cagney's lively incarnation of a fledgling FBI agent, that Hollywood could sell the desire for violence, thrills, and mystery in the most respectable forms.

The Thin Man and its five sequels, from *After the Thin Man* (1936) through *Song of the Thin Man* (1947), were only the most popular of the detective serials that sprouted on both sides of the Atlantic throughout the thirties. Spurred in England by protectionist laws mandating a minimal percentage of British-made films to be shown in each theater, even if these British products were "quota quickies," and in America by the rise of the double feature, which demanded a constant release of "programmers" to fill the bottom of double bills, studios rushed to release detective B films that traded on their heroes' and heroines' preexistent following. Dozens of literary detectives enjoyed active screen careers during the 1930s. At the end of the decade Sherlock Holmes and Dr. Watson, played by the inspired casting choices of Basil Rathbone and Nigel Bruce, made a triumphant return to the screen in *The Hound of the Baskervilles* [Fig. 5] and *The Adventures of Sherlock Holmes* (both 1939). Most active of all was Earl Derr Biggers's soft-spoken Charlie Chan, played by Warner Oland until his death in 1938, and then by Sidney Toler, who starred in a total of twenty-seven Fox features between 1931 and 1942. The smiling, self-deprecating, epigrammatic Chan, the globe-trotting Honolulu police detective who seemed eternally to be drawn into crimes outside his jurisdiction, appeared the final blow to the tough-guy milieu of the gangster.

One last source of detective films, however, suggested that America's appetite for tough heroes had still not been sated. Although the half-hour time slots of radio demanded brief, action-filled stories whose leading characters would not need to be established each week if they were already well-known, the radio detectives who made the most successful transitions to Hollywood tended to be tough guys themselves. Among the many crime-fighting heroes of radio, pulp writer Walter Gibson's mysterious character the Shadow, alias Lamont Cranston,[15] bolstered by the sinister associations with the criminal mind crystallized by his radio tag line ("Who knows what evil lurks in the hearts of men? The Shadow knows"), made perhaps the smoothest transition to Hollywood in a string of features and serials from 1937 through 1946. But Fran Striker and George W. Trendle's Green Hornet and the A-1 Detective Agency, created by Carleton E. Morse for *I Love a Mystery*, were not far behind. America's love affair with the detective hero continued, for better or worse, to be marked by its fascination with the dark side of human nature.

5. *The Hound of the Baskervilles:* Nigel Bruce and Basil Rathbone as the best-loved Watson and Holmes of all.

The Crisis in Hollywood Crime

Through the 1930s, American mass culture had treated criminals and their culture predominantly as exotica, glamorizing both the criminal masterminds who cracked safes and controlled the traffic in illegal liquor and the detectives whose well-advertised eccentricities gave them a similarly exotic cachet. As the decade drew to a close, however, the attitudes Hollywood seemed to encourage toward both fictional criminals and fictional detectives grew less straightforward and more conflicted. At the same time, in an even more fundamental shift, crime films grew more figurative, their criminals metaphors for a tangle of social forces and attitudes rather than heroic outsiders in their own right.

The gangsters played in the later 1930s by Humphrey Bogart illustrate this shift from the exotic criminal to the metaphoric criminal. After several years playing nondescript characters in the early 1930s, Bogart had left the screen for the stage, and it was in a stage role he had originated in 1935, Duke Mantee in *The Petrified Forest,* that he returned to Hollywood a year later. Mantee is the first of Hollywood's overtly metaphorical gangsters. Although he is by far the most commanding presence in Robert Sherwood's play and Archie Mayo's film (1936), his role is nothing more than a plot contrivance, a catalyst that allows the metaphysically weary hero Alan Squier (Leslie Howard) to sacrifice his own life and leave a legacy that will allow Gabrielle Maple (Bette Davis) to escape the existential paralysis Squier cannot.

Warner Bros. paired Bogart with James Cagney in three films in the later thirties: *Angels with Dirty Faces* (1938), *The Oklahoma Kid* (1939), and *The Roaring Twenties* (1939). In each of them, Cagney was the dynamic lead, whether as criminal or avenger, Bogart the dishonorable villain as social pathology. Bogart's Baby Face Martin was used to explain juvenile delinquency in *Dead End* (1937); his George Hally helped embalm the Prohibition era as historic Americana in *The Roaring Twenties*; but not until after he emerged from Cagney's shadow in *High Sierra* (1941) would his Roy Earle meld Squier's anachronistic pretensions to the gangster's atavistic grandeur. Unlike Cagney, whose appeal was direct, physical, and extroverted, Bogart, who could suggest depths of worldly disillusionment beneath a crooked shell, was the perfect choice to play gangsters designed to explore the ambiguities of nongangster culture: a stifling society's thirst for cathartic violence; the need to blame intractable social problems on outside agents or to project them onto a comfortably remote history; the recognition that the gangster's power, like the western gunslinger's, was for better or worse a reminder of a simpler time long past.

Better than anyone else before or since, Bogart incarnated the romantic mystique of the doomed criminal. He never played the nobly redeemable crook of Sternberg's *Underworld* or the dashing outlaw who flouts unjust laws – a figure popularized by Mae West (*She Done Him Wrong* and *I'm No Angel*, both 1933) and Errol Flynn (*The Adventures of Robin Hood*, 1938). Instead, Bogart's protagonists were ambivalent. Bogart villains like Roy Earle were sympathetic despite (or because of) their guilt, Bogart heroes like Sam Spade (in *The Maltese Falcon*, 1941) [Fig. 6] tainted with guilty knowledge. Bogart continued to trade on the mystique of the soulful criminal and the hero with a shady past, even when cast against type as the aging sailor Charlie Allnut in *The African Queen* (1951) or the obsessive Captain Queeg in *The Caine Mutiny* (1954). On the eve of John Huston's pivotal caper film *The Asphalt Jungle* (1950), Bogart would close the forties by starring

6. *The Maltese Falcon:* Humphrey Bogart as the private-eye hero tainted with guilty knowledge. (Bogart, Sydney Greenstreet)

in a pair of 1948 Huston films that confirmed the metaphoric power of the criminal, appearing as the psychotic Everyman Fred C. Dobbs in *The Treasure of the Sierra Madre* and as Lt. Frank McCloud in *Key Largo*, whose admonition to Americans to rouse themselves from their exhausted postwar apathy to battle the forces of evil represented by Johnny Rocco (Edward G. Robinson) makes it the most allegorical of all the great gangster films.

What made Bogart and his colleagues stop working exclusively for criminal gangs and go to work for cultural analysts who were using movie criminals as metaphors for American culture? The most obvious cause for this shift was the decline in high-profile organized crime, partly because of the repeal of Prohibition in 1933, partly because of the well-publicized success of the FBI. The adventures of *Scarface's* Tony Camonte and *"G" Men's* Brick Davis could fairly be claimed to be ripped from newspaper headlines; the gangsters played by Paul Muni in *Angel on My Shoulder* (1946) and James Cagney in *White Heat*

(1949) are self-consciously anachronistic, memoirs of a gangster culture whose day has passed.

As the journalistic currency of criminals declined, their literary matrix stood out in sharper relief. Ever since the coming of synchronized sound had encouraged Hollywood to turn to literary and dramatic sources, the great gangster films, like the great detective films, had all been based on literary properties; even *Scarface,* allegedly written from Chicago headlines, credited Armitrage Trail's novel as its source. But the crime films of the 1940s sprang out of a fictional tradition that was already hailed as more self-consciously literary despite its hard-boiled roots.[16] It may seem strange to claim Dashiell Hammett, Raymond Chandler, and James M. Cain as literary, but all of them had connections and pretensions to the literary establishment, and all of them – unlike fellow pulp writers Carroll John Daly and Erle Stanley Gardner – turned from action writers to literary stylists when they left the short story for the novel. The second paragraph of Chandler's first novel, *The Big Sleep* (1939), for example, is a classic of playfully metaphoric foreshadowing of the detective as disillusioned knight-errant that would have been blue-penciled from any of Chandler's submissions to *Black Mask, Detective Fiction Weekly,* or *Dime Detective:*

> The main hallway of the Sternwood place was two stories high. Over the entrance doors, which would have let in a troop of Indian elephants, there was a broad stained-glass panel showing a knight in dark armor rescuing a lady who was tied to a tree and didn't have any clothes on but some long and convenient hair. The knight had pushed the vizor of his helmet back to be sociable, and he was fiddling with the knots on the ropes that tied the lady to the tree and not getting anywhere. I stood there and thought that if I lived in the house, I would sooner or later have to climb up there and help him. He didn't seem to be really trying.[17]

Cornell Woolrich, the pulp writer who had an even greater impact on crime films of the forties, was no one's idea of a stylist, in either short forms or long, and yet his contribution to the crime film was equally metaphoric: a knack of tying particular crimes to a pervasive sense of urban paranoia and a claustrophobic compression of dramatic time. So powerful was the appeal of Woolrich's nightmare fantasies that apart from Erle Stanley Gardner, whose dozens of Perry Mason novels served as the basis for the 1957–66 television series, no crime writer approaches the number of Woolrich's source credits for movies. Films based on his novels and stories include *Convicted* (1938), *Street of*

Chance (1942), *The Leopard Man* (1943), *Phantom Lady* (1944), *Mark of the Whistler* (1944), *Deadline at Dawn* (1946), *Black Angel* (1946), *The Chase* (1946), *Fall Guy* (1947), *Fear in the Night* (1947), *The Guilty* (1947), *I Wouldn't Be in Your Shoes* (1948), *Return of the Whistler* (1948), *The Night Has a Thousand Eyes* (1948), *The Window* (1949), *No Man of Her Own* (1950) and its remakes *I Married a Shadow* (*J'ai épousé une ombre,* France, 1982) and *Mrs. Winterbourne* (1996), *Rear Window* (1954), and a pair of French adaptations directed by François Truffaut, *The Bride Wore Black* (*La Mariée était en noir,* 1967) and *Mississippi Mermaid* (*La Sirène du Mississippi,* 1969). The indirect influence of his fiction on other films noirs extends even further.

One reason filmmakers in this period were more aware of the literary traditions their work was following was that they were different filmmakers. The rise of Nazism and the coming of World War II had driven a generation of European filmmakers, including such important crime-film directors as Fritz Lang (*Fury,* 1936; *You Only Live Once,* 1937; *The Woman in the Window,* 1944; *Scarlet Street,* 1945; *The Big Heat,* 1953), Robert Siodmak (*Phantom Lady; The Spiral Staircase,* 1946; *The Killers,* 1946; *The Dark Mirror,* 1946; *Criss Cross,* 1949), and Billy Wilder (*Double Indemnity,* 1944; *Sunset Blvd.,* 1950; *Some Like It Hot,* 1959), to the United States, where they were joined by British émigré Alfred Hitchcock (*Rebecca,* 1940; *Strangers on a Train,* 1951; *Rear Window; Vertigo,* 1958; *Psycho,* 1960). Worldly, ambitious, and sophisticated, many of these European filmmakers managed to adapt to the big budgets of Hollywood studios while maintaining their sense of expressive visual style and their fondness for literate dialogue. Their attempt to use criminal plots to encapsulate the audience's whole world was hallowed by recognition from French critics, if not by American, as early as 1946, when the term *film noir* first appeared in print in describing the style of five crime films first released in 1944: *The Woman in the Window*, *Laura*, *Phantom Lady*, *Double Indemnity*, and *Murder, My Sweet.*

The noir cycle, which continued through the mid-1950s, featured amateur criminals – people who did not think of themselves as criminals at all – trapped in ordinary situations gone wrong, using everyday drives for love and success as the basis for criminal nightmares driven by the expressionistic psychopathology of everyday life rather than the imperatives of Depression economics. The weak hero sucked into a life of crime by the treacherous femme fatale, the tough private eye hoping to outwit the criminals who owned his city, the maze of rain-slick night streets leading nowhere, the hallucinatory contrasts between glaring white faces and deep black skies, the lush orchestral scores ratcheting up moments of emotional intensity still further – all of these figures were familiar to film-noir audiences not from the headlines, but from a mythic world created mainly by other movies.

When the inevitable reaction against the expressionistic world of film noir set in, it focused on style rather than figuration. The semi-documentary approach pioneered by the anti-Nazi thriller *The House on 92nd Street* (1945) flourished in the location shooting of films like *Kiss of Death* (1947), *Call Northside 777* (1948), and *The Naked City* (1948), with its you-are-there voice-over prologue and epilogue delivered by producer Mark Hellinger: "There are eight million stories in the naked city. This has been one of them." Although the crime film seemed poised to follow a new trend toward documentary realism, Robert Wise showed in *The Set-Up* (1949) that a realistic handling of mise-en-scène, coupled with the unfolding of the story in real time, could serve as the basis for a new, harder-edged expressionism, and it was this amalgam of realism and expressionism that sparked crime movies as different as *D.O.A.* (1950), *Sunset Blvd.,* and *Detective Story* (1951).

By the end of the decade, home-grown American critics were beginning to look more closely at the figurative power of popular films. While disclaiming any special artistry for individual Hollywood products, highbrow critics like Parker Tyler and Robert Warshow regarded Hollywood itself as a stage for repressed American cultural anxieties, which seemed to be running at an all-time high in the years immediately following the war, when the national identity the country had constructed for itself was in danger of collapsing along with the national project of winning the war. As Joseph Samuels (Sam Levene) prophetically tells Sgt. Montgomery, the anti-Semitic veteran who will soon murder him in *Crossfire* (1947):

> Maybe it's because for four years now we've been focusing . . . on one little peanut. The "win-the-war" peanut, that was all. Get it over, eat that peanut. All at once, no peanut. Now we start looking at each other again. We don't know what we're supposed to do. . . . We're too used to fightin'. But we just don't know what to fight.

It was time for the crime film, armed with its newly acknowledged metaphoric power to diagnose hidden social problems, to be pressed into service in shoring up a new national identity.

Criminal Culture and Mass Culture

Criminal subcultures had already been posed as social microcosms throughout the 1940s. More explicitly than any earlier prison film, *Brute Force* (1947) offered its prison as existential social metaphor for a meaningless, tragically unjust round of activities that would end only in death. The boxing cycle of the later 1940s (*Body and Soul*, 1947; *Champion*, 1949; *The Set-Up*), besides treating the ring as one more exotic milieu to be mined for its sociological interest, insistently equated it with one more inescapable prison.

White Heat inaugurated a cycle of films using crime melodrama to tame the omnipresent danger of the nuclear bomb. The power of *White Heat*'s psychotic gang leader, Cody Jarrett (James Cagney), is linked to uncontrollable technological forces like the steam generated by a railroad engine, the "white-hot buzz saw" that he feels inside his head, and the natural-gas refinery he invades in the film's climactic sequence. Faced with Jarrett's outlaw power, the police have recourse to superior technology of their own, pursuing Cody's mother in radio-directed cars and plotting, by means of a radio-tracking device, the course of the truck that takes the Jarrett gang to their last job. The subtext is clear: When threatened by technological nightmares, fight fire with fire.[18]

Interestingly, this subtext remains virtually unchanged in two later crime films that otherwise have little to do with each other, or with *White Heat*: *The Big Heat* (1953) and *Kiss Me Deadly* (1955). All three films use explicitly apocalyptic imagery both to indicate the dangerous extent of the criminals' threats and to depict the cleansing destruction of the criminals. In *The Big Heat,* the apocalyptic fury associated with the A-bomb's fearsome capacity to burn, maim, and kill individuals and whole communities is unleashed when Mrs. Duncan (Jeanette Nolan), a crooked cop's widow, is shot and murderous thug Vince Stone (Lee Marvin) scalded by the thug's former moll, Debby Marsh (Gloria Grahame). Debby's position beyond the pale of social morals and her own scalding by Stone – which has given the face of which she was so vain the half-scarred, half-beautiful look of a Dick Tracy grotesque – allow her a greater freedom to avenge herself than the upright, widower-cop hero Dave Bannion (Glenn Ford) could ever have. By killing Mrs. Duncan, Debby releases "the big heat" – intense police activity based on evidence against big-city crime boss Lagana (Alexander Scourby) and his organization that the cop's widow had safely stowed – which the film persistently links to images of cata-strophically uncontrolled power and the "traumatic consequences" of nuclear holocaust.[19] The much darker *Kiss Me Deadly* pits another social outsider, "bedroom dick" Mike Hammer (Ralph Meeker), against a lineup of criminal plotters and government conspirators, leading him literally inside the body of a dead woman for the key to what his secretary dubs "the Great Whatsit" – an atom bomb waiting in a locker of the Hollywood Athletic Club – while at the same time condemning Hammer's dim, brutal machismo, whose effects are as disastrous as the criminals' schemes.

In each of these films, as in the prison and boxing films of the for-ties, crime is used as a way of converting noncriminal but potentially unbearable social anxieties into entertainment by scaling down their threat from the global to the subcultural level, linking the threat to a series of charismatic heroes and villains who can encourage a strong rooting interest, and directing the audience's concern along the com-fortably generic lines of the crime film. Ten years earlier, the crime-reporter hero's editor in *Foreign Correspondent* (1940) had cut the Nazi threat in Europe down to size with the injunction, "There's a crime hatching on that bedeviled continent." Now films like *Kiss Me Deadly* showed how the crime genre could be enlisted to domesticate the equally imponderable threat of global holocaust.

The Asphalt Jungle (1950), released at the beginning of a new dec-ade, consolidated this tendency to define criminal subculture as a mir-ror of American culture. The cycle of caper films it exemplifies, from foreshadowings like *The Killers* and *Criss Cross* to full-blown later ex-amples like *The Killing* (1956) and *Odds against Tomorrow* (1959), used the planning and execution of a robbery that infallibly went wrong to dramatize the irreducible unreasonableness of life. Its aura of existen-tial despair made the caper film popular with European filmmakers, whose homages to Hollywood, beginning with *Rififi* (*Du Rififi chez les hommes,* 1955) and *The Swindle* (*Il bidone,* 1955), broadened into a wider and more complex mixture of nostalgia and critique with the coming of the French New Wave, which produced such notable crime films as *Frantic,* also known as *Elevator to the Gallows* (*Ascenseur pour l'échafaud,* 1958), *Breathless* (*À bout de souffle,* 1959), *Shoot the Piano Player* (*Tirez sur le pianiste,* 1960), *Alphaville* (1965), and *The Unfaith-ful Wife* (*La femme infidèle,* 1969). In the meantime, the doom-laden atmosphere of caper films was lightened in such British Ealing come-dies as *The Lavender Hill Mob* (1951) and *The Ladykillers* (1955), and the Italian *I soliti ignoti* (1958), a notable U.S. success as *Big Deal on Madonna Street.* Hollywood was slower to adopt a comic attitude toward the big heist, with the international coproduction *Topkapi* (1964, directed by *Rififi* alumnus Jules Dassin) the pivotal film, followed by *Gambit* (1966), *How to Steal a Million* (1966), and *The Hot Rock* (1972) and *Bank Shot* (1974), both adapted from Donald E. Westlake's caper novels about the comically frustrated thief John Dortmunder.

Far more surprising than the rise of the caper film as an anatomy of noncriminal society or its leavening through the comedy of ineptness is the enlistment of crime films to promote family values. The authority of the 1930 Production Code had become so shaky that it was successfully challenged by Fox, which released Otto Preminger's *The Moon Is Blue* without a seal in 1953, and Warner Bros., which released Elia Kazan's *Baby Doll* in 1956 despite the condemnation of the Legion of Decency. In the wake of the anticommunist witch-hunts of 1947 and 1950, however, calls for central control of the mass-entertainment media's content remained strong, particularly when those media targeted children. Psychologist Fredric Wertham's influential study *Seduction of the Innocent* (1954), attacking comic books, especially crime comics, as "an agent with harmful potentialities,"[20] provoked widespread public outrage and a Congressional investigation under the direction of Senator Estes Kefauver. In response, industry leader DC (Detective Comics), which published the adventures of Superman, Batman, Wonder Woman, and many of their superfriends, rushed to join other publishers in establishing a Comics Code that would preclude any government censorship, drawing a sharp line between code and noncode comics that would prepare the way for underground comics ten years later.

At the same time, the burgeoning popularity of television, which was rapidly taking control of the formulaic genres that would have been Hollywood's province only a few years earlier, created a demand for formula melodramas suitable for family viewing that could fit into slots of half an hour or an hour.[21] Some popular radio anthology programs like *Suspense* and *The Whistler* made successful transitions to television; others, like *Alfred Hitchcock Presents* and its successor *The Alfred Hitchcock Hour,* were created especially for the new medium. The mainstay of television programming, however, became the half-hour comedy or drama series that followed the adventures of a continuing character. This formula was ideally suited to the detective story, and between 1950 and 1960 Ellery Queen, Boston Blackie, Flash Casey,

Pam and Jerry North, Nick and Nora Charles, Mike Hammer, Charlie Chan, Philip Marlowe, and Mike Shayne had all tested the waters, where they were joined by the new detectives who headlined *Peter Gunn, Mannix, Richard Diamond, Private Eye, 77 Sunset Strip, Hawaiian Eye,* and *Surfside 6,* along with the indefatigable Perry Mason. In 1952, *Dragnet* brought LAPD Sgt. Joe ("Just the facts") Friday from radio to television, followed by *M Squad, Highway Patrol, The Untouchables, The Naked City, Ironside, Hawaii Five-O, Adam 12, The Mod Squad, Columbo,* and a dozen other police dramas. Although *The Defenders* frequently explored troubling moral ambiguities in the cases that came to its father-and-son law team, most crime series, whether they focused on private or police detectives, set their heroes problems that could be comfortably solved in less than an hour, thus emphasizing the cleaner, less troubling side of crime.

The Hollywood studios, increasingly embattled by competition from television, responded to the call for clean entertainment more subtly. Although Rhett Butler's memorable farewell line in *Gone with the Wind* (1939) – "Frankly, my dear, I don't give a damn" – had survived censors in and out of Hollywood, most studio releases of the fifties were no more violent or explicitly sexual than those of 1934, and scarcely more licentious in their language. The one way in which the movies could be cleaned up, in fact, was to harness antiauthoritarian genres like the crime film to images of authority. Hence *The Desperate Hours* (1955), which pits escaped criminal Glenn Griffin (Humphrey Bogart) against suburban father Dan Hilliard (Fredric March), turns the criminal melodrama into a poster for the American family, which Griffin's gang parodies on a one-to-one basis (authoritarian Griffin is paired with Hilliard, his shy kid brother with Griffin's teenaged daughter, their oafish sidekick with Hilliard's little boy). In particular, *The Desperate Hours* uses the dysfunctional criminal family to bolster its case for the imperatives of American patriarchy. Like Griffin's gang, which succeeds only until each member strikes out on his own, the Hilliards falter only when they disobey Dan, whose principled reluctance to kill turns into a source of strength at the film's climax, when he goes back to his home with an unloaded revolver the police have given him, relying on the fact that his son will trust him enough to run to the safety of his arms even though Griffin is holding the unloaded gun on him.

In the same way, the central characters in *Murder, Inc.* (1960), whose exposé of Louis "Lepke" Buchalter's Brooklyn murder-for-hire organi-

zation would have made Lepke and his lieutenants the main characters had the film been made contemporaneously with its Depression-
era action, are Joey Collins (Stuart Whitman) and his wife Eadie (Mai
Britt), whose marriage is stretched to the breaking point when the
contract killer Abe Reles (Peter Falk) makes Joey his unwilling accomplice. Though Lepke (David J. Stewart) ends up in prison with his gang
in tatters, the central question of the film is whether the weak, decent
Joey can extricate himself and Eadie from Reles's grasp. The film,
which subordinates the fate of its gangster empire to its solicitude for
the typical American couple it has dropped into their midst, plays like
Little Caesar with Rico's straight-arrow sidekick Joe Massara (Douglas
Fairbanks Jr.) as the hero.

The most complete transformation of all crime subgenres in the
1950s, however, is reserved for the lawyer film. Earlier movies had presented lawyer heroes as omnipotent or embattled; only in the fifties
did they become social prophets and social engineers. *Anatomy of a
Murder* (1959) casts James Stewart as Paul Biegler, an aw-shucks defense attorney whose alcoholic associate worries he may be "too pure
for the impurities of the law." *Inherit the Wind* (1960), which rehearses
the Scopes Monkey Trial of 1925, allows its Clarence Darrow hero Henry Drummond (Spencer Tracy) to range outside his judicial bailiwick
in such authoritative pronouncements as "You cannot administer a
wicked law impartially." By the time of *To Kill a Mockingbird* (1962), a
neighbor of Atticus Finch (Gregory Peck), the small-town Georgia lawyer who fights unsuccessfully to get an African-American acquitted
of an obviously trumped-up rape charge, can memorialize his heroic
failure to his children: "There's some men in this world who are born
to do our unpleasant jobs for us."

Films like these realign the lone heroes of the great Depression
genres not so much morally as institutionally. Now the greatest heroes
are those that stand for establishment values against hopeless odds.
By the time of *Experiment in Terror* (1962), the San Francisco Police
Department fulfills the same job the United States Army did in *Invaders
from Mars* (1953): the paternal, all-wise, all-powerful organization on
which imperiled heroes and heroines can rely more certainly than
family or friends. If this pattern is not a revelation of the fifties conformity satirized in films like *Pleasantville* (1998), it reveals how dear the
utopian ideal of social conformity remained as a wish of even such a
subversive genre as the crime film.

The Establishment on Trial

By 1960, it was clear that the movies had lost their battle with television as America's preeminent mass-entertainment medium. Despite Hollywood's brief flirtation with 3-D and its more lasting embrace of color and widescreen images beyond the scope of most television sets, movie receipts fell to an all-time low in 1963. Movie theaters could entice audiences away from the free entertainment they could find at home only by offering something television could not offer. In the crime film, that something was first violence, then sex. The increasing irrelevance of the Production Code ever since the challenges of *The Moon Is Blue* and *Baby Doll* invited Hollywood filmmakers to the greater explicitness the economic peril of the industry seemed to justify.

The first important film to accept this invitation was *Psycho,* whose director, Alfred Hitchcock, shot it in six weeks using a television crew and a shoestring budget of $800,000.[22] *Psycho* looked like nothing audiences had ever seen on television, or in movie theaters either. With its relentless omission of uplifting characters or subplots and its celebrated forty-five-second butchering of its heroine in an innocuous motel shower, it marked the beginning of a brutal new era in Hollywood filmmaking. By the time Hitchcock matched the violence of *Psycho* with the sexual candor of the rape in *Frenzy* (1972), however, the wave of explictness he had begun had left him behind. William Castle's low-budget horror films (*Homicidal*, 1961; *Strait-Jacket*, 1964; etc.) showed far more baroque violence than *Psycho,* and the sight of Janet Leigh in a brassiere, so daring in 1960, was soon dated by the sexual candor of Jane Fonda's Oscar-winning performance as the prostitute Bree Daniels in *Klute* (1971). By 1969, *Midnight Cowboy,* one of the first movies to be classified under the new MPAA ratings system established that year,[23] could become the first X-rated film to win the Academy Award for Best Picture.

Even as industry executives were nervously watching the slow growth of their box-office receipts through the later 1960s, they could not have predicted the explosive impact on the new Hollywood violence of the antiestablishment feelings sparked by the Vietnam War. As college students at Berkeley and Columbia demonstrated against racial injustice and the war and Mayor Richard Daley prepared to call the Chicago police out against antiwar protestors at the 1968 Democratic presidential convention, two films released during the summer

7. *Bonnie and Clyde:* Using thirties iconography to attack sixties authority. (Gene Hackman, Estelle Parsons, Warren Beatty, Faye Dunaway, Michael J. Pollard)

of 1967 unexpectedly reaped huge benefits from their antiestablishment tone: *The Graduate* and *Bonnie and Clyde*. Arthur Penn's flamboyant, affecting, and ultimately tragic saga of a pair of Depression-era gangsters, originally dismissed by reviewers as inconsistent and pointless, not only set new, post-*Psycho* standards for onscreen violence but helped identify a niche market of American teenagers who had previously had to make do with the likes of Pat Boone and Elvis Presley. Weighing Bonnie and Clyde's amoral killing against their youthful ignorance, the film managed to demonize the same American institutions as the gangster cycle of the thirties – the police, the banks, the law – but this time in metaphoric terms, using a pair of criminals from the thirties to attack the moral injustice of the draft and the violent injustice of the American experience in Vietnam [Fig. 7].[24]

At a time when images of the Vietnam War were playing on American television news every evening yet Hollywood was virtually ignoring the war – except for valentines like John Wayne's triumphalist *The*

Green Berets (1968) – *Bonnie and Clyde*, along with Sam Peckinpah's apocalyptic western *The Wild Bunch* (1969), used the metaphors of comfortably formulaic genres to tap into antiestablishment rage. Along with *Point Blank* (1967), John Boorman's coolly elusive story of a thief's vendetta against the Army buddy who betrayed him and the criminal organization that employs the buddy, it reaffirmed the primacy of the heroic loner after a decade in which crime films had been pressed into the service of communal values. And along with *The Graduate* and the cult hit *Easy Rider* (1969), it helped identify the youth audience – especially dating couples, who preferred films to television because moviegoing allowed them to get out of their parents' homes – as the most loyal of all movie audiences, and the one to whom the majority of Hollywood films would soon come to be directed.

In the meantime, Hollywood was courting other niche audiences. When *Shaft* (1971) revealed the extent of an underserved African-American audience by showcasing a black private eye and a title song by Isaac Hayes, the first African-American composer to win an Oscar, studios rushed to follow it with *Superfly* (1972), *Black Caesar* (1973), *Coffy* (1973), *Cleopatra Jones* (1973), *Black Godfather* (1974), *Foxy Brown* (1974), *The Black Six* (1974), and enough others to create a new genre: the blaxploitation film. The label aptly implied that the films were produced and marketed by white Americans for the sole purpose of attracting, even pandering to, a new audience. Certainly most of their stars – Richard Roundtree, Ron O'Neal, Fred Williamson, Pam Grier, Rod Perry, Tamara Dobson – proved a tough sell to white audiences.[25] But although this new infusion of ethnic talent, channeled almost exclusively into crime films pitting trash-talking heroes and heroines against the Man, was slower to cross over into the Hollywood mainstream than the sensibility of the European émigrés a generation before, the blaxploitation genre offered a new showcase to established African-American stars like Sidney Poitier, Bill Cosby, Harry Belafonte, Flip Wilson, and Richard Pryor (*Uptown Saturday Night*, 1974), gave a new impetus to interracial crime stories (*In the Heat of the Night*, 1967; *Across 110th Street*, 1972), and occasionally captured an authentic sense of ethnic rage (*Sweet Sweetback's Baad Asssss Song*, 1971).

It was only a matter of time before the growing rage against the establishment, as virulent as during the Depression but now unfettered by the Depression-era Production Code, spilled over into the portrayal of the police themselves. Only three years after *Bullitt* (1968) had set the saintly cop Lt. Frank Bullitt (Steve McQueen) between ruthless mob killers and equally ruthless politicians, and four years after *In the Heat of the Night* had been the first crime film to win a Best Picture Oscar, the Oscar-winning police drama *The French Connection* (1971) dispensed with *Bullitt*'s noble hero and *In the Heat of the Night*'s uplifting endorsement of racial equality in its annihilating portrait of the NYPD, personified in maverick cop Jimmy "Popeye" Doyle (Gene Hackman). Tireless, brutal, vicious, indifferent to the constraints of the law and his superiors, as violent as the druglords he pursued, Doyle represented both the ideally intuitive police detective popularized by decades of films since *"G" Men* and the audience's worst nightmares of the public abuse of authority.

The film's portrait of institutional authority was too lacerating to be simply recycled. Its 1975 sequel – in which Doyle, traveling to Marseilles in search of the French druglord (Fernando Rey) who eluded him at the end of the first film, is kidnapped, hooked on heroin, and then released to the French police, who hold him in secret while forcing him to go through the horrors of cold-turkey withdrawal – makes him far more sympathetic, even to restoring a speech attesting his fondness for Willie Mays that had been cut from the earlier film.

Meanwhile, *The Godfather* (1972) had rivaled *The French Connection*'s success at the Academy Awards, winning Oscars for Best Actor, Best Adapted Screenplay, and Best Picture, and exceeded Popeye Doyle's pull at the box office. This time, however, audiences and critics were responding not only to the film's portrait of a hero corrupted by the "family business" of organized crime, but by its nostalgic celebration of the strong, if ultimately tragic, ties among the Corleones. In a world in which no one can be trusted, the film seemed to suggest, family, for better or worse, is everything. Other crime films seemed equally ready to burrow into the past, either as a strategic retreat from the present (*Murder on the Orient Express,* 1974) or as a safely distant vantage point from which to explore the intractable contemporary problems of corruption and greed (*Chinatown,* 1974).

When movies turned again to establishment heroes, their criticism was more measured and equivocal. Even *Dirty Harry* (1971) and its four sequels (1973–88) gave its rogue cop better excuses for his reckless behavior than *The French Connection* had for Doyle's, from more dangerous criminal adversaries like the well-organized rogue cops in *Magnum Force* (1973) to a fistful of Christian analogues that helped establish his credentials as a traditional, though unexpected, moral hero. Yet the antiauthoritarian legacy of Vietnam left law enforcers of every stripe under a shadow, particularly after the Watergate scandal had the effect of criminalizing in the public imagination the entire executive branch of the federal government. Lawyers, the most obvious villains in the Watergate cover-up, fell to such a low point in public esteem that the most admirable Hollywood lawyer heroes were the anti-lawyers of . . . *And Justice for All* (1979), *The Verdict* (1982), and *My Cousin Vinny* (1992) [Fig. 8] and the nonlawyers of *Regarding Henry* (1991) and *The Pelican Brief* (1993). Even the blue-sky heroics of *Superman* (1978) and its three sequels (1981–7) gave way to the darker heroics of *Batman* (1989) and its three sequels (1992–7), in which the Dark Knight is repeatedly upstaged, like Dick Tracy, by villains more interesting than he is.

Criminal Anxieties, Criminal Jokes

As the 1990s wore on, however, it became clear that however cynical Americans may have grown about the justice system, they were even more frightened of criminals. After years of polls in which fewer than 10 percent of respondents listed crime as the nation's most important problem, it abruptly shot to the top of the 1994 Gallup Poll, with some 40 percent of respondents listing it as most important.[26] The recreational use of drugs, taken for granted by a generation of upper-class college students in the 1960s and 1970s, had been stigmatized by crack cocaine, whose low street price and well-publicized rush of euphoria made it the drug of choice among the black underclass. As legislators imposing mandatory minimum sentences, and police officers under heavy pressure to clean out crack houses and preserve decaying cities moved against the epidemic with a series of Wars on Drugs, the prison population skyrocketed. For the first time since Prohibition, a large number of Americans were jailed for an activity openly enjoyed by an even larger number. This time, however, public attitudes toward drugs were divided far more closely along class lines. America's inner cities, reeling from the effects of the exodus to the suburbs, were widely associated with poverty and crime. Unlike Prohibition audiences, who could always be relied on to find some point of contact with the fictional surrogates of the criminals who supplied liquor to every social class, citizens who endured or read about drug-related crimes like robbery and burglary now found themselves identifying with victims rather than criminals – not because members of the middle and upper classes had never used drugs, but because they had never used the

8. *My Cousin Vinny:* The antilawyer turned lawyer hero. (Marisa Tomei, Fred Gwynne, Joe Pesci)

highly addictive crack that was subject to the most severe criminal penalties.

Drug abuse, which had once been reserved for message dramas like *The Man with the Golden Arm* (1955) and *Bigger Than Life* (1956), had by now become a trope for corruption (*La Bamba,* 1987; *The Five Heartbeats,* 1991; *Casino,* 1995; *Basquiat,* 1996; *Boogie Nights,* 1997) and hard-core criminality (*GoodFellas,* 1990; *Rush,* 1991; *One False Move,* 1991; *Bad Lieutenant,* 1992; *Point of No Return,* 1993). One of the most striking differences between the 1932 *Scarface* and Brian De Palma's 1983 remake is between Tony Camonte, who makes a fortune by selling beer but is never shown drinking, and Marielito Tony Montana, shown at one point collapsing in a pile of his product, undone as much by consuming as by selling cocaine. The 1983 *Scarface* traded on the forbidden glamour of drug use as a token of the economic success that both confirmed the characters' arrival among the upper classes and prepared for their downfall [Fig. 9].

Audiences proved similarly conflicted in their attitudes toward screen violence. On the one hand, the violence of movies, along with that of children's television programming and video games, was in-

9. *Scarface* (1983): Marielito Tony Montana (Al Pacino) wasted by the drugs that mark his success.

creasingly condemned as a trigger for the violence of youthful "super-predators" and high-school terrorists. On the other hand, violence was more and more successful, and more and more in demand, in selling movies to a generation of teenagers who had grown up with remote controls that had sharpened their impatience, discouraged the deferred gratifications of slow-moving films, and reintroduced Mack Sennett's eighty-year-old principle of slapstick comedy: The introduction, buildup, and payoff of each joke had to take less than a minute.

These deepening divisions in audiences' attitudes toward violence, criminals, and the law – divisions, however often staged as debates among different people, that clearly ran deep within many individual audience members – produced a rich array of contradictory films and contradictory responses. In 1991, in a show of Academy unanimity matched only in 1934 and 1975, *The Silence of the Lambs* swept all four top awards, along with a writing Oscar; yet the film's success was anything but unanimous, blasted as it was by reviewers like Michael Medved who insisted that it was disastrously out of step with mainstream American values.[27] The ensuing decade produced important and hotly debated films about the relations between criminals and the police

10. *New Jack City:* An equal-opportunity drug culture. (Allen Payne, Wesley Snipes, Christopher Williams)

(*One False Move; Heat,* 1995), a continued updating of the neo-noir tradition in the erotic thriller (*Basic Instinct,* 1992; *Body of Evidence,* 1993), a postmodern renewal of the gangster film (*Reservoir Dogs,* 1991; *Pulp Fiction,* 1994), a return of the unofficial detective (*Devil in a Blue Dress,* 1995) and the innocent man on the run (*The Fugitive,* 1993), and the reemergence of the lawyer film (the John Grisham industry, with its prodigious influence on popular fiction as well as popular film).

Among the welter of these releases, a few developments stand out with particular clarity. First is the adaptation of the gangster film to the gangs sociologists and citizens alike find peculiar to the nineties: young, urban, African-American street gangs. The pivotal success of Spike Lee, whose films from *Do the Right Thing* (1989) to *Summer of Sam* (1999) tend to treat crime peripherally, encouraged African-American directors like Mario Van Peebles, John Singleton, and Ernest Dickerson to present their own versions of contemporary gang life. Van Peebles, whose father had made *Sweet Sweetback's Baad Asssss Song* twenty years earlier, followed the plot of *Scarface* surprisingly closely in *New Jack City* (1991), warning of the false promises of drug use and the culture it spawned [Fig. 10]. *Boyz N the Hood* (1991), which made Singleton the youngest director ever to be nominated for an

Oscar, was even more searingly realistic in its portrayal of the allure of gang life as the only community open to black ghetto kids, and the ambiguities surrounding two meanings of the word "gangs": the social units young people always tend to form, and the criminal organizations contemporary audiences use the term to identify.[28]

Unlike the blaxploitation films of the seventies, these films, though targeting primarily African-American audiences, had far more crossover appeal; but they were never as commercially successful as the series of comedy/action vehicles for Eddie Murphy (*48 Hrs.*, 1982; *Another 48 Hrs.*, 1990; *Beverly Hills Cop*, 1984, its sequels, 1987, 1994) and the salt-and-pepper team of Mel Gibson and Danny Glover (*Lethal Weapon*, 1987, and its three sequels, 1989–98). The box-office enthusiasm that greeted standup comic Murphy's debut as a foul-mouthed convict-turned-detective in *48 Hrs.* and the small effort required to turn him into a Detroit cop in the later franchise attested to audiences' hunger for antiauthoritarian authority figures [Fig. 11] – a hunger *Lethal Weapon*, which featured the relatively rooted family man Roger Murtaugh (Glover) barely restraining his "lethal weapon" police partner, the manic maverick Martin Riggs (Gibson), was designed once again to feed. The more modest success of the seven farcical *Police Academy* films (1984–94) showed that the formula demanded not toothlessly comical cops but wisecracking and independent action as the logical responses to dramatic tension and social oppression; the threat had to be as real as the release.

The most ambivalent of all nineties crime films, however, were the postmodern fables of David Lynch, Joel and Ethan Coen, and Quentin Tarantino. Lynch's *Blue Velvet* (1986), which mingled cloyingly saccharine glimpses of small-town Americana with horrific revelations about its psychosexual underside, marked a watershed in the history of criminal nightmares whose dark joke was that they seemed much more real than the supposedly normal surface above. The Coen brothers, beginning with *Blood Simple* (1984), set their seal on a new round of ironic crime comedies so dark that many audiences could not explain why they were laughing. Tarantino's startling *Reservoir Dogs* (1991), which uses the caper-gone-wrong to examine the nature of male posturing and male loyalty, attracted notice mainly for its unflinching violence, but his masterly *Pulp Fiction,* whose gangster heroes always had time in between their last round of killing and the next unanticipated trapdoor about to open beneath their feet to debate such moral quiddities as the meaning of a foot massage or the

11. *Beverly Hills Cop:* Eddie Murphy (center) as anti-authoritarian authority figure.

personality a pig would have to have to be edible, offered an exuberantly comic counterpoint to Lynch's nightmare vision of middle America. Tarantino's trademark moments – the plunging of a hypodermic into the breast of the untouchable, accidentally overdosed gangster's wife Mia Wallace (Uma Thurman), the double-crossing boxer Butch Coolidge (Bruce Willis) and his mortal enemy Marsellus Wallace (Ving Rhames) taken prisoner by a pair of homosexual rapists much more dangerous than they are, the accidental point-blank shooting of the gang member being asked by Vincent Vega (John Travolta) whether he believes in miracles – treat criminal violence as a cosmic joke whose point, like the threat of nuclear holocaust in *Dr. Strangelove* (1964), is precisely that jokes are an inadequate response to death, chaos, and annihilation. The nature of Lynch's and Tarantino's jokey send-ups of contemporary social anxieties by translating them into impossibly elaborate criminal plots inaugurated a hip new subgenre of ironic crime comedies like *2 Days in the Valley* (1996) [Fig. 12], *Happiness* (1998), *Lock, Stock, and Two Smoking Barrels* (1999), *Go* (1999), and *Nurse Betty* (2000).

As Hollywood addressed Americans' indecision about whether crime should be treated as a social epidemic or a sick joke by com-

12. *2 Days in the Valley:* Ironic crime comedy in the tradition of *Pulp Fiction.*
(Glenne Headly, Greg Cruttwell, Danny Aiello)

bining both perspectives in films like *Blue Velvet* and *Pulp Fiction,* popular fascination with the law soared to new heights. Although Americans regularly affirmed their disillusionment with courts and lawyers,
they responded eagerly to fictional representations of the law. Fueled
by Scott Turow's novel *Presumed Innocent* (1987), which turned a criminal prosecutor into the defendant in a high-profile murder case, and
John Grisham's *The Firm* (1989), which allowed a rookie lawyer to
disentangle himself from his mob-connected Memphis firm, the legal
thriller became a best-selling literary genre for the first time since Robert Travers's *Anatomy of a Murder* (1956). Nor was this triumph restricted to fictional courtroom drama. The success of Court TV and
the replacement of the heavily fictionalized television program *Divorce Court* by the real-life proceedings of *The People's Court* and *Judge
Judy* groomed a new audience for an apparently limitless succession
of unofficial Crimes of the Century, each of them minutely described,
analyzed, cataloged, and second-guessed in the news media by the
few legal experts who were not busy grinding out their own novels.
O. J. Simpson's two trials, for murder and for violating his murdered
wife Nicole Brown Simpson's and her late friend Ronald Goldman's

civil rights – the acknowledged landmark in this series of court cases – set a pattern for fairy-tale characters, exotic backgrounds, inexhaustible plot twists, an epic sense of scale and duration, strong partisan interests along preexisting lines of race and class, and a colorful array of legal personalities, most of whom wasted no time when the case was over in rushing into memoirs or novels revealing themselves even more fully to a waiting world. Secure in their knowledge that lawyers, loved or hated, are always opposed by other lawyers who can be hated or loved, audiences for this endless soap opera of real-life justice could find in it just the magic carpet to keep their ambivalence toward the law aloft indefinitely.

3

Critical Overview

Like comedies, westerns, horror films, and science fiction, the crime film has inspired dozens of volumes of critical commentary. It is difficult to write a coherent history of criticism of the crime film, however, especially because of its tendency to split into subgenres whose import is apparently only distantly related. The project of genre theory itself has depended throughout its history on the ascendancy of such critical methodologies as the structuralism of Tzvetan Todorov, which allows the systematic analysis of generic conventions, and the revisionist historicism of Rick Altman, which uncovers economic motives for the rise and fall of specific Hollywood genres. In the same way, critical responses to the crime film and its numerous subgenres have divided according to which modes of academic criticism have been fashionable from moment to moment: auteur criticism, mise-en-scène criticism, thematic criticism, structural criticism, psychoanalytic criticism, economic criticism, critical interrogations of race or gender or identity politics. Overlaid on these categories, however, is a different, surprisingly rigid series of categories dictated by the different crime subgenres themselves. The gangster film, the first crime subgenre to provoke serious commentary, tends to generate discussions of Hollywood mythmaking. Though this thematic strand continues in discussions of film noir, it is complemented by an equally strong thread of mise-en-scène criticism. Later, psychoanalytic and feminist approaches rediscover the film noir and grapple with the emerging erotic thriller. Still more recent critics deal with film noir in terms of economic or cultural history. Despite continuing debates about the value of these approaches, they share one thing in common: They are all anti-intentionalist, seeking the meaning of popular genres not in the avowed purposes of their creators but in something broader and deeper – universalistic myths, industrywide production styles, patriarchal hegemony, material or cultural forces beyond the creators' control and sometimes beyond their understanding.

This anti-intentionalist strain of criticism, though it remains the single leading note of most contemporary academic criticism, has never achieved anything like the same dominance in criticism of the detective film. Although criticism of detective fiction has long been influenced by structuralism, another anti-intentionalist school, structural analysis has never had a similar impact on criticism of the detective film. Instead, most commentary on detective films seems to have taken its cue from the rationalistic, hero-oriented bent of the films themselves. The result is an odd kind of auteur criticism, organized around the detective (or occasionally the roster of stars who have played the detective in different films) as auteur, and a strong tendency to accept the films on their own terms rather than analyzing them, individually or as a group, in any terms they do not explicitly invite.

One result of this difference is the production of two distinct kinds of genre history, an intentionalist history focusing on detective films and an anti-intentionalist history devoted to gangster films and films noirs. Jon Tuska and James Naremore can both be called historians of the crime film, since both attempt to root crime films in their cultural contexts, but Tuska's history is intentionalist, a chronicle of the facts and faces behind particular detective series, whereas Naremore's is a far more tendentious attempt to unmask the motives and influences of creators who may have been unwilling to acknowledge them, or indeed consciously unaware of them. For these reasons, criticism of crime films, like the films themselves, is more illuminatingly surveyed in terms of subgenres and the critical methodologies they have encouraged than in terms of a single discontinuous chronology. But isolating the leading tendencies in commentaries on the crime film from each other and tracing the development of each one produces a general, though often recursive, chronological history of crime-film criticism, a history best understood in the context of earlier theories of crime fiction.

Theories of Crime Fiction

Systematic criticism of the crime film was delayed by three obstacles. Early champions of film art like British documentary filmmaker and historian Paul Rotha tended to dismiss the established genres of Hollywood entertainment in favor of more ambitious, individual, original films that were the very antithesis of the crime film. Even among genres, the crime film continued to suffer neglect in favor of the western, which enjoyed a renaissance in the widescreen, Technicolor incarnations of the 1950s, because so many crime films were routine B-film "programmers"; *Double Indemnity* (1944), whose budget and Oscar attention made it Paramount's closest criminal analogue to *Shane* (1953), was not very close at all. Finally, Alfred Hitchcock's predominance in the suspense genre meant that when academic critics considered the crime film, they turned first to Hitchcock's films and the auteurist perspective they encouraged as products of a single director. For all these reasons, few critics writing in English paid close attention to the crime film before 1970.

By that time, criticism of the detective story, the first sort of crime fiction to have encouraged sustained critical analysis, had already gone through several distinct phases. As early as 1901, G. K. Chesterton had written in "A Defence of Detective Stories" that such stories are "the earliest and only form of popular literature in which is expressed some sense of the poetry of modern life," the romance of the modern city evoked so ably by Robert Louis Stevenson but neglected so completely by most other writers of serious literary pretensions.[1] A quarter-century later, after his Father Brown mysteries had captured the popular imagination, Chesterton added a prophetic dimension to his analysis of the genre's appeal: Since a detective story's movement from mystery to enlightenment is a prefiguration of the apocalypse, the moment when every earthly veil will be swept away, each mystery must be governed by a single unifying concept that makes its ending "not only the bursting of a bubble but rather the breaking of a dawn."[2]

The greatest influence of Chesterton's theological analysis of the detective story's appeal was indirect. In the opening chapter of *Trent's Last Case* (1913), E. C. Bentley burlesques the millenialism to which his friend Chesterton had alluded by showing the earth-shattering (yet ultimately inconsequential) results of the shadowy financier Sigsbee Manderson's shooting as the introduction to a case whose twists seem to mock human reason. The detective-story writers who followed Bentley, from the Britons Agatha Christie, Dorothy L. Sayers, and Margery Allingham to the Americans S. S. Van Dine, Ellery Queen, and John Dickson Carr, secularized Chesterton's emphasis on rationality as a prefiguration of a transcendental apocalypse, trivializing its theological overtones in the course of producing the influential recipe for the detective story as a comedy of manners for the characters and a civilized game of logical inference for the audience, all climaxing with a "Challenge to the Reader" made explicit in Queen's first nine novels (1929–35): an invitation to solve the mystery on the basis of the clues presented to detective and reader alike. The often highly formulaic interactions of the stock character types were nothing more than a pretense for the story's true action – "a hoodwinking contest," as Carr put it – between the enterprising author devising ingenious new means for murder and methods of concocting alibis and the wary reader determined to figure out the solution before it was revealed in the final chapter.[3] The principal theories of the formal or Golden Age detective story, as John Strachey dubbed it,[4] took the form of historical introductions to anthologies of detective short stories or lists of rules for authors to observe in order to play fair with the reader.[5]

It was not until the 1940s that criticism of the formal detective story came to focus on the moral import of these games. Nicholas Blake added to Chesterton's analogy between the revelatory denouement and the apocalypse the proposition that since readers of detective fiction identify with both detectives and murderers, the stories are folk myths whose aim is to purge postreligious audiences of guilt by reconciling "the light and dark sides" of their social attitudes.[6] W. H. Auden, agreeing with Blake that the detective stories appeal to their audiences' "sense of sin," argued by contrast that "the illusion of being dissociated from the murderer" in detective fiction, as opposed to the more literary novels of Dostoyevsky and Raymond Chandler, provides "the fantasy of being restored to the Garden of Eden" by using "the magic formula" of "an innocence which is discovered to contain guilt; then a suspicion of being the guilty other has been expelled, a cure effected, not by me or my neighbors, but by the miraculous intervention of a genius from outside who removes guilt by giving knowledge of guilt."[7]

In the meantime, a third phase of detective-story criticism had begun with Chandler's influential essay "The Simple Art of Murder" (1944). Unlike critics who defended the Golden Age formula of baffling mystery and rational detection as an intellectual game or a morally purgative ritual, Chandler announced in his frankly challenging opening sentence: "Fiction in any form has always intended to be realistic." Against the "badly-scared champions of the formal or the classic mystery who think no story is a detective story which does not pose a formal and exact problem and arrange the clues around it with neat labels on them," Chandler defended the hard-boiled private-eye stories of Dashiell Hammett, and by implication his own work, by arguing that they "gave murder back to the kind of people that commit it for reasons, not just to provide a corpse; and with the means at hand, not with hand-wrought duelling pistols, curare, and tropical fish."[8] Chandler's passionate partisanship of hard-boiled fiction's proletarian realism, ignoring the equally formulaic qualities of his own fiction,[9] established a conflict between realistic and ritualistic impulses – the tendency toward photographic or psychological realism versus the tendency toward the revelatory structure of dream, myth, and fairy tale – that serves as a backdrop for the theories of crime films that begin to emerge shortly thereafter.

Hollywood Mythmaking

Though neither of them names Paul Rotha directly, Parker Tyler and Robert Warshow, the first important critics to deal in English with crime films, both tackle his condescension toward genre films head-on. The two of them, writing soon after Chandler's "Simple Art of Murder," share the same project: to reveal the unconscious collective myths that play a much larger role than deliberate individual artistry in shaping Hollywood movies. As Tyler argues in *Magic and Myth of the Movies* (1947), "the lack of individual control" over any given Hollywood project, coupled with "the absence of respect for the original work" and "the premise that a movie is an ingenious fabrication of theoretically endless elasticity," all produce conditions more congenial to collective myth – "the industrialization of the mechanical worker's daylight dream" – than to individual art.[10] Tyler and Warshow ignore the avowed programs of individual filmmakers to examine the unconscious myths that underlie "what the public wants" – the collective tastes to which movies appeal.[11] Yet their approaches to the crime film could hardly be more different.

Tyler, America's first metaphysician of the movies, is an antigenre theorist for whom the narrative films produced by Hollywood studios constitute their own sovereign genre formed in response to its audience's needs and desires. Although most of the films Tyler discusses represent specimens of popular genres rather than aspirations to individual artistic achievement, he is less interested in the specificity of their genre markers than in their contribution to a transgeneric ontology of cinema. Tyler's analysis of *Double Indemnity,* for example, focuses on the relationship between Walter Neff and his boss Barton Keyes. The intimacy between the two men, he avers, is from the beginning an example of the insurance industry's psychopathology. Insurance salesmen like Walter make their living by marketing "the myth . . . that human wisdom has provided a method of safeguarding against certain consequences of accident or death," while at the same time claims adjusters like Keyes, who are "waiting to *invalidate* this myth," serve as "an ethical corrective" to the salesman's success in selling it. As the story unfolds, Tyler contends, Keyes appears more and more clearly as Walter's "sexual conscience," the unyielding figure who "*presides over his life as the hidden judge of his sexual claims as well as the insurance claims of his clients,*" and who condemns the "war psychology" whereby Walter "sells himself the idea of murderous violence as an aid to moral enthusiasm – in his case an enthusiasm for sex."[12]

Turning to *Mildred Pierce* (1945), Tyler compares it to *Citizen Kane* (1941) in compromising its identification of the camera eye with the "Universal Spectator" by failing to see just what the audience would most like to know: the identity of Rosebud, or of the person who fired the fatal shots into Monte Beragon (Zachary Scott). Both films depend on a single paradox: the substitution of "the rational or mechanical mystery" of the detective-story formula and the potentially omniscient camera eye for "the irrational or symbolic mystery of *the human soul*" for an audience that subliminally recognizes the incommensurability of these two sorts of mystery. Hence *Mildred Pierce,* whose story proceeds toward a climactic visualization of Monte's murder that finally identifies Mildred's daughter Veda (Ann Blyth) as his actual killer, works at the same time as "Mildred's dream of guilt" for having wished for Monte's death and created both the conditions under which he died and the executioner, the double of her younger self and her present desires, who is "a form of herself . . . [who] for some reason has taken on her incest crime."[13] As the detective apparatus of the film vindicates Mildred (Joan Crawford) in order to motivate a happy ending, her identification with Veda implicates her in Veda's guilt [Fig. 13]. Tyler's own implication is that this paradox, although it emerges with unusual clarity in mystery stories, is essential to all the dreams of Hollywood, essential indeed to the nature of the camera eye of narrative cinema.[14]

In "The Gangster as Tragic Hero" (1948), Warshow emphasizes by contrast the specificity of the gangster genre in posing a resistant alternative to the prevailing myth of optimism and social happiness that amounts to an unofficial imperative of democratic cultures. Unlike "'happy'" movies like *Good News* (1947), which "ignores death and suffering," and "'sad'" movies like *A Tree Grows in Brooklyn* (1945), which "uses death and suffering as incidents in the service of a higher optimism," gangster films express "that sense of desperation and inevitable failure which optimism itself helps to create." The gangster of Hollywood mythology – a figure much better known to most audiences than any actual gangsters – expresses the ethos of the city: "not the real city, but that dangerous and sad city of the imagination which is so much more important, which is the modern world." And his "pure criminality," which "becomes at once the means to success and the content of success," shows, through the rise and fall of his career, his futile attempt to establish his individual identity in a world whose only security is to be found in protective social groups, that "there is really only one possibility: failure. The final meaning of the city is anonymity and death." In the end, the gangster dies as the scapegoat of his conflicted audience, the man who represents both the capitalistic imperative to rise above others and the democratic imperative to remain equal to others. Hence "he is under the obligation to succeed," even though his audience knows that "success is evil and dangerous, is – ultimately – impossible." He does what no other movie hero can do: allows his audience to accept their failure as a moral choice by disavowing the corruption implicit in his fatal success.[15]

Genre versus Auteur

Tyler's and Warshow's work grows out of a tradition of American journalism that also produced the criticism of James Agee, Otis Ferguson, Manny Farber, and Pauline Kael. When film criticism entered American universities some twenty years later, however, it was not this journalistic impulse that predominated, but the sort of auteur criticism typified by Andrew Sarris's *The American Cinema: Directors and Directions, 1929–1968* (1968), with its notoriously precise ranking of directors from "Pantheon" status down through the ranks to "Strained Seri-

13. *Mildred Pierce:* The heroine (Joan Crawford) both contrasted and identified with her villainous daughter (Ann Blyth).

ousness" and "Less than Meets the Eye," and by François Truffaut's
book-length interview *Le Cinéma selon Hitchcock* (1966), translated as
Hitchcock (1967).[16] Even though the auteurist championing of popular
filmmakers like Hitchcock, which began with *Cahiers du cinéma* and
traveled to America through Sarris's *Village Voice* reviews and polem-
ical essays, eventually helped bring crime films to critical attention by
turning critical scrutiny from prestige studio productions like *Gone
with the Wind* and *The Wizard of Oz* (both 1939) to B movies like *Detour* (1945) and *The Big Combo* (1955), the immediate effect of auteur-
ism was to stifle any systematic analysis of popular genres. Not only
was genre study unable to compete successfully with the study of individual directors, but Hitchcock's long-standing popular success –
which Sarris and Truffaut urged to academic respectability – acted, as
Charles Derry has observed, to inhibit analysis of the suspense genre,
which was so often identified as that filmmaker's own exclusive province.[17]

The auteurist impulse remains primary in the first book-length critical study of the crime film in English, Colin McArthur's *Underworld U.S.A.* (1972). Noting the predominance of thematic and auteurist approaches in recent film criticism, McArthur defines his own approach to what he calls "the gangster film/thriller" as a focus on its "iconography," the leading visual and semiological codes that link gangster films like *The Public Enemy* (1931) and *Dillinger* (1945) to thrillers like *The Maltese Falcon* (1941) and *Dead Reckoning* (1947) and establish their world as common and distinctive.[18] But after four introductory chapters ("Genre," "Iconography," "Development," and "Background") in which this iconographic approach is intermittently maintained, McArthur proceeds to a director-by-director survey of Fritz Lang, John Huston, Jules Dassin, Robert Siodmak, Elia Kazan, Nicholas Ray, Samuel Fuller, Don Siegel, and Jean-Pierre Melville in which auteurist concerns predominate over genre analysis. McArthur concludes his discussion of Fuller's *Pickup on South Street* (1953), *House of Bamboo* (1955), *The Crimson Kimono* (1959), and *Underworld U.S.A.* (1961) by urging, in true auteurist fashion, that "with the possible exceptions of John Ford and Elia Kazan, no Hollywood film-maker has so consistently explored the American psyche. [Fuller] deserves to be taken seriously."[19] It was left to other critics to pursue McArthur's argument further from its roots in, and its ultimate allegiance to, the careers of individual filmmakers.

Thematic and Iconographic Analysis

Critics who read French were already familiar with the groundwork for a thematic approach to the crime genre laid by Raymond Borde and Étienne Chaumeton in their *Panorama du film noir américain* (1955). Noting film noir's leading points of departure from other films about violent death – its adoption of the criminal's point of view and fascination with the criminal's psychology, the moral determinism of the ambiguous and unstable criminal milieu, and the persistent oneirism that associates realistic individual details with constant suggestions of symbol, nightmare, and unbridled chaos – Borde and Chaumeton conclude that the goal of each of these devices is "to make the viewer coexperience the anguish and insecurity which are the true emotions of contemporary film noir. All the films of this cycle create a similar emotional effect: *that state of tension instilled in the spectator when the psychological reference points are removed.* The aim of *film noir* was to create *a specific alienation.*"[20] Borde and Chaumeton's distinctions both focused their study of representative noirs more sharply and helped give film noir a greater critical impetus than the larger genre of the crime film from which they wished to distinguish it.[21]

Fifteen years after Borde and Chaumeton's pioneering work, Raymond Durgnat returned to the project of thematic analysis in "Paint It Black: The Family Tree of the *Film Noir.*" Despite the essay's title, it does not establish a family tree of precedents for or influences on film noir; instead, it proposes eleven branch topics along which Durgnat briskly disposes some three hundred films from *Easy Street* (1917) to *2001: A Space Odyssey* (1968), this last on the grounds that "*film noir* is not a genre . . . and takes us into the realm of classification by motif and tone" rather than the subject of crime. "Only some crime films are *noir*," Durgnat contends, "and *films noirs* in other genres include *The Blue Angel*, *King Kong*, *High Noon*, *Stalag 17* . . . and *2001.*"[22] But Durgnat's eleven topics – "crime as social criticism," "gangsters," "on the run," "private eyes and adventurers," "middle class murder," "portraits and doubles," "sexual pathology," "psychopaths," "hostages to fortune," "blacks and reds," and "guignol, horror, fantasy" – are thematic rather than motivic or tonal, although a brief analysis of them reveals that they neither distinguish noirs from non-noirs nor, in their frequent overlapping and lack of parallelism, provide a systematic framework for defining film noir. Durgnat's work was accordingly most useful in suggesting topics for further research, encouraging discussion about the categorization of specific films, and provoking an alternative approach to the crime film. His thematic approach has been adopted by critics from Robert Porfirio to Glenn Erickson, even when they take issue with the specific categories Durgnat proposes.[23]

Restless critics seeking an alternative approach to Durgnat's thematics – intermittently promised by McArthur's description of his emphasis as iconographic and Durgnat's description of noir in terms of motif and tone rather than subject or genre – might have found such an approach already implicit in Charles Higham and Joel Greenberg's discussion, in their *Hollywood in the Forties* (1968), of "Black Cinema," which begins: "A dark street in the early morning hours, splashed with a sudden downpour. Lamps form haloes in the murk. In a walk-up room, filled with the intermittent flashing of a neon sign from across the street, a man is waiting to murder or be murdered."[24] As befits its context in Higham and Greenberg's survey of forties films, their discussion of noir iconography and their perusal of representative noirs from *Shadow of a Doubt* (1943) to *The Lady from Shanghai* (1948) is evocative rather than systematic.

The first theorist to attempt anything like an iconographic grammar of film noir is Paul Schrader, not yet a noted screenwriter (*Taxi Driver*, 1976; *Raging Bull*, 1980; *Bringing Out the Dead*, 1999) and director (*Hardcore*, 1979; *Patty Hearst*, 1988; *Affliction*, 1998). Agreeing with Durgnat that "*film noir* is not a genre," Schrader identifies it instead with "a specific period in film history, like German Expressionism or the French New Wave." According to Schrader, the flowering of noir in the 1940s and early 1950s depends on four leading influences: postwar disillusionment, the worldwide resurgence of an often harsh realism, the influence of Germanic expatriate directors and cinematographers, and the hard-boiled tradition of American writing exemplified by Chandler as novelist and screenwriter. Schrader divides the development of film noir into three overlapping phases. The first (1941–6), typified by *The Maltese Falcon* and *This Gun for Hire* (1942), is dominated by "the private eye and the lone wolf." The second (1945–9), ushered in by *Double Indemnity* and exemplified by *The House on 92nd Street* (1945) and *The Naked City* (1948), is "the post-war realistic period," focusing on "the problems of crime in the streets, political corruption and police routine." The third (1949–53), represented by *Gun Crazy* (1949) and *The Big Heat* (1953), is marked by the sort of "psychotic action and suicidal impulse" that eventually produces the deliriously climactic *Kiss Me Deadly* (1955), "the masterpiece of film noir," and "*film noir*'s epitaph," *Touch of Evil* (1958).[25]

This historical summary, however, is only a frame for Schrader's summary of the mise-en-scène that makes film noir coherent and memorable: the prevalence of nighttime lighting for interiors and exteriors alike; the preponderance of oblique angles and skewed lines over verticals, horizontals, and right angles; the tendency of the lighting and blocking to give inanimate objects as much emphasis as actors; the preponderance of portentous compositional tension over cathartic physical action; the "almost Freudian attachment to water" (particularly unrealistic in stories set in and around Los Angeles); the prevalence of romantic voice-over narration – like the memorable line with which Michael O'Hara (Orson Welles) introduces *The Lady from Shanghai:* "When I start out to make a fool of myself, there's very little can stop me" – to establish an unquenchable yearning for the past and a fatalistic frame for the present; and a rigorously confusing use of flashbacks and time shifts "to reinforce the feelings of hopelessness and lost time." These techniques work together, Schrader concludes, to "emphasize loss, nostalgia, lack of clear priorities, insecurity; then submerge these self-doubts in mannerism and style. In such a world style becomes paramount; it is all that separates one from meaninglessness."[26]

Schrader's emphasis on noir as a period and a style rather than a subject or genre is echoed by Janey Place and Lowell Peterson in "Some Visual Motifs of *Film Noir*" (1974), a brief but profusely illustrated catalog of visual devices that the authors divide into a distinctive "photographic style: antitraditional lighting and camera" (low-key lighting; movement of the key light off to the side; night-for-night shooting; increased depth of field; optical distortions of space and shape associated with wide-angle lenses) and an equally distinctive "directorial style: antitraditional mise-en-scène" (irregular or unbalanced figure placement; claustrophobic frames within the frame; doubling characters with shadows or reflections or inanimate objects in order to depersonalize them or suggest their hidden depths; withholding establishing shots or camera movements that would root the characters more securely in the frame and the space and world it presents).[27] Place and Peterson make a persuasive case for the decisive importance of such visual motifs to film noir, not only as signatures of individual auteurs but as expressions of a particular view of the world [Fig. 14].[28]

Structuralism and Beyond

By the mid-1970s, film noir had largely displaced the gangster film as the focus of crime-film criticism. Although most critics agreed that film noir was not a genre, the project of genre criticism itself was bolstered by the appearance of Stuart M. Kaminsky's *American Film Genres* (1974) and John G. Cawelti's *Adventure, Mystery, and Romance* (1976). As Tyler and Warshow had reacted against Paul Rotha, both Kaminsky and Cawelti broke explicitly with the auteurist assumptions that each work depended on a single authorizing creator and that the critic's task was aesthetic evaluation of different works and auteurs. As Kaminsky put it: "The genre approach need make no popular judgment. It is an examination of popular forms, an attempt to *understand,* not to '*sell*' films or directors."[29] The structuralist move from prescriptive to descriptive criticism is a reasonable response to a genre whose meaning is so completely generated by the conventions it shares with other members of the genre rather than its departures from them that, as Warshow had observed, "originality is to be welcomed only in the degree that it intensifies the expected experience without fundamentally altering it."[30]

Structuralism offers the most logical basis for genre criticism because it focuses on meanings within conventions shared widely throughout a given genre rather than on the transformation of those conventions within individual works. Although he never uses the term *structuralism*, Cawelti's bibliographical notes make it clear that his approach to the formulas of popular fiction owes a foundational debt to Northrop Frye's structural study of myths in his *Anatomy of Criticism* (1957).[31] By replacing auteurist critics' prescriptive faith in an authorizing creator, and timeless aesthetic standards with an anthropologist's interest in the anonymous productions of a given culture, the structuralist orientation redirected attention from the unique qualities of particular artworks to the contours of the popular genres they exemplified.

The first clear example of Frye's influence in the study of crime films is James Damico's 1978 invocation of Frye's analysis of romance in order to define film noir as a genre informed by an attitude and intent expressed through stock characters and a consistent armature of plot. Bypassing the attempt to seek thematic or stylistic denominators common to all noirs, Damico proposes "a model which embodies the 'truest' or 'purest' example of the type" from which more marginal noirs may be seen to diverge:

> A man whose experience of life has left him sanguine and often bitter meets a not-innocent woman of similar outlook to whom he is sexually and fatally attracted. Through this attraction . . . the man comes to cheat, attempt to murder, or actually murder a second man to whom the lover is unhappily or unwillingly attached (generally he is her husband or lover), an act which . . . brings about the sometimes metaphoric, but usually literal destruction of the woman, the man to whom she is attached, and frequently the protagonist himself.[32]

The structuralist impulse behind Damico's model provides a crucial link between the analysis of film noir and the more general commentaries on the crime film that lay ahead. Such a link would prove vital because criticism of the detective film, though nearly as voluminous throughout the 1970s, was taking a completely different course from the debate pitting myth against iconography in defining the film noir.

14. *Out of the Past:* Antitraditional mise-en-scène expressing a grim, romantically stylized view of the world. (Jane Greer, Robert Mitchum, Steve Brodie)

The defining presence of a detective hero had made the detective film seem less problematic from the beginning. Considering the formulaic nature of detective fiction, it was eminently predictable that its conventions would attract the attention of Tzvetan Todorov, the first-generation structuralist most interested in popular forms.

Todorov's essay "The Typology of Detective Fiction" (1966) postulates two alternative modes: the detective story of rational deduction and the *Série noire*, or thriller, which emphasizes suspense rather than curiosity and corresponds, as its French label indicates, to the film noir. Todorov proposes "the suspense novel," whose "reader is interested not only by what has happened but also by what will happen next," as a hybrid of the detective story and the thriller. The suspense novel presents a vulnerable detective "integrated into the universe of the other characters, instead of being an independent observer as the reader is." The mortal detective of the suspense novel, who can be either a fallible professional detective like Sam Spade or an innocent suspect who turns detective in order to clear his or her name, represents the genre's dissatisfactions with the detective formula and the

endeavor to renew that formula by retaining only its suspense elements.[33] Todorov's essay remains important today as the first attempt
to theorize a crime genre more comprehensive than the detective story, the thriller, or the suspense novel by mapping out the transformations of their shared conventions.[34]

Although George Grella, writing a few years later, treated the Golden
Age detective novel and the hard-boiled private-eye novel as equally
formulaic in a pair of essays on the myths of Edenic purity and corrupted romance that underlie the two formulas,[35] only three theorists
have reached outside the permutations of the detective-story formula
to the larger structuralist project Todorov outlines: Cawelti, in the
"Notes Toward a Typology of Literary Formulas" that introduces his
discussion of mystery fiction in *Adventure, Mystery, and Romance;*[36]
Gary C. Hoppenstand, in the typology of mystery and suspense formulas that frames his study *In Search of the Paper Tiger* (1987);[37] and
Charles Derry, in his typology of suspense films according to whether
they focus on criminals, detectives, or victims, and the extent to which
they include a strong detective figure as the exemplar of a rational
world order.[38]

In particular, the kind of structural analysis practiced by Todorov
has been much more influential in the criticism of detective fiction
than in the criticism of detective films. Instead, that criticism has been
dominated by quasi-auteurist studies, with the detective standing in
for the director as auteur. It was only a short step from film historian William K. Everson's *The Bad Guys* (1964), a lively categorical survey of movie villains ("the western outlaws," "the gangsters and the
hoods," "the psychos," and so on) folded into an opulent, oversized
collection of stills, to Everson's *The Detective in Film* (1972) – "an af-
fectionate . . . but certainly not comprehensive, introduction to the
field," as its author called it – which replaced many of the equivalent
photographs with more detailed historical information about the fictional heroes Charlie Chan, Dick Tracy, and the FBI, even though its
large format still suggested a coffee-table book.[39] The fan's impulse
toward appreciation that drives Everson also underlies Jon Tuska's
The Detective in Hollywood (1978), which again surveys the field detective by detective, from Sherlock Holmes and Philo Vance to the heroes
of *Dirty Harry* (1971) and *Chinatown* (1974). Although Tuska writes at
much greater length than Everson, the information he provides – biog-
raphies of detective-story authors, production and economic details

regarding particular films, anecdotes about and interviews with film-makers – steers clear of any systematic critical analysis.[40] The focus on typological characters as the genre's defining center of interest tends to accept these characters and the formulas they imply on their own terms, moving toward relative aesthetic judgments rather than analyzing them as structural or historical functions.

If critical commentary on detective films struggled to find expressive structures beneath the genre's recurrent figures, the combination of structural analysis and social history enabled Jack Shadoian to define "the gangster/crime genre"[41] more broadly yet more precisely than ever before in *Dreams and Dead Ends* (1977). Shadoian takes his cue from both Warshow's tragic myth and the brief sociological hints John Baxter had offered in the trenchant Introduction to his 1970 encyclopedia, *The Gangster Film*, which emphasized the interaction of social, criminal, and Hollywood culture rather than the simple reflection of any one by the other. Since "criminals are the creation of society rather than rebels against it," Baxter notes that audiences' relation to these urban wolves, whose personal and professional code is often indistinguishable from that of the paid enforcers of the law, is ambiguous, informed alike by "menace and glamour."[42] In answer to the question, "What does the genre do that can't be done as well elsewhere?" Shadoian expands this account to define the gangster as "the archetypal American dreamer" whose dreams rehearse the conflict between two blankly opposing national ideologies: the vision of a classless democratic society and the drive to get ahead. Echoing Warshow, Shadoian assigns central importance to the gangster's paradoxical drive for a success that will destroy him as surely as failure. Because neither gangsters, in their unappeasable thirst for success, nor their films propose any serious alternative to "the American way of life" whose shortcomings they dramatize, "they act on behalf of its *ideal* nature. If it could only work the way it is supposed to, there would be no problems." Hence the alluring, fearsome gangster – incorporating both the belief in egalitarianism and the possibility of a better life, both audiences' disillusionment with American society and their ultimate faith in its principles – is a contested figure on whom different periods can project their views of social utopia and social critique, from the limitless aspirations of *Little Caesar* (1930) to the claustrophobic nightmare of *The Killers* (1946), from the "romantic rage of selfhood" in *Gun Crazy* and *White Heat* (both 1949) to the more sentimental humanism of *Pick-*

up on South Street and *99 River Street* (both 1953), before tailing off in the nonrepresentational postmodernism of *Bonnie and Clyde* (1967), *Point Blank* (1967), and *The Godfather* (1972).[43]

Shadoian's eclectic readings of individual films, freely borrowing from mise-en-scène criticism, structuralism, and the historical analysis of gangster myths without committing themselves to any one of them, are echoed in three other synthetic studies that have become the standard narrative histories of their subgenres: Eugene Rosow's *Born to Lose: The Gangster Film in America* (1978), Carlos Clarens's *Crime Movies* (1980), and Foster Hirsch's *The Dark Side of the Screen: Film Noir* (1981). Rosow, whose sociologically oriented study devotes nearly half its length to films before 1930, argues for a close connection between the genre's changing appeal and the specific desires and demands of its changing audience. He is especially acute on the interrelations between organized crime and the business realities of Hollywood filmmaking, as in his observation that "success in the movie industry . . . was achieved in roughly the same way that bootleggers built and were continuing to build their empires" – that is, by former outsiders becoming "Robber Barons" through the ruthless enforcement of their monopolies.[44] Clarens, addressing a question much like Shadoian's – "What can be said to be the true intent of the crime film? To awaken in the viewer a civic conscience? To instill an awareness of a fallible society? To establish distance from a very real problem?" – defines his field more narrowly, despite his title, by excluding "the psychological thriller" that "deals with violence in the private sphere" (e.g., *Shadow of a Doubt, Kiss Me Deadly*) to produce a field basically corresponding to the gangster genre; but he surveys this field much more broadly, providing a comprehensive history studded with brief, pointed commentaries on hundreds of films.[45] Hirsch's volume is synthetic in still another sense, drawing on the work of most important earlier commentators on film noir in chapters that successively consider its literary and cinematic antecedents, its iconography, its narrative patterns, its leading performers and directors, and its influence on other films. Though Hirsch, steering a course between appreciation and analysis, does not attempt an original reconceptualization of noir, his frequent asides on such matters as the returning veteran as "the only character type in *noir* connected directly to the period" and the motifs that tie Hitchcock's films to the noir tradition have made his volume an oft-quoted guide to its subject.[46]

Feminist Critique

Even as Rosow, Clarens, and Hirsch were summing up an era in crime-film criticism, a new wave of feminist studies was calling into question that criticism's methodology. As an earlier generation of critics had rejected Rotha's tenets of originality and ambition, the new feminist theory rejected the content analysis of Molly Haskell, aptly summarized by Haskell's 1974 summary of female roles in films noirs: "In the dark melodramas of the forties, woman came down from her pedestal and she didn't stop when she reached the ground."[47] This revolt is fueled by the double influence of Marxist materialist aesthetics and Jacques Lacan's rewriting of Freud. Christine Gledhill explicitly invokes Marx in turning from the question, "What is this film's meaning?" (a question that assumes that meaning is immanent, objective, and readily available to the disinterested critic, a signifying function free of history and ideology) to the question, "How is its meaning produced?" which changes "*the project of criticism from the discovery of meaning to that of uncovering the means of its production*" – explaining why a genre or formula that has currency in a particular historical moment authorizes some meanings but not others. By changing the feminist critic's question from "Does this image of woman please me or not, do I identify with it or not?" to "*What is being said about women here, who is speaking, for whom?*" Gledhill and other feminists redirect the focus of genre theory from the content of stories, images, and conventions to the ideological conditions under which they were produced.[48]

Feminism's historical project is joined most decisively to Lacan's psychoanalytic theory in Laura Mulvey's influential "Visual Pleasure and Narrative Cinema" (1975). Asking how viewers can derive pleasure from potentially castrating images of women, Mulvey theorizes that movies address the fears of castration that images of women, who lack phalluses, arouse in (presumably male) viewers by allowing audiences the scopophilic pleasures of voyeurism and the narcissistic pleasures of identification with the human figures shown onscreen. Traditional narrative cinema, Mulvey argues, resolves the paradox between these two kinds of pleasure (looking at an image as object, looking at an image as representing a potentially engaging subjectivity) by casting woman as the object of a gaze that is "pleasurable in form" but "threatening in content." Patriarchal cinema neutralizes the potentially castrating power of women's images by fetishizing them, displacing their bodies or breaking them photographically into individually non-threatening pieces (as in *Morocco*, 1930), or making them the subjects of investigations directed by the male gaze (as in *Vertigo*, 1958) in order to reserve for men alone the position of active agents capable of demystifying and possessing potentially threatening women.[49]

Although Mulvey's theory, like Gledhill's, is intended to apply to all commercial films, it has particular applications to film noir, which assigns a central role to erotically charged images of powerful, fearsome women. Instead of joining Haskell in condemning these images as degrading, more recent feminists have used them to interrogate the allegedly invisible signifying practices of Hollywood cinema by unmasking its patriarchal agenda. Claire Johnston, identifying claims adjuster Keyes as the "signifier of the patriarchal order," sees *Double Indemnity* as a displaced oedipal drama in which Walter Neff kills Dietrichson, a negative father-surrogate, in order to take his place as head of his family and achieve at the same time the secure position of Keyes as the positive father.[50] Sylvia Harvey characterizes film noir as marked by "the strange and compelling absence of 'normal' family relations," which "encourage[s] the consideration of alternative institutions for the reproduction of social life."[51] Pam Cook, following Parker Tyler, argues in more general terms that Mildred's brutal assimilation to the patriarchal order in *Mildred Pierce* through the loss of her daughter and the deauthorizing of her narrative voice is one more example of the ways in which "the system which gives men and women their place in society must be reconstructed by a more explicit work of repression" exemplified by the film's narrative and visual systems.[52]

The resulting critique has been developed in two leading directions. In attempting to make room for women in film noir, Elizabeth Cowie has challenged "the tendency to characterize *film noir* as always a masculine film form" by valorizing the female unwilling killer of *The Accused* (1948), the obsessional heroine of *Possessed* (1947), and the fatally smitten heroine of *The Damned Don't Cry* (1950).[53] More often, feminist critics have sought to make room for female audiences by unmasking patriarchal motives behind noir conventions, even at the price of arguing that noir heroines onscreen are mere functions of male desire. Mary Ann Doane defines the femmes fatales who descend from Brigid O'Shaughnessy (Mary Astor), the treacherous client who nearly undermines Sam Spade (Humphrey Bogart) in his manly resolve in *The Maltese Falcon,* as "an articulation of fears surrounding the loss of stability and centrality of the [male] self. . . . The power ac-

15. *The Postman Always Rings Twice* (1946): Is the hero destroyed by the femme fatale, or by his own weakness? (John Garfield, Hume Cronyn, Lana Turner)

corded to the femme fatale is a function of fears linked to the notions of uncontrollable drives, the fading of subjectivity, and the loss of conscious agency."[54] James F. Maxfield is still more explicit: "The internal conflicts of the male protagonists are ultimately more important than external conflicts with other characters – even with the fatal woman. . . . The women are merely catalysts; in the end it is the men who are destructive to themselves"[55] [Fig. 15]. And Richard Dyer contends that "film noir is characterized by a certain anxiety over the existence and definition of masculinity and normality" – an anxiety that, since it cannot be expressed directly (for such a direct expression would admit the existence of the very problem it is the films' work to obscure), is marked by the threatening predominance of nonmasculine images to indicate the boundaries of categories that cannot be constructed in positive terms.[56]

As the feminist critique of Hollywood patriarchy has continued, it has been supplemented by the project Dyer suggests: an analysis of Hollywood images of masculinity. Frank Krutnik's *In a Lonely Street* (1991) explores the ways in which the conventions of film noir (a genre Krutnik restricts to "'tough' thrillers" of the 1940s) amount to a definition and defense of masculinity by allowing the hard-boiled hero to grapple with "the dangers represented by the feminine – not just women in themselves but also any non-'tough' potentiality of his own identity as a man." More generally, Krutnik maintains, the work of the "tough" thriller is to elaborate and resolve contradictions between the whole range of male desire and those desires admitted by a patriarchal culture of the period. A common though often unwilling way "tough" thrillers expressed this tension was to follow the normal Hollywood tendency toward heterosexual romance, since "the grafting of the love story onto the 'hard-boiled' detective story meant that the films had to confront . . . the question of how heterosexuality could possibly be accommodated within the parameters of such an obsessively phallocentric fantasy, without causing it to collapse."[57] The result was not only films like *Dead Reckoning,* in which the hero's love for the heroine is thwarted by his determination to avenge the dead buddy she killed, but films like *The Big Sleep* (1946), in which the hero is paired with a heroine who, though she first seems as devious as any femme fatale, miraculously turns out to be worthy of his trust and love, thus vindicating both his tough, wary professionalism and his openness to love against all odds.

Demystifications

The project of "making visible the invisible" that Annette Kuhn had claimed for feminist criticism – that is, disclosing unconscious, patriarchal, political, or otherwise unacknowledged motives that have shaped filmmaking practices – has had a much wider effect on film studies, and on studies of the crime film in particular.[58] By the time Carl Richardson made the Chandleresque announcement in *Autopsy* (1992) that film noir must balance its dark lack of sentimentality by incorporating "a greater element of realism" from which it departed at its peril, his forthright evaluations already seemed a rearguard action as quaintly dated as the mission of Chandler's knight of the mean streets. Richardson claimed categorically that "external reality [despite the psychologistic or deconstructive claims of Sigmund Freud,

Jacques Lacan, Christian Metz, Michel Foucault, Roland Barthes, and Jean-François Lyotard] is indifferent to minds that aspire to know it" and "unmoved by the incantations of the psychology-driven shamans who seek to master it." Hence Richardson, borrowing his critical framework from contemporary reviewers rather than "the biased perspective of post-1960s scholars, historians, and essayists," dismissed *Touch of Evil,* for example, because it "did not accurately reflect reality."[59]

Richardson's assumptions, which would have represented critical consensus of the detective film through most of its history, were far less representative of contemporaneous analysis of noir than J. P. Telotte's premise that noir is driven by "a compelling urge to understand, formulate, and articulate the human situation at a time when our old formulations, as well as the means of expression underlying them, no longer seemed adequate." Whether he is describing *The Killers* and *Sorry, Wrong Number* (1948), which "use so many subjective viewpoints that they ultimately seem to abandon all notion of an objective vantage or the possibility of ever synthesizing their multiple perspectives," or arguing that the despairing critique of the alienating force of contemporary culture in noirs from *The Big Sleep* to *Kiss Me Deadly* shows "how fundamentally our communications, even the movies themselves, carry a certain estranging force, one that renders all discourse precarious and every effort at human communication a risky wager against misunderstanding and alienation," it is clear that his notions of reality, textuality, and communication are far more tentative than Richardson's.[60]

For Telotte, film noir, by focusing on the problems of communication and narration, renders its own narrational strategies problematic at the same time it is dramatizing a world of annihilating isolation: "*Film noir* advances a sort of ideological criticism in itself, laying bare the systematic contradictions that our films usually cover up. In this way, it *reverses* how ideological structures like the genre film usually work, by embracing rather than disguising paradoxes, even talking about them structurally and thematically."[61] Other theorists, especially those writing under the aegis of poststructuralism, have made similar attempts to open new spaces in film noir by disrupting its transparent-seeming codes of narration and representation. Joan Copjec argues for a further problematizing of noir narration. Following Pascal Bonitzer's observation that the omnipotent voice of the archcriminal Dr. Soberin (Albert Dekker), in *Kiss Me Deadly*, falls silent in death almost as soon as it is assigned to an onscreen body, she concludes that "however contiguous it is with the diegetic space, the space of the voice-over is nevertheless radically heterogeneous to it." Riven by such irreconcilable divisions, film noir offers a critique of the "fetish- ization of private *jouissance*" created by displacing a social order based on oedipally regulated desire with a new order based on the un- ending drive for immediate pleasure. These films trace the "mortal consequences for society" when "we no longer attempt to safeguard the 'empty' private space . . . but to dwell in this space exclusively."[62] Marc Vernet similarly argues that "*film noir* . . . was meaningful only for French spectators cut off from the American cinema during the summer of 1946" in order to deconstruct the notion of film noir as an enduring critical category: "As an object or corpus of films, *film noir* does not belong to the history of cinema; it belongs as a notion to the history of film criticism."[63] And James Naremore, acting as a cultural historian rather than as a deconstructionist, has urged that noir is an "an antigenre" with a particular political agenda – to reveal "the dark side of savage capitalism" – more fairly associated with a literary sen- sibility, or "a nostalgia for something that never quite existed," than a corpus or genre of films.[64]

Naremore's project, in fact, is to valorize noir by demystifying it, showing the political and economic processes that link it to a much broader series of movements than cinema itself can accommodate: high modernism, political progressivism, reactions against the post- war blacklisting of suspected subversives, the fetishism of Hollywood images and genres, and a commodified past available for sale in the form of the overvalued Maltese Falcon from the 1941 film, a figure "originally intended to represent a worthless imitation . . . trans- formed into 'the stuff that dreams are made of,' if only because Hum- phrey Bogart touched it." It is a project thrown into particularly high relief by the contrary tendency of several recent histories, like Dou- glas Brode's *Money, Women, and Guns* (1995) and Marilyn Yaquinto's *Pump 'Em Full of Lead* (1998), to follow the conventions of detective- film criticism in accepting their genres on their own terms and remain close to the language of their original reviewers in analyzing them.[65] Naremore, by contrast, echoes Paul Kerr's suggestion nearly twenty years earlier, based on Kerr's analysis of film-industry practices, that noir was an "'oppositional' cinematic mode" whose battery of "realist devices" marked "an attempt to hold in balance traditional generic el- ements with unorthodox aesthetic practices which constantly undermine them" as part of a "negotiation of an 'oppositional space' within and against realist cinematic practice."[66]

In this project Naremore is joined by Jonathan Munby, who finds in the gangster film an oppositional analogue to film noir. Extending Naremore's argument beyond noir to theorize a continuing "legacy of dissidence" linking the 1930s gangster film with the noir tradition, Munby argues that the crime films that constitute "the transatlantic prehistory of film noir is constructed out of definitively discontinuous film forms," and that "the 1940s crime film cycle [therefore] represents not so much disengagement from the system as the *continuity of discontinuity* – the endurance of a dissenting tradition."[67] Both Naremore and Munby seek to broaden Kerr's economically based analysis by a broader appeal to the context of cultural studies, whose movement away from categorical generalizations toward political and economic revisions of film history seems likely to set the agenda for crime-film criticism for the foreseeable future.

Personal Books and Reference Books

Two sorts of study remain outside the line of development this chapter traces: belletristic personal, sometimes biographical, essays on crime films, and reference guides giving information about individual films or filmmakers. Although the two kinds of writing, which respectively reflect the anti-intentionalism of film-noir criticism and the intentionalism of detective-film criticism, may seem poles apart, several volumes show both impulses in full flower. Two books devoted primarily to crime fiction, for example, incorporate extensive entries on crime films as well: Chris Steinbrunner and Otto Penzler's *Encyclopedia of Mystery and Detection* (1976) and its unofficial successor, William L. DeAndrea's *Encyclopedia Mysteriosa* (1994), both of them especially thorough in treating film adaptations of famous fictional detectives from Sherlock Holmes to Horace Rumpole, and both of them, especially DeAndrea's, shot through with the personalities of their creators.[68] An even more eccentric reference is John Baxter's *The Gangster Film* (1970), devoted mostly to alphabetical listings, most of them only a sentence or two in length, of performers and filmmakers. The listings have long since been superseded by later, more comprehensive references, but Baxter's brief Introduction, cited earlier, remains important. The essays in *The Big Book of Noir* (1998), edited by Ed Gorman, Lee Server, and Martin H. Greenberg, range in their topics from cinema to literature to comic books to radio and television, and their approach ranges from productions notes to interviews to essays in interpretation and appreciation to lists of favorite films, making this volume the most eclectic of all reference books on noir.[69]

Other essayists on the crime film take pains to dissociate themselves from academic criticism or indeed any pretense to objectivity. In introducing *The Devil Thumbs a Ride and Other Unforgettable Films* (1988), a series of a hundred alphabetically organized essays, all originally written for *Mystery Scene* magazine, Barry Gifford acknowledges that he guarantees "only the veracity of the impression" each film made on him.[70] The poet Nicholas Christopher provides an equally personal traversal of film noir in *Somewhere in the Night* (1997).[71] Still more recently, Eddie Muller's impressionistic, supercharged *Dark City* (1998) declares its independence from the academy in its opening dialogue, a parody of *The Asphalt Jungle* (1950):

- Dix, what happened to the Professor? . . .
- *I killed him! I couldn't stand it anymore!* I couldn't take another minute of his blather about Judeo-Christian patriarchal structures and structuro-semiological judgments. My head was going to explode!
- My God, Dix – *what did you do?*
- Let's just say I deconstructed him.[72]

Other references seek greater balance or objectivity either by enlisting many contributors or by sticking closely to the data. Two examples of the first sort are among the essential references in the field. Its international scope and wide array of alphabetical entries on leading topics, writers, films, and filmmakers make *The BFI Companion to Crime* (1997), written by nine contributors and edited by Phil Hardy, the most comprehensive in scope, if not always in achievement, of all references on the crime film. More specialized, but equally useful within its field, is Alain Silver and Elizabeth Ward's *Film Noir: An Encyclopedic Reference to the American Style,* first published in 1979 and twice revised since.[73] Originally the work of twenty authors, the book is divided into some three hundred entries on individual films (a list that grows in its third edition to five hundred), each entry giving cast and production credits, a synopsis of the plot, and a brief critical commentary. The volume is lavishly illustrated with dozens of oversized stills. The editors' appendix on the relations between noir and the gangster film, the western, the period film, and the comedy is especially valuable, as are their indexes of noir directors, writers, cinematographers, composers, producers, and performers, and the supplementary essays added to each of the later editions.

Spencer Selby's *Dark City: The Film Noir* (1984), adopts a two-part structure that echoes Silver and Ward even as it marks a distance from their work. The first half of Selby's book, a series of summaries and interpretations of twenty-five key noirs, reads like an encyclopedia of analytical commentary; the second half, a more briefly annotated filmography of nearly five hundred more, reads more like a dictionary. Joseph J. Cocchiarelli reverses this procedure in his *Screen Sleuths* (1992), a filmography of some two hundred thrillers of varying stripes, followed by more detailed essays on a dozen of them. Robert Ottoson buttresses his 1981 analytical filmography of some two hundred films in *A Reference Guide to the American Film Noir: 1940–1958* by citing hundreds of contemporary reviews.[74]

James Robert Parish and Michael R. Pitts have produced not only a two-volume alphabetical reference on gangster films, *The Great Gangster Pictures* (1976, 1987), but a companion volume cataloging *The Great Detective Pictures* (1990) whose organization is similar but whose scope is even more sweeping. Pitts's three volumes on *Famous Movie Detectives* (1979–2001), following the auteurist pattern of detective-movie criticism, are organized around the fictional sleuths whose incarnations they trace, with individual chapters summarizing the literary and cinematic careers of detectives from Father Brown to Perry Mason. A more substantial work devoted to performers rather than fictional characters is Karen Burroughs Hannsberry's *Femme Noir: Bad Girls of Film* (1998), which collects forty-nine substantial essays on leading ladies of the genre, each combining historical background, a summary of noir appearances and contemporary reviews, a noir filmography, and a list of references.[75]

Finally, Larry Langman's and Daniel Finn's three volumes listing cast and production credits and summaries for over four thousand crime films from the 1890s through 1959 provide a salutary reminder of just how fragmented criticism of the crime film remains even at its most systematic: The Library of Congress has cataloged two of their works, *A Guide to American Silent Crime Films* (1994) and *A Guide to American Crime Films of the Forties and Fifties* (1995) under criticism of the detective and mystery film, with cross-references to gangster and police films and, in the case of the later volume, prison films, but the third, *A Guide to American Crime Films of the Thirties* (1995) under criticism of gangster films, with none of these cross-references.[76] Even at their most apparently cut-and-dried, analyses of crime films, like the films themselves, continue to resist any single synthesis or systematic overview.

4

Fury and the Victim Film

In Vittorio De Sica's great Italian neorealist movie *The Bicycle Thief* (*Ladri di biciclette,* 1948), Antonio Ricci (Lamberto Maggiorani) is a deliveryman whose bicycle, on which his new job depends, is stolen. With his little boy, Bruno (Enzo Staiola), in tow, Ricci scours Rome in search of the stolen bicycle, asking questions of dozens of people, but he fails to recover it and is nearly arrested himself when he tries to steal another bicycle he is mistakenly convinced is his. The film ends with father and son walking forlornly down the street away from the camera, accepting the fact that they will never see the bicycle again.

Legend has it that De Sica and his screenwriter, Cesare Zavattini, briefly shopped the idea of the film to Hollywood, only to be told that no studio would be interested unless Cary Grant were cast in the lead role. Whether or not it is true, this anecdote illustrates a fundamental contrast between European cinema and Hollywood genre films. If every crime story depends on a victim, a criminal, and an avenger, the victim is the structuring absence in American crime movies. The role of the victim of crime is so perennially unfashionable in Hollywood that it is hard to think of a single victim-hero, for example, in the years between 1919, when D. W. Griffith's *Broken Blossoms* shows Lucy Burrows (Lillian Gish) destroyed by her abusive boxer father (Donald Crisp), and 1944, when Gregory Anton (Charles Boyer) tries to drive his bride Paula Alquist (Ingrid Bergman) insane in *Gaslight* so that he can ransack her house for the jewels he failed to find when he murdered her aunt. In order for victims to be acceptable to American viewers, they have to played by the likes of Cary Grant, presumably because no matter how miserably Grant's character might suffer, he would still be the imperishably debonair Cary Grant.

This is not to say that there are no American movies about victims. *Gaslight,* for example, shows the influence on crime films like *Notorious* (1946) of the so-called weepies – dramas from the 1930s through the 1950s, intended for female viewers, in which variably innocent women suffered injustice at the hands of faithless men – by revealing that the man in question is not merely a cad but a killer. There have also been countless movies for nearly a hundred years whose main characters have been the victims of crimes, from the defeated southern gentry of *The Birth of a Nation* (1915) to the teenaged innocents of *Friday the 13th* (1980) and *Scream* (1996). Viewers have seen Hollywood stars of every stripe as victims of the nanny from hell (*The Hand That Rocks the Cradle,* 1992), the roommate from hell (*Single White Female,* 1992), the cop from hell (*Unlawful Entry,* 1992), the temp from hell (*The Temp,* 1993), the lawyer from Hell (*The Devil's Advocate,* 1997), and the loose-cannon government operatives from hell (*No Way Out,* 1987; *Absolute Power,* 1997; *Enemy of the State,* 1998). It is no wonder that Charles Derry, following Pierre Boileau and Thomas Narcejac's definition of the suspense novel as "*le roman de la victime,*" emphasizes the focus of "the suspense thriller" on "the innocent victim or pursued criminal."[1]

Even though these heroes and heroines may begin as victims, however, and even though viewers continues to perceive them as imperiled or embattled long after they have outgrown their early doormat status, their stories transform them from victims to far more traditional, more active heroes, usually by enabling them to kill their initially more menacing tormentors. In *The Accused* (1948), mousy psychology professor-turned-murderer Wilma Tuttle (Loretta Young) assumes, as Robert Ottoson has noted, the roles of "both Destroyer and Victim."[2] Even Babe Levy, the inoffensive graduate student played by Dustin Hoffman who is repeatedly set against his globe-hopping secret-agent brother Doc (Roy Scheider) in John Schlesinger's *Marathon Man* (1976), ultimately kills the sadistic Nazi dentist (Laurence Olivier) who has so memorably tortured him.

The film that most economically encapsulates Hollywood's determination to recast the passive victim as heroic avenger is *D.O.A.,* first released in 1950, little more than a year after *The Bicycle Thief,* and later remade as *Color Me Dead* (1969) and under its original title (1987) [Fig. 16]. In the original version, Frank Bigelow (Edmond O'Brien) is a

16. *D.O.A.* (1987): The doomed hero gets a new lease on life. (Meg Ryan, Dennis Quaid)

small-town accountant who is slipped a poisoned drink at a crowded, noisy San Francisco bar. By the time he learns he has been poisoned, nothing can be done to stop the poison's action – he will be dead in a day or two – but Frank, after the initial denial, shock, and depression brought on by this revelation, decides to use his last hours tracking down his killer. "I'm already dead," he says exultantly; and his death sentence, far from sidelining him in passive stoicism, gives him a new and unparalleled freedom of action.

The extended flashback that encloses Frank's entire story, from his initial poisoning through his detective work in tracing his killer back from the big bad city to an innocuous deed he notarized months ago to his final shootout with the man who killed him, might seem to guarantee a bleak tone to the film. Despite the often despairing look and fatalistic construction cinematographer-turned-director Rudolph Maté provides, however, it is clear that downing a lethal dose of poison is the best thing that ever happened to Frank. Only the inescapable threat of a death not merely impending but already accomplished frees Frank to ignore the social taboos that would otherwise prevent him from bullying the suspects who might know why he was poisoned, his inhibitions about his feelings for his loyal secretary Paula Gibson (Pamela Britton), and the institutional restraints against taking the law into his own hands. As a result of getting murdered but still being alive, in fact, Frank not only enjoys a unique indemnity against danger (since there is nothing anybody can do to him that will make his situation any worse) but has the opportunity to occupy all three major positions associated with crime fiction: victim, detective, and criminal (or at least dispenser of vigilante justice unencumbered by the law). In terms of the film's black-and-white morality, Frank's death is none too high a price to pay for the exhilarating privilege of serving as judge, jury, and executioner of the man who killed him. The film thus makes Frank's victimhood a position to be celebrated because it liberates heroic tendencies Frank has never before been able to show. The best victims, *D.O.A.* suggests, are those who come back fighting, exploiting the fact that their status as victims licenses in advance their most violent excesses – a premise adopted by both its remakes as well.

American films' preference for treating victims not as nobly stoic sufferers at the hands of criminals but as worms who turn on their tormentors suggests that Hollywood finds the status of victim inherently unstable and unsatisfactory. There are several reasons why this is so. The most obvious is the formal or structural incompleteness of the victim's story, which Aristotle recognized two thousand years ago required some reversal of fortune to be complete.[3] Viewers do not want to watch static heroes; either they want their heroes to fall from a

17. *Death Wish 4: The Crackdown:* The victim (Charles Bronson) turned avenger.

precarious height and become victims, like the outsized gangsters of *Little Caesar* (1930) and *Scarface* (1932), or they want heroic victims to move from suffering to action, like the wimps played by Dustin Hoffman in *Straw Dogs* (1971) and *Marathon Man,* and by Charles Bronson in all five *Death Wish* films (1974–94) [Fig. 17].

In fact, Hollywood's fondness for violent climaxes offers an even more compelling reason for its lack of interest in victims who consistently remain victims. Crime on American screens is played first and foremost for entertainment, and a criminal action is not simply an affront to the social order but a media event as distinct and formulaic as a Fred Astaire dance number. A film like *The Bicycle Thief,* treating an offscreen theft virtually unaccompanied by violence, then or later, would have even less chance in Hollywood today than in 1948. The violence of Hollywood crimes plays on viewers' ambivalence toward independence and institutional power, making these media events visually and aurally exciting even as it underlines their breach of the social order. More subtly, the opening violence prepares for still greater violence at the hands of the heroic avengers, even if they are yet to be introduced. After all, it is not just criminals who are violent anti-establishment figures. The historic American cult of independence and Americans' long attachment to strong heroes unbeholden to any system or community that might trammel their freedom or sap their resolve – from Huckleberry Finn to Han Solo – is faithfully expressed through Hollywood's prejudice in favor of antiauthoritarian, anti-institutional good guys played by the likes of Arnold Schwarzenegger and Steven Seagal. When ruthless criminals meet equally uninhibited avengers, the stage is set for climactic acts of violence that will outdo anything in the early reels, fulfilling viewers' desire for a crescendo of excitement.

Even so, neither viewers' desire for structuring reversals of fortune nor Hollywood's interest in violence as a way of making crime both emphatic and entertaining fully explains the American crime film's relative neglect of victims. Victims who act like victims appear throughout the genre; they are simply edged out by characters whose roles are more important, more dramatic, or more satisfying. In *Call Northside 777* (1948), reporter P. J. McNeal (James Stewart) becomes determined to clear Frank Wiecek (Richard Conte), who is serving time for killing a police officer. The film neglects many opportunities to linger over the victims of both the original crime and the miscarriage of justice McNeal is trying to correct; but since one is dead and the other in prison, it regards their suffering as static, simply a pretext for the hero's more dramatically satisfying detective work. One reason whodunits on and off the screen have focused for so long on murder is that murder is the only crime that utterly annihilates its victims, absolving the audience from worrying about them, and freeing viewers or readers to treat all the remaining characters as suspects locked in a potential duel with the detective in a contest that guarantees active roles for every participant. In man-on-the-run films from *Saboteur* (1942) to *The Fugitive* (1993), it is not enough for the wrongly accused heroes played by Robert Cummings and Harrison Ford simply to elude their pursuers; it is a cardinal rule of the genre (though one rarely observed by real-life fugitives from the law) that they must also clear themselves by turning detective in order to track down the real criminals [Fig. 18].

Whether they concentrate on criminals, avengers, or victims, Hollywood films focus on similar fantasies of active empowerment, from Frank Bigelow's license to execute his killer in *D.O.A.* to the apparent justification of D-FENS, Michael Douglas's unemployed defense contractor in *Falling Down* (1993), for taking down all the urban enemies who get in his way. The difference between the rousingly unlikely Everyman heroics of the doomed hero of *D.O.A.* and the pathetically

18. *The Fugitive:* Instead of simply escaping from the police, Dr. Richard Kimble (Harrison Ford) must track down the real criminal.

unconvincing self-justifications of D-FENS in *Falling Down* indicates that American movies do not necessarily approve this kind of empowerment; but they are clearly fascinated with it, whatever its costs, even at its most sociopathic [Fig. 19].

From their beginnings, then, American crime films have been less interested in winning viewers' sympathies for innocent victims than in exploring the possibilities of action available to those victims, the more apparently hopeless the better. These possibilities make an ideal subject for Hollywood because they provide a dramatic framework structured by an Aristotelian reversal and offer a wide range of powerfully straightforward emotional appeals (sympathy for the downtrodden, hope for their change to a more active role, exultation at their triumphs) while examining the problematic relations between passive and active roles, typically dramatized in crime films not only through the opposed roles of the victim and avenger but also through the opposition of victim and criminal. In showing victims rising to their own defense by striking back, crime films simultaneously reinforce strong, simple emotions proper to the given roles of victim, avenger, and criminal, and complicate these roles by showing how closely they are related. Whenever a victim turns avenger, chances are some element of the criminal will enter into this figure as well.

The reason why is obvious. Although there are a few movie criminals whose behavior is so vicious that viewers are never encouraged to see them as anything but monstrous (e.g., Michael Rooker's title character in *Henry: Portrait of a Serial Killer,* 1990), and a few others who are clearly saintly victims forced into crime rather than choosing it (Fredric March's Jean Valjean in *Les Misérables,* 1935), most Hollywood criminals fall somewhere between these two extremes. Bonnie and Clyde, Vito and Michael Corleone, and the sociopathic teenagers of *Kids* (1995) are all criminals, but their films all make some attempt to explain, and in some cases to justify, the choices that have made them as they are, in order to explore the relations between actions and reactions. To what extent are criminal actions simply reactions to the powerful forces of circumstance? The question of which actions count as actions, and which count only as reactions to the actions of others, is perhaps the most urgent moral question American movies ask, and one to which crime films give a unique pride of place.

Moreover, just as movies can scratch almost any criminal and find a victim who pleads the irresistible forces of poverty or family ties or bad companions or the system, movies can scratch the most passive victim and find a potential criminal. One way of drawing viewers into a greater intimacy with victims is to emphasize the pathos and injustice of their sufferings; another is to allow them to fulfill viewers' fantasies of heroic retaliation against the forces of evil; still another is to

19. *Falling Down:* The fascination of the sociopathic vigilante. (Michael Douglas, left)

show how deeply they have been brutalized by making them cross the line that separates law-abiding avengers from criminals. It would be surprising if Hollywood did not try all three tactics, often in the same movie.

Victim films turn on the questions of why bad things happen to good people, and what good people ought to do when they do happen. Although Hollywood has rarely been interested in the stoic acceptance of victimhood portrayed in *The Bicycle Thief* and *Broken Blossoms,* several options remain to Hollywood victims. They can suffer and die in an implicit indictment of their complicity with an immoral culture, as the heroines of *Looking for Mr. Goodbar* (1977) and *Star 80* (1983) are punished for having so internalized the woman-hating norms of their patriarchal cultures that they are incapable of breaking away from the men who prey on them. Alternatively, they can hire freelance avengers like the durable criminal attorney Perry Mason, guaranteeing a happy ending at the price of agreeing to have their suffering upstaged by their avengers.

Although Mason's clients fade comfortably into the woodwork once they place the burden of their cases on their infallible advocate, few victims who place their fate in the hands of the justice system find that system nearly as responsive. Rape victims Chris McCormick (Margaux Hemingway) in *Lipstick* (1976) and Sarah Tobias (Jodie Foster) in *The Accused* (1988) win legal vindication only after enduring harrowing legal ordeals that amount to a second violation. Heroes and heroines who lack the funds or the wit to call on the likes of Perry Mason, like the innocent suspects of such Hitchcock films as *I Confess* (1952), *Dial M for Murder* (1954), and *The Wrong Man* (1956), must be rescued by prayer or fate or sympathetic investigators or the criminal's overreaching.

Victims who willfully reject institutional justice to take a more active role in their own defense inevitably become both more heroic and more disturbingly complicit in the violence that threatened them in the first place. The surest way to guarantee their continued innocence is to isolate them completely from the justice system that ought to be redressing their grievances. Man-on-the-run films like *Saboteur* and *North by Northwest* (1959) work by estranging their heroes from both the criminals and the police. So too the blind heroine of *Wait until Dark* (1967), the embattled mathematician of *Straw Dogs,* and the pacifist graduate student of *Marathon Man,* all forced to their own defense by being cut off from the authorities on whom they are counting for help, strike back at the ruthless criminals who have been tormenting them without besmirching their straight-arrow credentials.

An especially potent image of this moral whitewash is the outlaw film, whose victims-turned-superheroes enjoy a continuing moral privilege whatever crimes they may commit against victims and a system more corrupt than they are. The Hollywood archetype is Robin Hood, the outlaw who defies the bullying Guy of Guisborne and the usurping King John by taking the blame for killing one of the king's deer, assembling a band of men that will represent a truer English society than the corrupt court, vindicating his counterculture's social credentials by winning the heart of the aristocrat Maid Marian, ransoming England's lawful king Richard the Lionheart from captivity, and earning pardon for all his merry men. Yet superheroes from *Batman* (1989) to *Darkman* (1990) and *The Crow* (1994) begin as victims too, and their victimhood gives their summary justice its moral authority.

Even avengers less noble will assume something of the superhero if the justice system they defy is sufficiently bankrupt. The heroines of *Thelma & Louise* (1991), forced to become robbers and fugitives by the men who victimize them, achieve heroic apotheosis when they drive their car off a cliff into the Grand Canyon, sealing their status as legendary fighters against patriarchy rather than insignificant, privately motivated killers and thieves. In the western *Bad Girls* (1994), the four heroines – less powerful, more dependent on men, but finally more successful – are equally dedicated to avenging the injustices visited on them by powerful men who take advantage of their physical weakness and their sexual vulnerability.

When victims work within the system, viewers' loyalties are typically divided between the hope that the system will be vindicated and the thirst for cathartic vigilante justice. A common way to resolve this conflict is to transform victims into heroic avengers whose vigilantism revitalizes a moribund justice system, as in *Marked Woman* (1937), *Saboteur,* or *Key Largo* (1948). The battleground of the defense or critique of the justice system can be as intimate as the American family. Although Charlie Newton (Teresa Wright) kills her murderous uncle at the end of Hitchcock's *Shadow of a Doubt* (1943), marking the final stage in her accelerated, enforced maturation, she does nothing to disturb the rest of her family's sense of him as kindly and charming, and her community mourns him as a saint. But William Wyler's *The Desperate Hours* (1955) uses the threat of victimization as a pretext for circling the wagons of domestic patriarchy when Dan Hilliard (Fredric March) finally succeeds in repelling the escaped convicts who are holding his family hostage by asserting his paternal authority over that of his criminal parody, authoritarian father-figure Glenn Griffin (Humphrey Bogart), and incidentally over his family itself, proving that, unlike his violent counterpart, father knows best.

D.O.A., substituting the fatally wounded individual's vengeance for that of the justice system (which is called upon in the final scene to provide tacit approval of his revenge), dramatizes the most common pattern among American victim films: reversing the hero's status as victim by showing the hero moving from victim to vigilante with both the system's and the viewers' implicit approval. But other films complicate the hero's progress from victim to avenger or criminal, as well as viewers' attitude toward that progress, in order to develop a critique of the relationship between action and reaction, social justice and private revenge. In *I Am a Fugitive from a Chain Gang* (1932), Paul Muni plays aspiring contractor James Allen, who is unjustly sent to prison in a carefully unnamed southern state. After bestial treatment by the prison trusties who supervise the chain gangs on which he is forced to work, he finally makes a successful escape, rising to become a noted contractor before he is identified and rearrested. Agreeing to return to serve one more year in the hated prison as a condition of clearing his record, he is denied release by the vindictive state authorities, stung by his public revelation of their prison culture's brutality. Escaping again from prison, Allen dynamites a bridge his pursuers must cross to reach him, annulling his dreams of constructive building. When he makes one final stealthy farewell visit to his former girlfriend Helen (Helen Vinson), she asks as he backs fearfully into the shadows, "How do you live?" Allen's chilling reply – "I steal" – is delivered over a black screen that emphasizes the film's radically unresolved ending, as if it were confessing its helplessness to conclude the story of this good man now eternally on the run because the state's brutality has made him a criminal.

Although James Naremore has aptly observed that, in later social-problem films like *Crossfire* (1947), "problems never appear systemic"[4] but rather seem to be aberrations that can be ascribed to individual psychopathology or maladjustment, in *I Am a Fugitive from a Chain Gang* and other social-problem films, especially common at Warner Bros. throughout the 1930s, the portrayal of the victim turned criminal is balanced by impeaching the system as the greatest criminal of all. Such films as *Black Legion* (1936), *Dead End* (1937), and *Each Dawn I Die* (1939) offered an obvious appeal to Depression-era viewers already suspicious of authority figures: politicians uninterested in the plight of the unemployed, industrialists indifferent to everything but their companies' profits, bankers reconciling their balance sheets by foreclosing on shaky mortgages, and courts and police officers dedicated to enforcing punitive laws. Instead of relying on the justice system of the constitutional government to provide moral authority for judgments about criminal action, such films dramatized the crisis of a system so deeply flawed that its fearsome powers had become separated from the moral authority that ought to give them their force.

In a world where the justice system is monstrously unjust, what is to prevent an innocent victim from turning into a criminal? Alfred Hitchcock's men on the run, like the hero of *D.O.A.*, are never confronted with this question because they enjoy the moral luxury (though the pragmatic handicap) of independence from a justice system that is indifferent to their plight and interested only in hunting them down. The only Hitchcock heroes and heroines whose moral decisions come under such remorseless scrutiny are those first presented as free agents. Alice White (Anny Ondra) has to live with her knowledge that not only did she kill the man who tried to rape her in *Blackmail* (1929) but that the attempt of her policeman-boyfriend, Frank Webber (John Longden), to protect her has sent Tracy (Donald Calthrop), a man innocent of that crime (though not of blackmail), to his death in her place. Alicia Huberman (Ingrid Bergman), who avenged her Nazi father's spying against the America she loved by agreeing to spy on the Nazis in *Notorious,* is married off to former suitor Alexander Sebastian (Claude Rains) by government agent T. R. Devlin (Cary Grant), who expects her to betray her bridegroom to him even though he will not admit he loves her himself. In *Rear Window* (1954), L. B. Jefferies (James Stewart), who begins by snooping on the neighboring apartments to pass the time while he is recuperating from a broken leg, becomes obsessively determined to prove that one of his neighbors has killed his wife. Retired police detective Scottie Ferguson (Stewart again), maddened by grief when he apparently let Madeleine Elster (Kim Novak), the woman he was hired to watch, fall to her death in *Vertigo* (1958), re-creates her living image as ruthlessly as the killer who first manufactured her alluring image by using her lookalike Judy Barton (also Novak), who loves him as hopelessly as he loved the dead Madeleine. Marion Crane (Janet Leigh), whose boyfriend Sam Loomis (John Gavin) refuses to marry her at the beginning of *Psycho* (1960), steals $40,000 from a lecherous client and runs off to meet the boyfriend. In every case Hitchcock asks just how far a victim can be pushed before losing the law's protection or the viewers' sympathy.

Hitchcock's most penetrating study of victimhood, *Suspicion* (1941), is his most ambiguous. Its passive heroine, Lina McLaidlaw (Joan Fontaine), is so enamored of her importunate suitor (later, husband) Johnny Aysgarth (Cary Grant) that she cannot believe that he is actually a liar, a cheat, and a thief. Eventually, however, she becomes convinced that he is planning to kill her. At this point in the film's source, the 1932 novel *Before the Fact* by Francis Iles (aka Anthony Berkeley), Lina, pregnant with Johnny's child, accepts the role of victim and martyrs herself to Johnny's scheming. The film, however, ends very differently. When Lina confronts Johnny with her suspicions, he convinces her he has planned suicide, not murder, and they return to the luxurious, unaffordable house he has rented for her with no plans for their future vicissitudes but a resolve to face them together. Whether Johnny is as innocent as he claims or as guilty as he acts, the film's title refers not only to Lina's attitude toward him but also to the film's attitude toward her. If Johnny is really as innocent as he claims of murderous impulses, then Lina's suspicions amount to a paranoid sense of persecution.

Is Lina an innocent victim or a paranoid schemer? In most cases, a film's logic would make the answer clear, at least at the fadeout; but *Suspicion* develops several different logics that seem to require contradictory endings. Viewers' sympathetic trust in the accuracy of her perceptions demands that Johnny be guilty, but their empathetic desire for Lina's happiness requires that he be innocent. The many indications of his guilt are so closely woven into the fabric of the film's representational vocabulary that he must be guilty; yet his guilt is so obvious from the beginning that the story requires an Aristotelian reversal that can be supplied only by his innocence. In removing Lina's impending death from the ending, Hitchcock guaranteed that whatever ending he provided would be read as inconclusive, because no possible alternative would be congruent with the film's contradictory logics. Once the film admits the possibility that Lina may be anything but a pure victim, her status becomes problematic.[5]

Though Hitchcock is more closely associated with the figure of the innocent victim than is any other filmmaker, the one who probes the ambiguous status of victims most profoundly is Fritz Lang. Hitchcock's films typically entangle heroes like Guy Haines (Farley Granger), in *Strangers on a Train* (1951), with killers who bring them under suspicion of guilt by the police even though they have done nothing wrong. Lang, however, more often follows the logic of the 1950 Patricia Highsmith novel Hitchcock adapted, in which Guy, overwhelmed by the insistence of Bruno Anthony (Robert Walker) that Guy repay the favor of Bruno's murdering his wife by killing Bruno's tyrannical father, eventually gives in to the pressure, kills the father, survives to mourn the villain's accidental death, and is eventually arrested. Lang's *You Only Live Once* (1937) covers some of the same territory as *Suspicion* and *Strangers on a Train*. Eddie Taylor (Henry Fonda), an ex-con repeatedly foiled in his attempt to put his past behind him, is eventually arrested for a fatal robbery he did not commit. Placed on Death Row, Eddie begs his wife Joan (Sylvia Sidney) to smuggle him a gun and uses it to break out of prison, killing in the process the priest who has come to bring him news of his pardon. Although the moody visuals of both the robbery and the breakout are shrouded in ambiguity – in a touch that might have come right out of a more hard-boiled version of *Suspicion,* Lang shows a gas-masked robber who may or may not be Eddie[6] – Eddie has clearly become a killer by the film's end. What is ambiguous is not whether he is guilty but exactly what his guilt means, who bears responsibility for it, and how different he is from any other citizen caught in the law's toils.

Lang first made his mark in the German silent cinema. The writer-director originally assigned to direct the groundbreaking *The Cabinet of Dr. Caligari* (*Das Kabinett des Dr. Caligari,* 1920), he was prevented from shooting the film, for which he provided the framing scenes that revealed its troubled narrator as insane, by his work on his first commercial success, the master-criminal tale *The Spiders* (*Die Spinnen,* 1919–20). Critical success followed with his allegorical *Destiny* (*Der müde Tod,* 1921). Through projects ranging from Wagnerian myth (*Die Niebelungen,* 1924) to science fiction (*The Woman in the Moon/ Die Frau im Mond,* 1929), Lang showed a particular gift for dramatizing psychopathology through architectural composition. This tendency reached its apotheosis in the futuristic dystopia of *Metropolis* (1927), whose mob scenes are choreographed with a precision that makes every one of hundreds of human bodies onscreen move like part of a single monstrous organism. Given Lang's fondness for projecting his characters' darkest fears and imaginings onto an oppressive mise-en-scène, it is no wonder that he returned repeatedly to two favorite stories. The first, *The Spiders*'s tale of a criminal conspiracy to conquer the world, pervades his German films (*Dr. Mabuse, the Gambler/Dr. Mabuse, der Spieler,* 1922; *Spies/Spione,* 1928; *The Testament of Dr. Mabuse/Das Testament des Dr. Mabuse,* 1933). The second, *Caligari*'s tale of a man hounded beyond endurance by nightmarish visual settings that figure both tyrannical administrators and the demons of his own mind, comes to full flower in his American films.

The theme of the man whose expressionistically rendered physical surroundings insistently reflect his own deepest terrors, which Lang's frame story made fundamental to *The Cabinet of Dr. Caligari,* was at the heart of his favorite film, *M* (1931), in which the psychotic child murderer Hans Beckert (Peter Lorre) is pursued both by the police and by the professional criminals whose livelihood has been threatened by the official crackdown he has provoked. Trapped by cluttered frames and menacing objects that mark him from the beginning as dangerous, the sweating Beckert – caught in a claustrophobic storage room by the criminals, who carry him off to a kangaroo court where he pleads an irresistible compulsion for the crimes he finds as repugnant as do his accusers – eventually stands revealed as the ultimate criminal-victim, whose inability to resist his impulses reflects the compulsive criminality of his whole society. *M* reveals Lang as the supreme architect of the troubled soul imaged by geometric visuals and monstrously threatening objects.

Although the nightmarish expressionism of *M* is more naturalized in the Hollywood films Lang directed after fleeing the Nazis in 1933, vigilantism and institutional justice are still set against each other, each indicting the other's shortcomings. In *Man Hunt* (1941), Captain Alan Thorndike (Walter Pidgeon), an English sportsman who is hunted down by Nazis after playfully stalking Hitler in Berchtesgaden, must acknowledge the violence within himself not only by killing his ruthless pursuer Quive-Smith (George Sanders), but by admitting that he did indeed want to kill Hitler after all. In *The Woman in the Window* (1944), Professor Richard Wanley (Edward G. Robinson), in the middle of an innocent but compromising meeting with Alice Reed (Joan Bennett), whose painting he has especially admired in a shop window, is attacked by her sometime lover, kills him in self-defense, and spends the rest of the film sinking deeper into guilty lies. In *The Big Heat* (1953), Sgt. Dave Bannion (Glenn Ford), whose wife has been killed by mobsters trying to stop him from looking into a dirty cop's suicide, nearly strangles the cop's widow, Bertha Duncan (Jeanette Nolan) before his guilt is taken over by the widow's double, spurned gangster's moll Debby Marsh (Gloria Grahame), who obligingly murders Mrs. Duncan herself.

Two of Lang's three westerns, *The Return of Frank James* (1940) and *Rancho Notorious* (1952), show heroes torn between their peaceful natures and their thirst for revenge; Vance Shaw (Randolph Scott) in the third, *Western Union* (1941), is a reformed outlaw whose heroic attempt to avoid both falling under the sway of and informing on his villainous brother marks him early on as a sacrificial victim to progress. In his more frequent tales of urban crime, Lang constructs moral mazes that begin by setting criminals against victims and end by muddying the distinctions between the two beyond any hope of reconstruction. In *While the City Sleeps* (1956), avid reporters compete for a promotion promised to the first to identify the sex killer who is terrorizing their city. One of them, Edward Mobley (Dana Andrews), ends up staking out his unwitting fiancée, Nancy Liggett (Sally Forrest), as bait for the murderer (John Barrymore Jr.), whose pathetically irresistible compulsion to kill, like Beckert's in *M,* makes him the film's most sympathetic character. *Beyond a Reasonable Doubt* (1956) stars Andrews again as Tom Garrett, a writer whose attempt to construct a misleadingly conclusive web of circumstantial evidence against himself in a recent murder backfires when Austin Spencer (Sidney Blackmer) – Garrett's editor, prospective father-in-law, and sole partner in this investigative ruse, who plans to deliver exculpatory evidence at Garrett's trial – is killed in a car accident. Fortunes are reversed once more when Spencer's daughter, Susan (Joan Fontaine), the loyal fiancée, realizes Garrett truly is guilty after all. In *Scarlet Street* (1945), the disquietingly named Christopher Cross (Edward G. Robinson), seduced by streetwalker Kitty March (Joan Bennett) into stealing from his employer, ends by killing her, allowing her abusive boyfriend, Johnny Prince (Dan Duryea) to take his punishment, and is left wandering the streets in a suicidal daze.

Lang's most notable films marry Hitchcock's portraits of heroes under the intense psychological strain of their moral complicity in crimes of which they are legally innocent to a broader analysis of institutional justice. In the first and greatest of all his American films, *Fury* (1936), Lang uses the conventions of the social-justice formula to link questions of individual and social complicity in crime. Social-justice films were popular throughout the 1930s because they fueled low-level paranoid fantasies by casting a critical eye on the moral authority of institutional justice; meanwhile, they anticipated Naremore's description of their diagnoses as unsystemic by implying that the worst abuses of institutional justice were taking place elsewhere, in California or some unnamed southern state. *Fury*, the most distinguished of all social-justice films, follows this pattern by attributing the most egregious abuses of the justice system to the fictitious faraway town of Strand, presumably but never explicitly on the California coast. At the same time, *Fury* achieves a resonance exceptional among social-justice films by subjecting its innocent victim to equally unsparing scrutiny.

Like Frank Capra's iconic Depression comedy *It Happened One Night* (1934), *Fury* features a pair of lovers separated by a big country one of them must cross to be reunited with the other. In both films, too, the course of the lovers' reunion is disrupted by their adventures among a group of quintessential Americans that lead to a discovery of an America they never suspected. But unlike *It Happened One Night,* which uses the image of the community singing together aboard the night bus to suggest that American society is at heart one big happy family, *Fury* – cowritten by Lang and Bartlett Cormack from an Oscar-nominated story by the more habitually comic screenwriter Norman Krasna – unmasks America as a mob whose bloodthirsty instincts are barely constrained by laws they are only too eager to pervert to their own vengeful ends.

The film begins with a lovers' farewell that establishes Chicago factory worker Joe Wilson (Spencer Tracy) as an American Everyman. Joe loves peanuts and dogs, wears a rumpled raincoat with a tear his all-American fiancée Katherine Grant (Sylvia Sidney) repairs with blue thread, and accepts the fact that, although he and Katherine have paused to fantasize in front of a shop window displaying a newlyweds' suite, he cannot marry her until the two of them have enough money to live on – a particularly poignant Depression wish. In this opening scene, however, every mark of Joe's endearing normalcy – his love of peanuts, the tear in his raincoat, his childish habit of mispronouncing the word "memento" as "mementum," the distinctive ring he accepts from Katherine – will end up betraying and entrapping him, first as the kidnapper the mob mistakes him for, then as the vindictive killer Katherine realizes he has become.

Having saved enough money from a service station he has opened with his brothers Charlie (Frank Albertson) and Tom (George Walcott) – whom he has shamed into quitting their errands for a local gangster – Joe, on his way to claim Katherine, is stopped by deputy "Bugs" Meyers (Walter Brennan) as he approaches Strand. Taken into custody as a suspect in the kidnapping of a young woman, Joe is trapped by the Everyman status that makes him – and "a million men," as he scoffs – fit the suspect's generic physical description. The trap snaps shut when Sheriff Tad Hummel (Edward Ellis) informs him that traces of salted peanuts were found in the envelope containing the ransom note, and Bugs matches a five-dollar bill Joe is carrying with one of the serial numbers from the ransom payment.

Despite Hummel's assurances, the law and its officers offer Joe scant protection from the hysterical rumors of his guilt that sweep through the town. Just after Lang cuts from a shot of three women gossiping about Joe to a close-up of chickens clucking, one woman asks, "But are you sure he's not innocent?" provoking the haughty response, "My dear young woman, in this country, people don't land in jail unless they're guilty." This ironic critique of America's presumed uniqueness reveals the totalitarian tendencies found even in places remote from Nazi Germany.

Just as Joe had earlier lectured his brothers by defining himself as everything they were not, the citizens of Strand can establish their self-righteous sense of themselves as ordinary, decent, hard-working

Americans only by contrasting themselves with a criminal scapegoat. Driven to a self-righteous fury, the townspeople take to the streets, surrendering their individuality to the identity that best suits them: members of a mob. After an ominous silence that ends with an alarming overhead shot of their assaulting the door with a battering ram, they storm the sheriff's office, where they overwhelm the few defenders and knock out the sheriff. Unable to reach the cell in which Joe, isolated and frantic with anxiety, is locked, the mob burns down the building. Katherine hears news of Joe's arrest that brings her running to the scene just in time to faint when she sees him at a barred window, surrounded by flames, as the eerily silent citizens look on in rapt approval. This scene, exploiting Lang's unparalleled gift for choreographing crowds, finally frames particular citizens of Strand as individuals once again; but the iconic poses in which cinematographer Joseph Ruttenberg freezes them – as gargoyles throwing stones, munching apples, hoisting babies to see the show, or simply watching in gleeful satisfaction – reveal how eager they are to surrender their individual moral judgment to the mob.

Yet Joe, whose innocence had been the focus of such intense pathos, is as capable of vengeful fury as his tormentors, as he reveals when he miraculously appears to Charlie and Tom and relates how he escaped from the explosion that destroyed the burning jail. He tells his brothers, "I'm legally dead, and they're legally murderers. . . . And they'll hang for it. . . . But I'll give them the chance they didn't give me. They'll get a legal trial in a legal courtroom. They'll have a legal judge, and a legal defense. They'll get a legal sentence, and a legal death."

What Joe sees as legal justice, of course, is a perversion of the justice system, which, he plans, like the mob, to hijack to suit his thirst for personal vengeance. Learning of the criminal lawsuit the brothers have urged against the twenty-two townspeople identified as part of the lynch mob, the citizens of Strand, though now claiming the protection of the law they had earlier trampled, continue to act like a mob by refusing to identify anyone as guilty, concocting false alibis for each other, and hiring out-of-town lawyers to make legalistic speeches about the corpus delicti. Now, however, Joe is recast as a tragic vigilante himself. As the trial wears on, Lang repeatedly cuts to reaction shots of Joe sitting in an anonymous rooming house raptly listening to news reports on the radio. The sparseness of the furnishings, the composition of the shots, and Joe's tense poses – first he is sitting hunched forward with his hands on his knees, then lying on a bed whose barred headboard is the most prominent background motif, then sitting in front of the headboard – precisely echo the physical details of the shots that figured his helpless isolation when he was in jail, gripping the bars as he strained to hear every offscreen sound that might telegraph the mob's next move. Now he is free and out of danger but still equally imprisoned by his own obsession with vengeance, which keeps him shut up alone, trapped in the frame, afraid to go out lest he be recognized, and compulsively listening for offscreen reports about the very same mob – until he smashes the radio in a fury that produces a silence just as ominous as the silence preceding the storming of the police station in which he had been imprisoned.

Joe is isolated even from Katherine, whom Charlie and Tom are keeping ignorant of his resurrection in order to make her a more effective witness to his death. But the strain that had maddened Joe with a thirst for revenge maddens Katherine in more clinical terms, first leading to her breakdown, then setting her against Joe. She has already noticed Tom wearing Joe's raincoat, whose telltale torn pocket she had mended with blue thread. Shortly after her testimony, she recognizes Joe's misspelling "mementum" on an anonymous note he sends to the judge, with the ring Katherine gave him, to establish his death beyond question; and she appears accusingly before him in the same low-angle full shot in a dark doorway as Joe's own return from the dead.

Joe's furious revulsion from Katherine's plea for mercy, his solitary evening on the town, is the film's apotheosis, a tour de force that epitomizes Lang's use of innocuous visual details to register the hero's frenzied isolation. Joe's dinner at a local restaurant is spoiled by the establishment's oppressive silence [Fig. 20]; he is troubled by a shop window whose display of furnishings for a newlywed couple echoes that of the window that had provided the film's opening image; he is haunted by a startlingly literal echo of Katherine's voice from the opening scene – "Are you planning to do a lot of running around in this room?" – reminding him that instead of running after Katherine, as he had promised, Joe is now running from himself. Seeking solace in a crowd, he finds that the cheerful noises he hears coming from a nearby bar are nothing but a radio; the bar is empty save for a bartender who, noting that midnight has brought a new day, inadvertently tears two sheets from his calendar instead of one. This accident leaves Joe staring at the number 22 – the number of defendants that his plot threatens with death.

20. *Fury:* Joe Wilson (Spencer Tracy) is alone wherever he goes, even in this intense face-off with a girl in a nightclub (Esther Muir), cut from the ending of the completed film.

Realizing that his irrational quest for legalized vengeance is dehumanizing him as surely as the mob surrendered its own humanity, and that they are presumably as haunted by his specter as he is by Katherine's, Joe is ready to show himself in the courtroom, in a final revelation – he drops the pretense of his death and Katherine returns to him – that was criticized from the film's first release as abrupt and unmotivated.[7] This ironically convenient ending is unsatisfactory precisely because it admits that the film's ruthless unmaskings have raised contradictions too deep to resolve. Not only have both middle America and Joe been revealed as morally inadequate in the eyes of the law; but the law itself, though it has persistently been set up as the force that protects individuals from each other and, ultimately, from their own most catastrophic impulses, has been unmasked as fallible and corrupt.[8]

Immediately after Sheriff Hummel first places Joe under arrest, Bugs goes to a barbershop in which one customer notes that "it's not possible to get a law that denies the right to say what one believes." One of the two barbers knows that freedom of speech is protected by the Constitution because he had to read it when he became a citizen; but the other, Hector (Raymond Hatton), is not such a defender of individual freedom: "People get funny impulses. If you resist them, you're sane. If you don't, you're on your way to the nuthouse, or the pen." Confessing that he has often been tempted, in shaving his customers, to cut their throats instead, he succeeds in frightening his customer into bolting his chair. Is the law an effective protection against the irrationally destructive impulses of individuals, or simply a guarantor of individual freedoms whose effect is to privilege a majoritarian mob as We the People? Such a question goes to the heart of a peculiarly American solicitude for individual rights under the law. In recapitulating the Founding Fathers' debate over the drafting of the Constitution, however, Lang seems far less confident than James Madison that laws enacted and enforced by individuals can rescue people from themselves, or from the mobs to which their selfishness and hysteria drive them.

The failures of law in the film are due in part to local corruption, a perversion of legal principle by private interest. As Sheriff Hummel waits helplessly for the National Guard to answer his call while the mob grows outside, Lang cuts away to show the ineffectual governor (Howard C. Hickman) overridden by the oily political advisor Will Vickery (Edwin Maxwell), who is concerned only for the governor's political popularity. But legal institutions are subject to far more insidious and systemic forms of perversion as well. Once Charlie and Tom, secretly fed information by Joe, succeed in building their case, they sit back and watch as woodenly noble District Attorney Adams (Walter Abel), at first frustrated in his appeal to the jury's "patriotism" by the staunch refusal of his witnesses to implicate anyone, brings into court a newsreel that shows key members of the mob in damning close-up. The episode has often been discussed as an example of the way cinema uses its evidentiary value to validate or to question its own fictional representational practices,[9] a confusion fostered by Joe's bitter observation to his brothers that he has watched movie footage of his death repeatedly in a theater even though he did not really die. The scene places less emphasis on cinema as the ultimate arbiter of legal truth, however, than on institutional justice clouded by personal vindictiveness; for as Adams smugly proclaims, he has called his witnesses only in order to entrap them in perjury before unveiling the

21. *Fury:* His brother Tom (George Walcott) is taken aback by the vindictive satisfaction Joe Wilson (Spencer Tracy) takes in cinematic evidence against the mob, in another scene cut from the film.

photographic evidence that has presumably been available to him all along. Every champion of justice, however pure his or her motives may be, is actually, like the mob, out for revenge [Fig. 21]. In calling on cinema as evidence in order to question not so much its own signifying practices as the motives behind its use, the film raises the question of whether justice is ever anything more than legally sanctioned revenge.

Along with its indictment of the American citizenry as at heart a mob, its Everyman hero as maddened by his quest for vengeance, and the justice system as arbitrary, corrupt, and vindictive, *Fury* indicts its viewers as equally complicit in the thirst for violence revenge that sweeps through Lang's world like a contagion. At the same time as the film shows the catastrophic results of Joe's obsession with vengeance, it encourages viewers to share that obsession by painting the defendants as such hateful targets, subversively re-creating the same attitude in viewers that the lynch mob had originally adopted toward Joe. Thus, even as the film unmasks the obsessive hatred behind Joe's fury, it urges that fury on the audience. By the film's climax, viewers who are in tune with the conventions of victim films are caught in the impossible position of wanting the twenty-two members of the lynch mob to be punished, even though they can see that the twenty-two are innocent of murder, and of wanting Joe to get revenge for his suffering, even though they can see that getting revenge will destroy him. Like Hitchcock in films from *Suspicion* to *Psycho,* Lang traps his viewers in the morally complicit judgments his dramatization of the victim's story has invited them to make.

Fury's greatest achievement, in fact, is not its dramatization of the evils of lynching or its unblinking representation of the way Joe's obsession with legal revenge has made him indistinguishable from the mob. Rather, it is Lang's creation of a lynch-mob mentality within viewers, who are forced by the film's disconcerting ending to acknowledge both their own implication in the impossible totalitarian dream of personal revenge cloaked as justice, and the uneasy knowledge that all institutions of justice are fueled by the desire for revenge. More ruthlessly than any other victim film, *Fury* forces its audience to choose between a collective identity that reduces them to a lawless mob and an individual identity as the equally lawless vigilante who alone can right the wrongs the system cannot punish.

5

The Godfather and the Gangster Film

Responding to his fretful, bedridden wife May (Dorothy Tree), who worries, "When I think of all those awful people you come in contact with, downright criminals, I get scared," double-dealing lawyer Alonzo D. Emmerich (Louis Calhern), who is about to be arrested for his part in a high-stakes jewel robbery in *The Asphalt Jungle* (1950), blandly reassures her: "Nothing so different about them. After all, crime is only a left-handed form of human endeavor." His remark neatly encapsulates the defining paradox of the gangster film: Even though professional criminals who come together for the express purpose of committing crimes are rough, unscrupulous, and fearsome, they are at the same time indistinguishable from ordinary citizens like Emmerich, both because Emmerich is so corrupt that he might as well be a gangster, and because gangsters cannot help imitating the society whose norms they set out to violate.

Although it could well be argued that every crime film is a critique of the society crime disrupts, the gangster film is especially concerned with the social order its gang mimics or parodies. This concern begins with the gangster film's obsession with rules. Some rules are so fundamental that they are virtually universal in gangster films. The authority of the leader, if the gang has a leader, is not to be questioned. Junior gangsters must pay due respect to their elders. Gang members are forbidden from socializing with the police or competing for each other's women. No matter how dishonest they are in their dealings with the law, gangsters must honor their debts to each other and refrain from betraying each other whatever the provocation. All disputes that arise within the gang must be settled within the gang, without appeals to any outside authority. In short, the gang is constituted as the supreme social authority that demands unquestioning loyalty.

Many gangster films, of course, go much further in tailoring these general rules to fit their individual gangs. Tony Camonte (Paul Muni), the self-made entrepreneur of *Scarface* (1932), lives by a code that reflects his reluctance to delegate authority: "Do it first, do it yourself, and keep on doing it." Sixty years later, Jimmy Conway (Robert De Niro) approvingly tells an apprentice hoodlum in *GoodFellas* (1990): "Keep your mouth shut, and don't rat on your friends" [Fig. 22]. In *Reservoir Dogs* (1992), Mr. Pink (Steve Buscemi) pleads with his colleagues to "be professional." Clyde Barrow (Warren Beatty) refuses to take a farmer's money in *Bonnie and Clyde* (1967), since he robs only banks, not the private citizens who use them. Big Jim Colfax (Albert Dekker), the gangleader in *The Killers* (1946), takes the lion's share of the loot off the top; the gangsters in *White Heat* (1949) and *Bonnie and Clyde* share equally in the proceeds; the technicians who pull off the jewel heist in *The Asphalt Jungle* are each paid a flat rate, "like house painters."

Setting down these rules does not, of course, prevent them from being broken, any more than the gangsters' knowledge of the law prevents them from committing crimes. Gangsters routinely scheme against each other, vie for each other's women, hold out each other's money, double-cross and kill each other, and betray each other to the law. Even when they are determined to follow their own rules, their debates over the rules can often stretch to ludicrous lengths, as when Vincent Vega and Jules Winnfield (John Travolta and Samuel L. Jackson), the two hit men in *Pulp Fiction* (1994), argue about whether giving their boss's wife a foot massage is morally equivalent to "sticking your tongue in the holiest of holies," or whether their escape from an inept drug dealer's bullets was "a divine miracle" or "a freak occurrence."

Pulp Fiction's characters, in fact, constantly illustrate the ways the gang's obsession with rules of conduct is echoed by the formula's own obsession with broader moral rules. Is there anything lower than a man who keys another man's car? How do you react when your boss's wife comes on to you while he's out of town, especially if you've already heard a rumor that the last man the boss caught flirting with her got tossed out a window? What loyalty do you owe a man you've double-crossed, a man who's been trying to kill you, if he's being held by the homosexual rapists you've just escaped? Should a specialist

22. *GoodFellas:* "Keep your mouth shut, and don't rat on your friends." (Robert De Niro, Ray Liotta, Paul Sorvino)

called in to help you dispose of a dead body have to say "please" when he tells you what to do? Though it is ironic that films and gangs organized around breaking the rules should be so preoccupied by the rules they establish in their place, it is eminently logical for gangsters to spend their time debating rules of conduct and morality, because in opting out of the social norms that everyone else takes for granted, they alone are forthrightly considering the question of what rules ought to be followed and why.

The gangster film's fascination with rules begins with the organization of the gang itself. Lone-wolf criminals like Skip McCoy (Richard Widmark) in *Pickup on South Street* (1953) may eventually learn that they are more social creatures than they knew, but they usually drift through their films with less interest in or awareness of social and moral rules because they have fewer commitments to honor. In both versions of *The Thomas Crown Affair* (1968/1999), the eponymous gentleman thief (Steve McQueen/Pierce Brosnan) has no loyalty to the accomplices he casually assembles and discards; only his romance with the insurance investigator on his trail (Faye Dunaway/Rene Russo) threatens to give him away. But gang members are bound from the beginning by rules dictated by the social structure of their particular gang. One reason these rules can vary so widely from one gangster film to the next is the varying basis of different gangs' social organization. Sometimes a gang, like the brood of Kate "Ma" Barker (Shelley Winters) in *Bloody Mama* (1970), is essentially a family. Sometimes, as in the ethnic white gangs of *The Public Enemy* (1931) and *Once Upon a Time in America* (1984) or the inner-city black gangs of *Boyz N the Hood* (1991) and *Menace II Society* (1993), ties among gang members are based on childhood friendships [Fig. 23]. Some gangs form around lovers like Bonnie and Clyde, or the paroled convict Carter "Doc" McCoy (Steve McQueen/Alec Baldwin) and his wife Carol (Ali MacGraw/Kim Basinger) in both versions of *The Getaway* (1972/1994); many, indeed, are restricted to attractive young couples on the lam, from Eddie (Henry Fonda) and Joan Taylor (Sylvia Sidney) in *You Only Live Once* (1937), to Bart Tare and Annie Laurie Starr (John Dall and Peggy Cummins) in *Gun Crazy* (1949), to Arthur "Bowie" and Catherine "Keechie" Bowers, the newlywed bank robber and his bride (Farley Granger and Cathy O'Donnell) in *They Live by Night* (1949) and its weddingless remake, *Thieves Like Us* (1974), to the sociopathic teen heroes of *Badlands* (1973) and *Natural Born Killers* (1994).

More organized gangs take the form of teams whose members all have a voice in their operation. Gangs like those in *The Public Enemy* and *Set It Off* (1996) can function like labor unions, forming a protective shield around members who would be more vulnerable to social pressures if they remained on their own, and giving them the power to stand up for themselves. When Big Jim Colfax convenes a meeting in *The Killers* to discuss the robbery of the Prentiss Hat Factory, every man present is given a chance to accept or reject the terms he proposes, and when a small-time thief named Charleston (Vince Barnett) announces that the job is too risky for him, he is allowed to leave with no hard feelings. In *Bonnie and Clyde,* gang members openly argue over who is to be counted as a member and how the take is to be split, sometimes overcoming the objections of both Bonnie and Clyde. Finally, Syndicate films from *The Big Combo* (1955) to *Point Blank* (1967) to *Casino* (1995) present organized crime organized in the most rigidly hierarchical and alienating way of all: as a business. The historical evocations of real-life gangsters in *The Cotton Club* (1984), *Billy Bathgate* (1991), and *Bugsy* (1991) all present them as aspiring businessmen, but the tendency is equally pronounced in many purely fictional treatments. In *The Asphalt Jungle* and *The Killing* (1956), gang members are

23. *Boyz N the Hood:* Gang loyalties based on childhood friendships. (Cuba Gooding Jr., Larry Fishburne, Ice Cube)

recruited specifically for the skills they bring to a proposed heist. Both Howard Hawks's *Scarface* and Brian De Palma's 1983 remake emphasize the gradual withdrawal of the gangleader from the day-to-day operations of the gang. By the time of *New Jack City* (1991), kingpin Wesley Snipes's involvement in his thriving cocaine empire seems to be limited entirely to executing traitors and consuming his own product.

No social model a gang adopts, however, will protect it from the moral imperative of Hollywood gangster films: Crime does not pay. This rule, with its corollary axiom that intelligent, morally responsible citizens never break the law, is responsible for gangster films' frequent emphasis on the question of why people turn to crime. Gangster films of the 1930s – as if to guard against the heretical suggestion that the inequities of the Depression could make a law-abiding citizen lose faith in the economic system – generated a heavily overdetermined series of explanations for crime, ranging from moral deviance (Tony Camonte and Marielito Tony Montana both willingly embrace the life of crime that makes them known as Scarface) to developmental deprivation (the bad kids of *The Public Enemy* grow up to be bad adults, and the Dead End Kids are at a similar risk in *Dead End* [1937] and *Angels with Dirty Faces* [1938]) to sociological determinism (*The Public Ene-my*'s gangsters are stereotypically Irish, the gangsters in *Scarface* and *Little Caesar* [1930] Italian)[1] to circumstantial accident, as in *They Made Me a Criminal* (1939), in which the persecution of prizefighter Johnnie Bradfield (John Garfield) produces a story that could more accurately have been titled *They Made Me Act Like a Criminal*. It was left to later generations to explore psychopathological explanations for crime in *Gun Crazy, Bonnie and Clyde, Badlands*, and *Natural Born Killers*. What is most remarkable throughout all these explanations is their unvarying insistence on the gangster's social deviance. Holly-wood never feels the need to explain why people become law-abiding citizens, only why they do not [Fig. 24].

Whenever a gangster's behavior is rationalized by explanations that assume criminals deviate from some social norm, Hollywood is affirm-ing the social order its audience accepts by reminding them that in-fractions against that order are stigmatized. When the criminal is a member of a gang that is utterly destroyed, however, the film's subtext becomes more complicated, since the destruction of any social unit, even a gang of criminals, that mirrors the larger society amounts to a critique of friendship, love, family ties, business ethics, or the social order as a whole. The movies' attitudes toward their "left-handed" so-cieties are still further complicated by the fact that gangsters have been presented throughout Hollywood history as heroic in their defi-ance of the law the movies are at such pains to affirm.

Hollywood's attitude toward gangsters was not always so morally complex – in *The Great Train Robbery* (1903), the criminals who carry out the robbery emerge no more clearly as individuals than their vic-tims among the trainmen or the passengers – but the steady move-ment of the American population from rural areas to big, strange cities increasingly populated by European immigrants soon caused the ur-ban gangster film to break away from the western. In the prairie settle-ments of the western, life may have been hard, but everyone knew who or what the enemies were: Indians, rustlers, natural disasters un-tempered by the amenities of civilization. In the new cities dramatized by the gangster film, by contrast, heroes and heroines isolated from their birth families and the communities in which they had grown up scrutinized every new arrival in the next apartment as a stranger and a possible threat. Such distance from one's closest neighbors, at once diminishing their humanity and magnifying their potential menace, tends to make them less empathetic. By the time of D. W. Griffith's *The*

24. *Natural Born Killers:* The enduring need to explain why people become criminals. (Juliette Lewis, Woody Harrelson)

Transformation of Mike (1912) and *The Musketeers of Pig Alley* (1912), the criminal heroes are already the most magnetic characters in their worlds, and it is not surprising to see them either ripe for conversion or at least capable of secretive good deeds. Later features like *Underworld* (1927) and *Thunderbolt* (1929) were frank celebrations of the gangster as tragic hero, proudly dignified by the stoic courage with which he meets his fate.

The gangster film enjoyed a remarkable flowering in the 1930s for three reasons. First was the premium that synchronized sound put on the genre's expressive sound effects: fast cars, threatening police sirens, the incessant chatter of guns that provide the auditory continuity substituting for music for most of the running time of the 1932 *Scarface*. Second was the opportunity sync sound offered gangster heroes to define themselves through pungent epigrams, from the sneering put-down of a rival gangster by Cesare "Rico" Bandello (Edward G. Robinson) in Mervyn Le Roy's *Little Caesar* – "He can dish it out, but he's got so he can't take it any more" – to Tom Powers's epitaph on himself in *The Public Enemy:* "I ain't so tough." Because of its demand for greater realism in dialogue, sync sound also unmasked the inarticulateness and the ethnic or immigrant inflections of gangster heroes like Tom Powers and Tony Camonte, making them seem even more alienated and vulnerable than their predecessors. Third and most important, however, was a development that had nothing to do with the rise of sync sound: the background of Prohibition and the Depression.

The Nineteenth Amendment to the Constitution – the Volstead Act, which took effect in 1920 – prohibited the sale or transportation of alcoholic beverages. By making every liquor purchase a criminal act, the Volstead Act transformed the American public's view of criminal culture. Instead of marginalizing criminals as lost souls on the other side of the tracks, Americans who wanted a drink were obliged to think of them as their suppliers, their associates, perhaps even their friends, without necessarily giving up their old opinion. Criminals were still Them, but they were increasingly Us as well; and a society that could not officially acknowledge its own dependence on smugglers and bootleggers prepared the way for an even more complex attitude toward criminals in its popular entertainment.

It was not until the onset of the Depression in 1929, however, when Prohibition was in its last years, that the availability of synchronized sound and the noncriminal audience's increased intimacy with criminal culture were sparked by the Depression's rapid polarizing of economic classes into the haves and the have-nots (basically, the employed and the unemployed) to produce gangster classics like *The Public Enemy, Little Caesar,* and *Scarface.* The heroes of these films may have been ruthless and even despicable, but they were living out the audience's dreams of economic power and revenge on the system. At first glance it might be hard to understand the appeal of *Scarface's* Tony Camonte. Tony's dim, boorish, ugly, disloyal side is painfully obvious in his pursuit of Poppy (Karen Morley), his boss's girlfriend, who shows up his lack of polish when, for instance, he unwittingly approves her description of his apartment as "gaudy" and his passion for jewelry as "effeminate." Yet Tony is as irresistible to the audience as he is to Poppy. His brutishness can be excused as childlike immaturity he may grow out of; his delight in violence, unforgettably displayed when he picks up his first machine gun and excitedly sprays the room with gunfire, is equally childlike; and his courage and rude wit place him above both his sniveling boss Johnny Lovo (Osgood Perkins) and Lt. Ben Guarino (C. Henry Gordon), the earnest, vengeful flatfoot determined to nail him. Even more important, Tony is acting as a Depression-era Horatio Alger, a self-made success in direct sales, one of the few avenues to wealth open to ordinary citizens in the thirties. Though the product Tony is selling is illegal, many members of his original audience would have sampled it regularly anyway, and their indulgence of Tony is compounded by his success in flouting both the law of the land and Johnny's cautious rule of staying away from the rival North Side mob. Tony is not only acting out the Depression audience's economic dreams of rising above the limitations of the authoritarian system represented in Hollywood films by centralized business, banks, courts, and police officers; he is also acting out viewers' far more equivocal desire to avenge themselves on the system that has kept them down.

Tony's status as an anticapitalist who ends up as the ultimate capitalist is rich material for a critique of capitalism as an economic system that cannot distinguish successful businessmen from career criminals. Not surprisingly, however, the public outcry against gangster films that led to the tighter enforcement of the 1930 Production Code beginning in 1934 focused on the seductive ways they glamorized the criminal hero's most sociopathic tendencies toward violence. The enduring appeal of the gangster's sociopathic behavior is made even more striking by the disinclination of most movie gangsters to offer any moral justification for their lawbreaking. *Set It Off,* one of the few gangster films to make a serious case for its protagonists' behavior, shows by implication why so few other films do so. Like other self-justifying gangsters, the four heroines of *Set It Off* do not think of themselves as gangsters; they are simply four friends struggling to make a living in Los Angeles as office cleaners. Fired from her job as a bank teller after her failure to trigger the silent alarm during a bank robbery has led to several deaths, Frankie Sutton (Vivica A. Fox) urges her friends, "We just takin' away from the system that's fuckin' us anyway." It is a system, as the film makes clear, that includes not only the Man – the police officers who mistakenly kill the kid brother of Frankie's friend Stony Newsome (Jada Pinkett Smith) – but men in general, from the car dealer who beds Stony in return for an advance in salary he promises her to the owner of the cleaning agency, who steals the take from the friends' second (and, as they had originally planned, final) bank job, forcing them to a third robbery with tragic consequences.

Like *You Only Live Once, They Made Me a Criminal, Carlito's Way* (1993), and *A Perfect World* (1993), *Set It Off* takes such pains to whitewash its criminal heroes as innocents whose actions are forced on them by an alienating society that it is hard to see them as criminals at all. From time to time, however, the film's assumption that its heroines and its audience have access to an intuitively correct code of justice that the system has betrayed is complicated, for example, by its more nuanced attitude toward the justice system represented by a kind but intransigent Child Protection caseworker and a cop – prejudiced against Frankie but remorseful about the death of Stony's brother – who is determined to keep the four suspects from getting killed. Even more telling are the differences the film develops among the four friends. Gentle Tisean Williams (Kimberly Elise) cannot even bring herself to participate in the first robbery; practical Frankie argues against targeting a well-protected downtown branch where the risks will be as big as the payoff; Stony is torn between her loyalty to her friends and the prospects of romance with a junior bank executive who works at the designated branch; hotheaded Cleo Simms (Queen Latifah) gets so deeply into the role of the gun-toting bank robber that she becomes a danger to all the others. Despite the different attitudes toward the law and lawbreakers the film explores, however, it ends by reaffirming the power of friendship among the four heroines, who would die rather than let each other down. Maintaining the friendships that have been formed under the gun, and under the heel of oppression, becomes the moral imperative *Set It Off* offers in place of following the rules of an unjust society.

Most gangsters, incapable of such unshakable loyalty to their friends, can offer no such sweeping justification for breaking the law. *Bonnie and Clyde*, which seems at first to offer its lovers as equally innocent, soon reveals them as shockingly damaged. Clyde Barrow (Warren Beatty) is a slick, insensitive, fast-talking salesman with no sense of moral responsibility and a harrowingly comical inability to see around the next curve. He is genuinely puzzled when a grocer he is robbing attacks him just for trying to get something to eat, and he thinks that by robbing banks instead of private citizens he can avoid hurting anybody. Bonnie Parker (Faye Dunaway), by contrast, is a sensitive, melancholic narcissist, a sociopath obsessed with thoughts of her impending death but indifferent to the death of the bank officer Clyde kills during a botched robbery. Yet for all their faults the couple remain, like Tony Camonte, the most appealing characters in their world. Even more than Tony's, their faults are those of youth, and their sterile West Texas landscape, which offers them nothing but a choice between dead-end rules and a hell-raising spree sure to bring the wrath of the authorities down on them, is so clearly a Depression-era refraction of the Vietnam-era draft that college audiences were ready to sentimentalize the lovers even more completely by adopting the 1930s fashions Theadora Van Runkle had designed for them.

Still other criminals justify their lawbreaking through their rejection not of the law as such but of particular laws proscribing particular crimes. Although practically all movie gangsters end up killing someone in order to raise the stakes of their lawbreaking, brand themselves as irredeemable, and create spectacular death scenes, these killings are incidental to the laws they set out to break. Bonnie and Clyde, like the heroines of *Set It Off,* are bank robbers; Tony Camonte is a bootlegger; Joe Morse (John Garfield), in *Force of Evil* (1948), is involved with the numbers racket; Harry Fabian, in *Night and the City* (1950/1992), is a small-time promoter. Except for the thrill-killers of *Badlands* and *Natural Born Killers*, few movie criminals use murder as a mode of social protest; murder (or the unintended deaths in *Force of Evil* and the 1950 *Night and the City*) simply represents the natural tendency of criminal plots to spiral out of control and the formula's imperative to inflate criminal infractions and their punishment to heroic status. Depression-era bootlegging films are especially likely to sympathize with their gangsters' original plots but not in the killings that are their inevitable results. These films reveal the ambivalence at the heart of the formula's attitude toward the law, and in particular toward the proposition that crime does not pay. Gangster films insist on this proposition, not because it is universally self-evident, but because it is constantly under suspicion by audiences eager to see their antiestablishment dreams of power and wealth acted out onscreen.

This ambivalence toward society's laws is dramatized even more directly by the primary conflicts in gangster films. Except for the flurry of antigangster films like *"G" Men* (1935) and the *Crime Does Not Pay* series (1935–47) shepherded through the Hays Office in the later 1930s, officers of the law are surprisingly marginal figures in most gangster films. The real threat to the gangs of *The Public Enemy* and

Scarface is not the impotent police force but rival gangsters; once Tony Camonte has wiped out the North Side gang, he is made vulnerable only by his grief at having killed his sidekick Guino Rinaldo (George Raft), who had secretly married Tony's sister Cesca (Ann Dvorak), and by Cesca's own death. Bonnie and Clyde are killed not by an official police force but by the collusion between a vigilante Texas ranger they have insulted and a gang member's father as outraged by his son's failure to achieve Bonnie and Clyde's notoriety as by his prominent tattoo. The gang members in *The Asphalt Jungle* are killed by each other, by the accident of bad luck, by their own flawed natures. The greatest danger to Big Jim Colfax's gang in *The Killers* is Big Jim himself, who eliminates each of them in order to cover up his plot to trick them out of the take from the Prentiss Hat Factory robbery. In Don Siegel's 1964 remake of *The Killers,* the authorities are even more invisible when Johnny North (John Cassavettes) is killed by another pair of hit men dispatched by his old boss, Jack Browning (Ronald Reagan), and it is the enterprising hit men, not the stalwart insurance investigator, who spend the film solving the puzzle of why Johnny did not run from them. *Point Blank* and *The Usual Suspects* (1995) show gangs similarly destroyed by criminal masterminds who clean house of possible rivals or assemble suicide forces to eliminate dangerous informants. *Mean Streets* (1973) marginalizes rival gangs along with the police, since every threat to Charlie (Harvey Keitel) and Johnny Boy Cervello (Robert De Niro) comes from within their own gang. Even in *Reservoir Dogs,* whose gangsters fret obsessively about the police officer who has infiltrated their gang, the undercover cop (Tim Roth) succeeds in killing only one of them; the others end up executing each other in a bloody, ritualistic finale.

The Grifters (1990) offers the bleakest view of criminal society of all. Although con man Roy Dillon (John Cusack) is seriously injured by a bartender he is trying to swindle out of ten dollars and Roy's mother Lilly (Anjelica Huston) is beaten and terrified by the bookmaker from whom she has been stealing, the real threat to Roy, Lilly, and Roy's lover Myra Langtry (Annette Bening) is each other. Throughout the film, the three grifters take turns trying to escape, betray, or kill each other; but only Roy realizes that since the essence of confidence schemes is "to take another pro – your partner, who's watching you" – his life of crime has poisoned every possible human relationship. The law is not Roy's enemy; if his every social relation is founded on a trust it is his vocation to betray, then everyone who tries to get close to him, from his lover to his mother, is the enemy.

The Grifters's unflinchingly bleak view of social relations is merely the logical extension of the gangster formula's treatment of society. Since gangsters who form outlaw societies in order to break the rules cannot help at the same time replicating the rules within their own countersocieties, what they take to be their primary conflict with the law will inevitably by mirrored and magnified as conflict within the gang. Gangster films resolve the resulting contradictions in one of three ways. The most conventionally reassuring films show the gangsters vanquished by the superior force or intelligence of the police; more challenging studies of career criminals explore their heroes' paradoxical combination of power and vulnerability by emphasizing their destruction at the hands of competing criminals to whom their life-style has made them vulnerable; and the films that use gang culture most directly as a means of analyzing the consensual culture of law-abiding citizens show gangsters destroyed by the contradictions among the different social roles they have been obliged to assume within their gangs.

The fatal effects of conflict among gangsters' different social roles are foreshadowed as early as *Scarface,* in which Tony Camonte's self-appointed role as his sister Cesca's protective guardian will end with his killing first her bridegroom Guino, his right-hand man in the gang, and later accidentally killing Cesca herself. *The Killers, Force of Evil, They Live by Night, Mean Streets, Once Upon a Time in America, New Jack City,* and *Casino* are all studies of the divided loyalties to which gangsters necessarily have committed themselves as gangsters. The fact-based *GoodFellas* is a particularly corrosive critique of the long-standing friendships that do not prevent gangsters from breaking their promises to each other or ratting each other out. But the most ambitious of all such studies, and the greatest of all American crime films, is the movie whose myth of honor among thieves *GoodFellas* seeks to correct: Francis Ford Coppola's *The Godfather* (1972).

The story of *The Godfather* begins with the success of Mario Puzo's bestselling 1969 novel. Paramount, which had acquired the rights to the novel before publication, found itself with an unexpected opportunity to revitalize the gangster film. First envisioning a quick, low-budget transcription, the studio hired screenwriter-director Francis Ford Coppola. Though he had shared a screenwriting Oscar for *Patton* in 1970, Coppola's credentials for the project were sketchy. While still a film student, he had begun a long apprenticeship with Roger Corman, the dean of low-budget independent producers. Coppola's first directorial credit was for Corman's horror film *Dementia 13* (1963); his second, the coming-of-age story *You're a Big Boy Now* (1966), was submitted as his M.F.A. thesis at UCLA. In between, he had collaborated on the screenplays of the Tennessee Williams sexual odyssey *This Property Is Condemned* and the World War II epic *Is Paris Burning?* (both 1966). Until he directed *The Godfather,* Coppola had been consistently more successful as a screenwriter than as a director; neither of the only two major studio releases Coppola had directed, the leprechaun musical *Finian's Rainbow* (1968) and the drama *The Rain People* (1969), had been successful at the box office.

Once he was brought aboard, however, Coppola moved quickly to take control of *The Godfather.* He fought for a budget big enough to finance location shooting for a key sequence in Sicily. He interested Marlon Brando, the preeminent screen actor of his generation, in the role of the aging Don Vito Corleone. He brought two cast members of *The Rain People* into the film: James Caan as the Don's oldest son, Santino "Sonny" Corleone, and Robert Duvall as his adopted son and *consigliere,* Tom Hagen. He asked that his younger sister, Talia Shire, be given the part of Connie Corleone, the Don's daughter. And he insisted, on the strength of an intense performance as a drug addict in *The Panic in Needle Park* (1971), on casting stage actor Al Pacino, virtually unknown in Hollywood despite his Obie and Tony awards for *The Indian Wants the Bronx* (1968) and *Does a Tiger Wear a Necktie?* (1969), in the pivotal role of Michael Corleone, the Don's youngest son.

Coppola kept the story faithful to the vision of Puzo, retained as co-screenwriter despite his lack of Hollywood experience, who maintained that *The Godfather* was essentially a film about a family that happened to be in crime rather than a crime film whose criminal organization happened to be that of a family. The film's anatomy of the conflicting roles the Corleone family demands its leading members play begins with its title, the first of a series of euphemisms forced on Paramount by the insistence of Italian-American lobbies that the film avoid the ethnically charged terms *Mafia* and *Cosa Nostra* in fictionalizing the five New York crime families whose existence was well known thanks to repeated journalistic exposés and Hollywood fictionalizations long before *The Godfather* ever went before the cameras. The film's forced ethnic sensitivity helped transform it into a masterpiece of innuendo in which innocent or neutral terms take on double meanings far more sinister than the ethnic slurs they had been pressed into service to replace.

As Michael, a returning World War II veteran, explains to his girl-friend Kay Adams (Diane Keaton) during his sister Connie's wedding reception, the daringly extended set piece that opens the film, standing as a child's godfather is a family relationship, a sacred relationship, that the Corleones take very seriously. In the Catholic Church, godparents are asked to take an active role in the religious education of their godchildren, and to act as the children's guardians if their parents die. These duties, however, are ironically remote from Don Vito's self-appointed responsibilities to his godson Johnny Fontaine (Al Martino), a washed-up singer. Vito, who has already released Johnny from an inconvenient contract to a bandleader by making the bandleader "an offer he couldn't refuse" – a choice between a $1,000 check and the loaded gun at his head – is about to intimidate a Hollywood producer into giving Johnny a career-reviving role in his new film by a combination of suave threats and shocking violence.

The contrast between the official and unofficial meanings of the term *godfather* – the spiritual advisor and guardian and the violently protective head of the Corleone interests – is developed visually throughout this opening sequence by the conflict production designer Dean Tavoularis and cinematographer Gordon Willis set up between the brightly lit exteriors, in which joyous wedding guests sing, dance, drink, and slip the bride and her groom Carlo Rizzi (Gianni Russo) envelopes of cash, and the somber, monochrome gold-lit interior of Vito's office, where the don sits listening to the petitioners who have come to ask him the favors Sicilian custom requires him to grant on his daughter's wedding day. Throughout this scene – the first of many contrasts the film sets up between the freedom and joy of exterior scenes and the entrapment of interiors, or of exteriors blocked and shot as if they were interiors – Don Vito manages to be at once generous, judicious, and unapologetically criminal [Fig. 25]. Although the undertaker Bonasera (Salvatore Corsitto) begs him to kill the boys who beat his daughter when she refused their sexual advances, Vito chides him: "You don't ask with respect." He agrees to have the boys beaten only when Bonasera asks him to "be my friend," calls him "Godfather," and kisses his hand. The scene, played in the hushed tones of a religious ritual, is the first of many parodies of such rituals that will mark the Corleones' growing distance from the ideals they embody.

The film's title is a pun in another sense as well. *The Godfather* is a generational history of the Corleone family that charts the changes in the family from the height of Vito's power to the coming of age of his three sons. Although Vito is widely identified as the film's title character, the title more accurately refers to a title, like that of president or pope, that migrates from one godfather to the next as Vito is succeeded by Sonny and finally Michael. Significantly, the Don's middle son, the sweetly ineffectual Fredo (John Cazale), who fails to prevent his father's near-fatal shooting by the henchmen of Virgil Sollozzo (Al Lettieri), is never considered to fill the role of Vito's successor; nor is Sonny, who is thrust into the position as Vito lies near death in a hospital room, ever referred to as the godfather. Vito's true heir is Michael, the clean-cut war hero who, despite capping the anecdote he tells his WASP girlfriend in the opening sequence, "That's my family, Kay. That's not me," ends as a far more ruthless godfather than his father ever was.

Woven through the film's saga of the Corleone family's fortunes from 1945 to 1952, which is driven by Michael's determination to execute the man he is certain will otherwise kill his father and his father's attempt to protect Michael from reprisals, is the question of what it means to be a member of a family. The question is first posed in the opening conversation between Bonasera and Vito and highlighted in Kay's question to Michael why Tom Hagen, whom he introduces as his brother, has a different last name from him. Even after Michael's explanation of how Vito adopted Tom, the question lingers: Is Tom a member of the Corleones? The same question will be asked of Kay, whom Michael insists, despite her objections and the red dress that jars with his family's wedding finery, on posing with them for a formal photograph at the very end of the wedding sequence. Even after her wedding to Michael years later, it is clear that Kay is not a Corleone. Neither is Connie herself, nor her mother, nor the wife Sonny casually betrays with a bridesmaid as the reception continues outside. The Corleone family excludes women from full membership; they can never act as freely or responsibly as the fathers and sons who are the family's core.

As Fredo and Carlo show, however, not every son can be a Corleone either. If family ties are measured by intimacy and responsibility, then Connie's husband Carlo, whom Vito tells Tom Hagen should be given a living but kept out of discussions of the family business, is not a Corleone, and Tom himself, as he points out to Sonny, is as much Vito's son as Sonny ever was. To make up for the attenuated ties to some disenfranchised members of the immediate family, the Corleones have

25. *The Godfather:* A crime boss at once generous, judicious, and unapologetically criminal. (Marlon Brando)

family ties to many people to whom they are not related by blood: Vito's *caporegimi* (lieutenants), his old Sicilian friends, Peter Clemenza (Richard Castellano) and Sal Tessio (Abe Vigoda); his dull-witted, fanatically loyal enforcer, Luca Brasi (Lenny Montana); and, most tellingly, Emilio Barzini (Richard Conte), Ottilio Cuneo (Rudy Bond), and the members of the other New York crime families.

Although it might seem absurd to take the term "crime families" as referring to relationships of genuine intimacy, it is an absurdity the film takes very seriously indeed. Sollozzo's attempt to kill Vito is based on his belief that Sonny, who had imprudently added a tactical question to his father's refusal of Sollozzo's offer to collaborate in selling drugs, will be more receptive to the partnership. What kind of businessman kills his prospective partner's much-loved father to cement their business relationship? The kind who is convinced, as Tom points out to Sonny, that with Vito seriously wounded, the survival of the Corleone family depends on their maintaining cordial official relations with the Five Families, who are likely to enforce a peace that forbids revenge for Vito's wounding in order to prevent the outbreak of full-scale gang warfare. The Corleone family, Sollozzo realizes, is ironically weakened by the very ties to the other New York families that are supposed to give it strength, and by the nobility of the Corleones' well-known commitment to any agreements they make with the other families.

Puzo and Coppola's view of the New York crime families as driven by an imperative of survival through cooperation makes Vito's world, with its handshake deals, its courtly nonaggression pacts, and its leaders' smug contrasts of their honorable behavior with the deals of politicians, remote from the Darwinian gang wars of *Scarface* and *Little Caesar*. Yet it is equally remote from the new world order Michael confirms in the film's climactic set piece, the baptism of Connie and Carlo's infant son Anthony (Sofia Coppola), when Coppola intercuts the murders Michael has ordered of the rival family heads with Michael's ritual vicarious promise, as his nephew's godfather, to renounce Satan and all his works and all his empty promises. The irony of this blasphemous christening focuses again on the distance between the two meanings of the word "godfather." Unlike his father, who is tragically caught trying to reconcile the two senses of the word by courteously declining Sollozzo's offer of a drug partnership because he feels it will degrade and imperil his family, Michael resolves the dilemma by ignoring the original force of family ties entirely. In acting to guarantee the safety of his family, Michael is making a mockery of the values he is most concerned to defend.

The Godfather tells the story of how Michael was brought to such a pass, the story of how Vito's olympian insistence on justice and family values gives way first to Sonny's impulsive, unquenchable appetite for vengeance, then to Michael's apparently more judicious, but actually more Machiavellian, handling of the family's struggles to adapt to a treacherously changing world. Michael's fate is shaped by the contradictions in his status in the family. Although the other families think him a "civilian" until his unexpected murders of Sollozzo and McCluskey (Sterling Hayden), the police captain Sollozzo has audaciously chosen as his bodyguard, Michael's crucial conversion comes earlier, in a deceptively quiet scene at his father's abandoned hospital bed. Realizing that Sollozzo has pressed police and hospital officials to eject Vito's bodyguards from the hospital so that they can finish the job of killing him, Michael gets a reluctant nurse to help him move Vito's bed into an unoccupied room, then tells his comatose father, "I'm here, Pop. . . . I'm with you now." All the subsequent corruption in the Corleone family stems from this moment of filial responsibility.

Despite his success in protecting his father, Michael argues to Sonny that since Sollozzo can save his own life now only by killing their father, he will keep trying unless he is stopped. "It's not personal," Michael concludes. "It's strictly business." The apparent contrast between the personal desires that continue to motivate Sonny and the business considerations that motivate Michael reveals still another contradiction lurking in the phrase "family business." The Corleones are connected to the other New York crime families, and for that matter to their own *caporegimi,* not by family ties but by business connections conducted as if they were family ties. Although the Corleones think of themselves as a family, they are better described as a family-run business, and it is the survival of the business, not the family, that is of paramount importance. Michael's "strictly business" rationale – sadly to be echoed at the film's ending by Michael's would-be betrayer Tessio to the capos who are leading him off to his own execution – is persuasive to Sonny because Sonny agrees that what's good for the Corleone business must be good for the Corleones, who have been schooled more successfully than any other gangsters in film history to put their family's welfare above their own.

Exiled to his family's idyllic ancestral village in Sicily after his assassination of Sollozzo and McCluskey, Michael attempts to settle down in an old-world marriage to Apollonia Vitelli (Simonetta Stefanelli); but once Apollonia dies in an explosion intended to kill him, everything Michael does for the rest of the film is calculated to ensure his family's safety by consolidating its power and destroying its enemies. Returning to America under a truce negotiated by his father, who has been thrown back into heading the family by the execution of Sonny, Mi-

26. *The Godfather:* Michael's first marriage as an abortive attempt at happiness. (Al Pacino, Simonetta Stefanelli)

chael abruptly marries Kay – their wedding, unlike his and Apollonia's, is never shown – after a single, chillingly dispassionate courtship scene. If his first marriage was an attempt at personal happiness and self-fulfillment [Fig. 26], his second is a marriage of convenience, an assimilationist fantasy evidently designed to bring him a step closer to his oft-proclaimed dream of making the Corleone family legitimate.

This quintessentially American fantasy of legitimacy through assimilation, generational survival, and the cultivation of a business dynasty most insidiously dramatizes Coppola's widely quoted remark that "the film always was a loose metaphor: Michael as America."[2] By the end of the film Michael has confirmed his promise as the heir to his father's family business. Armed with the advice Vito gives him just before his sentimentally peaceful death in his grape arbor, he repels a

27. *The Godfather:* Michael rejects Satan on behalf of the godson whose father he is about to have killed. (Al Pacino, Diane Keaton)

threat against his life. With his father dead, Michael moves swiftly in
ways his father never would have countenanced. Going a step beyond
his preemptive murder of Sollozzo and McCluskey, he orchestrates the
executions of the heads of all the rival families and of Moe Green (Alex
Rocco), the Las Vegas hotelier who refused to sell him the casino he
had sought as the base of operations for the Corleones' newly legitimate family business. He also avenges his brother Sonny by arrang-
ing the murder of Sonny's betrayer, Carlo, and wins the renewed loyalty of the family members who remain after his purge of the ranks.

At the same time, Michael's shocking betrayals expose the hollow-
ness of the Italian-American family values he espouses. Even viewers
who expect gangster heroes to be quick on the trigger are often ap-
palled by Michael's explicitly religious blasphemy during the christening sequence, when he covers his complicity in a gruesome series of
mob killings by promising to reject Satan on behalf of the godson
whose father he will send to his death later that same day [Fig. 27].

Michael's brusque denial of Connie's accusation that he had been planning to murder Carlo for all the years since Sonny's death is even more cold-blooded. Most troubling of all is the film's closing scene, in which Michael responds to Kay's demand that he tell her whether Connie's accusation is true first by angrily refusing to answer any questions about his business, then by assuring Kay that Connie's story is not true, moments before Clemenza and another capo enter, call Michael Don Corleone, kiss his hand, and quietly shut the door in Kay's face. Michael has ensured his family's survival and success, but only at the price of dishonoring his religious faith, his father's moral principles, his sister's happiness, and his wife's trust.

In one sense, Michael's exceptional personal heroism preserves his family business by destroying his soul. The film sets Vito's insistence on honor, respect, courtesy, and justice against Michael's uncompromising, deeply corrupted drive to do whatever it takes to ensure his family's survival. Vito's old-world gangster courtliness is set against his youngest son's vicious parody of the ritualistic rules of family life. The final scene between father and son, in which Vito speaks poignantly of his unfulfilled wishes for Michael as "Governor Corleone, Senator Corleone," heightens this contrast and presents Michael's whole life in terms of a road not taken, a life he should have led. In another sense, however, Michael is all too clearly Vito's legitimate heir, the don that Vito would have had to become if he wanted to protect his family from the conflicting loyalties between spiritual and temporal stewardship, blood relations and the extended family, family and business, Italian ways and American ways, that he had been cultivating for many years. As far back as the opening wedding sequence, the smiling presence of Carlo Rizzi, whose violence against his bride would finally lead to his murderous betrayal of Sonny, is a sign that the family's corruption is present, like the serpent in the garden, from the beginning.

The Godfather achieved extraordinary popular and critical success, winning Academy Awards for Best Picture, Best Adapted Screenplay, and Best Actor (Marlon Brando) and becoming the top-grossing film in Hollywood history until the days of Steven Spielberg. It launched Coppola on a meteoric career as the key American director of the 1970s, whose films ranged from the nightmare of surveillance paranoia *The Conversation* (1974) to the Vietnam restaging of Conrad's 1899 "Heart of Darkness," *Apocalypse Now* (1979), before the disastrous failure of his epic Las Vegas romance *One from the Heart* (1982) bankrupted his production company, Zoetrope Studios, and sent him back to the ranks of journeyman directors for such varied projects as the teen-angst films *Rumble Fish* and *The Outsiders* (both 1983), the historical gangster film *The Cotton Club* (1984), the time-travel romance *Peggy Sue Got Married* (1986), the home-front Vietnam War film *Gardens of Stone* (1987), the historical anecdote *Tucker: The Man and His Dream* (1988), whose tale of an independent carmaker buried by the establishment was a thinly veiled autobiographical parable, a florid adaptation of *Bram Stoker's Dracula* (1992), the comic fantasy *Jack* (1996), and the legal fairy tale *John Grisham's The Rainmaker* (1997).

Nonetheless, Coppola will undoubtedly be best remembered as the director and cowriter not only of *The Godfather* but of its two sequels (1974, 1990). Although the third film in the series, for all its grand scale and historical sweep, is memorable mostly as a pastiche of the first two, from its extended opening sequence at a festive celebration to its furiously crosscut climactic bloodbath, *The Godfather: Part II* is far and away the most successful sequel ever made, a dazzlingly complex reexamination of the relations between Don Vito (played as a young man by Robert De Niro, the only actor in screen history to win an Oscar for playing a role someone else had already been awarded an Oscar for playing) and his star-crossed son. Crisscrossing between Michael's ventures in Las Vegas and Havana just before the Cuban Revolution of 1958–9 and his father's rise to power half a century earlier in New York's Little Italy, *The Godfather: Part II* fleshes out the earlier film's mythic and psychological account of the Corleones' corruption with an incisive sociopolitical analysis of the family's evolution, even as it plumbs new depths of family betrayal in the name of family survival. When the film concludes after a poignant final flashback to Vito's birthday party in 1941, Michael, already a monster at the end of the earlier film, seems even more thoroughly damned by hopelessly entangling family loyalties his family's involvement in crime has dramatized but not created. It is not until the end of *The Godfather: Part III* sixteen years later, however, that he is finally permitted to die.

6

Double Indemnity and the Film Noir

The term *film noir* was first coined by French reviewer Nino Frank[1] when the end of the wartime embargo brought five 1944 Hollywood films – *The Woman in the Window, Laura, Phantom Lady, Double Indemnity,* and *Murder, My Sweet* – to Paris in the same week in 1946. All five films seemed to take place in a world marked by menace, violence, and crime and yet distinct from the world of the gangster cycle of the 1930s. In christening the young genre, Frank was thinking not so much of earlier movies as of earlier novels. The label *film noir* was adapted from Marcel Duhamel's *Série noire* translations for Gallimard of British and American hard-boiled novels. The private-eye stories of Dashiell Hammett and of Raymond Chandler, whose gorgeously overwrought prose made him the most obvious stylistic patron of noir, had broken the decorum of the formal detective story from Conan Doyle to Agatha Christie. But an even closer analogue was to be found in the breathless suspense novels of James M. Cain (*The Postman Always Rings Twice,* 1934; *Double Indemnity,* 1936) and Cornell Woolrich (*The Bride Wore Black,* 1940; *Phantom Lady,* 1942), which trapped their heroes in a nightmarishly claustrophobic world of evil.

Except for their common breeding ground in anonymous, claustrophobic cities that dramatized postwar alienation and disillusionment, noir heroes could not have had less in common with their gangster forebears. The principals of this new breed of crime films were not promethean challengers, or even professional criminals, defying the repressive institutions of their worlds, but hapless, sensitive, often passive amateurs who typically were seduced into criminal conspiracies through their infatuations with the sultry, treacherous heroines, femmes fatales who had no counterpart in the man's world of Hollywood gangster films. Unlike gangster films, which traced the rigidly symmetrical rise and fall of their outsized heroes, films noirs more often showed their heroes fatalistically sinking into a pit after the briefest of come-ons. The heroes of noir often dreamed of dabbling briefly in crime before returning to their normal lives, or found themselves trapped in the criminal plots of others despite their own innocence. In either case, the way back to normalcy was barred; they were so completely doomed by the slightest misstep, and their doom so openly telegraphed to the audience from the opening scene, that the very idea of heroism, even criminal heroism, became hopelessly distant.

Fueled from its first identification by the melding of its pop-cultural roots with the postwar disillusionment that made philosophical existentialism fashionable,[2] film noir has continued to enjoy more prestige than any other variety of crime film except for the gangster film, and has been the subject of more intense and enduring critical scrutiny; but it has also, for some of the same reasons, been the hardest sort of crime film to define. Steve Neale is only the most recent commentator to conclude that "as a single phenomenon, *noir* . . . never existed."[3] Even its duration has been the subject of considerable dispute, although most critics have bracketed it by John Huston's *The Maltese Falcon* (1941) and Orson Welles's *Touch of Evil* (1958), and many more have defined the decade after Nino Frank's list of 1944 films, ending with Robert Aldrich's *Kiss Me Deadly* (1955), as its heyday. As the quintet of films that first inspired Frank's label suggests, the label of noir has often been invoked to constitute a tradition of films that seem to have little in common with each other except for the crimes their characters commit.

Even commentators who agree in linking the rise of noir to the end of the war have offered dauntingly diverse theories of its origins. Michael Renov roots noir's misogynistic fear of treacherously powerful women in the looming return of GI's who would find that their jobs had often been taken by the women they had left behind.[4] Lucy Fischer links the films' concern with "psychoneurotic" victims of "male hysteria" to the war's legacy of shell shock.[5] Frank Krutnik, turning from psychoanalysis to economics, points out that the stylized visuals of noir were dictated in part by a 1943 ceiling of $5,000 on set construction per film imposed by the War Production Board, down from a prewar average of $50,000 for A pictures and $17,500 for B pictures.[6] Paul Kerr, arguing more broadly that film noir resists what Colin MacCabe calls "the homogenisation of different discourses by their relation to [the] one dominant discourse" of realism, ends his essay with the pointedly narrow premise that the stylized black-and-white visuals of noir marked a site of resistance to "the absorption of a color aesthetic within realism."[7]

Politically minded theorists have found no more comfort in their shared perspective. Both Carl Richardson and Thom Andersen link the decline of film noir in the 1950s to the decline of the Hollywood Left – Andersen has coined the term *film gris* to describe the films of blacklisted Hollywood leftists like Jules Dassin (*Thieves' Highway,* 1949) and Nicholas Ray (*Knock on Any Door,* 1949)[8] – but adopt sharply different definitions of and attitudes toward leftist filmmaking, whose drive toward realism was a prerequisite for its political critique. Mike Davis sees noir as using an "existentialized Marxism" to unmask Los Angeles as the "bright guilty place" Orson Welles presents in *The Lady from Shanghai* (1948), Dean MacCannell as driven by the tension between democracy and a capitalism grown stiff and antidemocratic, and Joan Copjec as arising more generally from "a split between power and those whom power subjects such that the very world of these subjects appears incomprehensible to them."[9]

This conceptual Babel has deep roots. From its beginnings as a critical term, film noir has overlapped with many other varieties of crime film. *Lady in the Lake* (1947), like most screen adventures of Raymond Chandler's hard-boiled gumshoe Philip Marlowe, is a noir detective story. *Brute Force* (1947) is a noir prison film. *Body and Soul* (1947) and *The Set-Up* (1949) are noir boxing stories. *They Live by Night* and *Gun Crazy* (both 1949) are noir tales of doomed lovers on the run. *The Killing* (1956) is a noir caper. *Possessed* (1947) is a noir weepie. These labels exploit one of the two main definitions of noir: a distinctive black-and-white visual style that emphasizes what Janey Place and Lowell Peterson have called "antitraditional" lighting, camera, and mise-en-scène and what David Bordwell, Janet Staiger, and Kristin Thompson have called "specific and non-subversive conventions derived from crime literature and from canons of realistic and generic motivation."[10]

The leading visual motifs of film noir, memorably summarized by Paul Schrader's dictum, following Frank's 1946 essay, that "compositional tension is preferred to physical action,"[11] are such well-known Hollywood visual conventions that many of them have become clichés parodists have used to evoke a whole era. Since they do not share the preference for balanced, harmonious visuals motivating the orthodox Hollywood practice of high-key lighting, noirs move and dim (or dispense with entirely) the fill light that normally complements the key light, producing a low-key, high-contrast, highly directional style of lighting and creating unbalanced visual compositions marked by dazzling, bleached-out whites amid pools of deep shadow that often conceal important onscreen spaces or expressions on characters' faces. Shooting nighttime exterior shots night-for-night produces rich, velvety blacks that provide a dramatic contrast to the heroes' garishly lit little world. The wide-angle lenses often used to extend depth of field exaggerate apparent depth within the image, so distorting the body of Kasper Gutman (Sydney Greenstreet) in *The Maltese Falcon* and the face of Hank Quinlan (Orson Welles) in *Touch of Evil* that the characters turn into gargoyles. At the same time, the coldly expressive mise-en-scène, a Hollywood refinement of the insistent expressionism of German silent films from *The Cabinet of Dr. Caligari (Das Kabinett des Dr. Caligari,* 1920) to *M* (1931), acts as a symbolic theater for hidden desires the characters can neither articulate nor satisfy, while confirming what Dana Polan has called "the radical externality and alterity of environment to personality."[12] A preference for angled shots disorients viewers and renders the world of the film more abstract, making the characters appear more menacing in low-angle shots and trapping them in their surroundings in high-angle shots. Sharply defined shadows and rain-slick streets create reflections that double and fracture the stable identities that would normally be incarnated in the actors' bodies. In extreme examples, characters' bodies are kept on one side of the screen, creating unbalanced masses that dramatize imbalances of power and the characters' alienation.

From its earliest formulations, the challenge of defining noir has been to theorize a relation between its visual conventions and the narratives of crime that have generated its leading alternative definition. Defining noir purely as a visual style would exclude such noir classics as *The Postman Always Rings Twice* (1946) and *Key Largo* (1948), as well as the Technicolor noir romances *Leave Her to Heaven* (1945) and *Niagara* (1953), and open the gates to hundreds of films that borrow noir's expressionistic visual style without its criminal plots, from the science-fiction terrors of *Invasion of the Body Snatchers* (1956) to the foiled middle-class adultery of *Brief Encounter* (1945) to the epic biography of *Citizen Kane* (1941), whose pioneering use of deep focus and expressionistic mise-en-scène has some claim to have inaugurated the noir visual style.[13]

The films more often invoked as the genre's precursors, however, are *Stranger on the Third Floor* (1940) and *The Maltese Falcon* – although, apart from their emphasis on crime, these two detective stories have little in common with each other. Certainly their visual styles could not be more different. *Stranger on the Third Floor* is a low-key-lighted nightmare about a witness who is afraid that his testimony has helped convict an innocent man of murder. The wide-angle interiors of *The Maltese Falcon,* by contrast, are evenly lit and traditionally balanced. Attempts to construct even the most rudimentary history of noir are therefore stymied by the competing claims of the style of individual shots and scenes and larger-scale narrative concerns.[14]

The troubled relations between style and narrative are focused in the five 1944 films that inspired Nino Frank's label in the first place. *The Woman in the Window* – with its story of how a man's fascination with a painting of a beautiful woman displayed in a shop window leads him first to an acquaintance with the woman herself, then suddenly to murder when the two of them are interrupted by her enraged lover, and finally to suicide when his frantic efforts to conceal the crime go increasingly awry – marries a noir plot to a visual style more geometric than moodily expressionistic. *Laura,* a handsomely designed, acidly literate whodunit with a velvety look and a haunting theme song, pits a middle-class cop who has also fallen in love with a portrait against the amusingly monstrous gallery of aristocratic suspects to the apparent murder of Laura Hunt; in both thematic and visual terms, it has even more tenuous links to film noir. *Phantom Lady,* best remembered for two remarkable sequences – the death of a murder suspect under the wheels of a subway train and a jam session in which a potential witness woos the heroine with an orgiastic drum solo, shot in the most evocative low-key-lighted style – is for most of its running time a much lighter suspense story about a secretary trying to free her accused boss from an equally photogenic prison. *Murder, My Sweet* [Fig. 28], though it makes the most consistent use of low-key visuals from its striking opening, is a parboiled private-eye story whose edge is softened by the casting of musical star Dick Powell as Philip Marlowe and by its incongruously happy ending. Of all the five films that inspired Frank, only *Double Indemnity*'s noir credentials have never been questioned, and the film may rightly stand, in its marriage of

28. *Murder, My Sweet:* The visual style of film noir coupled with a parboiled detective story. (Dick Powell, Ralf Harolde)

dark visuals and darker narrative to a pitch-black view of the world, as the founding exemplar of the genre, the film whose rigorously metaphoric structure reveals the logic that weds noir visuals to noir narrative.

The union of talents that produced *Double Indemnity* seems so inevitable in retrospect that it is surprising to recall its director's unlikely background. Although Vienna-born Billy Wilder had been collaborating on screenplays since Robert Siodmak's German semidocumentary *People on Sunday* (*Menschen am Sonntag,* 1930), his best-known credentials were as a writer of sophisticated Hollywood comedies like *Ninotchka* (1939) and *Ball of Fire* (1941). Neither of the previous films Wilder had directed, the romantic comedy *The Major and the Minor* (1942) nor the suspenseful war melodrama *Five Graves to Cairo* (1943), could have prepared audiences for the unrelentingly bleak cynicism of *Double Indemnity.* Ironically, this new cynicism, once revealed, would become the predominant note of such varied Wilder films as the alcoholic confessional *The Lost Weekend* (1945), the lurid Hollywood exposé *Sunset Blvd.* (1950), the acid journalistic fable *The Big Carnival* (aka *Ace in the Hole,* 1951), the POW comedy-drama *Stalag 17* (1953), the courtroom drama *Witness for the Prosecution* (1957), the Prohibition gangster comedy *Some Like It Hot* (1959), the acrid office romance *The Apartment* (1960), and the parodistic fantasy *The Private Life of Sherlock Holmes* (1970).

Wilder's regular collaborator, writer-producer Charles Brackett, declined to join him in adapting such a suspect property as *Double Indemnity,* which had been considered and rejected for filming even before its first publication. Cain's novella, based on the real-life 1927 Ruth Snyder–Judd Gray murder case, told the story of insurance salesman Walter Huff's unholy partnership with femme fatale Phyllis Nirdlinger (whose names were changed in the film) to kill her husband for the insurance money. The tale was widely criticized as not only sordid but socially subversive, offering, in the warning of the Hays Office, a blueprint for the perfect murder, though one with fatal consequences for both conspirators. Because Cain himself, under contract to Fox, was unavailable to write the adaptation for Paramount, Wilder asked noir godfather Raymond Chandler – who had never before worked on a movie even though he was now living in Hollywood – to collaborate with him. The results were a prickly working relationship but a definitive scenario that punched up Cain's dialogue, which Chandler found effective on the page but surprisingly flat in the ear, with some of Chandler's most florid verbal inventions.

Wilder and Chandler's coldly overwrought screenplay was perfectly complemented by art directors Hans Dreier and Hal Pereira. Dreier, like Wilder, was a veteran of German expressionist cinema who, in the course of rising to head Paramount's art department, had designed the atmospheric visuals for such striking films as *Underworld* (1927), *Thunderbolt* (1929), and *Dr. Jekyll and Mr. Hyde* (1931). Pereira, who would follow Dreier in 1950 as Paramount's supervising art director, was a unit art director working on his first big-budget film en route to later collaborations with Wilder and Alfred Hitchcock. For *Double Indemnity* they were joined by director of photography John F. Seitz, who had pioneered low-key-lighting effects for director Rex Ingram as early as *The Four Horsemen of the Apocalpyse* (1921) and *Scaramouche* (1923) before moving on to such Paramount properties as *This Gun for Hire* (1942) and *Five Graves to Cairo.*

The film wastes no time in establishing its leading visual and thematic motifs. A reckless midnight drive through the dark streets of Los Angeles to an office building, where Walter Neff (Fred MacMurray) slowly and painfully emerges from the car, ends with his elevator trip to the twelfth-floor offices of the Pacific All-Risk Insurance Company, where the camera follows him to disclose a few scattered cleaning women toiling among the rows of desks that line the vast floor below the iron-railed mezzanine where he stands. The scene inescapably recalls a prison yard, complete with prisoners working below a catwalk framed by iron bars, with Walter posed as a warden[15] – though Walter himself repeatedly refuses the role of enforcer to embrace the role of transgressing prisoner, as he makes clear in his opening words to a Dictaphone at his desk: "Office memorandum. Walter Neff to Barton Keyes, Claims Manager. Los Angeles, July 16th, 1938. Dear Keyes: I suppose you'll call this a confession when you hear it." The ensuing confession, which comprises most of the film, demonstrates that Walter, who ought to be as vigilant as his boss Keyes (Edward G. Robinson) in ferreting out bogus claims, has perpetrated one of his own by plotting with Phyllis Dietrichson (Barbara Stanwyck) to kill her husband, a Pacific All-Risk client, for the proceeds of an accident insurance policy for which they have tricked him into applying.

Although Walter is immediately established as an authority figure to whom the elderly elevator operator defers, and as a victim by virtue of the wound in his shoulder that slows him down and immobilizes his left hand, every detail of the mise-en-scène makes him a victim imprisoned in his own office, a status confirmed by the flashback structure that presents his story from the ironic viewpoint of someone who already knows how every scene will turn out and who often comments on the action from his informed point of view, as Walter does after his first encounter with Phyllis: "It was a hot afternoon, and I can still remember the smell of honeysuckle all along the street. How could I have known that murder can sometimes smell like honeysuckle?" His ironic commentary thus makes the Walter who appears on-screen a prisoner of his own discourse. Although he undertakes each of his actions as if it were freely chosen, he is trapped in the narrative shaped by his voice, which selects and dramatizes incidents precisely to the extent that they substantiate his confession to murder gone wrong. The extended flashback, preferably accompanied by the ironically informed voice-over echoed in different keys in *Laura* and *Murder, My Sweet*, became the defining narrative convention of film noir,

structuring such varied examples of the genre as *Leave Her to Heaven,*
Mildred Pierce (1945), *The Killers* (1946), *Out of the Past* (1947), and *The*
Big Clock (1948) before reaching its apotheosis in the flashback narrated by a corpse in Wilder's *Sunset Blvd.* – an ironic trope that survives, often in even more ironic guises, in such recent films as *Traces*
of Red (1992), *Casino* (1995), and *American Beauty* (1999).[16]

Walter's entrapment in his own narrative is telegraphed at every
point by the film's visuals. No sooner has he arrived at the Dietrichson
house in an attempt to get Dietrichson to renew his auto insurance
policy than he is confronted by Phyllis Dietrichson, alluringly toplit
with a white towel wrapped around her as she stands behind the
wrought-iron railing at the top of a staircase. Walter's voice-over com-
municates his immediate reaction: "I wanted to see her again, close,
without that silly staircase between us." He soon gets his wish to
break through the iron barrier when Phyllis, freshly dressed, trips
down the stairs to join him; but his pleasure that Phyllis has broken
through the boundary between them turns into a realization that he
has actually broken into a prison whose walls Walter first glimpses
when Phyllis asks how she can buy her husband an accident insurance policy without his knowing it [Fig. 29].[17] Throughout the rest of
the movie, the mise-en-scène will serve as a prison for the unwary,
foreshadowing the striking exterior landscapes in such later noirs as
Night and the City (1950), in which nocturnal London becomes a mirror
of Harry Fabian's feverishly shifting moods, and *On Dangerous Ground*
(1952), which balances the claustrophobic city against the natural settings to which the police hero pursues the suspect. Even after the stylized cityscapes of *Double Indemnity* shift to the more naturalistic, indeed documentary, urban exteriors in such later noirs as *Kiss of Death*
(1947), *The Naked City* (1948), and *D.O.A.* (1950), they still work to trap
the heroes in an urban jungle.

Wilder had originally planned to end the film with a sequence showing Walter's execution in the San Quentin gas chamber but scrapped
it after shooting because he became convinced it would be too intense
for audiences. Remarkably, however, the film manages to displace any
number of San Quentin's visual hallmarks – the iron bars, the ubiquitous railings, the guards hemming the prisoner in, the numberless
frames within the movie frame – onto more ostensibly neutral settings,
so that nearly every scene carries portentous reminders of Walter's
unspoken fate, a fate that becomes all the more ironically entrapping
because it is so obvious to the audience. Excising Walter's execution

29. *Double Indemnity:* The femme fatale (Barbara Stanwyck) and her victim (Fred MacMurray).

from the film also underlines one of its most cynical jokes: the absence from the film of any police officers, emphasizing Cain's belief in both *Double Indemnity* and *The Postman Always Rings Twice* that the officers sworn to uphold the law have much less interest in its enforcement than the insurance companies who stand to lose financially from any fraud.

Walter's office, with its prison yard, its railed catwalk, and the dark-painted wainscot and chair rail that segment the walls, offers the most obvious example of prison decor; but the dim Dietrichson living room is equally imprisoning, with its prominent striped shadows of venetian blinds on the floor, in an obvious echo of prison bars that resonates through the 1940s, and its clutter of furniture. Phyllis will trap Walter on the sofa in their second meeting, leaning forward confidentially to ask whether there isn't some way she could buy her husband an insurance policy without bothering him. Later, Walter and Phyllis will sit surrounding Dietrichson (Tom Powers), her leg cocked at him like a rifle, as he unwittingly signs the policy. Walter's own apartment, when Phyllis arrives there to seduce him into helping her, is shrouded in nearly complete darkness. Even Jerry's Market, the innocuous grocery store where Phyllis and Walter meet twice, first to plan the details of the murder and then to quarrel about submitting the insurance claim, is designed with a threatening geometry that recalls Fritz Lang's most menacing storefronts in *M*. In some shots the camera watches a stone-faced Walter and a sunglassed Phyllis pointedly not looking at each other, isolated by their togetherness, as stacks of canned goods loom ominously behind them; in others, Wilder uses a high camera angle over the tops of the aisles of foodstuffs that hem in the conspirators, as he did in the early shot of the prison yard that is Pacific All-Risk, to pin them to the spot with a God's-eye view that sees them exactly as they are despite their best efforts to hide.

Even when characters are not obviously menaced by the mise-en-scène, they eagerly surrender to the tyranny of the many symbolic objects on which their murder plot depends. A close-up of the index card Walter sticks under the clapper of his telephone bell illustrates how completely his alibi for the evening depends on such apparently trivial objects as the doorbell, the telephone bell, his rate book, and the car he leaves in the garage to be washed. Just after Phyllis and Walter have dumped Dietrichson's body – his neck having been broken by Walter, who had hidden in the back seat of Dietrichson's car and then masqueraded as him on the train to San Francisco – Phyllis is unable to restart the car. A tight close-up of her alarmed, dead-white face, before Walter warily reaches across and gets the engine to turn over, is a sudden reminder of the killers' helpless dependence on the car's reliable operation. The recipe for the perfect murder that exercised the Hays Office depends so completely on the flawless operation of mechanical devices that it makes the murderers automata themselves, simultaneously dehumanizing them and emphasizing their fetishistic attachment to other objects that speak the desires their dialogue cannot express.

Just as the definitive noir narrative device is the extended flashback and its definitive scenic icon the shadows of venetian blinds, the ultimate noir fetish is the revolver, echoing Chandler's own self-mocking dictum for narrative structure ("When in doubt have a man come through a door with a gun in his hand"[18]). In one of film noir's most notable legacies from the gangster film, handguns are used so inveterately to establish and alter the balance of power in noirs from *Murder, My Sweet* to *Touch of Evil* – reaching a climax in the aptly titled *Gun*

30. *Double Indemnity:* Walter (Fred MacMurray) admires the fetishistic anklet worn by Phyllis (Barbara Stanwyck).

Crazy and in *The Big Heat* (1953), in which the revolver framed in isolation just after the credits fires the shot that sets the whole story in motion – that the fetish can be inverted or satirized in *The Maltese Falcon* and *The Big Sleep* (1946), whose private-eye heroes regularly ignore or disarm villains who depend on their artillery, and *Kiss Me Deadly,* whose sociopathic private eye is forced to find new ways to hurt the suspects he interrogates after the police confiscate his gun.

The revolver puts in only a cameo appearance in *Double Indemnity*, but just as the film displaces the trappings of San Quentin onto other settings that become equally threatening, it offers many substitute fetishes for the handgun: the engraved anklet, shown in seductive close-up as Phyllis descends the barred stairs, that first attracts Walter to her [Fig. 30]; the Dictaphone into which Walter pours his solitary confession; the matches he repeatedly uses to light Keyes's cigars when Keyes unfailingly cannot find matches of his own. The anklet stands in for Phyllis's nearly nude body, which Walter had glimpsed moments before at the top of the stairs. The Dictaphone takes the place of the absent Keyes, allowing Walter to reveal himself with an intimacy he could never achieve face to face with his trusting boss. The matches do double duty: They reflect both the imbalance of power between scheming Walter and his gulled, albeit suspicious, boss – an imbalance powerfully redressed in the most tender scene in this chilly film, the final moment when the wounded Walter, collapsed in the Pacific All-Risk doorway, is unable to light his cigarette, and Keyes bends to light it for him – and the affection the two men could never express to each other without violating Hollywood taboos against male homoeroticism, and for that matter against men's ability to speak their love.[19] Although similar uses of cigarettes to establish emotional intimacy are too numerous to cite, *Out of the Past* offers a virtual catalog of such images, from the good-girl heroine who carries matches even though she does not smoke to the startling echo of *Double Indemnity*'s final scene, when the jittery hero takes a lighted cigarette from the mouth of a cabbie friend, draws on it, then offers it back.

Trapped equally by the Los Angeles territory through which he must move to sell or be sold and by the objects on which his murder plot and his sense of himself depend, Walter often pauses to illustrate the ways he and other characters are trapped by frames within the frames. The first objects Walter picks up in the Dietrichson home are a pair of framed portraits of Dietrichson and his daughter Lola (Jean Heather), who will soon become the direct and indirect victims of his plot. When Walter later takes Lola to meet her boyfriend Nino Zachette (Byron Barr), first Zachette, then Lola, is framed within his car window. The most memorable of these framings, however, comes earlier, when Walter watches Phyllis apply lipstick after dressing to meet him in their first scene together, and the mirror in which she is watching herself reflects the two of them as they really are: Walter unguardedly giving Phyllis the once-over, Phyllis apparently ignoring him and looking only at herself.

Such mirroring effects, unmasking the characters' true natures, trap them by confronting them with their own doubles, revealing fissures within themselves they can neither overcome nor fully acknowledge. In fact, it is the motif of doubling rather than darkness that is the keynote not only of *Double Indemnity* but of film noir as a genre, the theme that links noir's crime narratives with its visual hallmarks.[20] The pattern begins in *Double Indemnity* with matched pairs of characters who dramatize alternative responses to similar pressures. Hence Lola Dietrichson, first shown competing with Phyllis in a game of Chinese checkers neither of them wants to play, is the good girl to Phyllis's femme fatale, and Keyes, who consistently dresses in black and white, is the straight-shooting insurance man consistently set against his

31. *Double Indemnity:* The hero (Fred MacMurray) trapped by his knowledge of his guilty double (Barbara Stanwyck).

failed protégé Walter's rogue salesman, who always dresses in non-committal gray suits, except when he is impersonating the man he is planning to kill. But these external doubles are only a sign of a deeper psychological doubling that is revealed by Walter's incautious gaze over Phyllis's shoulder while she tellingly remarks, "I hope I've got my face on straight" (indicating that her face is simply a mask assumed for the occasion), and he replies, "It's perfect for my money" (indicating that he is only too eager to accept the mask at face value without looking deeper). This sort of doubling is represented in different terms when Phyllis, coming to visit Walter's apartment after the murder, hears Keyes inside and hides behind the apartment door as Keyes comes out into the corridor, trapping Walter between the two people who are contending for his soul. As Walter poses before the blank door with Phyllis and Keyes on either side of him, the film asks which Walter will prevail: Phyllis's conspirator or Keyes's employee? It answers this question when he shields Phyllis from Keyes, waving her in back of the door with a telltale hand [Fig. 31].

The motif of doubling each character with an alter ego that is re-vealed to the audience but kept secret from the other characters is il-lustrated by the film's constant framings of characters with shadows that reveal their hidden desires. Every time Walter enters the Dietrich-son home, he is preceded by his shadow, which lingers a moment after each time he leaves. Much later, as Phyllis sets the stage for her shooting of Walter, she is doubled with a shadow on the wall behind her that shows her split nature. Even the costuming develops this mo-tif by revealing a side of Phyllis her words and actions do not. Unlike Walter and Keyes, whose dress changes little in the course of the film, Phyllis follows the unwritten dictate for Hollywood heroines of chang-ing her clothes for every scene. She is first shown wrapped in a white towel, then changes into a dress that, following Cain, is described as "pale blue" in the screenplay[21] and photographs off-white. In their sec-ond scene together, she wears a white blouse figured with large black flowers and black slacks; later that night, at Walter's apartment, she has changed to a clinging white sweater and black slacks; and at the supermarket the next time they meet she is wearing a gray coat that she also wears for the murder. The next time she appears, summoned to the insurance office by Keyes's ineptly blustering boss Edward S. Norton (Richard Gaines), she is in mourning for the husband she helped kill, complete with a black coat, hat, and veil. Having begun as an angelic vision beneath ethereal toplighting, Phyllis grows gradual-ly darker and darker as she pulls Walter into her murder plot. At this point, however, the pattern reverses itself, and her remaining scenes show her in successively lighter costumes until the scene in which she shoots Walter while wearing off-white lounging pajamas. Far from re-vealing her true nature, then, Phyllis's outfits, like her makeup, mere-ly project the identity she has chosen for a particular effect, and the effect she wishes to create in these later scenes is that she has dis-entangled herself from her husband's murder, leaving Walter holding the bag.[22]

Phyllis's carefully cultivated alter ego, which reveals the split be-tween her public personality and her unspeakable private desires, is not the film's foremost doubling. Indeed, *Double Indemnity* presents so many doubles, beginning with its title, that it rivals the much better-known pattern of persistent doubles in Alfred Hitchcock's *Shadow of a Doubt* (1943) and *Strangers on a Train* (1951). Like Hitchcock's films, Wilder's frequently develops its action through pairs of scenes. Walter visits the Dietrichsons' house twice, hoping to get Dietrichson to renew his auto insurance; Phyllis balances the pattern by visiting Walter's apartment twice. There are two scenes in Jerry's Market, two with Nino Zachette, and two with Mr. Jackson (Porter Hall), the interloping witness who speaks with Walter on the train. In the final showdown between Walter and Phyllis – a scene in which Walter reminds himself and her of the first time they met in the same room – two shots are fired, one by (and into) each of the conspirators. In each case the effect of these doubles is the same: The first term sets up a tension whose source the second reveals, whether that source is Walter's lust for Phyllis or his determination to kill the lover who cannot quite bring herself to fire the second shot that would kill him.

The dialogue, like that of *Shadow of a Doubt,* is liberally salted with clues to the characters', and the film's, irreducible duality. Dietrichson puts his signature to the fatal insurance application in response to Walter's direction: "Both copies, please." "Sign twice, huh?" says Dietrichson, dutifully inking his death warrant. Later, as Phyllis, driving her husband to the spot where he is to be killed, asks him to be careful on his broken leg lest he end up with one leg shorter than the other, Dietrichson sulkily responds, "So what? I could break the other one and match 'em up again." Both cues point directly to the crucial doubling, like the pairing of Charlie and her uncle in *Shadow of a Doubt,* around which all the others are arranged: Walter's impersonation of Dietrichson on the train in order to suggest that he has died in an accidental fall from the observation car's rear platform, thus qualifying the death for the double-indemnity payout stipulated by the accident insurance policy.

Walter's murder plan, which depends on his taking the place of the man he has just killed, succeeds at a deeper level than he realizes. When Dietrichson breaks his leg just a few days before he is scheduled to take the train to his Stanford reunion, Walter insists that the murder wait, because "it's all worked out for a train." Phyllis, though, encourages her husband to take the train anyway, convincing Walter that "with the crutches it's much better" because most potential witnesses, noticing the crutches rather than the man himself, will give a wide berth to a man with his leg in a cast. Walter's plan, that is, does not so much involve substituting himself for Dietrichson as it does reducing Dietrichson metonymically to his crutches and then substituting Walter-on-crutches for Dietrichson-on-crutches. But the scheme backfires in two ways. First, Dietrichson's failure to submit a claim for his broken leg alerts Keyes to the possibility that Dietrichson never knew he was carrying the policy – a possibility that must, sooner or later, lead him to Walter. Second, Walter's masquerade succeeds all too well in its aim of displacing Walter's own identity onto a pair of crutches. As Walter walks home from the successful murder, he becomes irrationally convinced that "everything would go wrong. It sounds crazy, Keyes, but it's true, so help me: I couldn't hear my own footsteps. It was the walk of a dead man." It is not until much later that Walter will realize that his impersonation of the crippled Dietrichson is only a preparation for Phyllis's treating the two of them identically, since she plans to seduce Zachette into killing Walter just as she seduced Walter into killing Dietrichson. Walter's successful murder has thus made him at the same time a victim of his accomplice, as the film's opening image so powerfully illustrates: As the credits roll, the silhouette of a man on crutches comes forward from deep space to approach the camera, eventually filling the screen. Is the man Dietrichson or Walter? In the harsh backlight that effaces every trace of individual personality, there is no way of knowing, just as there is no way of telling the difference between the killer adopting the crutches his lover has offered him and the victim whose fate predicts his own.

The criminal-victim Walter incarnates so economically is the central figure of film noir, even more central than the femme fatale who so often tempts him to his doom. In its most straightforward form, this figure is beguiled into crime by a seductive heroine whose guilt is so patent that it may seem to swallow his own, a villainous heroine like Kitty March (Joan Bennett) in *Scarlet Street* (1945), Kitty Collins (Ava Gardner) in *The Killers*, Kathie Moffat (Jane Greer) in *Out of the Past*, Elsa Bannister (Rita Hayworth) in *The Lady from Shanghai,* or Annie Laurie Starr (Peggy Cummins) in *Gun Crazy.* But there are many other ways to establish a criminal's victimhood that do not depend on the machinations of a femme fatale. In *High Sierra* (1941), hard-luck ex-con Roy Earle (Humphrey Bogart) is an honorable crook trapped in a world he cannot escape. In *A Double Life* (1947), Anthony John (Ronald Colman) is such an obsessive actor that he cannot stop playing Othello. The professional skills the boxer heroes display in *Body and Soul* and *The Set-Up* still leave them the helpless prey of deeper-dyed criminals outside the ring. *Kiss of Death* casts the ex-con struggling to go straight (Victor Mature) as the suffering Christ, a victim of luck and circumstance who is redeemed by his heroism and the love of a good woman. In the more typical *In a Lonely Place* (1950), the hero (Bogart again) is sacrificed to the violent rages he cannot resist, even though he is vindicated of the murder of which he is accused (and of which, in the film's source novel, he is guilty). The hero (Tyrone Power) of *Nightmare Alley* (1947) rises, like his gangster forebears, from obscurity to wealth and success, only to fall precipitously to the status of a "geek," the freak-show attraction he had first defined himself against. *Night and the City* engages its hero (Richard Widmark) in a complex series of treacherous relationships that unmask successively darker depths of his ambition, until finally the last veil is torn away to reveal his surprising and touching nobility. The roles of criminal and victim combine still more problematically with the role of avenging detective in the troubled-cop heroes of *On Dangerous Ground*, *The File on Thelma Jordan* (1949), *Where the Sidewalk Ends* (1950), and *Detective Story* (1951).

Despite its reliance on a femme fatale, *Double Indemnity* invokes several of these patterns. Walter presumably sees himself as sacrificed to Phyllis's sinister plot, which reduces men to anonymous cripples, and a generation of critics have followed him in emphasizing the powerfully disruptive agency of the femme fatale in noirs from *Murder, My Sweet* to *Kiss Me Deadly*. Almost equally often, however, the heroes' involvement in crime stems from their infatuation with heroines who are technically innocent of any crime, like Alice Reed (Joan Bennett) in *The Woman in the Window* and Pauline York (Rita Johnson) in *The Big Clock*. The prisoners in *Brute Force* are all doing time because of the women in their lives, even though those women appear only in flashback. Even heroines who are technically innocent, like Laura Hunt (Gene Tierney) in *Laura* and Mary McLeod (Eleanor Parker) in *Detective Story*, suffer intensive investigations into their alleged wrongdoings and continue after their vindication under a lingering cloud of guilt because of their sexuality, which makes every female, even the dutiful helpmeets of *Body and Soul, Kiss of Death*, and *The Set-Up*, nonmale outsiders in a world of male power and desire.

Dividing noir heroines into those who are stigmatized as evil and those who are idealized into impotence does not absolve the male heroes of guilt, as *Double Indemnity* shows, but simply externalizes it. After all, noir heroes like Walter do not, as they would no doubt prefer to believe, lose their identities to strong women; rather, they fall victim to a radical split within themselves that would ensure their self-alienation even without the catalyst of the femme fatale they blame for their troubles. Walter's law-abiding double Keyes shows this split at its most benign in the scene in which he is introduced, when he describes the "little man" inside him who "ties knots in my stomach" every time a fraudulent claim crosses his desk. Walter clearly has a healthy respect for the moral compass that keeps Keyes on course, even though Keyes's little man is never shown giving the boss anything but pain. Keyes's Manichaean, black-and-white view of the world is clearly dictated by his uncompromising conscience. At the same time, his comical thralldom to this tyrannical force hints that the price of socialization may be pathological self-alienation.

Walter laughs at Keyes's little man, but he has a diminutive tyrant of his own: Phyllis, who dictates his every action just as assuredly, often without lifting a finger. When Phyllis reschedules her second appointment with Walter to a less convenient time, he muses in voice-over: "I had a lot of stuff lined up for that Thursday afternoon, including a trip down to Santa Monica to see a couple of live prospects about some group insurance. But I kept thinking about Phyllis Dietrichson and the way that anklet of hers cut into her leg." As he speaks, the scene dissolves from a midshot of Walter in his office to a close-up of Phyllis's legs as she runs down the stairs to greet Walter, lounging with a witless grin outside her front door. So powerful and immediate is her hold over him from the beginning that the film does not even need to show him changing his mind; his reaction is as unconscious and involuntary as Keyes's.

The central doubling in *Double Indemnity,* then, is of Walter Neff with himself, the man whose motives he cannot explain and whose actions he cannot accept. By doubling Walter with each of the other main characters – Keyes as the good angel who cannot save him for a socially productive life, Phyllis as the bad angel who seems to bear the primary responsibility for his crimes, Dietrichson as the foretaste of the future he blindly embraces – the film might seem to empty Walter of the very possibility of agency. Yet the opposite is the case: As is revealed by the split between the active, foolhardy Walter who is shown within the flashback and the contemplative, powerless Walter who narrates the story in intermittent voice-over, the film focuses so obsessively on the problem of Walter's agency that all the other characters – from Phyllis and Keyes down to Lola, Zachette, and the elevator operator – become projections of his fear and desire, modeling attitudes and admonitions among which he feels powerless to choose.

This problem is not an invention of film noir. Its most trenchant expositor is Saint Paul: "That good that I would, I do not; but the evil which I would not, that I do" (Romans 7:19). It is at the heart of Poe's short stories, and it emerges with startling immediacy in Stevenson's story "The Strange Case of Dr. Jekyll and Mr. Hyde" (1886) and Freud's theory of the unconscious before flowering visually in the Weimar cinema in which Wilder and art director Hans Dreier first worked. Indeed, the major strain in German expressionist cinema from *The Cabinet of Dr. Caligari* to *M* is the displacement of psychological conflicts that would be hopelessly deadlocked onto external conflicts that offer some hope of resolution. This keynote of self-alienation distinguishes *Double Indemnity* and the noir tradition it inaugurates from Hollywood genres like the western and the musical, which are also constructed around the external doubling of good guys and bad guys or quarreling lovers, brought together respectively by ritual gunfights or dance numbers. The difference is that in westerns and musicals, the heroes' doubles remedy the heroes' incompleteness, either by giving them an outlet for their contradictory desires (as John Wayne's characters fight villains in order to domesticate a western landscape in which he himself is too wild to live comfortably) or by providing them with mates who complement their natures even as they fulfill their desires (as a character played by peerlessly graceful Fred Astaire finds its perfect partner once again in mates played by the more openly sexual Ginger Rogers). In film noir, external doublings and couplings do not complete the heroes but merely entrap them more deeply by emphasizing their self-alienation. Hence Phyllis observes to Walter that the very conspiracy that has brought them together forces them apart: "It's so tough for you. It's like a war between us." Keyes, as usual, is more pungent in theorizing two conspirators:

> Sometime, somewhere, they've got to meet. Their emotions are all kicked up. Whether it's love or hate doesn't matter. They can't keep away from each other. They think it's twice as safe because there are two of them. But it's not twice as safe. It's ten times twice as dangerous.

In the view of the unmarried Keyes, the social life figured by romance is one more trap; the wise man would shun all others and retreat into himself with only his little man for company. Yet Keyes's helpless servitude to this little man, who brings him to Walter's begging for some peppermint or a bicarbonate, shows that even a solitary existence would still be too crowded for comfort: There is no refuge from the tyrannical superego, the Lacanian Law of the Father, that demands unquestioning obedience without conferring any secure sense of the self the world of film noir so mercilessly splits.

7

Basic Instinct and the Erotic Thriller

wenty-five years after the film noir cycle ended with *Kiss Me Deadly* (1955) and *Touch of Evil* (1958), noir returned with a vengeance in 1981 with *Body Heat* and a remake of *The Postman Always Rings Twice,* which mark the resurgence of a new cycle of neo-noirs defined alike by their borrowings and their distance from the earlier cycle. Retro genres, by definition, must offer something new to distinguish themselves from their models, and the something in this new cycle is sex. The self-alienation that had been noir's keynote had not necessarily been driven by sex – as Christopher Nolan demonstrated in his neo-noir *Memento* (2000), whose backward scene-by-scene trajectory into the past cleverly dramatizes its avenging hero's loss of short-term memory – but sex is what the new cycle was selling.

The newly resurgent neo-noirs are driven by three developments in the sociology of American sexuality: the sexual freedom made possible by the widespread availability of contraception and abortion; the replacement of the Hays Office's 1930 Production Code by the Motion Picture Association of America's system of age-appropriate ratings, beginning in 1969; and the dramatic political and social changes provoked by the women's liberation movement in the 1970s. Just as issues concerning women's empowerment were coming to the fore for the first time since the years immediately following the war, the film industry was undergoing a revolution in its portrayal of sexual behavior. No longer bound by the restrictions of the Production Code, filmmakers were free to present sexual relationships more frankly. At the same time, the discovery of the youth audience's economic power, with the success of *The Graduate* and *Bonnie and Clyde* in the summer of 1967, led to a movement away from a mass-marketing strategy, which had dictated that virtually every film Hollywood released had to be suitable for family audiences, to a niche-marketing strategy, which allowed studios to target more specific audiences with different releases, promoting some films as family fare and others as suitable for adult audiences only.

The emergence of a full-blown neo-noir cycle was accelerated by two further developments in the 1980s: the isolation of HIV, the virus that causes AIDS, and the explosion in home video technology, which led not only to a renascence of low-budget pornography but to the proliferation of low-budget sex/suspense features starring such direct-to-video stars as Shannen Doherty, Shannon Tweed, and Shannon Whirry.[1] These developments broadened the range of explicitly sexual behavior presented on Hollywood screens, but at the same time encouraged an ultimately censorious attitude toward that behavior in much the way that Cecil B. DeMille's biblical spectacles from *The Ten Commandments* (1923) to *The Sign of the Cross* (1932) had done in the generation before the code.

Although the new license in sexual frankness left its mark on many genres, from the soap-opera anomie of *Making Love* (1982) to the explicit period biography of *Henry and June* (1990), it found a particularly hospitable genre in the newly resurgent crime film, whose built-in moral categories allowed audiences to indulge forbidden sexual fantasies without ever forgetting how likely they were to be punished. Because the central figure of this new generation of crime films, the fatally alluring, often naked body of the female star,[2] points both toward and away from its noir antecedents, the films are less accurately called neo-noirs than erotic thrillers.

The indispensable importance of female nudity to the noir revival is nowhere more clearly figured than in *Body Heat.* In its central situation, writer-director Lawrence Kasdan's debut film is a loose reworking of *Double Indemnity.* Both films concern an unremarkable hero, Ned Racine (William Hurt, in the Fred MacMurray role) ensnared in a conspiracy to kill the husband (Richard Crenna) of his lover (Kathleen Turner) for love and money, and both turn on the adulterous wife's treachery toward both husband and lover. Although *Body Heat* is shot in color, its desaturated monochrome visuals (overexposed in the lunchtime scenes at a stifling diner, restricted to one color at a time everywhere else) pay constant homage to film noir's black-and-white visual style, an homage frequently underlined by Turner's timeless outfits as Matty Walker and the anachronistic fedora she gives her lawyer-lover Ned Racine as a gift.[3]

Sex is what marks *Body Heat*'s distance from *Double Indemnity*. It is a difference registered at every point from Ned's first meeting with Matty, in which she challenges him to lick off the cherry ice she has spilled on her dress. Unlike Wilder, who had cowritten and directed one of the coldest films in Hollywood history, Kasdan chooses heat as his leading metaphor for pent-up desire. As Ned's cop friend Oscar Grace (J. A. Preston) tells him, "When it gets hot, people try to kill each other. . . . After a while people think the old rules are not in effect. They start to break them, figuring nobody'll care, because it's emergency time." And Kasdan replaces Wilder's and Chandler's gaudy verbal sparring with the X-rated needling of Oscar and Assistant District Attorney Peter Lowenstein (Ted Danson).

The main difference is of course in the sex scenes themselves. Unlike *Double Indemnity,* whose representations of sex are limited to a few fatal kisses, a possibly postcoital cigarette in Walter's apartment, a fetishized vocabulary of accessories like Phyllis's anklet, and endless repetitions of the endearment "baby," *Body Heat* wastes no opportunity for its attractive leads to make love on camera or just off. In the film's most startling echo of its progenitor's imagery, Ned breaks into Matty's locked house by throwing a chair through a window and climbing into what will become the prison of his own sexual desire as he pushes up her skirt and lowers her to the floor. Later they will be discovered naked in Matty's bed, on the floor, and in a bathtub filled with ice water. Like Bob Rafelson's remake of *The Postman Always Rings Twice, Body Heat* links the violence of its principals' sexual encounters to a general breakdown of social inhibitions. The atmosphere of steamy sexual license is so pervasive that it seems perfectly logical for Ned to encounter Matty twice outside her house ready for action, greeting her the first time with a cheery, "Hey, lady, wanna fuck?" and the second with an even more forthright invitation to oral sex.

The authentic dangers that turn out to be involved in both these encounters seem minor compared to the languorous pleasures of sex to which Ned is invited as a participant and the audience as voyeurs. Unlike *Double Indemnity,* whose narrative frame casts Walter's every action in a flashback that allows Walter, and encourages viewers, to pass prospective judgment on his behavior, *Body Heat* contains no

32. *Body Heat:* Coexperiencing the betrayal of Ned (William Hurt) by the femme fatale, Matty (Kathleen Turner).

such coercive frame.[4] The film relies instead on the less coercive implications of its imagery of uncontrolled, consuming fire and the intertextual allusions of its plot, dialogue, and mise-en-scène. Instead of knowing from the beginning that the hero is doomed, "the viewer," as Silver and Ward point out, "coexperiences [the hero's] betrayal"[5] [Fig. 32] by being encouraged to enjoy the sex scenes, which continue even past the murder of Edmund Walker (Crenna), as titillating spectacles that apparently bare all, even though they present the heroine far more deceptively than anything in Wilder's clinically dispassionate film.[6]

The result is a deeply divided attitude toward sex, which is first presented as more seductive than anything shown in the era of the Production Code, then revealed as more treacherous. Ultimately, the hero's seduction is used in the service of a deeper masochism than that of earlier noirs, since he is more clearly a victim of the femme fatale. *Double Indemnity* may blame the corruption of its mediocre hero on the femme fatale, but there is no doubt that by the time they shoot each other, he has indeed become fatally corrupted. *Body Heat,* by contrast, is constantly making excuses for Ned, the inoffensive dope who is originally drawn to Matty by her come-on line, "You're not too smart, are you? I like that in a man." Instead of planning their double-indemnity payoff together, Ned finds himself persistently double-crossed by the treacherous Matty.

Even when his trust in Matty disintegrates, however, Ned never turns on her. He greets her admission that "I'm greedy, like you said. . . . If you never trusted me again, you'd probably be smart" by resuming their affair under his law-enforcement friends' eyes, and tells Matty in their final showdown, "Keep talking, Matty. Experience shows that I can be convinced of anything." Ned's love never loses its essential innocence, not even after he kills Edmund, since the film presents the murder as a fight to the death between the slightly built killer and a ruthless, alert victim packing a handgun. Afterward, Lowenstein concludes, "That Edmund Walker was a really bad guy. The more I hear about him, the gladder I am that he's dead," and frames Oscar's bulldog determination to arrest Edmund's killer anyway by remarking that Oscar is "the only person I know like that. Sometimes it's a real pain in the ass, even for him," presenting Oscar's quest for justice as more deviant than Ned's inoffensive murder of a really bad guy.

The strongest plea for Ned's witless innocence, and therefore the most damning condemnation of Matty's guilt, has its basis in a remark Edmund makes about the difference between two kinds of people: the ruthless ones who are willing "to do what's necessary – whatever's necessary" – and the spineless ones who aren't. Ned admits to being a spineless person himself. In the film's final sequence, after Ned, now in prison for the murder, has realized that Matty has escaped, he tells Oscar, who dismisses the possibility of any such deep-laid plans: "That was her special gift. She was relentless. Matty was the kind of person who could do what was necessary – whatever was necessary." Hence Matty is cast alongside her murdered husband as one of the ruthless predators who feed on innocent victims like Ned.

Erotic thrillers like *Body Heat* are even more determined than films noirs to exculpate their male heroes at the expense of their femmes fatales. The sexual politics of this asymmetry, noted as early as Rita Hayworth's song "Put the Blame on Mame" in *Gilda* (1946), may seem anachronistic in the days after women's liberation; but the fear of powerful women, stirred by dramatic gains in women's political and economic power during the 1970s, is even deeper in erotic thrillers than in the noirs of forty years earlier, given both sharper definition and heightened moral ambivalence by the genre's emphasis on sex.

Fatal Attraction (1987) indicates the complex ways viewers' contradictory attitudes toward sex are projected onto the femme fatale but not her male counterpart. Glenn Close, who plays the femme fatale to Michael Douglas's philandering husband, had already starred in *Jagged Edge* (1985), which managed to reverse the genders of *Body Heat's* criminal-lover story without sexually fetishizing either her or her co-star, Jeff Bridges, who plays murder suspect Jack Forrester. In one sense, *Jagged Edge* presents a feminized view of the erotic thriller, focusing on the treacherous psychological promise of romance rather than the duplicitous visual spectacle of sex. In another, however, it suggests that feminized erotic thrillers are simply a contradiction in terms, since the fetishization that is the genre's defining marker, irrelevant as it is to the interests of female audiences, stipulates a target audience of heterosexual males.[7] No Hollywood hunk, it might seem, can take the place of Kathleen Turner, since no slice of beefcake can arouse the same response as a fetishized female.

Nor, it might seem, can Glenn Close, whose career has been founded on playing strong women who refuse to be defined by men; but *Fatal Attraction* shows how even Close, by virtue of her character's very determination to avoid being bound by male desire, can anchor an erotic thriller. Despite its persistent echoes of the Puccini opera *Madama Butterfly, Fatal Attraction,* which unfolds like a male nightmare of adultery, more closely resembles Fritz Lang's *The Woman in the Window* (1944), which it echoes in somewhat the same way that *Body Heat* does *Double Indemnity:* All four films concern men who are beguiled into lethal relationships with femmes fatales, but the later film in each pair allows the male lead to survive, albeit morally compromised, at the price of utterly demonizing the female. When New York attorney Dan Gallagher (Michael Douglas) – whose family, like Professor Wanley's in *The Woman in the Window,* is out of town on a visit – follows a recent acquaintance, editor Alex Forrest (Close), back to her loft for some scorching sex, he thinks he is enjoying a one-night stand. But beginning the next morning, when she phones him at home and begs him to come back to her, Alex keeps making demands on him, luring him back to her loft, slitting her wrists when he insists on leaving, then phoning him at work and at home to announce her pregnancy, pretending an interest in buying his apartment that allows her to get his new, unlisted phone number from his unsuspecting wife, Beth (Anne Archer), throwing acid on his Volvo, and following him to his family's new suburban home to kill his daughter Ellen's rabbit, take Ellen (Ellen Hamilton Latzen) out of school to an amusement park, provoke the frantic Beth into a near-fatal car crash, and finally attack Beth in her bathroom. Dan apparently drowns Alex in the bathtub, and when she rises from beneath the water, Beth shoots her dead.[8]

The film splits into two parts that accurately reflect the attraction/repulsion to sex so characteristic of the genre. The first part, which follows the story of screenwriter James Dearden's 45-minute British film *Diversion* (1979), introduces Dan to the joys of flirting, romantic pursuit by an alluring woman and the uninhibited coupling he is evidently barred from at home, despite Beth's attractiveness and willingness, by his family responsibilities. (In the film's opening scene, all three Gallaghers are shown in various states of undress, emphasizing both Dan and Beth's sexual desires and their sexual frustration.) But this fantasy of fulfillment is only a prologue to the film's second movement, which multiplies the disastrous consequences of Dan's adultery. Alex's tactics escalate from whimpering for Dan's companionship and providing a surrogate family for him to breaching his domestic sphere and threatening his wife and daughter. At every stage, the film catalogs all the ways Dan's adultery is fetishized, not by the visual spectacle of Alex's body, but by his overinvestment in the one-night stand that makes him vulnerable to Alex's pleas and threats. It is not Alex's sexual allure that binds Dan to her, but the same passivity that led Dan into the affair in the first place [Fig. 33]. Long after his initial attraction to Alex is gone, Dan is held prisoner first by his inability to say no when she asks him to spend the rest of the weekend with her, then by his cowardly acceptance of her term "adults" to describe people who can enjoy sex without commitment, then by his guilt about his participating in the affair and her attempting suicide, then by his apprehension lest she reveal the affair to his wife, and finally by his realization that the family he is reluctant to abandon for her gives him much more to lose than she does.

Alex's power, in other words, stems not from her specularized body (which the film, like *Jagged Edge,* treats with surprisingly chaste restraint) but from Dan's feelings about her and about the threats to his sense of himself his affair with her represents. This power, however, based as it is on male perceptions of the female rather than on the female herself, is the very essence of fetishism. Soon after his initial cou-

33. *Fatal Attraction:* Another weak hero (Michael Douglas) trapped by his own passivity between his inamorata (Glenn Close) and his wife (Anne Archer).

pling with Alex on her kitchen sink, Dan's associations with sex turn overwhelmingly negative; yet that does not prevent them from operating as fetishes – it merely makes them negative fetishes for which he still, by virtue of the patriarchal values that made him susceptible to Alex in the first place, must bear responsibility.

Fatal Attraction has been read as an anti-AIDS parable, a defense of embattled family values (most audiences, no matter how sympathetic they may have been to forlorn Alex, recoil from her when she directs her vicious attentions from Dan to his innocent family), and an exorcism of unregulated female sexuality.[9] It is also, in its uneasy medley of soft-focus sex and hell-hath-no-fury horror clichés, an unusually revealing portrait of its target audience's contradictory feelings about the pleasures and dangers of sex, the difficulty of connecting them, and the inevitability of attributing their contradictions to the fetishized femme fatale. Jack Forrester in *Jagged Edge* needs to be unmasked as a cunning, heartless manipulator who uses sex and the trappings of sex to keep his hold on money and power, whereas Alex Forrest needs to be exorcised, not simply unmasked, because her sexual allure is real, not assumed, and because merely casting her out would allow audiences to disavow all the male desires and activities that endowed her with power by fetishizing her in the first place. A cycle of films determined to ratify beleaguered ideals of masculinity while acknowledging that the power of female sexuality depends on these very ideals, whether specular or psychological, must end by turning in redoubled fury on the guilty heroine, producing a misogyny more intense than anything in *Double Indemnity.* For if the matrix of postwar noir is American anxiety over unbridled political power, focused and inverted by the nightmare fantasy of the powerful woman, the matrix of the erotic thriller is cultural anxiety over unbridled access to sex, focused and inverted by the nightmare fantasy of the castrating liberated woman figured in even more strikingly misogynistic terms than the femme fatale of film noir because she represents a much broader range of threats. Besides seeking the economic parity of women who supported the wartime economy on the home front, these women demand access to capital, control of their sexuality, an equal voice in sexual politics, and a subversive access to patriarchal power or its female equivalent. Hence a man like Dan Gallagher is profoundly shaken when his one-night stand refuses his offer to finance an abortion and demands a share of his domestic life because he is to grant her sexual freedom only as far as it leaves his own unabridged. The heroines of contemporary erotic thrillers, who claim traditionally male sources of power as their own, provoke a male sexual panic that is truly global, revealing itself in undifferentiated paranoid hysteria.

The ultimate male nightmare of the castrating heroine to date is Sharon Stone's Catherine Tramell, the seductive heroine of Paul Verhoeven's *Basic Instinct.* Virtually overnight since its opening in 1992, the film has been recognized as a landmark even by commentators who deplore its sexual explicitness, its sexual politics (it was picketed by gay activists protesting its characterization of its amoral heroine as bisexual), or its sexual manipulativeness. It succeeded in becoming one of the top moneymakers of 1992, garnering Oscar nominations for editing (by Frank J. Urioste) and music (by veteran Jerry Goldsmith) and putting both its director and its female star on the map for good, without ever establishing its respectability.

The gap between the film's high profile and low respect has continued to mark the later development of its director, cinematographer, and screenwriter. Verhoeven, who had previously been best known in America for the violent action films *RoboCop* (1987) and *Total Recall* (1990), had already rehearsed for the project with the sexually explicit historical drama *Flesh + Blood* (1985), his American debut, and *The Fourth Man* (*De Vierde man,* 1979), an art-house thriller from his native Holland that explored a gay writer's obsession with an alluring widow whose publicity stills showed her wielding a pair of scissors like a butcher knife. Jan de Bont, who had shot all Verhoeven's earlier films, changed careers immediately after *Basic Instinct* to become the director of such action spectacles as *Speed* (1994) and *Twister* (1996). But the most dramatic gap between notoriety and respect is illustrated by the later trajectory of Joe Eszterhas, who was paid three million dollars for his screenplay – a coup that launched Eszterhas, who had earlier written *Jagged Edge,* on a round of upscale exploitation films that would include *Sliver* (1993), *Showgirls* (1995), and *Jade* (1995).

Most audiences, however, were less interested in the film's production credits than in the opulently displayed bodies of Stone and Michael Douglas. Douglas, the actor-producer who had won an Oscar for playing the take-charge Gordon Gekko in *Wall Street* in 1987, the same year *Fatal Attraction* was released, confirmed his status as the leading man who made sex look most unpleasant (a status that, first suggested in *Fatal Attraction,* would turn into a joke with his starring role as the executive sexually harassed by Demi Moore in the 1994 *Disclosure*). In *Basic Instinct,* however, he was sensationally out-acted, or at least out-undraped, by Sharon Stone, previously best known for her roles as the hero's ostensible loving wife in *Total Recall* and the sexually predatory journalist in *Year of the Gun* (1991) – a role that had given the clearest hint of what she was capable of, and how she would be typed beginning with *Basic Instinct.*

No film has ever succeeded in making sex look at once so alluring and so glum. From its opening sequence, the film is a castration fantasy that conducts a running critique of the titillation it is marketing. It begins not with a confession like Walter Neff's that turns the rest of the story into a fatalistic flashback, nor with an ambivalent metaphor like the fire burning uncontrolled outside Ned Racine's window in *Body Heat,* but with a nude scene showing a blonde woman, whose face is obscured, tying her lover's hands to a headboard, making passionate love to him, and then stabbing him to death with an ice pick she has hidden under the covers. Like innumerable earlier movie scenes showing a crime being committed without revealing the culprit,[10] it plays on audiences' attraction to scenes of sex and death while keeping them uncertain how they are supposed to feel about the suspects who may have been involved in these scenes.

This opening murder of retired rock star Johnny Boz (Bill Cable) not only kicks off the film's plot but frames its paranoia in visual and thematic terms as well. The monochrome gold light in which de Bont bathes this tableau of murderous rapture persists throughout the film's interior scenes, relieved only by the strategic use of blue sky and water in the film's exterior shots, the slate blues of the police interrogation room walls and Douglas's shirts, and the blue neon lights that keep popping up in diners and nightclubs. Except for these blue notes – which gradually recede along with the low horizon lines of the film's early exterior shots – the visual style is dominated by flesh tones.

The masking of the killer's face in an opening scene, which gives voyeuristic viewers otherwise complete access to her body, suggests why fleshtones will be so important: because the human face, with its promise of psychological depth, will be systematically displaced throughout the film by the specularized body as a locus of identity. Even the uncomfortably tight facial close-ups and two-shots with which early dialogue scenes are studded do not reveal what the characters are thinking or feeling; they merely suffuse the screen with more flesh tones, reducing each face to flesh. Giving the killer's breasts and blonde hair more visual prominence than her concealed face does not, of course, allow her to be easily recognized; instead, it equates her with all women who can be so fetishized by a male gaze turned paranoid.

The film's opening scene, establishing both a voyeuristic interest in sex and a grim tone from the beginning, provides an interpretive frame for the action that is neither as coercive as the flashback structure of *Double Indemnity* nor as open-ended as the symbolic frame of *Body Heat.* In its radical ambivalence, charged with both voyeurism and admonition, it encourages an attitude of doubt and dread toward every sexual activity – a notion the film defines broadly enough to include virtually all the behavior it puts on display – until the very last shot.

A second, equally ambiguous interpretive frame is provided by the novels written by Catherine, the principal suspect in Boz's murder, under the pseudonym Catherine Woolf: *The First Time,* which fictionalized the deaths of her parents years ago; *Love Hurts,* which predicted the Boz murder in uncanny detail; and the one she is just beginning, *Shooter,* which she intends as a portrait of Nick Curran (Douglas), the lead detective investigating the murder. Catherine's brazen openness about the basis of her books in real experiences, and her insistence that only someone who wanted to frame her would kill someone in a manner she had outlined so precisely, make Nick uncertain just how to interpret them, even when, incredibly, he allows his partner Gus Moran (George Dzundza) to enter a building in which the manuscript of *Shooter* has just predicted Gus will meet his death.

The film's third interpretive frame is intertextual. *Body Heat* invoked *Double Indemnity* and other noirs at so many points that only an audience as naïve or besotted as Ned would have failed to recognize Matty's femme-fatale heritage. *Basic Instinct* is even more heavily indebted to earlier films. The fear of a woman who kills the men with whom she has sex echoes the central premise of *Black Widow* (1987), and the casting of Douglas inevitably recalls his similar role in *Fatal Attraction*. When Nick discovers that Catherine's friend Hazel Dobkins (Dorothy Malone) is an ex-convict who had killed her husband in 1956, alert viewers will recognize the reference to the year Malone had given her Oscar-winning performance as the nymphomaniac Marylee Hadley in *Written on the Wind* – a reference that allows the film to echo its opening reduction of the killer to a golden body by reducing Malone's character to the actress's earlier performance as a man-hungry tramp. The film's most important echoes, though, are of *Vertigo* (1958), through not only its exploration of gender but also its evocative music – particularly the chromatic descending phrase introduced over the main title, with its persistent denial of resolution in the tonic key – and its San Francisco setting, especially when Nick, in a grotesquely souped-up version of James Stewart's dreamlike pursuit of Kim Novak's Rolls-Royce, weaves in and out of traffic on a sheer hillside expressway behind Catherine's death-defying Lamborghini. None of these references, however, helps audiences decide how to react to the film's frequent presentations of sexual couplings by indicating whether Catherine is innocent or guilty. The overgalvanized chase scenes show Nick, like *Vertigo*'s Scottie Ferguson, tailing a suspicious woman in the hopes that her adventures will explain her behavior. Like Scottie, however, Nick sees only a series of tableaux in which the mysterious heroine reveals alternative versions of herself rather than the heart of her personal mystery. Since both sequences are staged by their heroines, neither voyeuristic pursuit can provide the psychological demystification that is its pretext. Like the teasing opening murder, these sequences simply create a climate of suspicion dispersed over every female member of the cast.

The film's suspicions focus on Catherine because of her frankly predatory sexuality while linking her vampirish sexual habits to subtler but equally sinister forms of possession. Nick is obviously taken aback by Catherine's wealth (she inherited an estate worth $110 million when her parents died), her magna cum laude Berkeley degree in psychology and literature (figured here as the credentials for world-class manipulation), her effortless mastery of self-presentation, her amused detachment from the case, and her refusal to accept either of the roles he would like to assign her: grieving lover or murder suspect. More directly threatening is her announcement, "I use people for what I write. Let the world beware," and her subsequent disarming revelation to Nick, "I'm using you for my detective in my book. You don't mind, do you?"

The film's best-known set piece, in which Catherine sits with aplomb and without underwear, her legs spread, as the sweating police interrogate her, pits her charismatic sexuality against male institutions of power whose interest in regulating it is outweighed by lubricity. Her forthright refusal to put out her cigarette – "What're you going to do, charge me with smoking?" she taunts the cops who are interrogating her – makes the male inquisitors in the no-smoking interrogation room look like monkeys because, even as she invites the male gaze that ought to disempower her by reducing her to an object, she turns the tables on her accusers. She challenges their rules by refusing to follow them – or by throwing them in their faces, by her mastery of their lie-detector test. She refuses to play the role of prey to Nick's institutional predator, calling him by his first name throughout the scene and taunting him with personal remarks; and by courting the gaze of her interrogators through the way she poses for them, she challenges their right to question her at all by revealing their interest in her as ultimately scopophilic. It is no wonder that even more than the three sex scenes that structure the film's narrative – the murder of Johnny Boz, the re-enactment of that murder by the episode halfway through in which Catherine ties Nick's hands to her bedpost but then does not kill him, and the final scene that finds Nick and Catherine in bed once more – Catherine's brazen challenge to the legitimacy of the police interrogation has become the film's hallmark [Fig. 34].

Catherine, however, is only the most prominent of the film's femmes fatales. Her friend Hazel long ago had killed her family with a knife that had been a wedding gift. Her lesbian live-in companion Roxy Hardy (Leilani Sarelle) had killed her brothers with their father's razor at the age of sixteen. Even her apparent opposite, Nick's lover, police psychiatrist Dr. Beth Garner (Jeanne Tripplehorn), who ought to be cast as

34. *Basic Instinct:* The frank sexuality of the heroine (Sharon Stone) challenges the legitimacy of the police hero (Michael Douglas) in and out of bed.

the good girl, turns out to be implicated in the mystery as someone who was briefly Catherine's lover when they were students at Berkeley, and who may have killed one of the old teachers she shared with Catherine with an ice pick.

The dispersion of suspicion over a wide range of suspects is hardly an innovation of *Basic Instinct,* since, as a defining trope of the mystery story, it turns up in films as different as *Laura* (1944) and *The Last*

of Sheila (1973). What makes *Basic Instinct* stand out from other whodunits is the sexual tension aroused by the hero's sleeping with two
of the suspects, either of whom could be planning to kill him. Not
even the reckless affair Det. Frank Keller (Al Pacino) conducts with
Helen (Ellen Barkin), the leading suspect in *Sea of Love* (1989) [Fig.
35], produces an equivalent sense of sexual paranoia; for even though
the film initially casts Beth in a therapeutic role as Nick's counselor
and lover, makes her the widowed victim of violence (her husband
was shot to death five years ago), and shows her consistently offering herself as subservient to Nick, evidence against her continues
to mount. She has changed both her name and her hair color since
her student days at Berkeley; she knew Catherine much better there
than she originally admitted; and according to Catherine, it was Beth
who obsessively imitated and stalked Catherine, not the other way
around. After Nick shoots Beth when he finds her on the scene of
Gus's murder, the police discover a mountain of new evidence point-
ing to her as the killer, and many viewers leave the theater believing
in her guilt.

Given the pall of suspicion the film goes out of its way to cast over
every female in the cast, why is Nick so attracted to them, especially
to Catherine, who makes no secret of the fact that she simply intends
to use him for her new book? The interrogation scene pointedly suggests that when it comes to seductive women, men don't think with
their brains; but even if Nick's only attraction to Catherine were sexual, the sex would not be half as good if her effrontery did not provide
him with a risk he clearly enjoys. Although Nick assures both Catherine and Gus that his interest in her is professional, her unrelentingly
provocative behavior reveals a more insidious lure: his recognition of
Catherine as his more successful double. Even when he is nominally
assigned an adversarial role toward Catherine, as detective to her suspect, he finds himself echoing her dialogue tags (most memorably,
"What're you going to do, charge me with smoking?" when he sits in
the same chair to be questioned about the murder of his nemesis, Lt.
Marty Nilsen [Daniel von Bargen]) and adopting her habits, returning
to the smoking and drinking he had given up, cornering Beth over her
protests for a bout of rough sex that not only reveals his frustration
at Catherine's aloofness but borrows her way of expressing it. When
Gus tells Nick that Catherine doesn't have any friends who haven't
killed anyone, he is rather tactlessly forgetting that this description
applies to Nick himself, who has shot four bystanders, two quite re-

35. *Sea of Love:* Another compromised cop, another reckless affair. (Ellen Barkin, Al Pacino)

cently, on the job. After initially considering Catherine an adversary who provides a rationale for his professional identity, Nick is eventually forced to see her as the untrammeled self he longs to be.

As she warns him, however, theirs is an unequal twinship [Fig. 36]; for if Catherine, in accord with her plans to feed on Nick as material for her novel, increasingly succeeds in getting inside Nick's head until she knows him better than he knows himself, Nick never succeeds in getting inside her any way but physically. Early on, Nick recognizes that he is overmatched, but he soon manages to forget this knowledge. He is humiliatingly doubled with Catherine's alternative lover, Roxy, when he finds that she has watched what Nick, though not Catherine, calls "the fuck of the century," and has often watched Catherine in bed with Catherine's knowledge and consent. Although he caps a second wild car chase, after almost being run over twice, by killing Roxy, the car's driver (believing she is Catherine), he had never succeeded in rattling her into thinking he has taken her place in Catherine's affections, the way she obviously rattles him into suspecting that Catherine has marginalized his male sexuality by staging their coupling expressly for Roxy's benefit – just as she had earlier danced with him in Johnny Boz's club in order to make Roxy jealous. If his affair with Catherine is, as Nick believes, a race between his attempt to build a case against her and her attempt to embalm him in her novel and then move on, there can be no doubt who wins: She not only remakes him in her own image, completes the book, and briskly dismisses him, but succeeds so completely in turning his suspicions from her to Beth that, after shooting Beth dead, he resumes his affair with Catherine.

Unlike the doomed lovers of *Double Indemnity,* then, Nick and Catherine are not evenly matched partners; they more closely resemble the female plotter and the male patsy of *Body Heat.* The film treats its violent rondelet of sexual couplings as a game whose roles absorb its participants so fully that they can never return to their former identities. As Gus points out to Nick when he expresses his appetite for playing along with Catherine, "Everybody she plays with dies." By the end of the story, Nick, practically alone of Catherine's partners, has not died; but he has paid for his relationship with Catherine with the loss of his privacy (his troubled history is about to be revealed to the world in the forthcoming *Shooter*), his peace of mind, his former lover and therapist, his best friend, and his professional standing.

The film's final scene aptly indicates what it means to gain Catherine in this game of sex by pointedly failing to resolve the problems Nick's suicidally heedless infatuation with Catherine has raised. Nick and Catherine are in bed in a scene staged as their final reenactment of Johnny Boz's murder. When they have finished making love, they wonder what they're going to do next as Nick invitingly presents his back as a target; Catherine, after trailing her hand under the bed, sweeps her arm up in passionate rather than murderous intent; and the film fades from a shot of their exhausted faces to black. But in-

36. *Basic Instinct:* An unequal twinship in which the woman (Sharon Stone) wields the icepick.

stead of presenting the closing credits, Verhoeven fades in after a few long seconds on the identical shot, then tilts down further to show Catherine's hand dangling again under the bed, inches above an ice pick she has presumably left there (although skeptical viewers are free to think that Beth, who has been in Nick's apartment often enough, left it there instead). Catherine withdraws her hand without touching the ice pick, suggesting over a second and final fade that she will not kill Nick this time; maybe she never will. It is in that *maybe* that *Basic Instinct* locates all hope for love, friendship, even satisfying sex. Having survived the deaths of their closest friends and lovers, maybe Nick and Catherine – he certainly a killer, she presumably one as well – will live happily ever after. Maybe Nick has left behind the haunted loner who killed four bystanders while working as a cop. Maybe Catherine is not the killer he thought she was. Maybe.

Why are the rituals of courtship and romance systematically reduced to the poisonous games these lovers play? The film presents Catherine's castrating power as a transgressive inversion of Nick's institutional power by showing her unfairly seizing advantages he assumed, equally unfairly, were his by right. Yet Nick's identity is so bound up in his job that his initial self-confidence is really a confidence in the legal system that has allowed him to use lethal force in life-or-death situations, made his therapist-lover obligingly submissive to him, and enlisted her official authority in forgiving or covering up his fatal lapses in judgment. The femme fatale's charismatic individual power is nothing more than a backlash against the institutional power of patriarchy, which would guarantee, whatever the heroine's behavior, an imbalance of power between men and women. In such an unbalanced world, love is all but impossible, and sex at best a dangerous game rife with possibilities for bullying, counterattack, and betrayal, at worst an invitation to personal annihilation in the pursuit of power needed to sustain even the most opportunistic relationship. No wonder that R. Barton Palmer, whose reading of Catherine as guilty of murder but largely sympathetic makes him perhaps the most optimistic commentator on the film, concludes that it "ends by endorsing a true love based on shared psychopathology."[11]

Unlike films noirs, erotic thrillers, freed from the Production Code's demand that evil be punished, are often too deeply divided between their critique of patriarchy and their complicit invitation to voyeurism to resolve this dilemma by killing off the licentious heroine. Increasingly, in the trajectory from *Body Heat* to *Basic Instinct,* they condemn their patriarchal heroes without abating their execration of their femmes fatales. Two recent films, however, suggest that even if love between men and women may be impossible in a world that is patriarchal, misogynistic, and voyeuristic, films need not simply reproduce these values uncritically themselves.

John Dahl's *The Last Seduction* (1994), first made for HBO, offers a villain who is so resourceful in triumphing over her negligible male adversaries that her criminality becomes heroic. After a spat in which her face is slapped by her husband, Clay (Bill Pullman), a Manhattan medical resident who has just scored $700,000 in a drug deal, hard-charging sales-force supervisor Bridget Gregory (Linda Fiorentino) walks out on him with the money, apparently on the spur of the moment and for no reason other than the slap, and goes to ground in tiny Beston, outside Buffalo. Stopping for gas, Bridget ridicules the crude come-on of insurance claims adjuster Mike Swale (Peter Berg), who tells her, "I'm hung like a horse," in reply to which she sits him down, opens his fly, and gropes him in search of "Mr. Ed." Eventually, however, she allows him to buy her a drink and take her home as a "designated fuck" whose companionship will keep her off Clay's radar. In an ingenious series of maneuvers, she manages to foil both of the detectives Clay sends after her and inveigles the unwitting Mike into a plot to murder him. When Mike balks at the last minute, she kills Clay herself, pinning the crime on Mike, and rides off into the sunset rich and free.

The film plays like *Body Heat* seen from the femme fatale's point of view. The only excuse it offers for Bridget's behavior is the stupidity and venality of her male adversaries. Even though Bridget is as duplicitous and brutal as Matty Walker, the film suggests, she deserves to beat the men she is playing because by adopting the stereotypically male habits of sexual aggression, dirty talk, frank lack of romantic commitment, and lust for power and money, she is getting revenge for generations of patriarchal abuse of women. Bridget deliciously sends up the romantic attitudinizing that is supposed to keep her responsive to men, as when she responds to Mike's complaint that she doesn't feel anything for him by saying, "You're different from the others, Mike. I feel that maybe I could love you. I don't want that to happen. Really. – Will that do?" No matter that Bridget does not consider herself a sister to the women who paved the way for her role reversal, or that she studiously snubs all the neighbors, women and men alike, who offer her greetings on her first morning in Beston. Her right to revenge is confirmed by her ruthlessness and wit and her victims' weakness.

Clay, who is just as criminal without being just as clever, is Bridget's natural prey; but Mike, in the film's most cunning gender reversal, is an equally fitting victim. Although he talks constantly of his longing for romantic commitment, the film never forgets that Mike, reeling from the disastrous marriage that took him briefly to Buffalo before tossing him back on Beston, sees Bridget mainly as a prop to his masculinity. "How long does it take to grow a new set of balls?" he muses to his drinking buddies as Bridget, whom he calls "a new set of balls," walks in. When Bridget begins at one point to tell him the truth about herself, he stops her, insisting it's just another lie, then tells her that he needs her to restore his sense of himself: "You've been out there. You came here, and you chose me. So I was right. I'm bigger than this town." Viewers are invited to revel in the irony of the romantic Mike's selection by someone who demonstrates how disastrously out of his league he is when he leaves his despised small town for Buffalo (where his bride, Trish, turns out to be a transvestite male played by the porn actress Serena) or New York (where Bridget, by briefly playing the role of the wife he hates, tricks him into releasing his rage just long enough to ensure that he will take the fall for Clay's murder). Male and female viewers alike are invited to enjoy this castration fantasy as exhilarating rather than disturbing because the male victims are so carefully distinguished from the presumably less insecure audience.

The Last Seduction, like *Basic Instinct*, works not by redressing the social inequalities between men and women but by inverting them, allowing the femme fatale to earn her payday by usurping traditionally male habits in order to play on the masculine insecurities of the hero. Andy and Larry Wachowski's *Bound* (1996) goes a step further by playing to Nick Curran's most paranoid fantasy, taking men out of the equation altogether. By casting Gina Gershon in the role of the innocent sucked into a dangerous conspiracy by an alluring woman with criminal connections – a role traditionally played by men from Burt Lancaster in *The Killers* (1946) to Don Johnson in *Goodbye, Lover* (1999) – the film recasts in lesbian terms the anatomy of male–female power games that dominate both films noirs and erotic thrillers. Once ex-con rehabber Corky (Gershon) and her next-door neighbor Violet (Jennifer Tilly) team up to fleece Violet's lover Caesar (Joe Pantoliano) of two million dollars in Mob money, the key question the film's convoluted plot keeps raising is whether the two conspirators can trust each oth-

37. *Bound:* Conspirators (Gina Gershon, Jennifer Tilly) drawn together, for better or worse, by their similarities.

er, or which one will betray the other one first. In a heterosexual noir or erotic thriller the answer would be foreordained, since although men can rage murderous through erotic thrillers like *Crimes of Passion* (1984), *Body Double* (1984), *Consenting Adults* (1992), and *Sliver,* men rarely betray the women with whom they conspire to break the law. The role of double-crossing criminal conspirator is reserved for women in such films as *Out of the Past* (1947), *Criss Cross* (1949), *Body of Evidence* (1993), *Romeo Is Bleeding* (1993), and *Palmetto* (1998).[12] This time, however, there is no way of telling which of the two females will crack first.

As it turns out, neither does. Even though Violet seems at first to harp on the cultural differences between them – "A truck. Of course," she says when she hears that Corky drives a 1962 Chevy pickup, and later responds to Corky's drink of choice, "Beer. Of course." – the two are bound together from the beginning, for better or worse, by their similarities [Fig. 37]. Violet seduces Corky by admiring Corky's tattoos and inviting her to touch the tattoo on Violet's own breast. Much later, as Violet refuses to tell the suspicious Caesar the name of the person she has telephoned after the money has disappeared, he identifies

Corky by the telephone he hears ringing next door. Caesar, maddened as he is by Violet's refusal to betray Corky, cannot know that the two women have already passed up repeated opportunities to sell each other out. Corky could have driven off with the briefcase that Violet tipped her off would be full of cash; Violet could have stayed behind and tipped Caesar off about Corky's break-in instead of going to the liquor store; Violet could have given Caesar Corky's name earlier. The two women not only flimflam Joe out of the money he is minding for his higher-ups and so endanger his life, but also outrage his sense of sexual propriety by forging a bond that is closer than his bond with Violet.

Corky is an obvious butch whose idea of romance is picking up women in gay bars, Violet a femme who has been living with the same man for five years; Corky is a thief who is identified with physical labor, Violet a passive–aggressive seducer who seems to have learned her behavior from studying every erotic thriller since *Body Heat.* Despite the differences in their status and habits, though, they are alike under the leather jackets they wear so differently and inside their hyperaesthetically stylized visual world, from the opening sequence – a tour of a closet interior that comprises a delirious exercise in fetishism – to the climactic shooting of the villain that becomes a study in white. Less like the heterosexual lovers whose failures litter the noir and neo-noir landscape than like the besieged family members of *Fatal Attraction,* Corky and Violet are capable of forming a team whose members can trust each other because they see themselves in each other too completely ever to be fooled by superficial differences. The film's final exchange confirms this sense of teamwork while ruling it out for heterosexual couples. As they drive off in Corky's brand-new truck after killing Joe and pocketing the money, Corky asks Violet, "You know what the difference is between you and me, Violet?" "No," replies Violet dutifully. "Me neither," says Corky.

The happy ending of *Bound,* like Bridget's subversively enjoyable rout of her male victims in *The Last Seduction,* suggests that insecure men, not treacherous women, are the real villains in films noirs and erotic thrillers. Unlike men, these films suggest, women do not oppress or victimize people, justifying their power by perpetuating it in patriarchal institutions, in order to reassure themselves about their sexual identities. Women may be greedy and ruthless, but since these traits are rarely gendered as female, the men they outwit are equally immoral, simply more vulnerable because their access to institutional power gives them more to lose, and because their masculinity makes them more vulnerable both to the heroines who play on their insecurities and to the audiences who are willing to sacrifice them as hostages to the gender wars. *Bound* in particular suggests that the motivic doubling of Walter and Phyllis in *Double Indemnity* as an image for Walter's own irreducible duality can be read in still another way: as a more general representation of woman and man, doomed to failure as a couple by social and cultural inequalities that can be mended only if they exchange forgiveness and start over again. Lesbianism, *Bound* suggests, is not deviant; heterosexuality is, because its couples are divided by the very forces that unite them, from criminal conspiracies to sexual difference. If the alleged attraction of psychosexual opposites makes love go round (and round and round) for the repressed heroes of film noir, the erotic thriller raises the stakes by dramatizing the global paranoia men feel not only for the women on whom they depend for the sex they crave, but for the possibility that women could ever undermine cherished ideals of masculinity by showing how nightmarish it would be if they ever acted as badly as men.

8

Murder on the Orient Express, Blue Velvet, and the Unofficial-Detective Film

I t is commonplace to observe that films noirs, whose criminals are amateurs, differ in crucial ways from gangster films, whose criminals are professionals. It is equally true that the different kinds of character who are called on to solve crimes – officials of the justice system like lawyers or the police, licensed private detectives who make their living investigating crimes, unofficial detectives who work neither for the justice system nor as salaried independent contractors – emphasize problems so different that they generate distinctive subgenres within the crime film. Films featuring officers of the justice system are organized around problems of institutional justice (What should society do with suspected or convicted criminals?), films featuring private investigators around problems of professionalism and masculinity (What sort of man makes the best detective?), and films featuring amateur detectives around problems of knowledge (What is the solution to the mystery?).

Throughout the century since the vogue of Sherlock Holmes, unofficial detectives have played a leading role in the history of the detective story. Although Edgar Allan Poe had produced the first detective story, "The Murders in the Rue Morgue," as early as 1841, it was the Holmes stories – *A Study in Scarlet* (1887), *The Sign of the Four* (1890), and especially the series of short stories Arthur Conan Doyle published in the *Strand,* beginning with "A Scandal in Bohemia" in 1891 – that provoked a torrent of imitators in England and America who first made the detective story an established literary genre. The Holmes formula pitted a heroically eccentric detective not so much against a criminal (Holmes's best-known criminal quarry, Professor

Moriarty, appears directly in only one of his sixty cases) as against a baffling mystery. The detective, by dint of close observation and a sharp analytical mind, makes a series of logical inferences that lead him or her ahead of the official police to the criminal. To the figure of the idiosyncratic unofficial detective, the so-called Golden Age of the British detective story – represented between the two world wars by the likes of Agatha Christie and Dorothy L. Sayers – added a stylized, enclosed setting (typically an English village or country house) and a strong emphasis on baroque, ingenious mysteries. In the work of the Anglo-American mystery writer John Dickson Carr, these mysteries often took the form of puzzles so intricately clued that their explanations required footnotes referring back to earlier passages. How could a man have been strangled in the middle of a wet tennis court by a murderer who walked away from the scene without leaving footprints? How could a murderer make a loaded gun leap from its wall mount and kill someone else? How could a man threatened by his long-dead brother be shot to death alone in a guarded room, and a third brother be fatally shot at close range in the middle of a deserted street? In novels like *The Problem of the Wire Cage* (1939), *The Man Who Could Not Shudder* (1941), and *The Three Coffins* (1935), Carr posed one impossible crime after another for readers alert enough to follow the chain of evidence to solve. In America, the pseudonymous Ellery Queen (Frederic Dannay and Manfred Lee) made the invitation to readers interested in following the evidence explicit in a series of novels beginning with *The Roman Hat Mystery* (1929), each featuring a "Challenge to the Reader" before the closing chapters that asked readers to solve the crime on the basis of logic and the evidence before the detective announced his or her own solution. These novels, like those of Carr and the American S. S. Van Dine, were often illustrated with floor plans of the murder chamber or line drawings showing how a room could be locked from outside by an enterprising criminal. In a series of "Crime Dossiers" published in the 1930s, Dennis Wheatley went even further, including such bits of physical evidence as spent matches, locks of hair, and scraps of bloodstained draperies for readers to comb for clues. Even after fads like footnotes, Queen's "Challenge to the Reader," and the "Crime Dossiers" passed, the unofficial-detective story remained for many years primarily a logical conundrum, like a crossword puzzle for detectives and their brainier readers to solve.[1]

Throughout this period, many fictional detectives were brought to the screen. Sherlock Holmes led the field in 1903 in the American Mu-

toscope short *Sherlock Holmes Baffled.* The American actor-playwright
William Gillette's stage play *Sherlock Holmes* was filmed with Gillette
(1916) and again with John Barrymore (1922), and by 1923 the hawk-
nosed detective had appeared in some fifty brief British adaptations
of Conan Doyle's stories. With the coming of synchronized sound,
Holmes was joined in short order by S. S. Van Dine's Manhattan aristocrat Philo Vance (*The Canary Murder Case,* 1929), Agatha Christie's
self-important Belgian Hercule Poirot (*Alibi,* 1931), Stuart Palmer's vin-
egary schoolteacher Hildegarde Withers (*The Penguin Pool Murder,*
1932), Ellery Queen's logician Ellery Queen (*The Spanish Cape Mystery,* 1935), Rex Stout's gargantuan Nero Wolfe (*Meet Nero Wolfe,* 1936),
and even the teenaged detective Nancy Drew, ghostwritten under the
name Carolyn Keene (*Nancy Drew, Detective,* 1938).[2] Most of these detectives starred in a whole series of films during the 1930s and early
1940s; yet the formal detective story, the mystery organized as a puzzle for the audience to compete with the detective in solving, never
achieved the eminence in Hollywood that it did on the printed page.
At the height of their popularity in bookstores, Philo Vance and Ellery
Queen were still largely restricted in their sleuthing to second features. Even Sherlock Holmes, given new life by Basil Rathbone in Sidney Lanfield's elaborate 1939 production of *The Hound of the Baskervilles,* soon declined to a series of wartime "programmers" directed by
Roy William Neill for Universal (e.g., *Sherlock Holmes and the Secret
Weapon,* 1942) before Rathbone was driven from the role by his ac-
curate, if overdue, fears of typecasting in 1946.

Although unofficial detectives have long been a staple of Hollywood
crime films, then, they have seldom been its most distinguished ava-
tars. No less an authority than Alfred Hitchcock averred to François
Truffaut that he had no appetite for detective stories "because as a
rule all the interest is concentrated in the ending." The Master of Suspense added, "I don't really approve of whodunits because they're
rather like a jigsaw or crossword puzzle. No emotion. You simply wait
to find out who committed the murder."[3] Even though many Hitchcock
films incorporate elements of the whodunit, and no filmmaker is identified more closely, however misleadingly, with the mystery film, Hitchcock only made one true detective story: the British talkie *Murder!*
(1930).

Hitchcock's aversion to the formal detective story is best explained
by noting the ways in which the presence of a powerfully charismatic
detective hero like Sherlock Holmes and the emphasis on physical

evidence, logical inferences, and a puzzling mystery focused on the single question "Whodunit?" give such detective stories a most un-Hitchcockian spin. All crime films deal with violent disruptions in the social order and threats to the safety of ordinary characters like *Fury's* Joe Wilson, whose dilemmas dramatize the audience's own nightmares of social and epistemological breakdown; but the dominance of a heroic detective like Holmes goes far to counterbalance those threatening elements by presenting a benevolent restorer of order, apparently omniscient and omnipotent, who leaves an impression even more powerful than the mysteries he solves. The opposition between the mysterious crime and the heroic detective reveals a deeper polarity at the heart of the whodunit between the entertainingly threatening elements associated with the mystery and the reassuringly domestic elements associated with the detective. The pleasure many readers take in Sherlock Holmes, for example, has less to do with the tales' incidental mysteries, which come and go from story to story, than with the constant presence of Holmes and Dr. Watson, whose enduring solidity provides a counterweight to the threat of mystery and violent death.

The details of Holmes and Watson's domestic life provide a pattern for many unofficial detectives who follow. Holmes, who thinks of himself as an ascetic scientist who has no interest in women, carries traces of the aesthete as well: He plays the violin, uses cocaine, and affects irregular hours and irregular companions. Watson, by contrast, represents the most stolid strain of the good Englishman: loyal, courageous, sentimental, and invincibly unimaginative. Their headquarters at 221b Baker Street are so minutely described, from the fifteen steps up to their landlady Mrs. Hudson's second floor to the Persian slipper for Holmes's tobacco, that readers insisted the place must be real, and sixty years after Doyle's death, a Sherlock Holmes museum was opened in what had heretofore been a fictional address.

All these domestic touches provide a countervailing weight to the menace of criminal activity that predominates in most crime fiction. The emphasis on the everyday rituals of the detective's life allows the stories to deal with the darkest threats imaginable – personal betrayal, the theft of irreplaceable objects, unexplained violence, mysterious death, the ultimate breakdown of logic and reason – within a formula as sanitized as that of the comic strip or the weekly sitcom, the only other surviving fictional modes that routinely depend on recycling the same heroes from story to story. The ritual of reassurance begins with

the very presence of stock detectives protected from death or destruction by the guarantee that they will return in the next installment,
and continues in each fetishized detail of the detectives' domestic
lives that anchors the series against the vicissitudes of mystery, crime,
or history itself. So complete is the emphasis on the unchanging pole
of detectives' cozy households, in fact, that even today mystery stories solved by unofficial detectives are often labeled by their publishers as "cozies," often over the protests of their own authors.

The plots of these stories, whose emphasis on the class distinction
within a stable, enclosed society in which everyone knows everyone
else has made the formula a particular favorite among British authors,
are often as cozy as their heroes' lives. The discovery of a beheaded
corpse that cannot be identified would be a grisly shock in real life;
yet the tone of Dorothy L. Sayers's first novel, *Whose Body?* (1923), is
so facetiously literate that the headless corpse becomes an abstract,
cerebral puzzle, the opening move in a game of deception that will end
in the detective's vanquishing the criminal by sheer force of intellect
and personality. The light, detached, often playful tone of Golden Age
British writers from E. C. Bentley to Georgette Heyer encourages readers to follow the characters' lead in treating even the most outré cir-
cumstances as bloodless clues. Crime is no longer a danger to individuals and an affront to society, but the pretext for an entertainingly
recondite mystery that can be solved by readers willing to suspend
their emotional commitments to the characters completely enough to
evaluate each of them clinically as possible suspects. Because the unofficial detective has by definition no ties to the justice system,[4] the
problems of legal justice can be waived, and criminals confronted with
the truth of their broken alibis and unsuccessful red herrings consid-
erately break down and confess, or even more obligingly commit suicide, sparing the state the expense and the ethical questions a trial
might entail. This freedom from the more disturbing problems of menacing violence and the more problematic issues of institutional justice
allows unofficial detective stories from *The Thin Man* (book and film,
1934) to *Young Sherlock Holmes* (film and novelization, 1985) to adopt
an optimistic, triumphalist, often broadly comic tone, with the detective's star power guaranteeing a happy ending.

Nowhere is the whodunit's tendency to smooth the rough edges of the
crime story more obvious than in Sidney Lumet's 1974 film version of
Agatha Christie's *Murder on the Orient Express.* Christie's novel, first

published in 1933 as *Murder in the Calais Coach,* had represented a turning point in the career of her hero, Hercule Poirot, who, after his retirement from the Belgian police, had enjoyed a career as a private detective in novels from *The Mysterious Affair at Styles* (1920) to *Thirteen at Dinner* (first published in Britain as *Lord Edgware Dies,* 1933). Accompanied by his endearingly dense Watson figure, Capt. Arthur Hastings, Poirot had repeatedly come out of retirement from his second career to solve a wide variety of cases. *Murder on the Orient Express,* however, finds him returning from a trip to the Mideast without Hastings and turning his back on a paying client by refusing the American businessman Samuel Ratchett's commission to find out who has been sending him threatening letters. When Ratchett is stabbed to death in his berth on the exclusive trans-European train, Poirot is urged to take charge of the investigation until the authorities arrive.

   Lumet came to the film from a background of dramas that explored the weight of the past and of social pressures on individual behavior. His first film, the one-set drama *12 Angry Men* (1957), plumbed the dynamics of a jury whose members could not agree on a verdict in an apparently routine case. *Long Day's Journey into Night* (1962) and *The Pawnbroker* (1965) presented characters mired in long-standing family struggles or Holocaust memories they could not escape. The caper film *The Anderson Tapes* (1971) took a deterministic view of a newly formed gang's attempt to loot a posh Manhattan apartment building even as its members were under surveillance by various government agencies. The police hero of *Serpico* (1973) was an honest New York cop battling corruption in his department as he was transferred from one hostile precinct to the next. Lumet, however, seemed to approach *Murder on the Orient Express* as a holiday from the agonizing ethical dilemmas of his earlier films, an excursion preceding the close analysis of morally flawed pillars of the justice system that would become his hallmark in such later films as *Prince of the City* (1981), *The Verdict* (1982), *Q & A* (1990), *Guilty as Sin* (1993), and *Night Falls on Manhattan* (1997). Beginning with its art-deco credits, *Murder on the Orient Express* announces itself as a vacation from the strenuous moral analysis of other crime films – a respite marked by the persistent emphasis of the reassuring pole of domesticity over the threatening pole of mystery and violent death.[5]

   The film might be taken as a textbook example of Hitchcock's strictures against the screen whodunit. Hitchcock had complained that everything that happens in a whodunit is reducible to a mere prologue to its climactic revelation of guilt. This revelation in Christie's novel is a high point of mystery's Golden Age. Realizing that the presence of so many characters connected with the unsolved kidnapping of little Daisy Armstrong five years earlier cannot possibly be coincidental, Poirot declares that the twelve suspects who have shared the fatal coach with him and Ratchett are all guilty (or, more precisely, that only one of the thirteen possible suspects is innocent): They have constituted themselves a jury to punish a crime the justice system could not. The novel is therefore powerfully inventive in a peculiarly limited way. It is not notable for an extraordinarily unified or resonant plot like *Oedipus the King*, or for any special inventiveness in the way of incident, or even for ingenuity on the part of its criminal plotters. The cleverness is Christie's success in devising a rationale for her mystery that, as G. K. Chesterton had urged, could be explained in a few sentences and grasped in a moment. Forty years before Hollywood would become notorious as the town where movies were outlined on luncheon napkins, Christie had perfected the high-concept mystery. Novel after novel that she published between 1920 and 1940 turned out to be organized around a single brilliant device for concealing, then revealing, the criminal pattern; but with the exception of *The Murder of Roger Ackroyd* (1926), whose narrator was unmasked as the murderer, none of her concepts was more simple or successful than the secret of *Murder on the Orient Express*.

The film follows Christie's strategy of reducing the murder of Ratchett (Richard Widmark) to the status of an intellectual game by revealing early on that he was actually Cassetti, the criminal mastermind behind Daisy Armstrong's kidnapping and murder, marking him as a victim not worth mourning – and incidentally gesturing slyly at the checkered persona of Widmark, who had made his reputation by playing a series of stylishly brutal hoodlums in films from *Kiss of Death* (1947), his spectacular debut, to *Pickup on South Street* (1953). It departs from Christie, however, in reframing her intellectual puzzle in more overtly visual, and ultimately sociocultural, terms.

The very nature of Christie's novel involves the containment of potentially disturbing threats in an enclosed space. Whereas a filmmaker like Elia Kazan might have opened the story's setting beyond the single railway coach, and a noir stylist like Robert Siodmak or Jules Dassin might have emphasized the claustrophobic confines of the space, Lumet's approach is consistently decorative. He begins with a gauzy prologue, a montage showing the 1930 kidnapping of little Daisy Arm-

38. *Murder on the Orient Express:* The evocative sequence leading up to the train's departure. (Martin Balsam, Albert Finney)

strong (an event to which Christie's novel only alludes), and proceeds to a sumptuously designed opening of the present-day story five years later, set mostly in the spacious, atmospheric train station at Istanbul [Fig. 38]. The moments leading up to the Orient Express's departure for Europe are crammed especially full of exotic detail, as Lumet provides passersby in turbans, burnouses, fezzes, yarmulkes, and Chinese dress to mingle briefly with the stars. From the moment the train pulls out of the station, however, the film becomes an exercise in one-set cinema. Except for the exterior shots showing the train stuck in a picturesque snowbank that makes it impossible for the investigating authorities to reach it, every scene is structurally the same scene – Poirot interrogating the suspects in Ratchett's murder in a series of midshots and close-ups – set against the same paneled interiors.

Lumet and his Oscar-nominated collaborators, production designer and costumer Tony Walton and cinematographer Geoffrey Unsworth, deal with their opulent but static set by reframing the story in crucial new ways. Lumet is much less interested in visual space as such than, say, Orson Welles; instead he focuses on two centers of visual interest:

the stars' meticulously detailed costumes and their famous faces. From starchy tweeds to flashy furs, the screen is filled with a parade of extravagant period costumes; but it is the stars themselves who consistently command attention [Fig. 39]. Following the lead of John Huston's *The List of Adrian Messenger* (1963), which had dressed up its mystery by putting well-known stars into impenetrably heavy disguise for a teasing finale, *Murder on the Orient Express* assaults its audience from almost the beginning with A-list star power. Many of its stars – Vanessa Redgrave as unassuming Mary Debenham, Sean Connery as bluff Colonel Arbuthnot, Wendy Hiller as ugly old Princess Dragomiroff, Lauren Bacall as fur-draped American tourist Harriet Hubbard, Michael York and Jacqueline Bisset as the Count and Countess Andrenyi – are given showy entrance tableaux. Ingrid Bergman as missionary Greta Ohlsson and John Gielgud as Ratchett's butler, Beddoes, are allowed star turns that won them British Film Academy awards for their performances. Many of the roles are reshaped for, or by, their performers. In an Oscar-winning turn, Bergman makes Christie's colorless Ohlsson a missionary who, since being "born backwards," has spent her life "teaching little brown babies more backwards than myself." Mrs. Hubbard is remade from a quietly rambling American dowager to an obnoxious loudmouth to suit the aggressive talents of Bacall. Anthony Perkins as Hector MacQueen, Ratchett's secretary, is playing a thinly disguised version of his indelible screen persona, Norman Bates.

This emphasis on star power goes far beyond visually showcasing the film's cast. By shifting attention from the characters to the stars who play them, the film displaces the whodunit's dualistic approach to character (everyone seems smilingly innocent, but since one person must be a dissembling murderer, everyone is suspect) onto a more reassuring dichotomy between actor and role. The film's advertising posters exploited this dichotomy even before the audience arrived in the theater by asking the question, "Can Ingrid Bergman commit murder?" When Colonel Arbuthnot, stung by Poirot's suspicions of such a "woman" as Mary Debenham, retorts witheringly, "Miss Debenham is not a woman – she's a lady," the implied question that arises is not whether Miss Debenham is really a lady, but whether a lady can really commit murder. By confounding its characters with the actors and actresses who play them, the film consistently shifts questions of innocence and guilt from personal, psychological terms to the more broadly cultural, visually accessible terms of social class, public persona, and celebrity framed by its status as star vehicle.[6]

39. *Murder on the Orient Express:* Stars as scenery. (Jean-Pierre Cassel, Anthony Perkins, Vanessa Redgrave, Sean Connery, Ingrid Bergman, George Coulouris, Albert Finney, Rachel Roberts, Wendy Hiller, Colin Blakely, Michael York, Jacqueline Bisset, Lauren Bacall, Martin Balsam)

This reframing of the story's mystery by the terms of the film's production is echoed by its use of its period setting. Christie's novel – obviously inspired by the 1932 kidnapping of the baby of Charles Lindbergh, the aviator whose 1927 solo flight over the Atlantic had made him a hero – is set, like the film, in the early 1930s. Whereas Christie treats her setting as unobtrusively contemporary, however, the film emphasizes what has now become its remote historical period in a thousand ways, through costumes, hairdos, interior decor, and quaint vanished customs. The very presence of the anachronistic butler played by the iconic Shakespearean Gielgud frames the film's era as reassuringly as the repeated shots of the locomotive's belching smokestack. To the novel's original exoticism of place and class reassuringly remote from those of its middle-class target audience, the film thus adds the nostalgic framing of a remote historical period. Even the film's indirect allusions to the fatal Lindbergh kidnapping, separated from its audience by forty years and a murder conviction, become nostalgic in this context. This consistently archaeological

handling of the material broadens what might have seemed the limited narrative interest of Christie's whodunit, in which Poirot's round
of interviews with the suspects is merely a prelude to his revelation
of who killed Ratchett, by making every knickknack, every cigarette
butt, every motive and gesture, every telltale scrap of evidence potentially important not only as a clue to Ratchett's murder but as a
window on a painstakingly re-created world.

The result of this exotic, visually decorative reframing of the mystery is that the story's denouement, which Christie had compressed
into a few revelatory sentences, now sprawls to nearly half an hour
in a sequence that dissipates the elegant central concept that makes
Christie's novel a classic whodunit in favor of Poirot's comprehensive
review of the often confusing visual evidence, dozens of brief flashbacks showing clues the audience may have missed, and a longer
flashback of Ratchett's murder presumably intended to satisfy 1970s
viewers' greater appetite for violence. Despite its box-office success,
the film did not revive the formula of the classic whodunit; instead,
it inaugurated a new cycle of star-studded period whodunits, often
based on Christie's novels (*Death on the Nile,* 1978; *The Mirror Crack'd*,
1980; *Evil Under the Sun,* 1982; *Appointment with Death*, 1988), in which
cadres of stars competed for the chance to upstage Christie's high-
concept plots. In a final triumph of cultural embalming over the brain-
teasing pleasures of the great whodunit series, these films, all of
whose settings were originally contemporary to their author and their
initial reading audiences, were invariably set in an upper-class past,
a Never-Never Land that might as well have been called the Agatha
Christie period [Fig. 40].

Though these films might seem to bear out Hitchcock's criticism of
the puzzle mystery – they typically displace the intellectual concepts
(the narrator is the killer, all the suspects are in it together) with which
Golden Age writers domesticate their murderous plots in favor of a
continuous flow of eye-catching details (period trappings, exotic settings, noteworthy casting choices) that domesticate the story's threatening elements still further – many of Hitchcock's own films suggest
another approach to the mystery plot. Mystery films like *Blackmail*
(1929), *Rebecca* (1940), *Spellbound* (1945), and *Rear Window* (1954) re-
define the balance between the normal life of the detective hero and
the crimes that interrupt it by the simple expedient of making the hero
an unwilling, personally involved detective. The difference is not be-

40. *Death on the Nile:* Different stars, but the same shot – a return to the Agatha Christie period. (Simon MacCorkindale, Mia Farrow, Jack Warden, Maggie Smith, Bette Davis, Jon Finch, Olivia Hussey, George Kennedy, I. S. Johar)

tween unofficial and official detectives but between *habitual* unofficial detectives like Hercule Poirot and Nancy Drew and one-time detectives like Richard Hannay (Robert Donat), the reluctant hero of *The 39 Steps* (1935).

If the presence and power of a continuing unofficial detective push the mystery in the direction of the television sitcom, substituting a one-time unofficial detective reverses that pattern, pushing the mystery away from a domestic routine and toward melodrama and suspense. Because there is no guarantee that the hero or heroine will survive the film, the potential consequences of investigation become much more deadly. Holly Martins (Joseph Cotten) is betrayed by his oldest friend in *The Third Man* (1949). Audio technician Jack Terri (John Travolta) hears the woman he loves being killed in *Blow Out* (1981). The investigator heroes of *Mr. Arkadin* (aka *Confidential Report,* 1955), *Don't Look Now* (1973), and *The Parallax View* (1974) are killed, along with virtually the entire cast of *And Then There Were None* (1945; remade twice as *Ten Little Indians,* 1966, 1975). In the most nihilistic twist of all, the two assassins of Don Siegel's *The Killers* (1964), who also serve as investigators into the past of the man they have just murdered, are gunned down at the end of the film, leaving most of the main characters dead. Even when such films have happy endings, their resolutions are inevitably more tentative than the endings that Holmes and Poirot promised from the beginning. When the protagonists of *Klute* (1971), *Body Double* (1984), and *The Vanishing* (1993) survive the threatening criminals in their films, their survival is hard-won, because they could just as easily have been killed.[7]

Whether or not one-time detectives are killed or suffer lasting harm, the constant threat of danger gives their adventures a far less comic and optimistic tone than the adventures of Sherlock Holmes. Because the hero is often forced to investigate the case by his or her own connection to it, the investigation is marked by intimate emotional involvement rather than aloof intellectual detachment. The mystery is not a puzzle to be solved or a game to be played but a menace to the detective and his or her loved ones, and the casting of suspicion on one suspect after another calls into question the detective's previous, often long-standing relations with them all. Suspicion thus functions not as an intellectual tease for a detective who has no personal stake in which of a number of interchangeable suspects is guilty, but as an expression of paranoia about which apparent friend is really a liar, a betrayer, or a killer.

Instead of balancing the remote menace of crime against the detective's cozy domestic life, these films undermine any possibility of domestic stability by tainting the domestic sphere with criminal elements. Because the key witness in *Klute* is a threatened prostitute whose household is a savage parody of the missing suburban husband's idyllic domestic circle, the investigation of her sordid life-style turns into a searching critique of the suburban verities to which her world was first opposed. Unlike whodunits like Sayers's *Gaudy Night* (book 1935; TV film 1987), which valorize the social and intellectual snobbery of a closed collegiate circle by showing the calamitous results of its tainting by a malicious interloper, mystery stories shorn of larger-than-life continuing detectives and the domestic values they represent accommodate a much more critical view of the social establishment. Hence the unmarried, housebound photographer in *Rear Window,* becoming obsessed with a neighbor who may have killed his wife, may be rationalizing his own fears of marriage; and the rival newspaper reporters chasing down leads to the serial killer in *While the City Sleeps* (1956) are jackals willing to sacrifice anything, including the women they love, for a crack at a corner office and another few dollars a week.

Hitchcock's *Shadow of a Doubt* (1943) turns the conventions of the unofficial detective story to typically subversive ends. The story revolves around the visit of Charles Spencer Oakley (Joseph Cotten) to his sister's family in cozy Santa Rosa, California. Both his sister, Emma Newton (Patricia Collinge), and his niece and namesake, Charlotte, called "Charlie" (Teresa Wright), adore him, but the film begins to drop increasingly emphatic hints that there is something wrong with Uncle Charlie, until his niece's trip to the newspaper file in the local library reveals the truth about him: He has made his money as the "'Merry-Widow' murderer," a man who has romanced, robbed, and murdered a series of wealthy widows.

Although Charlie functions as the unofficial detective of *Shadow of a Doubt,* piecing together clues to her uncle's criminal past, Charlie's lack of Poirot's semiofficial status produces two vital differences from whodunits like *Murder on the Orient Express.* Even though the police are uncertain whether the Merry Widow murderer is Uncle Charlie or another man they are pursuing in New England, Charlie's story is not really a whodunit, since she has access to damningly conclusive evidence against her uncle that the police do not. Even before the film makes it clear that Uncle Charlie is the killer they seek, the question it poses is not "Whodunit?" but "What happened?" or "What's the matter with him?" The only character in the film to fall under suspicion of wrongdoing is Uncle Charlie; the question is simply whether those suspicions are justified, and what he has done to justify them.

The other difference is even more crucial. It is only the first half of *Shadow of a Doubt* that is a mystery story. Once Charlie confirms her suspicions about her uncle, the story shifts gears from puzzle to suspense story, as Charlie's panicky attempts to get her uncle to leave Santa Rosa reveal her struggles in coming to terms with the man the film has gone to extraordinary lengths to set up as her double. How can Charlie turn on her uncle without denying part of herself? Is her attempt to shield her mother from unpleasant publicity really an attempt to disavow her own closeness to the uncle she cannot accept any longer? How can she ever return to the sheltering safety of Santa Rosa now that Uncle Charlie has invited her to see the world as "a foul sty" and forced on her a nightmarish complicity with his guilt? Have the unwholesome secrets she has shared with him poisoned her life forever, as they would presumably poison those of the victims of incest whom her nightmarish domestic dilemma ("don't tell Mom") constantly evokes? These uncomfortable questions about the relation between the detective and the criminal, which are at the heart of *Shadow of a Doubt,* are all beside the point for Sherlock Holmes, who never needs to confront the nature of his often surprisingly intimate relations with criminals.

Forty years after Hitchcock's microscope revealed small-town America's fascination with the charismatic criminal hero it could survive only by destroying, David Lynch returned to the dark side of the suburbs with *Blue Velvet* (1986), in which Jeffrey Beaumont (Kyle MacLachlan), called home from college by his father's heart attack, discovers the evil beneath the smiling surface of idyllic Lumberton, North Carolina, where, according to a WOOD radio announcer, "people really know how much wood a woodchuck chucks." Writer-director Lynch was already well-known for two cult favorites, the surrealistic shocker *Eraserhead* (1977) and the scattershot science-fiction epic *Dune* (1984), as well as for *The Elephant Man* (1980), which used its pitiably deformed hero as a lightning-rod for Victorian hypocrisy.

If *Murder on the Orient Express* marks its director's attempt to frame a murder mystery in the most comfortably domestic terms possible by embalming its characters in exotic period detail, in the faces of well-known stars, and in a reassuringly remote historical past, *Blue Velvet* marks its director's most sustained attempt to emphasize the polarity between the domestic and threatening terms in which such stories can be framed. The film's rigorous stylistic duality established Lynch's territory once and for all as the crossroads between the hyperreal and the surreal, the intensely ordinary world and the realm of nightmare. He would return to this familiar territory in the demented road film *Wild at Heart* (1990), the Chinese boxes *Lost Highway* (1997) and *Mulholland Drive* (2001), and especially the groundbreaking television series *Twin Peaks* (1990–1). All these projects confirmed Lynch's most recognizable trademarks as an extreme visual and auditory stylization that weighted every moment of his stories with potential meaning and menace, a motivic counterpoint between florid melodrama and the apparently normal quirks of ordinary people, and the repetition of banal images or dialogue tags to a frighteningly incantatory point (as in *Blue Velvet*'s harrowing use of the Roy Orbison song "In Dreams" and its repeated, prophetic line of dialogue, "It's a strange world"). To *Murder on the Orient Express*'s use of violent death as an extraordinary event that temporarily disrupts the calm order of the everyday world and provokes a teasing mystery the detective must solve, *Blue Velvet* adds the sense of mortality as a condition that links aggressor, victim, and detective in an unholy and disturbing economy of desire. Death is everywhere in Lynch's film, not because so many people die, but because so many of them are blasted by the mortal flaws that reduce them to a kind of death-in-life.

The film begins a world away from this dark vision, with cinematographer Frederick Elmes's montage of overexposed, deeply saturated color shots designed to showcase the picture-postcard beauties of Lumberton. As Bobby Vinton's rendition of "Blue Velvet" substitutes for the diegetic sound proper to the images, Lynch cuts from a brilliant blue sky against which red roses are glowing to a fire engine passing down the street, one firefighter waving in dreamlike slow motion, to a second close-up of flowers and then to a crossing guard before settling on a neat white frame house whose owner, Tom Beaumont (Jack Harvey), is watering in the backyard with a garden hose. Everything is perfect – until an unnoticed kink in the hose keeps Mr. Beaumont from pulling it closer, and he claps his hand to his neck with a silent cry and falls to the ground. As his nerveless hand continues to clutch the hose, Lynch adds two macabre touches: a dog runs up and drinks from the fountain of water, and an impossibly close track-in to the grass reveals, courtesy of Elmes and sound designer Alan Splet, the suddenly overwhelming sights and sounds of myriad insects bustling and chomping in the alarmingly active world beneath Mr. Beaumont.

Having already undermined perfect Lumberton as an idealized world that maintains its pristine suburban image by denying the unpleasant realities that coexist within its orbit, Lynch is ready to immerse Mr. Beaumont's son, Jeffrey, in the other world that opens before him when he finds a severed ear crawling with ants in a vacant lot near his home. Taking his gruesome discovery to his neighbor, Det. John Williams (George Dickerson), he finds that although Williams refuses to discuss the ear with him, his less circumspect daughter, Sandy (Laura Dern), is happy to link it to a case involving Dorothy Vallens (Isabella Rossellini), a nightclub singer who lives on the other side of the tracks on Lumberton's notorious Lincoln Street. When Jeffrey, hungry for "knowledge and experience," hatches a plan to break into Dorothy's apartment, Sandy demurs, but Jeffrey argues that they will be protected by their spotless reputations. Dorothy's languidly erotic rendition of "Blue Velvet" in the Slow Club, where she performs as "the Blue Lady," does indeed seem to mark her as poles apart from Jeffrey and Sandy, who have gone to watch her before carrying out their plan; yet the heart of *Blue Velvet* is the relationship that develops between Jeffrey and Dorothy, a relationship that begins even as Jeffrey is watching her perform in the Slow Club. "I don't know if you're a detective or a pervert," Sandy says to Jeffrey as she drops him outside Dorothy's place at the Deep River Apartments. Jeffrey smirks: "That's for me to know and you to find out." The choices between these two alternatives are hopelessly muddled once Dorothy discovers Jeffrey in her closet [Fig. 41] – where he has overheard a phone call she took from Frank Booth (Dennis Hopper) and Don, later revealed as her kidnapped husband – forces him at knifepoint to strip, then quickly returns him to her closet when Frank arrives to torment her in ways that go far to explain her own alternately seductive and masochistic behavior toward Jeffrey. Even after Frank has left, Jeffrey's terror continues when Dorothy rejects his tenderness – and his solicitous concern for the husband and son who are shown in a photograph she keeps hidden under her sofa – and begs him to hit her.

Jeffrey's shockingly perverse sexual initiation destroys his peace of mind because it prevents him from thinking of himself as simply one of the good guys. The more completely Angelo Badalamenti's disturbing musical arrangements undermine the normal associations of the visuals (as Jeffrey is mounting the dark stairs to Dorothy's apartment for a later rendezvous, a lighthearted Bobby Vinton is reprising "Blue Velvet") or ironically intensify them (as in the heavenly choirs that repeatedly accompany Jeffrey's romantic scenes with Sandy), the more completely Jeffrey loses his sense of his own innocent identity. He cannot go to Det. Williams with his suspicions that Frank has kidnapped Dorothy's husband and son in order to make her his sex slave because he does not want to get Sandy (or himself) in trouble; he tells Sandy that his world is shattered by the very existence of people like Frank; and at the same time, though he is ever more closely to drawn to Sandy, he cannot help returning to the fascinating and pitiable Dorothy. Swearing that he wants only to help her, Jeffrey is soon seduced anyway.

Sandy and Dorothy represent opposed and incompatible aspects of Jeffrey's sexual desire. Her blond hair, soft lighting, and pastel outfits mark Sandy, who "both makes possible Jeffrey's quasi-incestuous relationship with Dorothy . . . and provides a safe alternative to it,"[8] as conventionally attractive, Jeffrey's future suburban helpmeet, whose appropriate musical accompaniment is teen ballads, the film's subdued theme music (which returns only during two scenes in which

41. *Blue Velvet:* Jeffrey (Kyle MacLachlan) about to come out of the closet at knifepoint.

she and Jeffrey are walking the streets of Lumberton together), or weirdly uplifting liturgical music. When Sandy tells Jeffrey of a dream in which a dark, loveless world was brightened by the arrival of thousands of robins bearing "this blinding light of love," her recitation is accompanied by organ music from the church whose stained-glass windows are framed in romantic soft focus behind her. Dorothy, by contrast, is associated exclusively with forbidden sexuality. She dresses entirely in black, red, or dark blue; her face, with its heavy coating of rouge and lipstick, is as fetishized as her wardrobe, especially in the extreme close-ups that repeatedly show her parted lips; her deep, mournful voice bespeaks sex as a painful ritual to be suffered, not consecrated in a church. No one would ever describe Dorothy, as Jeffrey describes Sandy, as "a neat girl" with whom it would be a pleasure to fall in love; she is rather the sex partner Jeffrey can neither acknowledge nor resist.

The price of Jeffrey's seduction becomes horrifyingly clear when Frank catches him leaving Dorothy's apartment and, in the film's most hallucinatory sequence, takes him for a joy ride with Dorothy and several more willing friends, gloating to him, "You're like me," threatening to kill him if he tries to "be a good neighbor to her," and concluding: "If you get a love letter from me, you're fucked forever!" Smearing lipstick on his own face, Frank kisses Jeffrey, gags him with the strip of blue velvet, and beats him unconscious. What makes this sequence so frightening is not only Frank's brutality but the way he persistently breaks down the psychosexual distinctions on which Jeffrey's sense of himself and his world depends. Frank, during his earlier visit to Dorothy, had bridled when she called him "Baby," insisting on being called "Daddy"; yet moments later he was telling "Mommy" that "Baby wants to fuck," conflating in himself the roles of father and son, child and adult, offspring and sex partner. In treating Jeffrey like Dorothy, Frank is attacking the even more fundamental distinction between men and women and revealing the terrifyingly unlimited aggression that stirs his sexual appetite. As he declares exultantly to his drug supplier, Ben (a bravura turn by Dean Stockwell), "I'll fuck anything that moves!" Face to face with the identifications with both Frank and Dorothy that have been forced on him, Jeffrey spirals down into chaos. The moral side of Jeffrey's confusion surfaces when he goes to report his evidence of Frank's drug murders to Det. Williams and recognizes the officer's partner, Det. Tom Gordon (Fred Pickler), as Frank's accomplice. Can Jeffrey trust Williams himself, who has always been studiously noncommittal in his reactions, and who wears a holstered gun even around his home? The complementary perceptual side of Jeffrey's confusion is illustrated at key points in the film by the recurrent visual image of a flickering candle (associated with Frank's tag line, "Now it's night"), and the roaring sound associated first with the insects under Mr. Beaumont's back and later with Don Vallens's severed ear.

The ultimate sign of this chaos, and the sequence in which all the different aspects of Jeffrey's life he has struggled to keep separate collapse into one another, comes when Jeffrey and Sandy leave a party at a friend's house and realize they are being followed by another car. The driver who has been sounding his horn and ramming Jeffrey's convertible is not, however, Frank but Mike (Ken Stovitz), Sandy's aggrieved boyfriend, who simply wants to beat Jeffrey up for stealing his girl. The collision between Frank's monstrous evil and Mike's small-town intrigue becomes complete when Mike catches sight of Dorothy stumbling nude from around the corner of Jeffrey's house and says in stupefaction, "Is that your mother?" Driving off in confusion, he leaves

Jeffrey and Sandy to deal with Dorothy, who throws herself into Jeffrey's arms and calls out to him in despair as "my secret love." The power of this sequence depends not only on its horrifyingly funny sense of anticlimax – Jeffrey is in danger not of being unmanned and killed by a dangerous psychotic, but only of being punched out by a high-school rival, and the sequence ends with Sandy, stung by the revelation of Jeffrey's relationship with Dorothy, slapping Jeffrey's face – but on its vertiginous sense of reframing. It is reassuring to find that Jeffrey is not in real danger, but it would have been reassuring in its own way to have the car chase framed by Jeffrey's knowledge of Frank and the generic expectations that knowledge would arouse. What is far more disturbing is the presence of blankly contradictory contextual frames that forestall the audience's wish to know how they are to interpret each threat and revelation.

The film's climactic scene, in which Jeffrey returns to Dorothy's apartment to find both her husband and Frank's partner-in-crime, Det. Gordon, dead moments before Frank arrives on the scene, forces Jeffrey to kill Frank in self-defense, completing his descent from Lumberton's overidealized suburban utopia to the acceptance of his own mortality, his ability to kill the man who was about to kill him. Having accepted his own dark side by killing Frank and acknowledging to Sandy his desire for Dorothy, Jeffrey is ready for the impossibly happy ending the film provides. A brightly lit scene back at the Beaumonts' house shows Tom Beaumont, miraculously recovered, barbecuing in the backyard with Det. Williams as their wives chat in the living room and Jeffrey and Sandy scrutinize a robin, presumably a fulfillment of Sandy's prophetic dream of light and love, perched on the kitchen window. But the robin's meal, a large insect still protruding from its mouth, is a reminder that even the most dreamlike landscapes are still stippled with ugliness and death. This reminder is complemented by the closing montage that complements its opening framing sequence: another slow-motion shot of the passing fire engine, another close-up of red roses against a blue sky, and finally a slow-motion shot of Dorothy's freed son, Donny, never before seen in the film, running playfully to his mother as her mournful voice is heard singing the closing line to the title song: "And I still can see blue velvet through my tears." Just as Jeffrey's attempt to keep his position as amateur sleuth distinct from the part of him that responded to the other side of the tracks leads inevitably to his acknowledgment of the dark desires he shared with Frank Booth, the film ends by disclosing that the dark secret at the heart of Dorothy's Deep River apartment is a woman moved by courage, nobility, and maternal love.

The different terms in which they frame their mysteries put *Blue Velvet* worlds apart from *Murder on the Orient Express*. Lumet's film maintains a strict opposition between detective and criminals; Lynch's everywhere announces their interpenetration. Lumet emphasizes specific details of mise-en-scène over Christie's high concept; Lynch is so interested in the thematic import of his dualities that he neglects the most elementary plot points. He never explains, for example, why Jeffrey feels drawn to return to the climactic scene in Dorothy's absence, why the criminals had brought her kidnapped husband back, how Don Vallens and Gordon had gotten killed, how Dorothy was able to escape to appear at the Beaumonts' house, or why Frank returned in disguise to the apartment. More generally, Lynch offers no explanation for Frank's sexual pathology, and none for Dorothy's other than her corruption by Frank's demands, or the bug-eating robin's implication that Frank's brand of sexual terrorism is as natural as Jeffrey's tenderness. *Murder on the Orient Express* is driven by the visual possibilities of clues to the characters' cultural status, *Blue Velvet* by a nightmare logic uninterested in clues except as triggers of nightmare associations [Fig. 42].

Still, these films are linked by more than their detective figures, because the nature of detection inevitably reveals the intimacy between transgressors and avengers. Since *Blue Velvet* gives Jeffrey, like *Shadow of a Doubt*'s young Charlie Newton, an evil double he can neither acknowledge nor deny but only destroy, the film raises the question of whether Jeffrey's psychosexual nightmare, like Charlie's, has been a phenomenally aberrant experience or simply a parable for the normal rite of passage to sexual maturity. When Charlie is reassured by Jack Graham (Macdonald Carey), the police-detective-turned-suitor who is Charlie's safe alternative to Uncle Charlie, in the film's celebrated last line – that the world is "not quite as bad as that, but sometimes it needs a lot of watching. It seems to go crazy every now and then, like your Uncle Charlie" – is he suggesting that Uncle Charlie is a freak of nature, a historical aberration like the contemporaneous Adolf Hitler, or as natural a part of the order of things as Charlie and Graham? It is a deeply subversive question for both the adult Charlie and the audience.

42. *Blue Velvet:* The nightmare logic behind the rape of Dorothy (Isabella Rossellini) by Frank (Dennis Hopper).

Even *Murder on the Orient Express* ends by revealing the links between detectives and criminals. Ratchett, the threatened victim who first solicits Poirot's help, is really a criminal himself. The innocent suspects from whom Poirot must pick the criminal are all guilty. Their shared guilt impeaches that order as criminal throughout. The detective deputized to identify the criminal for the absent authorities instead agrees to let them go, since the friend who authorized his investigation agrees with him that the victim, not the killers, is the true criminal. Even the film's concluding tableau, a ritual series of toasts among the passengers who have succeeded in killing Ratchett, celebrates homicide rather than detection as the therapeutic restorer of the social order thrown into chaos by the kidnapping of Daisy Armstrong. Whether as spectacularly as *Blue Velvet* or as unobtrusively as *Murder on the Orient Express,* the unofficial detective film, however resolutely it separates the detective from the criminal, cannot help showing how each lives in the other.

9

Chinatown and the Private-Eye Film

I n his landmark 1944 essay "The Simple Art of Murder," Raymond
Chandler made no secret of his impatience with Golden Age detective stories. He dismissed as hopelessly farfetched, despite its
similarity to the screenplay he coauthored for that year's *Double Indemnity,* a tale by Freeman Wills Crofts in which "a murderer by the
aid of makeup, split second timing, and some very sweet evasive action, impersonates the man he has just killed and thereby gets him
alive and distant from the place of the crime." And the solution to
Agatha Christie's *Murder on the Orient Express,* he concluded, was "the
type guaranteed to knock the keenest mind for a loop. Only a halfwit
could guess it."[1]

Certainly the hard-boiled story Chandler advocated and practiced,
with its rough-and-tumble maze of tough "janes," tougher private eyes,
wholesale violence, and official corruption, seems poles apart from
the orderly world of Hercule Poirot Chandler satirized in his semiparo-
distic story "Pearls Are a Nuisance" (1939) and throughout the series
of novels beginning with *The Big Sleep* (1939) that upend their conventions of the suspects' class-bound isolation from the outside world
and the detective's interrogations as a civilized game. The hard-boiled
formula, like its near-contemporaries jazz and musical theater, is a peculiarly American invention, and one linked especially closely to the
California landscapes of its two best-known practitioners, Chandler
and his progenitor, Dashiell Hammett.

California had been a magical site for American dreams ever since
the days of Spanish explorers' search for the mythical land of El Do-
rado – a search that might have seemed, in this land of mild weather

and bountiful natural resources, to come closer to success than any-place else on earth. The rush of prospectors sparked by the discovery of gold in 1848 added a new layer to the California legend. Even travelers disappointed in their search for gold stayed to enjoy the region's agricultural opportunities, and as early as 1850 California was admitted to statehood, an isolated western outpost of U.S. sovereignty surrounded for years afterward by nonstate territories. The construction of the first transcontinental railroad in the 1860s, a project financed largely with eastern capital but built by immigrant laborers, established at a stroke the power of the state's agricultural exports, its rich and unstable mixture of Latino, Chinese, European, and Native American inhabitants, and the growing importance of industrial capital – in this case, the wealth of the Union Pacific – in its politics. The infant movie studios that settled in Hollywood beginning in 1911, drawn by cheap labor, varied outdoor locations, reliable weather, and the proximity of nearby Mexico as a refuge from legal actions, confirmed the status of California as the nation's dream factory: a modern utopia of glamour, wealth, ambition, and ease that hid beneath its surface the cynicism and disillusionment of every disappointed dreamer and every dream merchant who knew what hard work it was to manufacture the myth of the California Eden.

The California landscape was a natural setting for a new kind of detective story, a kind that owed as much to the strenuous dime-novel action of western heroes like Buffalo Bill as to the more sedate powers of reasoning displayed by amateur detectives from Sherlock Holmes to Hercule Poirot. Although the state was proudly conscious of its vanguard role as the westernmost outpost of American culture, even its largest cities retained much of the flavor of frontier towns, in which institutional justice often seemed a long way off, and strong men in the role of urban cowboys took up arms to right wrongs the justice system could not, or would not, touch.

For all his proclivity to violence, the California shamus is most at home in the contemporary frontier of the big-city landscape. Even audiences who have seen only a handful or private-eye films are familiar with the iconography of the California city immortalized in the 1940s mise-en-scène of *The Maltese Falcon* (1941), *Murder, My Sweet* (1944), and *The Big Sleep* (1946): the dark streets slick with rain, the alleys and doorways hiding small-time hoodlums, the contrastingly overdecorated homes of the hero's nouveau-riche clients, the eternal nighttime skies, and the noirish high-contrast lighting that throws every threat into sharp relief. The private eye's office is invariably located on the second floor of an office building, presumably for the sake of an evocative view from windows that frame the cityscape as both picturesque and menacing.

The very existence of the private eye, the urban cowboy who has pushed as far west as the Pacific will allow, is a double scandal to the social order California idealized. A true Eden would have no need of the police, since no one in Paradise would ever commit a crime; but even in a fallen world, there would be no work for hard-boiled detectives if the police did their job properly. Sometimes the police are overwhelmed by a powerful ring of professional criminals, as in *Heat* (1995); sometimes their bureaucratic routines are too unimaginative to allow them to keep up with an unusually resourceful criminal, as in *The Usual Suspects* (1995); but more often they are simply incompetent or hamstrung by political or personal corruption that makes them unwilling to do their job. It is only the incompetence and corruption of the police that keep the private eye in business.

The hard-boiled dick's typical client – often wealthy, and always wealthier than the proletarian hero who wears his working-class membership like a badge of honor – hires the hero to recover either an irreplaceable artifact redolent of magical powers, or a missing person, or, as in *Murder, My Sweet* and *Out of the Past* (1947), both at once. Even though the police cannot be brought into the case or are uninterested, the client's world, which has been thrown into turmoil by the absence of something uniquely precious, will be restored to equilibrium by its return. Almost as soon as the hero takes the case, however, he finds that these assumptions are wrong because the case for which he has been hired is fictitious, misleading, or only a small part of a much more labyrinthine case that ineluctably leads to murder. The client, who originally described the police as too indiscreet or indifferent to call in, is often correct; but the client's deceptiveness about his or her motives, the stakes of the mystery, or the danger involved means that the client cannot be trusted either. The private eye is therefore left in the perilous position of an independent contractor whose deepest loyalty is not to the client but to the case. Hence the obligatory scene halfway through *The Big Sleep* in which Vivian Sternwood Rutledge (Lauren Bacall) tries to buy Philip Marlowe off the case, telling him that he's done the job for which he was hired, only to have him respond that he won't quit until he's uncovered every last criminal secret, including her own. *Kiss Me Deadly* (1955) pushes this professional dedication to a frightening extreme, as Mike Hammer (Ralph

Meeker), working without any client and motivated as much by greed as by vengeance, defies the confiscation of his gun and his license, repeated attempts on his life, and the scorn of his secretary, Velda (Maxine Cooper), in an ultimately futile pursuit of what Velda witheringly calls "the Great Whatsit."

The deceptive nature of the private eye's caseload is an apt indication of the treacherous nature of his world, a world in which criminals are neither marginal, socially deviant monsters like Frank Booth in *Blue Velvet* (1986), nor suavely deceptive private individuals like the killers in Agatha Christie, but professional criminals or their unwilling conspirators: criminals who have the force of money and powerful institutions (criminal gangs, corrupt city governments, even the police force) behind their transgressions. What seemed at first a conflict between good guys and bad guys simply conceals a deeper conflict among the good guys – the private eye, his client, the police force, the local government, the justice system – who are fighting instead of supporting each other. Hence private-eye films tend to be sharply critical of the society they represent, a society whose pretenses to civilization are unmasked not only by the criminal intrigues that make up the hero's daily work, but by the private eye's running conflicts with his supposed allies. Even if the case ends with a roundup (or, more often, a body count) of killers and gangleaders, the original social evils – the inequalities aggravated by unbridled capitalism, the dependence of developers on crooked deals, the government's abuse of power – are only contained, never resolved. Greed and lust remain, waiting to erupt again as soon as the final credits have rolled. A private eye's work is never done.

If the hard-boiled story's resulting attitude toward justice, as first developed in *Black Mask* and other American pulp magazines of the 1920s and 1930s, is cynical, the glamorous veneer of the California settings and the heroic figure of the private eye nonetheless lend the formula strong elements of masculine romance epitomized in Raymond Chandler's famous description of the private eye in "The Simple Art of Murder" as a man

> who is not himself mean, who is neither tarnished nor afraid. . . . He must be a complete man and a common man and yet an unusual man. He must be, to use a rather weathered phrase, a man of honor, by instinct, by inevitability, without thought of it, and certainly without saying it. He must be the best man in his world and a good enough man for any world. . . . He has a range of awareness that startles you, but it belongs to him by right, because it belongs to the world he lives in.[2]

Chandler's idealistic evocation of the private eye makes it clear that he embodies all the contradictions of California urban culture. Although his job sets him against the official powers of his world, he represents all that is best in that world. He is a free-lance warrior, a man of honor whose sexual morality is flexible and whose mastery of violence is one of his most formidable weapons. His incessant wisecracking is both a guarantee of his disempowered status and a means of asserting what limited individual power he can, a mark of the personal charisma that is his primary defense against the epidemic institutional corruption he faces. He is, in short, that paradoxical figure, the perfect commoner, the man of his culture who becomes a hero because he so completely expresses the contradictions of that culture.

Two qualities of the private eye are especially paradoxical: his professionalism and his masculinity. The private eye is a working stiff whose attachment to his job is obsessive, even though he is often criticized for his lack of loyalty to his employers; but private eyes, though they seem barely to survive from job to unprofitable job, are luckier in their employment than police officers because they have the luxury of independence – they answer to no one but a succession of clients they can tell off and threaten to quit at will, instead of being a cog in a machine that is itself helpless or corrupt. Their films nearly always glamorize their cowboy independence, even when they present private eyes who are estranged from their wives (*Harper,* 1966; *Night Moves,* 1975), aging and ailing (*The Late Show,* 1977), psychotic (*Kiss Me Deadly*), sadly ineffectual (*The Conversation,* 1974), disconnected from their surroundings (*The Long Goodbye,* 1973), or utterly damned (*Angel Heart,* 1987). Since private eyes often, in their pursuit of the truth, break both the law they are trying to uphold and their promises to the client who is paying them, their success amounts to a critique of institutional law and the nature of employment under capitalism. At the same time, the private eye, for all his up-to-the-minute realism and violence Chandler praises, is a more old-fashioned figure than either the gifted amateur detective or the bone-weary cop. Often his disinterested professionalism makes him an anachronistic knight-errant who slays modern dragons on behalf of damsels seldom worth rescuing. If Humphrey Bogart's Sam Spade seems perfectly attuned to the world of treacherous criminals in double-crossing pursuit of the Maltese Falcon, Bogart's Marlowe, in *The Big Sleep,* seems far too good for his world, virtually the only man of integrity in a landscape teem-

ing with gamblers, blackmailers, pornographers, and their equally de-
generate victims whose families have clawed their way up the slopes
of Los Angeles' social elite. A generation later, *The Long Goodbye* goes
still further in presenting the unlikely casting choice of Elliot Gould
as Marlowe caught in a time warp, a survivor from the forties whose
hangdog alienation from his 1970s orbit is by turns outrageously unrealistic, satiric, and oddly touching in its nostalgia. Abandoned by his
persnickety cat and betrayed by both his client and the old friend who
dropped him into the case, Gould's Marlowe, who spends his days going through the motions of a job he does not want to do and does not
seem to be very good at, is a man with nothing but his work to keep
him going.

The popular image of the private eye has less to do with his idealized, often obsessive professionalism, however, than with his masculinity. Far more than films about police detectives or amateur detectives, hard-boiled films regard detective work as a test of what Frank
Krutnik calls the private eye's "self-sufficient phallic potency."[3] This
convention is so deeply ingrained in private-eye films that it is hard to
appreciate how arbitrary and strange it is. Since private eyes are hired
to solve mysteries by gathering information – tasks that are accomplished by most real-life private detectives primarily over telephones
and computer modems – there is no reason to assume that testoster-
one ought to be a prerequisite for the job. The recent proliferation of
novels about female private eyes (Marcia Muller's Sharon McCone,
Sue Grafton's Kinsey Millhone, Sara Paretsky's V. I. Warshawski, et al.)
suggests that women can do the job as well as men; but Hollywood
has never accepted this argument because a search by computer or
phone for a missing person or object would be so visually and morally
dull. In hard-boiled movies, the missing objects or people the detective is asked to recover are never simply missing; they always turn out
to be involved in a criminal plot. Standing up to the criminal conspirators requires a hero who is undeterred by violence, capable of using
his fists and guns in the requisite action scenes, untrammeled by inconvenient personal attachments that might slow him down or cloud
his judgment, and obsessively devoted to the job at hand – in short,
a man. In *V. I. Warshawski* (1991), the only important film to date about
a female private eye, Kathleen Turner, as the heroine, spends most
of her time alternately acting like a stereotypical male – chasing suspects, shooting at them, mouthing off at them, and getting beaten up
by them – and assuring the audience that she's really a woman by

showing maternal devotion to her client, a teenaged girl, and flashing her legs.

The hard-boiled film's celebration of masculinity achieves an exceptional concentration in the archetypal *The Maltese Falcon* (1941), already the third film version of Dashiell Hammett's novel (following *The Maltese Falcon* [aka *Dangerous Female*], 1931, and *Satan Met a Lady*, 1936). Hired to find his client's missing sister, Sam Spade (Humphrey Bogart) avenges as well the death of his partner, Miles Archer (Jerome Cowan), who grabbed the case from him only to be decoyed into a dark alley and shot. The story's tangled series of lies and betrayals revolve around the characters' highly competitive search for the legendary Maltese Falcon, a jeweled statue that has so often been stolen from its rightful owners over the past four centuries that title to the storied treasure can evidently be established only by possession. In the end, the statue over whose possession Archer and two others were murdered turns out to be a fake, its legendary association with the Holy Grail a bitterly ironic sign of the corruption of the search for truth and value in contemporary San Francisco. Although the defeated villains seem philosophically resigned to resuming their years-long search for the real falcon, the talisman's origin as a tribute to Charles V from the Knights Templars after their sack of Malta suggests that this magical object was hopelessly corrupted by the brutality of armed conquest from the moment of its creation.

Lacking any transcendent value to inspire his search, Spade is left with only his personal code to distinguish himself from the criminals with whom the search has allied him. Spade's treacherous client Brigid O'Shaughnessy (Mary Astor) is a femme fatale who uses her wiles to lure men to their destruction, and each of the other men seeking the falcon – gardenia-scented Joel Cairo (Peter Lorre), jovially paternal Kasper Gutman (Sydney Greenstreet), and ludicrously incompetent gunsel Wilmer Cook (Elisha Cook Jr.) – is clearly marked as homosexual. It is Spade's status as nonfemale and nongay that rescues him from full complicity in the film's villainous conspiracy. Spade is admirably, heroically masculine *because* he is not female or homosexual; and in the zero-sum economy of hard-boiled movies, the vindication of Spade's sexual prowess requires that all other sexual possibilities be impeached. Hence the private eye's manliness must constantly be confirmed through conflicts with asexual or bisexual characters – or, far more often, with female or gay male characters – whom the film leaves demystified, disempowered, defeated, and dehumanized.[4]

43. *Devil in a Blue Dress:* This shot is just about all that remains of the novel's interracial romance. (Denzel Washington, Jennifer Beals)

This defense of masculinity places debates about sex and power at the heart of all but a handful of hard-boiled films. It is true, of course, that *The Thin Man* (1934) combines a hard-boiled mystery with an intermittently lightsome celebration of the cockeyed domestic life of private eye Nick Charles (William Powell) and his wife, Nora (Myrna Loy). More recently, *Devil in a Blue Dress* (1995), shorn of the interracial romance that had capped Walter Mosley's 1990 novel [Fig. 43], uses race to displace sex as the matrix of the film's conflicts, focusing almost exclusively on the survival of Ezekiel "Easy" Rawlins (Denzel Washington), the unemployed aircraft worker who serves as the film's reluctant hero. In the white man's world he finds himself investigating, cops and crooks alike can beat him half to death without a reason, and asserting his identity requires a perilous tightrope dance between the Uncle Tom subservience white men demand and the reflexive brutality of his old friend Mouse (Don Cheadle), whose propensity for violence becomes disturbingly necessary to Easy's success [Fig. 44]. But most private-eye films, like films noirs and erotic thrillers, are anatomies of masculinity.

Since the hero's masculinity is always reaffirmed at the cost of marginalizing or annulling other sexual possibilities, the private eye's investigation typically focuses on discrediting seductive femmes fatales like Brigid O'Shaughnessy, Velma Valento (in *Murder, My Sweet*), or the Sternwood sisters (in *The Big Sleep*). Sometimes the hero's love–hate relationship with women is dramatized by the presence of both good and bad heroines, like the double heroines of *Murder, My Sweet* and *Out of the Past;* more often, his ambivalence is simply projected onto a single heroine, whose ambiguity expresses both his desire to possess her and his fear of the power her sexuality gives her. The price of resolving the hero's ambivalence is the heroine's demystification, and often her destruction as well. Not even death can protect an enigmatic female from the private eye's continued unsparing exposure, as Philip Marlowe shows in *Lady in the Lake* (1947) in his continuing inquiries about the drowned Muriel Chess, and Mike Hammer shows in *Kiss Me Deadly* in his determination to follow the murdered Christina Bailey's injunction to "remember me," even to violating her corpse after death by retrieving a key she had swallowed.

Although the private eye's aggressive masculinity, shored up by his discrediting of alternative sexualities, becomes his most distinctive trait in later hard-boiled films – turning into a running joke as early as the endless parade of willing women in *The Big Sleep* – it also becomes, especially in the wave of revisionist hard-boiled films that follow the women's-liberation movement of the early 1970s, the subject of a searching critique. In these ironic reconsiderations of masculine heroism, the male habits that allow a private eye to succeed at his work – professionalism and abstract idealism; the kind of dualistic moral thinking that categorizes suspects, solves cases, and confirms the hero's embattled masculinity through zero-sum contrasts; the violent skills that allow the hard-boiled hero to hold his own in a hostile world; and the freedom to follow a case wherever it leads – turn out to make him unfit for anything else. *Kiss Me Deadly,* appearing fifteen years before the flood of revisionist hard-boiled films, begins its prophetic critique in the opening scene, as Christina (Cloris Leachman), the fleeing hitchhiker who Mike Hammer (Ralph Meeker) has picked up, recovers from her terror long enough to dismiss him as just one more example of "Man, wonderful Man," incapable of loving anything but himself and his sports car. The film goes on to suggest that Ham-

44. *Devil in a Blue Dress:* Easy (Denzel Washington, right) is forced to depend on his volatile friend Mouse (Don Cheadle).

mer's expertise as "a bedroom dick" and his sadistic propensity for violence both stem from his neurotic contempt for the feminized culture represented by the film's constant references to ballet, opera, classical music, and modern art.[5] *Harper* makes the inability of Lew Harper (Paul Newman) to commit himself to his wife (a character absent from *The Moving Target*, the 1949 Ross Macdonald novel on which the film was based) into one of its most important themes. By the time of *Night Moves*, it seems inevitable that no film would burden a private eye like Harry Moseby (Gene Hackman) with a wife if it did not plan to make an issue of his ruined marriage.

It was at the height of this highly critical reconsideration of the private eye's authority and potency that Roman Polanski's *Chinatown* was released in 1974. The film's Oscar-winning screenplay, credited to legendary script doctor Robert Towne, looks back nostalgically, as John Cawelti noted not long after it appeared,[6] to the glory days of the private eye in 1937, the year in which its story is set, at the same time it presents a penetrating critique of the hard-boiled hero and the values he represents. The vehicle for this ambivalent critique is pastiche: The film is a catalog of both private-eye and historical-period clichés whose meanings are renewed and often inverted by their ironic handling. Both *Chinatown*'s bumptious hero, J. J. ("call me Jake") Gittes (Jack Nicholson), and the case he gets swept up in are defined by their echoes of the past.

As even its title ends up indicating, however, *Chinatown*, for all its nostalgic invocation of a double past – the formative years of the City of Los Angeles and the celluloid heritage of the California shamus – is an exceptionally bleak film, a record of unrelieved failure. Despite his pertinacity, his detective skills, and his unexpected idealism, Gittes does not realize the monstrous nature of the crime he is investigating until it is too late to stop its corruption from spreading still further. He can neither persuade the police to arrest the killer he unmasks nor save the life of the heroine he has come to love. *Chinatown* is much more than an ironic valentine to the hard-boiled detective of the thirties; though it is patterned by a series of reversals, deceptions, and betrayals, its deeper structure of revelations, the variety of roles in which it casts the hero and heroine, and its intricate mixture of tones make it the most complete detective film of all. Yet the most urgent question the film poses about Gittes is why this hard-boiled dick, who seems to wear so lightly the mantle of so many Hollywood private eyes before him, is doomed to failure.

The film's balance of celebration and critique of the private eye begins in its opening scene, after its black-and-white art-deco credits, backed by Jerry Goldsmith's haunting trumpet melody. The teasing possibility that the whole film will be shot in black-and-white continues in its opening shot, a riffle through a series of black-and-white still photographs of something Bogart never would have been shown looking at: a man and a woman having sex. Gittes is presenting them to Curly (Burt Young), his latest client, a weeping skipjack who suspected all too accurately that his wife had been cheating on him.

Gittes's next client, identifying herself as Evelyn Mulwray (Diane Ladd), wants to hire Gittes to follow her husband, who she says is involved with another woman. After token protest Gittes agrees and follows Hollis Mulwray (Darrell Zwerling), the Chief Engineer of the Los Angeles Department of Water and Power, through a dazzlingly pictorial array of locations, from the hot, spacious interior of the county courthouse, where Mulwray insists that a dam that drought-stricken local farmers claim is necessary to their livelihood is doomed to collapse; to a dry riverbed where Mulwray waits for hours until the night brings a torrent of water through the spillway; to Echo Park, where

Gittes photographs Mulwray rowing with a mysterious young woman; to the Almacondo Apartments, where he meets the young woman again. The one place Mulwray never leads Gittes is his home, for reasons that will soon become obvious.

Throughout these dreamlike opening sequences, the range of locations could not be further from the mean streets of Chandler's Los Angeles. Cinematographer John A. Alonzo's brilliant outdoor skies and low horizon lines create dazzlingly picturesque vistas virtually unique in hard-boiled films. The handsome, airless interiors designed by Richard Sylbert seem to recede forever into deep space in widescreen framings that undercut the customary visual dialectic between exterior and interior space, or more generally between nature and culture, so vital in different ways to *Fury* (1936), *The Godfather* (1972), *Double Indemnity* (1944), *Basic Instinct* (1992), and *Blue Velvet* (1986). The absence of the ubiquitous sepia/gold lighting increasingly used to shoot historical dramas gives the film's vistas a fresh, contemporary look despite the careful period costumes Gittes wears and the automobiles he passes on the street; and the pacing of these early scenes, in which Gittes intently watches Mulwray sitting oblivious and equally still in the distance, is so deliberate that they become hypnotic. The picture-postcard mise-en-scène presents southern California at its most seductive, with only a few reminders that *Chinatown* is a private-eye film: the class struggles portended by the farmers' outrage at Mulwray's refusal to build a dam that would ensure irrigation for their crops, the hints of a political establishment polluted by big money, Gittes's crassly astringent urban sensibility.

At the same time, the slow pace of these scenes and their lack of action serve as a reminder that what Gittes is doing is nothing but *watching,* harking back to the prehistory of the private eye, when detectives were expected to be skilled observers rather than men of violence [Fig. 45]. These early sequences, in which Mulwray seems to be doing nothing but *being watched,* seem to fit Laura Mulvey's proposition that cinema is organized around male voyeurism and fetishism as neatly as the corresponding sequences in Hitchcock's *Vertigo* (1958) in which Scottie Ferguson (James Stewart) watches Madeleine Elster (Kim Novak).[7] Both men, bewildered by the apparent lack of purpose behind their quarry's activities, become fascinated with the possibility of discovering or constructing such a purpose, and the obsessive quality of this fascination is conveyed in both films by the surreal beauty of the widescreen California landscapes to which the watchers seem indiffer-

45. *Chinatown:* A hero (Jack Nicholson) who does nothing but watch.

ent. If Gittes is following a man rather than a woman, it is a man whose lack of masculinity, already foreshadowed by his effeminate bowties, his self-effacing manner, and his mildly ineffectual arguments against the new dam, will become steadily more apparent as the film proceeds, apparently confirming Gittes's own manliness through the private eye's formulaic algebra of contrast.

What is most out of place amid the ethereal beauty of the California locations in these opening sequences is the earthy sensibility of Gittes, who seems more realistically drawn than Chandler's twentieth-century knights because he cracks dirty jokes, acknowledges without shame that the mainstay of his business is sordid divorce work, and seems, despite the oleaginous assurance of his glad-handing professional manner and the bravado of his flashy dress outfits, a parvenu little removed from his dim "associates" Duffy (Bruce Glover) and Lawrence Walsh (Joe Mantell), or even proletarian clients like Curly. Gittes, the film seems to suggest, is no chivalric anachronism like Philip Marlowe; he is the real thing, a working stiff whose work happens to take him to hotel bedrooms.

46. *Chinatown:* The glacial Evelyn Mulwray (Faye Dunaway) as the hero first sees her.

No sooner, however, has the film replaced the normal visual duality between nature and culture with a thematic duality between its dream-like landscape and its down-to-earth hero than it begins to complicate it. Rumors about Mulwray's scandalous affair, leaked to the newspapers, bring Gittes an icily menacing visit from the real Evelyn Mulwray (Faye Dunaway) [Fig. 46], which forces him to acknowledge that he has not only, in classic private-eye form, been decoyed into taking the wrong case, but has taken it for the wrong client, since the client on whose behalf he followed Mulwray was obviously not his wife. Gittes's mistake not only starts his relationship with Evelyn Mulwray off on the wrong foot but forecasts his deeper failures to come, after her husband's drowned body is pulled from the spillway Gittes had watched him visit.

Once Gittes and Mrs. Mulwray tacitly agree to support each other's stories about her having hired him to follow her husband, the plot seems settled in a familiar groove: a dead husband, an alluring widow, a hard-boiled outsider on the make. When Gittes retraces Mulwray's steps by returning to the spillway that night, the signature scene that follows adds the one ingredient that has so far been missing from the film's hard-boiled stew: onscreen violence. After Gittes is nearly drowned in the unexpectedly torrential runoff, his retreat is interrupted by crooked ex–Ventura County sheriff Claude Mulvihill (Roy Jenson) and Mulvihill's little white-suited companion, identified in the film's credits only as "Man with Knife." As Mulvihill beats and then holds Gittes up, his sidekick takes out a switchblade knife, accuses Gittes of being nosy, and then unhesitatingly slits his nose.

This scene confirms the film's hard-boiled credentials, reminding viewers that despite its leisurely opening it is still a story in which criminal corruption will be figured as violent action. In addition, it connects Gittes to a Hollywood tradition of physically suffering private eyes. Philip Marlowe, who began life in Chandler's *The Big Sleep* by eyeing a stained-glass window over the door of the Sternwood mansion showing a naked woman tied to a tree and rescued by a knight, has to be rescued from bondage himself by the hard-bitten dame for whom he is looking. Other screen Marlowes get shot up with dope (*Murder, My Sweet*), slugged and forced off the road (*Lady in the Lake*), or run down by cars (*The Long Goodbye*). Mike Hammer, widely regarded as the toughest private eye of all, begins *Kiss Me Deadly* by being pulled from his car, beaten, and put back in the car to get sent over a cliff; miraculously surviving the fire that kills his passenger, he is available to be beaten again, tied to a bed, and drugged in a later scene before getting shot in the film's incendiary climax. Jeff Bailey (Robert Mitchum), one of the few Hollywood private eyes to avoid serious injury during his film, ends *Out of the Past* shot dead by the femme fatale he thought he could outwit. The ritual torturing of the private eye, of course, has the effect of giving him a personal stake in his case, justifying in advance any extralegal actions he might take in the name of

47. *Chinatown:* The disfigured nose of Gittes (Jack Nicholson) marks his vulnerability and rationalizes his suspicions of treacherous women.

personal revenge; but it also confirms his status as a former or potential victim whose heroic status is hard-won and liable to be revoked, particularly when he falls into the clutches of a treacherous woman [Fig. 47].

In addition, the nose slitting in *Chinatown* is so sudden, disproportionate, and graphic that it marks a disturbingly absolute contrast with the serene California landscape through which Gittes has been moving. The abrupt outburst of violence is Gittes's first glimpse of the nightmare world lurking beneath the painterly surface of *Chinatown*'s widescreen visuals. In the most shocking touch of all, the character who slits the hero's nose is played by the film's director, Roman Polanski, who brings to it a dark history of his own. Born in Poland, Polanski was eight years old when his parents were forced into the concentration camp where his mother soon died. Escaping from Cracow's Jewish ghetto, he wandered the wartime countryside seeking refuge with a series of Catholic families. Although he survived to be reunited with his father when his camp was liberated, he never forgot the episode in which German soldiers pretended to use him for target practice.

Throughout Polanski's early films, a deadpan sense of absurdity is linked to unbridled terror in the manner of Jerzy Kosinski's Holocaust novel *The Painted Bird.* A few years after Polanski's award-winning surrealistic short *Two Men and a Wardrobe (Dwaj ludzie z szafa,* 1958) brought him to international notice, his first feature, *Knife in the Water (Nóz w wodzie,* 1962), established a tone of lowering, often blackly comic menace he broadened in both Britain (*Repulsion,* 1965; *Cul-de-Sac,* 1966; *Macbeth,* 1971) and the United States (*The Fearless Vampire Killers,* 1967; *Rosemary's Baby,* 1968). His acknowledged specialty was brooding tone poems that seemed to translate Poe's unity of effect into cinematic terms. Already his literal transcription of *Macbeth,* which treated Shakespeare's supernatural horrors as metaphors for the normal transfer of power, had confirmed his reputation for onscreen violence. Yet Polanski, as later films from *The Tenant* (1976) to *The Ninth Gate* (1999) would confirm, was more often a poet of anomie who preferred to keep violence, as in *Rosemary's Baby,* largely offscreen, reserving it for moments in which it expressed and released, for example, the pent-up psychological tension of the fearfully repressed heroine of *Repulsion.* It is all the more gruesome and ironic, therefore, that here, in his first film following the ritual murder of his actress wife, Sharon Tate (the star of *The Fearless Vampire Killers*), by Charles Manson's deranged crime family, he casts himself not as the victim of senseless violence but as its perpetrator, marking a confusion between villains and victims at the heart of his distinctive contribution to the private-eye genre.

The director's attack on his star, the first extended nighttime sequence in the film, marks a pivotal point in the film's visual design as well. Although the events thus far have taken place over at least three days, they have been shot as if over a single extended afternoon interrupted only by Mulwray and Gittes's nocturnal vigil at the spillway. Similarly, the two days that remain in the story's time scheme will be compressed, after Gittes's lunch the following day with Evelyn's father, Noah Cross (John Huston), into a single endless night, as exterior skies will gradually darken, horizon lines will rise, color palettes will shade to oppressive monochromes (especially during Gittes's visit to an orange grove), and the spectacular interior depth characteristic of the film's early scenes will shrink as claustrophobic interior spaces (most memorably in the tightly framed interiors at the house of Evelyn's late impersonator, Ida Sessions) close in around the hero.

This sense of creeping enclosure is emphasized in several ways. When Gittes returns to the Department of Water and Power to accuse Mulwray's deputy, Russ Yelburton (John Hillerman), of having set up his boss for the scandal Gittes's investigation unleashed in order to discredit him and take over his job, he discovers that Mulwray had once owned the city's water supply in partnership with patriarchal Noah Cross. Then, smilingly accepting Gittes's "nasty reputation," Cross offers nothing to allay the detective's suspicion of having been a cat's-paw in a conspiracy to destroy Mulwray – only a handsome amount of cash to "just find the girl" with whom Gittes had photographed Mulwray, and an ominous view of Evelyn, his daughter: "You're dealing with a disturbed woman who's just lost her husband. . . . You may *think* you know what you're dealing with, but believe me, you don't." Evelyn's own attempt to hire Gittes to solve her husband's murder is undermined by the telltale twitches that more and more often cross her beautiful but no longer placidly reposeful face.[8]

Gittes's attempt to track down the reason for Mulwray's murder takes him from the Hall of Records to a sun-parched fruit grove in the valley – where his car is literally trapped amid rows of orange trees – and to the Mar Vista Inn and Rest Home, where dozens of fading old men and women sit and doze, pinch the nurses, or work on a patchwork quilt, unaware that the county records to which Ida Sessions alerted Gittes identify them as the proprietors of a fifty-thousand-acre empire that would be fabulously valuable if current plans to bring water to the valley were completed. Each stop in this stage of Gittes's journey of discovery is organized around images of complicit mortality. Together they provide an ironic critique of the opening identification of Los Angeles with the new Eden, replacing the picture-postcard exteriors and spacious interiors with landscapes ripe with intimations of death, the corrupting force of money and culture, and the fragile natural resources – here figured most powerfully by the ubiquitous images of water – despoiled by human machinations.

Gittes's far-reaching odyssey over the external landscape, however, only begins a voyage of self-discovery that intensifies when he takes Evelyn Mulwray to bed. Everything he has done up to this point in the film has been eminently consistent with his role as a vintage thirties private eye. Though he is more brash and coarse, more self-centered and even stupid than Bogart's heroes, his feral intelligence, his eye for the main chance, and his suspicion of women mark him as the legitimate descendant of Marlowe and Spade. But just as Marlowe's refusal to be bought off by Vivian Rutledge marks a turning point in *The Big Sleep* – the moment at which Marlowe stops acting as the Sternwood family's hired help and begins to act like an isolated, impersonal instrument of justice – Gittes's new status as Evelyn Mulwray's lover marks a crucial stage in his relationship with Evelyn and in his status as a hard-boiled hero. From now on, Gittes will not simply follow the self-righteous professional code of the incorruptible private eye; beneath his shop-soiled cynicism, he will disclose surprisingly quixotic depths of idealism toward the client he loves but cannot trust. The fragility of their relationship is indicated by how early their lovemaking comes in the film: far too soon to give it the terminal, perhaps redemptive force that it would carry at the conclusion.

Instead of being sanctified by the romantic pairing of the scrappy detective and the safely domesticated heroine, as it is in Philip Marlowe's first four screen incarnations (*Murder, My Sweet; The Big Sleep; Lady in the Lake; The Brasher Doubloon,* 1947), the ending of *Chinatown* is defined by a pair of horrifying revelations: first Evelyn's sobbing confession that the mysterious young woman with whom Gittes had photographed Mulwray was not simply "my sister" or "my daughter" but "my sister *and* my daughter," the product of Evelyn's incestuous union with her father; then Cross's guileless confession that he killed Mulwray to cover up his involvement in a scheme to inflate the value of outlying land he has secretly purchased by manipulating the Los Angeles water supply in order to force the expansion of the city's boundaries. Asked by an incredulous Gittes what more he can possibly hope to buy with whatever additional money he can amass from this fraudulent scheme, Cross replies, "The future" – revealing for the first time the link between his two monstrous crimes: incest with his daughter and land fraud on an epic scale. Cross, whose first name invokes the patriarch of the Flood (a role already played by Huston in his own 1966 film version of *The Bible*), has "water on the brain" – a phrase Gittes used to describe the son-in-law he'd been tailing. Cross, however, has his daughter on the brain as well. The link between water and daughter is a fertility run amok under Cross's monstrously paternal determination to control the future of his family and his city, whose destiny he wishes to guide with a fond solicitude ultimately unmasked as incestuous. As a monster who gives new resonance to the term "city father," Cross reveals the catastrophic sexual and social power of paternity gone mad in the climactic street scene in the city's

48. *Chinatown:* The desperate Evelyn Mulwray (Faye Dunaway) as the hero last sees her, with Katherine Cross (Belinda Palmer, left).

Chinatown, in which Evelyn, fleeing with her sister-daughter Catherine from the patriarchal monster she has just failed to kill [Fig. 48], is killed by a police officer's warning shot.[9]

   Why does Gittes, with the best will, fail in his attempt to help Evelyn escape her father and the patriarchal law he has suborned? As he had earlier told Evelyn, that's just the way it is sometimes; it's the jinx of Chinatown, where he once before lost a woman he was trying to help. The broad implication of Gittes's remark is that Chinatown is his whole world, a place where nothing ever goes right; but the film offers several more probing explanations for Gittes's failure. A former owner of the city's water supply, a man who has committed incest with his daughter and presumably has designs on his granddaughter as well, has killed his daughter's caretaker husband in order to push a fraudulent and unsafe dam through the city council. The new Chief of Water and Power is in Cross's pocket; the police indicate they are willing to join him. Everywhere Gittes turns, he is met by more conspirators and musclemen, from Cross's hireling Mulvihill and his knife-wielding companion to the white-haired director of the Mar Vista Inn and Rest Home. Even the elderly residents of Mar Vista are unwitting participants in the scam. Moreover, when Gittes meets the orange growers Cross's people are driving from their land, perhaps the only truly innocent victims in the film, they turn on him in a rage and beat him. It is no wonder that his credentials as a white knight cannot survive such an onslaught.

As the film's seductive visual design makes clear, nature itself is against Gittes. He is doomed not simply by the conflict between nature and culture figured by the fight over the dam and the gradual narrowing of the film's widescreen vistas till even the final street scene traps the characters, but by the fact that the natural world, through which he thinks he is free to move in the film's spectacular opening sequences, is already a commodity corrupted by acculturation. Father figures as different as Cross and Mulwray have engineered the natural-seeming landscapes as brutally as they have manipulated Evelyn, whose name marks her as a daughter of Eve in more ways than Gittes can understand. His only choices are to become a monstrous father like Cross or to follow in substitute-father Mulwray's steps as a victim.[10]

Gittes is trapped, finally, by the film's historical roots. Setting the film during the period invoked by so many earlier private-eye films, a move that casts such a nostalgic glow over its opening scenes, ends up working powerfully against Gittes, for it ensures an outcome he is powerless to prevent. Just as the recursive flashbacks in films noirs cast a noose around the heroes caught in plots their voice-over narration already recognized as traps, California's history becomes a fatal flashback for Gittes – an image made even more powerful by its frankly mythic roots in the hard-boiled hero's heyday, years after the actual Los Angeles water scandals of 1923, but long before viewers might have assumed the modern urban rot that marks the hard-boiled genre set in. Viewers know from the first that Gittes is trapped in history. No matter what he does, Los Angeles will end up building the dam, annexing the valley, and enriching a few visionary conspirators; the battle between farmers and city dwellers over water rights will continue to the present day; and the city's political future will be dominated, like its past, by greed and the lust for power. In philosophical terms, tracing the city's corruption back to its founding years creates a growing sense of fatalistic doom surrounding the embattled hero; in mythic terms, California's history as a second Eden has included monstrous serpents from the very beginning; in pragmatic terms, Gittes is neither smart enough nor powerful enough to prevent the rape of the valley by a power broker whose ultimate aim is to control the future. The tide of history cannot be stemmed by a single hero, however noble.

Not that Gittes is the noblest hero under the California sun. He is hotheaded, venal, crude, and, like Mike Hammer, too busy calculating the angles ever to see the big picture. It never occurs to him to question the relationship between Mulwray and his mysterious companion. He pries Evelyn's darkest secret out of her in a mere defensive gesture, in order to defend himself from the victimhood of arrest. Even knowing that Noah Cross has masterminded a gigantic fraud against the city, he still naïvely thinks he can face him down, first confronting him without weapons or backup, then shouting Cross's guilt at police officers determined to ignore him.

Gittes fails, however, not because he is a poor specimen of the private eye, but because he is a perfect specimen. His cynicism, his impulsiveness, even his bullying brashness, makes him good at this job. He probably would never have looked beyond the story Ida Sessions told him if he were not so easily inflamed and so heedless of his own safety. Gittes's failure therefore amounts to a critique of the whole tradition he incarnates, because despite his grating lack of polish, he shares the features that make most private eyes successful.

What he does not have is a way of thinking about other people as people. He is egregiously blind to the true nature of the gentle dreamer Hollis Mulwray. More damningly, he never appreciates Evelyn Mulwray's complexity. Since he persists in treating her only as a suspect in a case, he can think of her only as innocent or guilty. When she acts innocent, he treats her with tender concern; when she acts guilty, he recoils in baffled fury. Since the many lies Evelyn tells him mark her as a femme fatale, Gittes generally treats her as one, following the resolutely present-tense orientation of all private-eye films in not asking why she is behaving as she does, or what claims she might have on him despite her complicity. Echoing Spade's climactic remark to Brigid when she asks him if he loves her ("I won't play the sap for you"), Gittes repeatedly turns against Evelyn because he fears becoming her victim. Even his tenderness toward her works against their union, for it reveals a vulnerability he must cover up by outbursts of rage.

Gittes never sees that it is not necessary to whitewash Evelyn to understand her. Certainly she is deeply complicit in her husband's murder. She has known for years what a monster her father is, yet does everything she can to protect him because of the secret they share. When she tells Gittes about her relationship with her father, he immediately switches gears, thinking of her as a victim rather than a femme fatale, despite the fact that she does nothing but shake her head when he asks if her father raped her.[11] In truth, Evelyn is neither femme fatale nor victim; she is a woman whose childhood has left her with a fatal attraction for powerful men – Cross, Mulwray, Gittes himself – who cannot protect her from themselves, a woman whose deepest secret is that her entire identity depends on men. For all his righteous indignation at Noah Cross, Gittes never realizes the extent to which his relationship with Evelyn, which turns into an equally devouring, equally disastrous love, echoes her father's. This pairing of hero and villain, together with the film's presentation of the femme fatale as the ultimate victim, is its most annihilating condemnation of the private eye's masculine heroism. In what amounts to a historical summary of the hard-boiled hero's progress from Philip Marlowe's masculine heroism to Mike Hammer's hypermasculine hysteria to the paralysis of *The Conversation*'s Harry Caul (Gene Hackman), *Chinatown* suggests that the irreducible complexity of the people pressed into service as suspects and criminals and detectives, and the irreversible contamination of natural resources by cultural imperatives, guarantee the failure of any possible quest for justice and truth.

10

Bullitt and the Police Film

T he conventional behavior of police heroes, from their maverick attitudinizing to their ubiquitous car chases, is so well established that it is easy to forget how dramatically it departs from the behavior of most police officers in literature or life. Police detectives had existed as early in prose fiction as Dickens (Inspector Bucket in *Bleak House,* 1852–3) and Wilkie Collins (Sergeant Cuff in *The Moonstone,* 1868); Georges Simenon's indefatigable Inspector Maigret had debuted in 1931; and Sidney Kingsley's grindingly realistic play *Detective Story* had premiered on Broadway in 1949. But the conventions of the genre laid down by the Commander Gideon police-procedural series of J. J. Marric (aka John Creasey) beginning in 1955, and by *Cop Hater,* the first of Ed McBain's 87th Precinct novels, the following year were the emphasis on the daily routines of a given group of police officers, rather than their rare dramatic breakthroughs, and on the presentation of several overlapping cases simultaneously. Together these two innovations conferred a soap-opera sense of endlessness on the routines of McBain's and Marric's fictional police departments. These cops struggle to bring each one of their assignments to a successful conclusion as if the case in hand is uniquely important, even though they know it will be followed by numberless further crimes. The emotional keynote of literary cops is the sentiment expressed by Lt. Clancy at the outset of Robert L. Pike's novel *Mute Witness* (1963): "He was tired and he knew it."[1] Like the soap-opera continuity of the police squad, this tonality has been a hallmark of TV programs from *Police Story* (1973–7), created by best-selling police novelist Joseph Wambaugh, to *Law and Order* and *NYPD Blue,* but rarely of feature films.

Seldom have police films followed actual experiences of police offi-cers any more closely. Hollywood films regularly feature police heroes as independent, despite their uniforms, as any private eye. When the police outside Hollywood movies are seeking a criminal, their watch-word is routine, their most potent weapons are informants and data-bases, and by far the most probable outcomes of their search are that they will not find a likely suspect, or that they will find such a suspect, arrest the suspect, and turn him or her over to the court system for processing, arraignment, and trial. Both of these outcomes are high-ly unlikely in most police films. Instead, loose-cannon cops from *"G" Men* (1935) to *The Rock* (1996) typically pursue suspects in chase se-quences with guns blazing on both sides, leaving in their wake a high body count and impressive property damage; and suspects, instead of being taken into custody, tried, and convicted, are last seen snarl-ing their defiance or getting carried out in a body bag.

Most audiences' nonmovie experiences of the police are remote from this scenario, not only because police work is rarely as exciting or as conclusive as Hollywood suggests, but because few citizens ex-perience police officers as crime-solving presences in their own lives. Most of them encounter the police more often as minor public ser-vants or intimidating enforcers of traffic laws than as heroic solvers of serious crimes. If it is true that most audiences are as afraid of the police as Alfred Hitchcock claimed he was himself,[2] then the heroic cops Hollywood manufactures might seem designed specifically to al-lay their fears. Even so, movies do not simply substitute viewers' fear of the police – which arises from their sense of themselves as poten-tial lawbreakers and their consequent hostility toward the laws they may have broken and the justice system designed to punish them – for these other attitudes, as Hitchcock, himself a shrewd creator of movie cops, was the first to recognize. Instead, viewers bring to police films a set of sharply ambivalent attitudes toward the heroes of the law-enforcement establishment – an ambivalence on which private-eye films capitalize by making the incompetent or corrupt police the hero's adversaries in the search for justice. Hollywood police officers represent at once the human face of the law's front lines and its most threatening aspects, the vulnerability and the power of the justice sys-tem. They evoke both audiences' solicitude for the laws that make so-cial order possible and their skepticism about the failings of the law.

Throughout the history of the Hollywood police film, this ambiva-lence, whereby audiences see themselves as both defenders and victims of law enforcement, plays out through a series of running debates over the issues of power and justice. The peculiar status of police heroes, who are both individuals and representatives of the social will, makes their enabling myth social rather than psychological or transcendental: that the police force's institutional power coincides with a shared ideal of social justice, so that, as in war movies, what George N. Dove calls its "paramilitary" might makes right.[3] Police films, assuming that the power individual citizens have relinquished to all the social institutions the police represent is moral and just despite their potentially coercive force, endorse social conformity on the grounds that centralized social power ultimately benefits all citizens because the body of officers that enforce it is a representative microcosm of the larger society. All police films take this assumption as their point of departure, and most of them conclude by reaffirming it emphatically; but virtually all police films call it into question sooner or later as well by raising doubts about the efficacy of police power, the morality of police justice, or the authority of police culture.

This ambivalence is powerfully figured by Detroit cop Alex J. Murphy (Peter Weller), the half-man, half-machine law-enforcement hero of *RoboCop* (1987). The cyborg is an especially apt figure for Hollywood police officers because it shatters the apparent unity within both their individual bodies and so many of the unitary metaphorical bodies the police force as a corps of individuals and an incarnation of social norms ideally incorporates. The ideal of professionalism, for example, is as important a touchstone in police films as in private eye films from *The Maltese Falcon* (1941) to *Chinatown* (1974), but it is defined in terms of a more amorphous body of work to be done. Unlike both amateur detectives and private eyes, the police do not choose their cases; they are powerless to turn down a case they do not like, and behind each case loom nothing but more cases. Hence the Hollywood cop's professionalism, unlike the private eye's, is not pegged to the body of any particular case but rather to a patient dedication to whatever cases may arise, a constant availability for tedious or dangerous front-line duty. The ubiquity of crime for the weary police is made most explicit in the famous closing lines of *The Naked City* (1948) – "There are eight million stories in the naked city. This has been one of them." – but it is acknowledged more briefly in any number of other police films, for instance in the endings of *The Big Heat* (1953) and *Fort Apache, the Bronx* (1981), which leave their heroes just as they are embarking on new cases. Reimagining crime in *RoboCop*'s terms, as an incessant social condition rather than an aberrant intrusion into the apparently Edenic world of *Murder on the Orient Express* (1974) or *Blue Velvet* (1986), recasts crime-solving heroes as more stoic organization men (or women) whose heroism depends less on their individual initiative than on their willingness to accept the challenges of a world they did not make and cannot control.

Most stories of unofficial detectives and private eyes take the form of mysteries whose solution is withheld from both readers and heroes. In police films, mystery plays a much more minor role. For every whodunit like *Laura* (1944) starring a police detective, there are a dozen films like *RoboCop,* in which the police hero knows who is responsible for the crimes he is investigating but is powerless to make an arrest. Criminals are more often shown at work, and their identities more often known to the police from the beginning, as in *The Untouchables* (1987), which begins with a scene that establishes Al Capone (Robert De Niro) as not only the man behind Chicago's crime wars but simply the most powerful man in the city. Questions about power are more equivocal than questions about knowledge because power relationships, unlike individual guilt, can never be definitively discovered; they must be continually renegotiated. An enabling convention of detective stories from *Oedipus the King* to *Murder on the Orient Express* is that the truth shall set you free; that is, a community that faces the darkest truths about itself will enjoy greater freedom and happiness than a community that suppresses those truths. But police films, which focus on power instead of knowledge, can offer no such assurance, since, as Elliot Ness (Kevin Costner) learns in *The Untouchables,* power can always be trumped by greater power without any necessary moral sanction [Fig. 49].

The popular image of the police force is one of authoritarian power most economically encapsulated in abbreviated references to the corporate body of the police as "the force." In movies like *RoboCop* and *The Untouchables,* however, the police are frequently shown as powerless before a greater malignant power. Jim Malone (Sean Connery), the beat cop who takes Ness under his wing, is represented in life and death by a talisman on his key chain, a medal depicting Saint Jude, the patron saint of impossible causes; and on the face of it, a Hollywood police officer's job is indeed impossible, not only because cops are confronted with supercriminals from Capone to Hannibal Lecter (Anthony Hopkins) in *The Silence of the Lambs* (1991) and *Hannibal* (2001) to John Doe (Kevin Spacey) in *Se7en* (1995), but because each case is followed inevitably by an endless parade of other cases.

49. *The Untouchables:* Police power (Sean Connery, Kevin Costner) trumped by the greater power of Al Capone's bodyguards.

Nonetheless, viewers routinely assume the police will succeed. Sometimes their confidence is justified by their knowledge of history, as in *The Untouchables,* in which audiences' awareness of how Capone was actually brought down makes an ironic joke of the apparently pointless efforts of Oscar Wallace (Charles Martin Smith) to prove Capone guilty of tax evasion. Other times, audiences rely on internal foreshadowing and narrative logic, as in *One False Move* (1991), in which it is clear early on that the three criminals fleeing from Los Angeles to faraway Star City, Arkansas, are actually running into the arms of the law. Even when they have neither history nor any specific foreshadowing to guide them, however, audiences' experiences of films whose stars are cast as police officers will be framed by their experience of generic conventions in myriad earlier police films, which predict, with remarkably few exceptions, the success of the police, at whatever cost, in identifying and apprehending or destroying the criminals.

How can the job of policing be at once so hopeless and so assured of success? This question mirrors a deeper contradiction in viewers' attitudes toward the majesty of the law, their suspicion of the very legal system they are counting on to protect their welfare. The opening situation of most police films typically engages viewers' fears of the

50. *L.A. Confidential:* An ill-assorted police team (James Cromwell, Guy Pearce, Russell Crowe, Kevin Spacey) that has not yet begun to work as a team.

law's powerlessness, the weakness of the authority that gives it moral and legal force, and the resulting lawless chaos; the final resolution reflects their confidence in the law and the justice of its tactics, however violent, even lawless, they may seem. It is a primary task of police films to mediate between these two attitudes, expressing audiences' skeptical fears about the justice system while leaving them ultimately confident in its workings.

The most obvious device for mediating between these two contradictory attitudes is a plot that explains how the powerless police gain enough power to challenge the apparently invincible criminals. This reversal is trivialized in countless films that show that although the bad guys have more guns, the good guys have better aim; but the moment of reversal is often a pivotal moment in the police film. In both versions of *Scarface* (1932, 1983), the criminal heroes are defeated by the sheer numbers of the police. Since numbers alone rarely evoke a sense of heroism, however, police films prefer to show their law-enforcement heroes triumphing by virtue of their superior technology, as in *"G" Men* and *White Heat* (1949), or superior teamwork, as in *The Untouchables* and *L.A. Confidential* (1997), which sets a well-

51. *Se7en:* Police officers (Brad Pitt, Morgan Freeman) led on by the criminal they are pursuing.

organized gang of criminals against an initially disorganized gang of police officers [Fig. 50]. Such films emphasize from the beginning strengths implicit in the police, and by extension the communities they represent and the authority that empowers them, by showing these strengths developing out of earlier weaknesses. Alternatively, instead of showing the police growing stronger, films may show the criminals growing weaker, as in police officers' use of variously complicit informers or the criminals' confessions. Such films, which predicate the power of the police on the weakness of criminal transgressors, more disturbingly compromise the duality between the police and the criminals by emphasizing the dependence of police work on the weakness or even the active collusion of criminals like John Doe in *Se7en* [Fig. 51].

The ideal police force would be as perfect in its justice as in its power over criminals, and a founding convention of the police movie is the alliance of police power with social justice. But most police movies follow victim movies like *Fury* (1936) and private-eye movies like *Chinatown* in challenging this convention, usually by giving the police hero a personal stake in the case at hand because the criminal has either breached the sanctity of his domestic sphere (*The Devil's Own*, 1997) or killed his partner (*The Narrow Margin*, 1952) or taken his wife hostage (*Die Hard*, 1988) or left him for dead (*RoboCop*). Such a personal stake makes the hero's pursuit of the villain more compelling for the audience than the abstract conflict between social good and transgressive evil. At the same time, however, emphasizing the officer's personal interest in the case unmasks the status of institutional justice as institutionalized revenge more interested in repaying insults and injuries than in restoring the social order. To what extent is justice anything more than vengeance sanctioned by superior power? This question, which has troubled Western literature at least since Aeschylus' *Oresteia* nearly twenty-five hundred years ago, is at the heart of the police film.

The most obvious challenge to the alliance of police power and institutional justice is the figure of the corrupt cop, who has fascinated Sidney Lumet in *Serpico* (1973), *Prince of the City* (1981), *Q & A* (1990), and *Night Falls on Manhattan* (1996). Equally dangerous are the loose-cannon cops like fanatical Pete Davis (Ray Liotta) in *Unlawful Entry* (1992), whose dedication to their mandate to serve and protect goes too far. Human emotions of any sort, from greed to desire, threaten to compromise the Hollywood cop's prescribed dedication to ideals of justice.

Police officers who embody motives above suspicion, by contrast, are routinely cast as loners. The lonely isolation of the Hollywood cop is the most immutable of all the genre's conventions. Police officers in movies never have happy, stable family lives for long. Hurricane Dixon (Bill Paxton) in *One False Move* is hiding from his wife and daughter his sexual involvement with one of the criminals he is hoping to capture; Elliot Ness has to rush his wife and daughter out of Chicago in *The Untouchables* after they are threatened by Frank Nitti (Billy Drago); the wife of Dave Bannion (Glenn Ford) is killed by a car bomb intended for him in *The Big Heat;* Det. Jim McLeod (Kirk Douglas) ends up investigating his own wife in *Detective Story* (1951). More often, the hero is a loner from the beginning, a man whose private life is deviant, dysfunctional, or nonexistent. The hero of *Tightrope* (1984), New Orleans Police Inspector Wes Block (Clint Eastwood), has sexual tastes as kinky, though not as homicidal, as those of the killer he is chasing [Fig. 52], and LAPD detective Vincent Hanna (Al Pacino) is just as obsessive as the thief Neil McCauley (Robert De Niro) he is paired against in *Heat* (1995) [Fig. 53]. Even the more gentlemanly Mark Mc-

52. *Tightrope:* Wes Block (Clint Eastwood), a cop whose demonstration of handcuffs to Beryl Thibodeaux (Geneviève Bujold) hints at sexual tastes that are as kinky as those of the criminal he is chasing.

Pherson (Dana Andrews), the lead detective in *Laura,* has no better way to spend his nights than to return to a murder scene and stare at the painting of a dead woman. Like the western hero, the police hero is deprived of a domestic life in order to marginalize him from the social body he is supposed to be defending, even as his alienation reinforces his professional dedication.

For such heroes, whose dedication often amounts to an obsession, the ultimate isolation is estrangement from their professional colleagues, and most police films isolate their heroes in exactly this way. The isolation is often institutional, emphasizing the conflicts between the executive branch of the law the police represent and the legislative and judicial branches. Legislators, lawyers, and judges, like cops themselves in private-eye movies, are often cast as the real enemies of society because they will not give investigative agencies the power they need (the FBI agents in *"G" Men* have to petition Congress for the right to carry firearms) or because they are so ready to stand up for

53. *Heat:* A historic pairing of Al Pacino and Robert De Niro as a cop and his equally obsessive criminal double.

the rights of suspects, rather than the conflicting rights of the larger society, that they help obviously guilty suspects go free.

Often, the heroes' isolation is both institutional and personal, as when Arizona deputy sheriff Walt Coogan (Clint Eastwood) pursues a suspect to the urban jungles of New York in *Coogan's Bluff* (1968), or when Clarice Starling (Jodie Foster), the FBI-trainee heroine of *The Silence of the Lambs,* feels estranged from her boss, Jack Crawford (Scott Glenn), both because he is a full-fledged agent and because he is a man, as he reminds her by his thoughtlessly sexist behavior at a backwoods autopsy. Lt. Ed Exley (Guy Pearce) and Sgt. Wendell "Bud" White (Russell Crowe), the two heroes of *L.A. Confidential*, are feuding over the ambitious Exley's testimony and White's refusal to testify against the officers who rioted during Exley's brief stint as watch commander. The Los Angeles cops staking out Star City, Arkansas, in *One False Move* look down their noses at Hurricane Dixon, the country-boy sheriff who dreams of hitting "the big time" by joining the LAPD.

The most radical isolation between police heroes and their world is achieved by driving a wedge between them and the corruption of

54. *Cop Land:* Sylvester Stallone as a paunchy Everyman. (Robert De Niro, Stallone)

untrustworthy colleagues in their own departments. In *The Big Heat,* Dave Bannion runs so far afoul of his superiors in investigating the death of a bent cop that he is driven from the force to become the dispenser of his own brand of vigilante justice; only the timely intervention of disillusioned gun moll Debby Marsh (Gloria Grahame), who does him the service of killing blackmailing cop-widow Bertha Duncan (Jeanette Nolan), saves him from becoming a murderer himself. Movies like *Serpico, Witness* (1985), and *Cop Land* (1997) set their cleancut heroes at odds with corruption on a grand scale, modeling the few cops who are not on the take on the private eyes who would be their enemies in *The Maltese Falcon* and *Chinatown.* Each of these three films marks its hero's physical body off from the body of untrustworthy colleagues arrayed against him. *Cop Land* casts beefcake Sylvester Stallone against type as paunchy and partially deaf [Fig. 54]. *Serpico* shows Al Pacino, first seen in his well-pressed uniform graduating from the police academy, growing increasingly scruffy and bearded, looking more and more like the lowlifes he is supposed to be catching and less and less like the well-groomed but crooked colleagues who are supposed to be backing him up. *Witness* shows wounded Philadelphia cop John Book (Harrison Ford) dressed in Amish clothing as he preaches nonviolence to the corrupt colleague who, hearing of this supposedly Amish farmer's telltale fistfight, has left the big city to find and kill him.

These films, which fracture the unity that might be expected to prevail among all police officers, help to explain why, unlike movies in which cops figure only marginally, police films rarely show their heroes in the uniforms that express their professional solidarity. More often, they blur the distinction between the police gang and the criminal gang in order to recast the solitary heroic cop in the mold of the lone-wolf private eye who can be trusted precisely because he is not part of the corrupt establishment. The ironic result is that police officers, the very embodiment of the justice system's threateningly monolithic power in private-eye films, often feel hopelessly alienated from or victimized by the system they are supposed to incarnate when they are the heroes of their own movies.

The most common remedy for this disaffection is the camaraderie cops conventionally share with their partners in films like *Lethal Weapon* (1987) and its sequels, which show the overlapping influence of the buddy film; but relations between partners even as close as detective sergeants Martin Riggs (Mel Gibson) and Roger Murtaugh (Danny Glover) are typically marked by conflict [Fig. 55]. Quarrels between oil-and-water cops forced into partnering each other are a staple figure of films as different as *The Laughing Policeman* (1974), *Dragnet* (1987), *Rising Sun* (1993), and *Rush Hour* (1998). More serious are the moral and jurisdictional disputes between the virtuous Mexican narcotics cop Ramon Miguel "Mike" Vargas (Charlton Heston) and the high-handed American Capt. Hank Quinlan (Orson Welles) in *Touch of Evil* (1958), and the fights over turf and tactics between Ed Exley and Bud White, two of the few Los Angeles cops who are not dirty, in *L.A. Confidential.*

Still more disturbingly, police movies often raise questions about police justice by presenting dedicated cops pushed to, and sometimes over, the edge. Det. Sgt. Mark Dixon (Dana Andrews) spends most of the running time of *Where the Sidewalk Ends* (1950) trying to cover up his accidental killing of a robbery suspect. *On Dangerous Ground* (1952) shows Jim Wilson (Robert Ryan) hounding a young criminal from the city to the countryside, and ultimately to his death. As the punch line of his seven-deadly-sins series of murders, John Doe, the

55. *Lethal Weapon 3:* Comic conflict between oil-and-water cops (Mel Gibson, Danny Glover).

villain of *Se7en,* kills the wife of David Mills (Brad Pitt), one of the two detectives on his trail, out of his envy of Mills, goading Mills into killing Doe himself out of wrath. Even clean-cut Elliot Ness, moments after pulling Frank Nitti to safety in *The Untouchables,* throws him off a roof-top when Nitti brags that he will never do time for killing Jim Malone. Mills and Ness, dazed with shock and grief, kill Doe and Nitti out of an anger and hatred fostered by their job that has become too personal; but Wilson and Dixon cause the deaths of the criminals in their films out of professional obsessions, workaholism run amok.

The ultimate example of professional dedication gone wrong is the police officer as vigilante killer, the conceit behind *Magnum Force* (1973), in which Harry Callahan (Clint Eastwood) sheds his normal quasi-vigilante role to battle an even more murderously vigilante wing of the San Francisco Police Department. But the opposite conceit is equally familiar: the undercover police officer whose success and sur-vival depend on playing a role that represents the opposite of his or her true nature, as Hank Fallon (Edmond O'Brien) worms his way into the confidence of his cellmate Cody Jarrett (James Cagney) in *White Heat* by taking over the nurturing, reassuring role of Cody's late mother despite his personal revulsion from Cody. The most memorable recent portrayals of undercover cops have emphasized the destructive conflicts between their institutional loyalties and the requirements of their criminal roles. *Donnie Brasco* (1997) turns on the unwilling betrayal by undercover cop Joe Pistone (Johnny Depp) of his trusting mentor Lefty, played with elegiac dignity by the iconic Al Pacino [Fig. 56]. *Rush* (1991) plunges rookie narcotics officer Kristen Cates (Jennifer Jason Leigh) into a nightmarishly successful masquerade when she gets hooked not only on heroin but also on her undercover partner, Raynor (Jason Patric). Most searing of all is *Reservoir Dogs* (1992), which sets its jewel thieves' insistent professionalism against the growing intimacy between one of their leading figures, Mr. White (Harvey Keitel), and the mortally wounded Mr. Orange (Tim Roth). As the film gradually reveals, both the police and the criminals are so deeply immersed in a culture of violence that it is only by violent actions – playfully scrapping with each other like puppies, accusing each other of betrayal, defending each other at gunpoint, taking hostages – that they can establish any connection with each other.

Even police officers who stay on the right side of the law can fall under suspicion, such as James "Brick" Davis (James Cagney), the rookie FBI agent whose background as a lawyer educated by a mobster patron makes his FBI superior Jeff McCord (Robert Armstrong) constantly suspicious of him in *"G" Men.* One False Move's Hurricane Dixon is forever compromised by his long-ago seduction of African-American shoplifter Lila Walker (Cynda Williams) and his refusal to acknowledge her son Byron as his own – acts that fostered Lila's criminal rebirth as Fantasia, whose drug-dealing friends provoke a tide of violence that challenges the self-congratulatory good-versus-evil dichotomies on which Hurricane has built his comfortable life. *"G" Men* and *One False Move,* like all police films, feed on audiences' anxieties about power and justice, which occupy the same central position in police films as heterosexual male audiences' psychosexual anxieties in private-eye films. *"G" Men,* produced at a time when a strong executive branch under President Franklin Roosevelt was attempting to pull the nation out of widespread economic chaos, and released with the imprimatur of FBI director J. Edgar Hoover, mounts a spirited defense of the recent empowerment of FBI agents and their moral authority. The most problematic police films appear at times when the police, and institutional authority generally, are under suspicion, and especially when these suspicions are rooted in still deeper genera-

56. *Donnie Brasco:* The undercover cop (Johnny Depp) and his unwitting mob mentor (Al Pacino).

tional conflicts concerning authority and the law. The crucial period in the Hollywood police film is the late 1960s and early 1970s, not only because it is a period of unprecedented economic freedom and formal experimentation in American films generally,[4] but because a spate of rioting in Watts (1965), Detroit (1967), Newark (1967), and on innumerable college campuses – culminating in the National Guard's killing of four students at Ohio's Kent State University (1970) – fed public debate about both police tactics and the legitimacy of the government they represented.

Three films – *Bullitt* (1968), *Dirty Harry* (1971), and *The French Connection* (1971) – focus this debate indelibly. All three feature rogue cops who are at odds with judges, lawyers, politicians, and their own bosses or colleagues. All three express skepticism about institutional power and justice by asking when law-enforcement officers are justified in breaking the law in order to uphold the moral law that gives legal laws their authority, and all three conclude by endorsing the vigilante cop over the system that has failed them and the society they are sworn to protect. What distinguishes the three films from each other is the strikingly different attitudes they adopt toward their rogue heroes.

The most straightforward of the three is William Friedkin's *The French Connection* because its attitude toward its hero is the easiest to understand. Jimmy "Popeye" Doyle (Gene Hackman) is the unlikeliest defender of the law imaginable, a nightmare vision of the modern urban cop designed to appeal to viewers' most paranoid fantasies about the police. As he moves through a New York landscape Martin Rubin aptly describes as "relentlessly drab, sordid, ugly – a virtual wasteland,"[5] it becomes obvious that Popeye, like Hank Quinlan in *Touch of Evil,* is a great detective but a lousy cop, a man whose obsessively honed skill in detective work has destroyed whatever social instincts he may have had – instincts that may well be a luxury modern police officers, beset alike by resourceful drug dealers and widespread drug use even among movie audiences, can no longer afford. Popeye's social responsibilities are so impossible, and his single moral imperative of chasing criminals until he catches them is so inadequate, it is no wonder that, in the film's most celebrated sequence, he is nearly as heedless of the law as the killer he chases through streets and subways crowded with innocent bystanders, many of whom become casualties of the chase.

If Popeye is the nightmare cop hopelessly at odds with his department and the society he is sworn to protect, Inspector Harry Callahan (Clint Eastwood),[6] in Don Siegel's *Dirty Harry,* is a more even-handed representation of the officer who is not afraid to take the law into his own hands. Universally reviled by his superiors and the mayor of San Francisco, Harry is still the cop they call on when a extortionist sniper calling himself Scorpio (Andy Robinson) begins killing citizens virtually at random and demands a payment of $100,000 to stop. The film's suggestion that Harry, though he may look no better than Scorpio at first, is actually his opposite is developed by the shifting contexts in which its title comes up. When Harry's new partner, Chico Gonzalez (Reni Santori), first asks the other cops how Harry got his nickname, a colleague tells him, "Harry hates everyone." Later, Chico decides that an episode of opportunistic voyeurism – Harry interrupts their pursuit of Scorpio to peek through a window at a lovemaking couple – explains his nickname. Still later, after Harry has saved a would-be suicide from jumping off a building by punching him into submission, he tells Chico, "Now you know why they call me Dirty Harry – every dirty job that comes along." Finally, as Lt. Bressler (Harry Guardino) is laying down dangerous restrictions for the blackmail payment, Chico tells him, "No wonder they call him Dirty Harry. Always gets the shit end of the stick." What originally seemed like Harry's personal dirt becomes, on reflection, society's dirt; he has been tarred with it only because he is forced to shovel it every day. Especially in view of the film's factual basis,[7] the revelation changes Harry from the "pig bastard" Scorpio calls him to the messianic answer to real-life San Francisco's prayers, the one man who has the sense and the guts to say, when he's told that his torture of Scorpio and his unauthorized search of his room have broken the law: "Well, then, the law is crazy!"

Though Harry and Popeye are the two best-known examples of loose-cannon cops in Hollywood history, Lt. Frank Bullitt is more problematic than either of them, not only because he is the progenitor that makes their films possible, but because his film, by presenting him as the most unexceptionally heroic of the three of them, raises the most difficult questions about the audience's ambivalence toward the law. No one at Warner Bros., the studio that released *Bullitt,* expected such ambiguities from the film's director, Peter Yates, a British stage veteran making his Hollywood directorial debut, even though Yates's subsequent career would mark him as one of the most enduringly unpredictable of Hollywood directors. Denied auteur status because of the lack of thematic or stylistic unity in such commercial projects as *For Pete's Sake* (1974), *Mother, Jugs & Speed* (1976), and *The Deep* (1977), or even in the three films written by Steve Tesich – the offbeat teen comedy *Breaking Away* (1979), the janitorial noir *Eyewitness* (1981), and the historical docudrama *Eleni* (1985) – Yates has consistently subordinated himself to his stars in the emotionally charged backstage theatrics of *The Dresser* (1983), the legal thrills of *Suspect* (1987), and the tear-jerking generational wisdom of *Roommates* (1995).

Warners hired Yates to turn Robert L. Pike's novel *Mute Witness* into an action vehicle for its star, Steve McQueen, whose company, Solar Productions, produced the film. A familiar presence on American screens ever since *The Blob* (1958) and the television series *Wanted: Dead or Alive,* which began its run the same year, McQueen had shot to stardom as the action heroes of *The Magnificent Seven* (1960) and *The Great Escape* (1963). Coolly charismatic onscreen and off, McQueen charmed fans in the 1960s and 1970s as a loner of preternatural silence and bodily repose, even in the most strenuous action sequences, who filled his holidays by racing cars and motorcycles and

did his own stunt work in *The Great Escape*. In *Bullitt*, which sent Mc-
Queen to the top of the Hollywood box-office list, he is cast in his most
enduringly popular role, the thinking man's (and woman's) action star,
but one whose body, like those of so many of his other roles, incarnates a world of contradictions.

McQueen's star persona demanded that the lead role be radically
reshaped for him. Pike's hero, Lt. Clancy, is a lonely, weary New York
cop already on the outs with his nemesis, Assistant District Attorney
Chalmers, who got him transferred out of his old precinct after Clancy
shot a prosecution witness who came at him with a gun. Burdened
with a reputation as "trigger-happy,"[8] Clancy is still detailed to protect
a West Coast mobster who has agreed to come east and testify for
Chalmers. The hero Pike created would have been perfectly suited for
Gene Hackman or Clint Eastwood; veteran screenwriter Harry Kleiner
and newcomer Alan R. Trustman retooled the character, now renamed
Lt. Frank Bullitt, for McQueen by giving him an understated heroism
that first brings him to Chalmers's attention. Clancy and his world are
as ordinary as possible; Bullitt and his world are both ordinary and
subtly glamorized. In shifting the scene from New York to San Francisco, Kleiner and Trustman provided a surprisingly large number of
roles for African Americans but deracinated the ethnically shaded colleagues Pike had given his hero and created a more romantic setting
for him, memorably photographed by William A. Fraker – a setting
with the potential for a chase sequence as unforgettable as Popeye
Doyle's.

The film begins with a dark screen, a visual homage to noir that is
soon filled with a nocturnal cityscape whose neon lights prominently
feature the word "Chicago." The credit sequence, which shows a mob
break-in at the offices of John and Peter Ross, is edited so elliptically
that it is nearly impossible to tell what is happening until the sequence's only line of dialogue: "He's your brother, Pete. If you can't
find him, we have people who will. And you're paying for the contract." But a cut to a high overhead shot of San Francisco establishes
another world. The California exteriors are routinely sun-drenched
and saturated in color, and shadows uniformly crisp, unlike those in
the city's foggy, smoggy real-life prototype. Even when the film treats
the streets of San Francisco as a maze of urban canyons, as it frequently does, they look picturesque rather than claustrophobic. The noirish world of Chicago mobsters the credit sequence so economically
evoked is nothing but a tease – and so is that threatening remark

about Pete Ross's brother, and indeed the following sequence, in which a man enters a hotel asking for Johnny Ross's mail.

Immediately thereafter, Bullitt is sought by Walter Chalmers (Robert Vaughn) to protect Johnny Ross (Felice Orlandi), a witness who is testifying in a Senate subcommittee hearing against the Chicago mob because, as Bullitt's boss, Capt. Sam Bennett (Simon Oakland), tells him, "You make good copy, Frank. The papers love you," and Chalmers wants to associate himself with a popular and successful officer in his political plans. Though he disapproves of Chalmers's arrangements to safeguard Ross by installing him in a room at the seedy Hotel Reynolds, whose big windows open to a freeway outside, Bullitt accepts the job. But Stanton (Carl Reindel), the officer on the graveyard shift, is gunned down and Ross critically wounded by a pair of assassins Ross has just let into the room himself by surreptitiously slipping the chain lock, setting Bullitt at odds with Chalmers, his true adversary, for the rest of the film.

The clash between the two men is presented as a battle of ideologies. Chalmers's top priority is clear: to get Ross's testimony. He presents the image of the law enforcer as politician, sensitive only to public opinion and his own chances for publicity and power. Bullitt's priorities are more personal and mutable. His first priority, Stanton's survival, switches to a second as soon as doctors assure him that Stanton is out of danger: waiting for Ross to regain consciousness so that he can ask him why he unlatched the door to his hotel room. In both cases, Bullitt's underlying concern is for the welfare of his own men, who have been betrayed by the man they were supposed to protect, a concern that emerges starkly in his confrontation with Chalmers at the hospital. Their argument swiftly degenerates into a battle over who was responsible for the attack, the officers who let down their guard or the informer who knew where to send the killers.

What is most remarkable about this confrontation is a question that haunts the whole film. Given the diametrically opposed views of the law's responsibilities it presents, why do audiences invariably take Bullitt's side? On the face of it, Chalmers's view seems more generous and unselfish: If Ross testifies, the Organization and its criminal activities will collapse. By contrast, Bullitt is interested only in looking after the welfare of his own colleague, finding out who had him shot, and, after Ross dies without regaining consciousness, switching to a third priority: pretending Ross is still alive and in hiding in order to draw the killers out into the open instead of letting Chalmers shut down the case. Although Bullitt's view seems both narrower and more punitive, viewers never fail to adopt it as their own, treating Chalmers throughout the film as a thorn in the side of Bullitt's more high-minded idealism.

This problem does not arise in *The French Connection* because Friedkin's film makes such a clear distinction between Popeye's finely honed detective intuitions and his lack of conscience that audiences have no trouble distinguishing between his professional heroism and his social bankruptcy. The problem is central to *Dirty Harry,* but it is more simply resolved by the film's contention that laws arising from the Miranda ruling have unfairly hamstrung law-enforcement officials who, whatever their excesses, deserve better laws to enforce. *Dirty Harry* may load its cop's case against a dangerously liberal judiciary, but it is essentially a logical case.

Bullitt, by contrast, establishes its police hero's moral credentials more indirectly, for example, by reserving to him the role of detective along with the customary role of avenger. Although the film shows the faces of the hit men early on, it does not reveal who hired them, or how their employer knew where to find Johnny Ross. Keeping this information secret is crucial to the film's sympathetic presentation of Bullitt, for it makes him, like Hercule Poirot and J. J. Gittes, the only character who is committed to finding out the truth the film tantalizingly withholds from the audience.

More pervasively, the film invites audiences to side with Bullitt through a visual logic that builds on the contrast between darkly deceptive Chicago and sunny, scenic, but equally violent San Francisco. Even in his first, and his only cordial, scene with Chalmers, Bullitt is set against the oily political climber and his equally well-dressed party guests by his informal black turtleneck, nondescript jacket, and rumpled raincoat. If Chalmers is clearly identified with a sanctimonious upper class, however, Bullitt's proletarian status is far more ambiguous than that of his fictional prototype, Lt. Clancy. The film gives him an improbably beautiful and exotic girlfriend as a mark of his sophistication. Just before the attack on Johnny Ross, Bullitt and Cathy (Jacqueline Bisset) enjoy an evening at the Coffee Cantata in a sublimely 1960s dinner-date sequence that showcases Bullitt as a man who, despite his proletarian job, can appreciate the finer things in life. Clearly he is a political outsider by choice and temperamental inclination, not by maladjustment, inadequacy, or social deprivation.

A closer look at Bullitt's body (one the film is happy to provide through a much greater number of full shots than any other character gets) shows that he is not Chalmers's opposite but rather a uniquely pansocial figure who alone can mediate between the untrustworthy world of political power Chalmers represents and the equally treacherous lowlife world of Johnny Ross, the fleabag hotel where Chalmers stashes him, and the unnamed hit men (the only characters in the film even more laconic than Bullitt) who come after him. Straddling the space between equally dangerous enemies above and below him on the social scale would seem to be a perilous activity, yet Bullitt seems completely at home in his job, largely because he seems so completely at home in his body. After introducing him in bed, the film shows him in the first of many full shots, sleepy but eminently self-contained, wearing camouflage pajamas that identify him with American soldiers dutifully fighting the politicians' war in Vietnam while erasing any specific marks of his own social class. Bullitt might seem scarcely more civilized than Popeye Doyle when he purchases a pile of frozen TV dinners at a local grocery store, ignoring a produce sign that says "fresh today." But his purposeful movements in stacking the dinners, reflected later in the rows of sweaters neatly arranged in his apartment, are so graceful and economical that he avoids the specifically proletarian associations of Popeye's primitive home life or Harry Callahan's Robert Hall outfits.

The narrow line Bullitt walks between proletarianism and saintly purity is challenged most sharply not by Chalmers, whose attempts to seize the moral high ground are undermined by his own transparently self-serving hypocrisy, but by Cathy, whose pointed questions to her lover after she has stumbled over a female corpse Bullitt has found in San Mateo in his investigation of Ross's movements ("Do you let anything reach you – really reach you? Or are you so used to it by now that nothing really touches you? . . . How can you be part of it without becoming more and more callous? Your world is so far from the one I know. What will happen to us in time?") mark the only time anyone ever penetrates Bullitt's still façade even momentarily. Often gruff but never raising his voice, he keeps his distance from other characters by maintaining a self-contained silence. Building on McQueen's legendary screen persona of stoic understatement, the film, for all the excitement of its action sequences, presents Bullitt's normal mode as the Zenlike repose of the tightrope walker, so that his silence, which resonates throughout several long sequences without dialogue, again seems to express deliberate choice rather than inarticulateness or social incapacity. When his partner Det. Sgt. Delgetti (Don Gordon) first arrives at Bullitt's apartment with his assignment, the two men exchange hardly a word because they do not need to talk. Later, Bullitt looks steadily into the eyes of Stanton's wife over his hospital bed, but he says nothing because there is nothing to say. Stanton was betrayed, but not by Bullitt, who is committed to doing everything he can, even if it means breaking the law, to find and punish the killers.

The complex nature of the audience's attachment to Bullitt – the combination of admiration for his dedication, acceptance of his hooded emotional remoteness, dependence on his detective powers, hatred of his enemies, and respect for his physical self-possession that the film invites – is essential to the success of the film's most famous addition to Pike's novel, a car chase over the hills of San Francisco. Although this chase both lacks the kinetic intensity and the moral complexity of the chase sequence in *The French Connection,* it illustrates even better than William Friedkin's sequence why car chases have been staples of police films from *"G" Men* to *RoboCop,* from *White Heat* to *Heat.*

Of all the different kinds of crime film, police films depend most on establishing ongoing moral tensions that need to be periodically dissipated. Pitting good cops against evil killers allows the audience to take sides unreflectively, waiving for the moment the more complex problems that are raised, for instance, by the conflict between Bullitt's and Chalmers's views of the law. Moreover, police films feature a hero who is always potentially in danger, so that the dangers of the chase express the dangers implicit in every move the hero makes, as in the suspenseful earlier episode in which Bullitt chases one of the killers through the hospital basement while trying to avoid getting killed himself [Fig. 57]. Police films can use chases to remind the audience of the closeness between the police heroes and the world they are protecting, from the nightscapes of Chicago to the hills of San Francisco, even as they exploit that world's potential as an exotic mise-en-scène. Police films, emphasizing questions of power over questions of knowledge, can use chases to dramatize the difficulties of catching identifiable criminals, or to transform the question of whodunit into the question of "howcatchem"[9] by having the chase reveal the criminals' identities. Police films permit extended chases between criminals who cannot afford to be captured and police pursuers who will take thrill-

57. *Bullitt:* The athletic hero (Steve McQueen) chases his ostensible enemy through the hospital.

ing risks to capture them because they are all too used to cutting legal corners in the course of their job.

Yates controls the tension of *Bullitt*'s chase sequence not only by prolonging it to ten minutes without dialogue but by dividing it into four distinct segments: (1) the two minutes during which the killers tail Bullitt's car to a menacing saxophone cue; (2) the one minute of cat-and-mouse reversal after Bullitt shakes them and turns up behind them; (3) the three minutes, signaled by the cutting off of the music in a roar of revving engines, of Bullitt's high-speed pursuit of the hit men through city streets, accompanied only by diegetic sound effects that emphasize the physical immediacy of the chase without telling viewers how to feel about it; and (4) the four minutes after the two cars leave the city's hills for a highway on which they must swerve to avoid oncoming cars while trading shots and trying to run each other off the road. The sequence depends throughout on the contrast between the hit men's anonymous black sedan and Bullitt's stylish Mustang, which functions as an extension of his body – tenacious, vulnerable to gunfire, but as triumphantly youthful, individual, and charismatic as James Bond's Aston Martin.

The effect of this sequence is express and relieve through a physical catharsis the moral and psychological tension of the film's conflict between Bullitt and the absent Chalmers and to dispel the threat posed by the two killers, but at the same time to preserve and intensify the mystery of who hired them and how they knew where to find Ross. From beginning to end, the chase is structured by a progressive simplification, as the deceptively subtle tailing of each party by the other yields to the no-holds-barred chase that rejects deception for lethal force.[10] This progression tells audiences it is time, and suggests that it is morally appropriate, to exchange the ethical subtleties of Bullitt's argument with Chalmers about moral responsibility for the simpler satisfactions of rooting for the good guy against the bad guys, even as the final image of the burning gunmen preserves the mystery of how they got to Johnny Ross. The chase sequence transforms viewers' experience from the ideational commitment of rooting for Bullitt to the kinesthetic sensation of holding their breath on his account without resolving the moral problems implicit in identifying with law enforcers rather than lawmakers.

Although the film will provide Bullitt with still another extended chase after his ultimate prey – the wily Johnny Ross, who paid a double he intended to have killed at the Hotel Reynolds to throw both the mob and the law off his trail – the film's unsettlingly wordless epilogue, its most audacious addition to (or subtraction from) the crime genre, deprives the film of its obligatory conclusion, the detective hero's explanation of the evidence. The closest to such an explanation the film comes is Bullitt's earlier riposte to Chalmers's demand for a public statement from him that Ross died in Bullitt's custody: "You sent us to guard the wrong man, Mr. Chalmers."

The film's true climax is not Bullitt's killing of Johnny Ross or his nonexplanation of the mystery, but his final confrontation with the

58. *Bullitt:* The self-contained hero (Steve McQueen) confronts his real enemy, the hypocritical prosecutor (Robert Vaughn), at the airport.

unapologetic Chalmers, who attempts to press his claim on the tarnished Ross's testimony by telling Bullitt that even though his star witness has now been proved a killer who faked his own death, he is still determined to get him to testify [Fig. 58]. "The Organization – several murders – could all do us both a great deal of good," he adds. "We both know how careers are made. Integrity is something you sell the public. . . . We must all compromise," with a scorchingly quiet reply: "Bullshit. Get the hell out of here now." By this time, Bullitt's emphatic rhetoric (the word "bullshit" was rarely heard in 1968 movies) on behalf of the pancultural cachet of law enforcement over the rule of law the film reserves to the gratingly upper-class Chalmers and his minions is backed by the dangerous physical actions that gives his words their authority.

Why should viewers trust such an enduringly laconic and self-contained hero rather than his superiors and counterparts in the legislature and judiciary? The film gives him an integrity it denies his superiors, a personal concern for his professional colleagues, and just enough proletarian markers to establish him as a working stiff doing his job even as it glamorizes the hero, his hometown, and his job at any number of strategic moments. Like films from *"G" Men* to *One False Move, Bullitt,* with its hero who is both emphatically middle-class and essentially classless, links the contrary drives toward individual empowerment and communal welfare it is the work of the police film to unite.

11

Reversal of Fortune and the Lawyer Film

More than any other figure in the Hollywood imagination, more even than the maverick cop, the lawyer embodies viewers' ambivalent attitudes toward the law. Ever since the American public became aware that "a distressing number of the Watergate villains, including the President, were lawyers,"[1] disillusionment with lawyers as overpaid hairsplitters who ride roughshod over the truth in defense of their well-heeled and amoral clients has spawned a thousand late-night comedy monologues. When special prosecutor Kenneth Starr issued his historic report on President Clinton's alleged perjuries about his dalliance with Monica Lewinsky, each side was quick to attack the other's tactics as legalistic, as if the practice of law were itself contemptible. Recent movie lawyers have accordingly included Kevin Lomax (Keanu Reeves) in *The Devil's Advocate* (1997), which makes explicit the widespread implication that lawyers are in league with the devil [Fig. 59], and Fletcher Reede (Jim Carrey) in *Liar Liar* (1997), which chooses a compulsively untruthful lawyer as the person who would be most comically hamstrung by his disappointed son's magically granted wish that he be forced to tell the truth for a single day.

Even as lawyers are universally vilified in the public imagination, they occupy a position of unprecedented popularity in American culture. From Scott Turow to John Grisham, from TV's *Law and Order* to its *The Practice*, from *Primal Fear* (1996) to *A Civil Action* (1998), from Johnnie Cochrane to Christopher Darden to Marcia Clark, from Kenneth Starr to Bill Clinton, lawyers have never before held such sway over the popular imagination. Real-life jurists from Judge Wapner to

Judge Judy have become television stars, and an increasing number of cable franchises allocate an entire television channel to Court TV. Certainly some entries in the recent torrent of legal fiction and non-fiction – for example, the films *Trial by Jury* (1994) and *The Juror* (1996), following the lead of *12 Angry Men* (1957), which pit the heroic ordinary citizens of the jury against a system that seems to be rigged against justice – cast lawyers as bogeymen. More often, however, Hollywood prefers to focus on idealistic lawyers, especially those who originally plied their trade in John Grisham novels adapted for the screen, who win justice for their clients against impossible odds. For fictional lawyers, the 1990s seem to be the worst of times that are also the best of times.

This ambivalence is nothing new. Over the years, in fact, lawyers have modeled and evoked a wider range of attitudes toward the justice system than any other single figure. How dramatic these mood swings have been can be illustrated by fictional representations of the archetypal lawyer hero. Erle Stanley Gardner's Perry Mason has been played by dapper Warren William, in a series of Warner Bros. features (e.g., *The Case of the Howling Dog,* 1934), as a wily legal tactician; by Raymond Burr, in the CBS television series that ran from 1957 to 1966, as a staunch defender of the innocent; and, in a series of television movies that brought back Burr from 1985 to the star's death in 1993, as a stern reminder of a tradition of legal probity endangered by a new generation of lawyers.

Nor are the changing attitudes Mason has reflected limited to questions of morality, for, like all criminal investigators, Hollywood lawyers offer images of power as well as images of virtue or vice. Warren William's Mason – respected by the district attorney, trusted by his clients, worshiped by his faithful secretary – is a paragon of personal power. When Alfred Hitchcock presents one of his rare lawyer heroes in *The Paradine Case* (1947), however, he makes Anthony Keane (Gregory Peck) into a victim who is undone by the depth of his advocacy for his client, the mysterious widow Maddalena Paradine (Alida Valli), which crosses the line to a ruinous infatuation and a romantic rivalry with Andre Latour (Louis Jourdain), the valet he is convinced has murdered Mrs. Paradine's husband. Because lawyers, well paid as they often are by clients who never call on them except when they are in trouble, are so often assumed to occupy a privileged position in society and the legal establishment, they are ripe for the reversals that play to audiences' revenge fantasies by making them outcasts or victims in films like *The Verdict* (1982), *Presumed Innocent* (1990), *The Firm*

59. *The Devil's Advocate:* A lawyer hero (Keanu Reeves) literally in league with the Devil (Al Pacino).

(1992), *A Time to Kill* (1996), and *Witness for the Prosecution* (1957; based on a 1949 story and 1954 play by Agatha Christie), in which the magisterial Sir Wilfrid Robarts (Charles Laughton) takes a client he has proved to his own imperious satisfaction is innocent, only to be flimflammed by both the client and his resourceful wife.

Instead of being figured as simply powerful or powerless, lawyers can be shown as evenly matched sparring partners, as in the proto-feminist comedy *Adam's Rib* (1949), which asks whether an aggrieved wife who shoots her philandering husband in the arms of his mistress is entitled to the same unwritten legal defense that a man in her position has long been able to claim in attacking his wife. The twist here is that Adam Bonner (Spencer Tracy), the assistant D.A. prosecuting Doris Attinger (Judy Holliday), is married to her defense attorney, Amanda Bonner (Katharine Hepburn). Despite their amusingly different views of gender politics, both partners, in their different ways, ultimately reveal their respect for the law as it is written and their sense of the underlying ideals of social justice for which the law is all too often an imperfect instrument.

Despite its comic mode, *Adam's Rib* provides an unusually explicit illustration of the contradictory nature of movie lawyers. Movies can readily capitalize on viewers' ambivalence toward lawyers because movie lawyers, unlike cops, private eyes, amateur detectives, gangsters, or the heroes and heroines of films noirs and erotic thrillers, are routinely opposed by other lawyers. The ambivalence toward social authority that has to be worked into police films by isolating heroic loner cops like Frank Serpico or Elliot Ness from a corrupt or uncaring force is built into the adversarial system of American justice, since lawyers represent both the values with which viewers most sympathize and those they find most repugnant.

Movie lawyers are not, of course, always set against other lawyers of equal stature. The Crown Prosecutors who oppose the barristers in *The Paradine Case* and *Witness for the Prosecution* are colorless figures who never hold the screen. The prosecutors in *Primal Fear* and *The People vs. Larry Flynt* (1996) are consistently upstaged by the defense attorneys, even when they are the attorneys' former lovers. In *To Kill a Mockingbird* (1962), Atticus Finch (Gregory Peck), repeatedly shown in dominating low-angle shots even though his children are watching him from a gallery above, towers over everyone else in the courtroom, so that the lone hero's antagonist becomes the whole depersonalized system of racist justice in 1932 Georgia rather than the attorney and any single opponent. The heroic attorney in *Erin Brockovich* (2000) is not even an attorney but a filing clerk who hates lawyers so much that she takes on their role herself.

More typically, however, the impossibly heroic attorneys in *Anatomy of a Murder* (1959), *Inherit the Wind* (1960), *Sergeant Rutledge*

(1960), *The Verdict, A Few Good Men* (1992), *Philadelphia* (1993), *John Grisham's The Rainmaker* (1997), and *A Civil Action* are opposed by lawyers whose oily smugness is equally impossible, so that the audiences' interest in rooting for a heroic lawyer, usually a fledgling or a has-been, is fueled in large part by their interest in rooting against other lawyers who are much more closely implicated in the system. Films as different as *JFK* (1991), *My Cousin Vinny* (1992), *In the Name of the Father* (1993), and *Amistad* (1997) express the hope, familiar from police movies, that heroic individuals incarnating the best principles of the justice system can triumph over the imperfections of the system as it is.

It may seem odd for lawyer films to emphasize the injustices of the justice system, but a founding convention of these films is that any system that puts citizens on trial, holding their actions up to the measure of the law, is open to question itself, particularly in those films that present an innocent defendant or some other miscarriage of justice. The lawyer's official role, held in contempt in gangster films and police films alike, is to represent the law to individual citizens accused of wrongdoing, and to represent those citizens to the legal system. In practically all lawyer films, the hero is a criminal defense attorney who represents an overmatched David against the state's Goliath [Fig. 60]. Even films like *The Verdict, The Firm, A Civil Action,* and *Erin Brockovich,* which focus on noncriminal law, retain this David-and-Goliath structure by inflating the power of the hero's adversaries – which, in *The Verdict,* include a hospital, a battery of wealthy doctors, specialist deponents, insurance companies, the most fearsome law firm in Boston, and the Catholic Church. Since the constant implication is that any system with so much power must be corrupt or unfair, lawyer films use the very power of the law as an argument against its unquestioned moral authority.

Even more obviously than other crime films, lawyer films are irreducibly dualistic. The most emphatic dualism, of course, is between the positions of the two opposing lawyers – in criminal trials, the prosecution story and the defense story – but there are many others as well. *Sergeant Rutledge,* a western that puts a black cavalryman on trial for rape and murder, depends on a visual contrast between the dark, claustrophobic world of the courtroom, which brands First Sgt. Braxton Rutledge (Woody Strode) as a criminal, and the increasingly open, natural world of the flashbacks leading up to the trial, which show Rutledge as brave, loyal, selfless, and ultimately helpless to save

60. *The Verdict:* Shirt-sleeved Frank Galvin (Paul Newman) takes on the Boston Goliath Edward J. Concannon (James Mason) before Judge Hoyle (Milo O'Shea).

his life by deserting the 9th Cavalry, which he calls "my home, my real freedom, and my self-respect." Hence the design of the film, alternating low-ceilinged interiors with low-horizoned exteriors, closely echoes that of its black-and-white predecessor *Stagecoach* (1939), also directed by John Ford and photographed by Bert Glennon. The contrast confirms the judgment of Rutledge's lawyer, Lt. Thomas Cantrell (Jeffrey Hunter): "It is this court that stands on trial, and not Sergeant Rutledge."

Lawyer films frequently load further dualities onto this dualistic matrix. *A Few Good Men,* beginning with a case against a pair of Marines for a hazing prank that ended in death, pits the plea-bargaining compromiser Lt. Daniel Kaffee (Tom Cruise) not only against court-martial prosecutor Capt. Jack Ross (Kevin Bacon) but against his own ally, the feisty, principled Lt. Cmdr. JoAnne Galloway (Demi Moore) [Fig. 61]; the authority of the Navy defense attorneys against that of the Marine prosecutors; official authority (the meeting at which the Marines were ordered not to take reprisals against a despised informer) against un-

61. *A Few Good Men:* Lt. Kaffee (Tom Cruise) fights with everyone, even allies like Lt. Cmdr. Galloway (Demi Moore).

official (the clandestine order immediately afterward to institute a "Code Red" against the informer); orders from one's legal superiors against individual conscience, and hence individual against group welfare; and finally the authority of the Marine command against that of the court. So powerful are these conflicts that Lt. Col. Matthew Markinson (J. T. Walsh) is destroyed by them, and even Kaffee's two clients obtain only a split verdict on their actions.

Inherit the Wind goes still further, taking the 1925 Scopes Monkey Trial, which indicted a Tennessee schoolteacher for teaching Darwin's theory of evolution, as the basis for an epic battle of worldviews. In one corner is the creationist prosecutor, oracular Matthew Harrison Brady (Fredric March), representing the transcendent authority of divine law, the Bible as central text, faith, preaching, patriarchal authority, pietistic rural values, and the weight of the past. In the other is the evolutionist defense attorney Henry Drummond (Spencer Tracy), representing the authority of human law, the Constitution as central text, rationality, analytical cross-examination, avuncular self-deprecation, progressive urban values, and the promise of the future. Though the film has its share of courtroom pyrotechnics, the real action of the film is in the speeches the two titans hurl at each other.

Though few courtroom dramas take on as much sociocultural baggage as *Inherit the Wind,* it is the business of all lawyer films to explore conflicting views about morality and power – in effect, to raise the question of what gives legal authority its authority – by projecting those conflicts onto the courtroom. Most lawyer films end up in the courtroom for the same reason that most westerns end up in a climactic shootout: because the arena of the courtroom is the seat of powers in conflict and the site of the heroic individual agon. Just as the western shootout is supposed to eliminate every distraction in favor of a purified, disinterested contest of power, skill, and nerve, the courtroom is supposed to be a sheltered arena free of distractions or prejudice that will allow the best man (or, in films like *Suspect* [1987] and *Music Box* [1989], the best woman) to win. The complication essential to courtroom drama, however, is the suspicion that the institutional justice system is biased against women (*Adam's Rib*), or people of color (*Sergeant Rutledge, To Kill a Mockingbird*), or more generally that justice under the law is not congruent with moral justice (*The Accused,* 1988). Even assuming, as lawyer films generally do, that the best client and the best lawyer has the best case, the law itself may not recognize that superiority. The courtroom thus aims to test the social status quo to which the law by its nature appeals.

The space of individual courtrooms customarily expresses both a general aspiration to impartial justice and the specific prejudices of the justice system in any given film. British courtrooms place prisoners in the dock, an elevated platform that isolates them and emphasizes their importance; but American courtrooms seat the accused alongside their attorneys, giving them much less prominence, so that once Perry Mason's cases go to trial, his clients generally fade to insignificance. Instead, Hollywood courtrooms, divided between architecturally balanced tables for the two opposing sides and symmetrically placed seats for the spectators who uniformly fill the space behind them, emphasize their equality under the law and their deference toward the law, represented by the elevated judge's seat they all face. This seat, even more than the person who occupies it, represents the law's authority, as Daniel Kaffee indicates when he pauses before it before leaving the empty courtroom at the end of *A Few Good Men.* Movies that diminish its visual importance invariably imply that the judge in their particular case is insignificant (*Inherit the Wind, To Kill a Mockingbird*) or corrupt (*Presumed Innocent*).

Courtroom decorum is as rigidly prescribed as courtroom space. Witnesses swear to tell the truth; defendants and spectators are enjoined against unseemly outbursts; attorneys for both sides, who frequently object to their adversaries' questions as irrelevant, leading, or immaterial, are forbidden from offering testimony themselves under the guise of questioning witnesses; and juries are routinely ordered to disregard what they have just heard. Yet all these rules are constantly broken; indeed, their breaches provide much of the courtroom drama's allure. The judge in *Sergeant Rutledge* begins by ejecting his wife from the court, then is forced to readmit her when she is called as a witness. Both lead attorneys in *Inherit the Wind* are more interested in making speeches, and both attorneys in *Anatomy of a Murder* are more interested in denouncing each other's narrow-mindedly legalistic tactics, than any of them is in the job of examining the witnesses who are supposed to establish the facts of their cases. The defense attorney calls the prosecutor to testify in *Inherit the Wind,* and the judge comes down from his bench to testify in *Fury* (1936). Witnesses rush to incriminate themselves in *Sergeant Rutledge* and *A Few Good Men.* Perry Mason, who has an uncanny knack of evoking confessions from witnesses even when he is not questioning them on the stand, is constantly accused by his favorite television adversary, the outraged District Attorney Hamilton Burger (William Talman), of turning the courtroom into a circus. This transformation is more literal in *Adam's Rib,* when defense attorney Amanda Bonner asks a female weightlifter to lift Amanda's husband, the prosecuting attorney, off his feet during one of their many arguments.

Every breach of courtroom decorum rehearses a conflict between the conventions established to administer justice and an attorney's plea that those conventions unfairly stifle an individual client's rights. A well-ordered courtroom indicates the audience's faith in the system; the more frequent and turbulent the violations of decorum, the more openly that faith is challenged. In extreme cases, the system designed to evince the truth seems to work only when it is ignored (*12 Angry Men, Trial by Jury, The Juror*) or has broken down completely. In *Presumed Innocent*, Sandy Stern (Raul Julia) gets the charges against his client dismissed by obliquely threatening to expose the judge (Paul Winfield) to prosecution for bribery; in . . . *And Justice for All* (1979), Arthur Kirkland (Al Pacino) brings his defense of his old adversary Judge Henry Fleming (John Forsythe), an accused rapist, to a climax by insisting that his client is guilty ("He told me so himself"), guaranteeing a mistrial for the client and disbarment for himself. Justice can be served, these films imply, only when lawyers exceed their legal authority. In *Adam's Rib,* which argues that the same legal defenses should be allowed to men and women, Amanda Bonner in effect steps outside of her judicial role to become an ad hoc legislator arguing the case on the basis of what the law should be. At the end of *Witness for the Prosecution,* the virtually deserted courtroom serves as backdrop to the murder of Leonard Vole (Tyrone Power) by his enraged wife, Christine (Marlene Dietrich), after her plan to free him by unmasking as perjury her testimony attacking his alibi backfires when he declares his attachment to another woman. Finally, the courtroom setting proclaims, justice has been done, but only because Christine has acted as her husband's executioner, condemning and killing him when the law would not. The film puts a last, comical twist on this breakdown of the law before the imperatives of justice in Sir Wilfrid Robarts's announcement that he will be delighted to handle Christine's defense, suggesting that for him, the law is nothing but a game.

Sir Wilfrid had first taken her husband's case because he had convinced himself of Vole's innocence by watching his eyes react without blinking to the bright light Sir Wilfrid's monocle was reflecting into them. In whodunits like *Witness for the Prosecution, Sergeant Rutledge,* and *Presumed Innocent,* which leave the question of the guilty party's identity open until the end, it would undoubtedly be useful to have a special line on the truth, even if Sir Wilfrid is grievously misled in believing he has it. But when questions of motivation rather than the identity of the perpetrator are in dispute, as in *Adam's Rib, Anatomy of a Murder,* or *A Few Good Men,* privileged access to the truth is less important than the ability to sell one's story to a jury.

Thinking of lawyers as gamesters or salespeople implies a more cynical approach to the law than most Hollywood movies are comfortable affirming in the end. Instead, lawyer movies like *To Kill a Mockingbird* typically open a space between the historical specificity of an individual law or courtroom, which may well be inadequate, corrupt, or dated, and the presumed generality of the moral law on which the audience can be counted to share. More ambitious films like *Inherit the Wind* and *A Few Good Men* use courtrooms to stage broader cultural conflicts without unequivocally endorsing either side, though even these two films, for example, clearly assume that their audiences will root for the defense.

Even when they present value systems in collision, Hollywood courtroom dramas end by appealing to allegedly universal moral norms that have less to do with transcendental authority, historical tradition, or the legal precedents of particular social orders than with a surprisingly simple ideology of Hollywood entertainment. The unbroken rule is that David trumps Goliath; the underdogs always have moral right on their side. Hence the few are always more justified than the many, the poor than the rich, the lower class than the upper class, the powerless than the powerful, the individual than the system.

The constancy with which Hollywood champions underdogs goes far to explain the changes in lawyers' fortunes since the coming of synchronized sound. Attorneys of the 1930s and 1940s are first and foremost successful professional men and women who may be admired for their success (*Counsellor-at-Law*, 1933; the Perry Mason movies) or victimized because of it (*The Paradine Case*). In general, films of this period, regarding lawyers as anything but underdogs, project their attitudes toward the law onto its representatives, from the constant writs of habeas corpus submitted by Johnny Lovo's shyster lawyer, Epstein (Bert Starkey), in *Scarface* (1932) to the background as an unsuccessful lawyer that prepares Brick Davis (James Cagney) for an FBI career that suits his idealism better in *"G" Men* (1935). *Adam's Rib* provides perhaps the most comprehensive celebration of the attorney's material success before *The Firm*. Its lawyer couple enjoys an upper-crust life-style including a beautiful Manhattan apartment, a country house, and servants who prepare everything from morning coffee to dinner. Freed of financial constraints, they can concentrate on the important business of alternately bickering and flirting with each other over whether the existing laws concerning criminal assault should be enforced or rewritten. There is, however, no lawyer genre coeval with the gangster genre or film noir because films starring lawyers are relatively rare during periods in which the law's authority is generally accepted; lawyers are neither clearly David nor Goliath.

Because the legal formula relies on conflicts about the most fundamental institutional values, its appeal is greatest in crises of belief – not simply belief in the legal system, but belief in authority generally. The civil rights movement provides just such a pivotal moment in the later 1950s. Fifteen years earlier, *The Ox-Bow Incident* (1943) had used the conventions of the western to present a cautionary tale of what happens when well-meaning citizens constitute themselves a lynch mob; it provided a warning against fascism, endorsed the authority of the American legal system, and incidentally made a hero of Gil Carter (Henry Fonda), the lone cowboy who argues against the lynching. The more optimistic *The Caine Mutiny* (1954) shows that system vindicating the necessity of a naval mutiny against the paranoiac Captain

Queeg (Humphrey Bogart). A series of films contemporaneous with the original *Perry Mason* television series – *Anatomy of a Murder, Compulsion* (1959), *Inherit the Wind* – present underdog lawyers as heroic social prophets and engineers. *Sergeant Rutledge* and *To Kill a Mockingbird* stigmatize racial bigotry to make explicit the pattern beneath all these films: the fear of existing laws as coercive and unfair, coupled with faith in heroic lawyers as advocates for those oppressed by the law and architects of better laws.

The years following Watergate dramatically reverse this view of lawyers as embattled champions of the underdog. . . . *And Justice for All* offers a scathing portrait of a justice system so dysfunctional (one judge is suicidal, another on trial for rape, attorneys on both sides under constant investigation) that no one could serve its distorted offices in good conscience; the only ethical choice is to denounce it and opt out, as Arthur Kirkland does by fingering his own client. When Raymond Burr returned as television's Perry Mason in 1985, it was as a comfortable paterfamilias, a blast from a past when lawyers could still be heroes because they fought the power.

The other option open to defenders of would-be heroic lawyers was to argue that they were not really lawyers. Washed-up alcoholic Frank Galvin (Paul Newman) in *The Verdict* and fish-out-of-water Brooklyn shyster Vinny Gambini (Joe Pesci) in *My Cousin Vinny* are antilawyers; the attorney heroes of John Grisham are nonlawyers. Mitch McDeere (Tom Cruise), a Harvard Law graduate recruited by the sinister Memphis firm of Bendini, Lambert and Locke in *The Firm,* does not even pass the bar exam until the film is nearly over [Fig. 62]. Darby Shaw (Julia Roberts), the heroine of *The Pelican Brief* (1993), is a law student whose brief speculating on the reason for the murders of two Supreme Court justices leads to the murder of her lover, Tulane Law professor Thomas Callahan (Sam Shepard), and forces her to take flight in a series of breathtaking high-fashion chases that make her look anything but lawyerly. The heroine of *The Client* (1994) is a troubled, maternal attorney (Susan Sarandon) whose incongruous name, Reggie Love, suggests, as Atticus Finch did thirty years earlier, that the best lawyers are mom and dad writ large. Even in Grisham's more orthodox courtroom dramas, *A Time to Kill* and *John Grisham's The Rainmaker*, the lawyer heroes, Jake Brigance (Matthew McConaughey) and Rudy Baylor (Matt Damon) and their allies are unseasoned, raffish, or cast-off types set against powerful, corrupt legal insiders like D.A. Rufus Buckley (Kevin Spacey) and Leo F. Drummond (Jon Voight), who

62. *The Firm:* Cruise again, as a lawyer hero who has not even passed the bar exam.

are apparently more representative of the justice system. Julia Roberts's eponymous heroine in *Erin Brockovich* represents the antilawyer (trash talk, sexy clothes, unlimited empathy) who is also a nonlawyer. (Her herculean efforts on behalf of her boss's pro bono clients are bracketed by two memorable remarks: "I hate lawyers. I just work for 'em," and "Tell her I'm not a lawyer. That may help.")

Even in an age noted for its skepticism about the law and its contempt for lawyers' morality, there are other ways to make a lawyer into a hero. If Grisham sets his nonlawyer or barely lawyer heroes against the legal establishment, his contemporary Scott Turow, in a series of novels as notable for their differences from one another as Grisham's are for their formulaic similarities, puts his lawyer heroes through a wide variety of paces. The film version of his best-known novel, *Presumed Innocent,* offers a textbook case of how contemporary filmmakers can breathe new life into the dualities of the lawyer film – in this case, by using a series of analogies between sex and the law to explore the range of roles the prosecutor Rusty Sabich (Harrison Ford) must assume.

More and more completely, the film muddles the distinction between heroic lawyers like Rusty who have respect for the law and corrupt lawyers like Nico Della Guardia (Tom Mardirosian) who, as Rusty announces, "fuck the law for politics." The professional and sexual career of Carolyn Polhemus (Greta Scacchi), the manipulative lover Rusty is accused of killing, unmasks respect for the law as fucking, and fucking as the pursuit of power. It is a lesson Rusty does not learn until he loses the power of his office and realizes that if he declines to use the law to fuck his enemies by beating back Nico's challenge or challenging his boss, Raymond Horgan (Brian Dennehy), himself, the law does not thereby remain pure; someone else merely uses it to fuck him. Like sex, the law is in itself neither bad nor good; it is merely one more medium for human relationships based on lust and power. But in Rusty's bleak world, in which the only possibilities open to anyone are to fuck or be fucked, the law becomes simply the most powerful tool of oppression and the most transparent expression of the universal will to power. Lawyers like Rusty Sabich are no more or less guilty than anyone else; they are simply people with greater opportunities to seize power, and more to lose if it is used against them [Fig. 63].

Presumed Innocent soft-pedals its lawyer hero, and incidentally casts him as David against the Goliaths in his old office, by giving him a variety of roles that do justice to his representative humanity, forcing him to shift from one reasonable but impossible role (prosecutor, politician, detective, husband, father, lover, client, officer of the court) to the next, and showing the compromises each role exacts. A more direct and radical critique of the stereotype of the contemptible lawyer, and the conventions of lawyer films generally, is *Reversal of Fortune* (1990), a film remarkable for its refusal of the melodrama *Presumed Innocent* handles so resourcefully and expertly. In *Reversal of Fortune,* a well-known, well-heeled, self-publicizing, and potentially despicable lawyer takes on the appeal of one of the most hated men in America, already convicted of attempted murder in a trial that cast him in a truly villainous light, and secures for a him a new trial that will ultimately reverse his conviction – all without losing the audience's sympathy, and while scarcely entering a courtroom.

Where *Presumed Innocent* is impassioned and involving, *Reversal of Fortune* is clinically detached in its handling of the question of whether jet-setting socialite Claus von Bülow injected his beautiful, wealthy, pill-popping wife, Sunny, with a near-lethal dose of insulin. This detachment begins with the film's opening helicopter shot of the Rhode Island coast, moving toward Clarendon Court, the von Bülows' estate,

63. *Presumed Innocent:* Harrison Ford as a lawyer hero no more or less innocent than anyone else. (Raul Julia, Bonnie Bedelia, Ford)

and then tracking down a hospital corridor toward the open door of the room where Sunny von Bülow lies in an irreversible coma, attended by round-the-clock nurses who monitor her condition, bathe her, and turn her body to prevent bedsores, leaving her, as she puts it in disembodied voice-over, "brain dead, body better than ever."

If the resulting air of otherworldly detachment seems remote from Hollywood, it is no surprise that director Barbet Schroeder, like his cinematographer, Luciano Tovoli, had trained in Europe. The French director, best known to American audiences for the more melodramatic but equally chilly *Single White Female* (1992), had followed teenaged dropouts in *More* (1969) and *The Valley Obscured by the Clouds* (1972), then explored the sexual underworld of *Maîtresse* (1976) and the criminal underworld of *Tricheurs* (1984) before making his American debut with *Barfly* (1987). The unsettling force of *Reversal of Fortune*'s opening sequence, with its gliding, weightless camera and its crisp exterior shadows, depends as well on its suppression of live sound in favor of the quiet, vaguely sinister music of Mark Isham. The combination of Isham's darkly self-effacing score, the brightly lit Rhode Island exteriors, the antiseptic hospital corridor filled with silent people, and the sense of penetration from a mysterious exterior to the secrets hidden behind Sunny von Bülow's door, her hospital room bathed in spectral, blue-filtered light, provide both a foretaste of the film's narrative plan – a series of movements from outside to inside, from the surface to the secrets beneath – and a hint that this plan, like that of Joseph Conrad's story "Heart of Darkness," or of *Citizen Kane* (1941) or *Psycho* (1960), offers an analytical critique rather than an example of the empirical method, for there is no ultimate truth to be found.

The true auteurs of the film are its three lead actors and its two screenwriters. The most unlikely of these is Alan Dershowitz, who not only wrote the book on which the film is based but was himself the star of that book, a factual account of his success in winning an appeal of Claus von Bülow's attempted-murder conviction. Dershowitz, at the time a professor at Harvard Law School and the coauthor of two textbooks and a volume of reminiscences, has since become far more widely known as a legal analyst, novelist, and social polemicist; but it was the publication of *Reversal of Fortune* (1986) that first made his abrasive, self-promoting figure known outside the legal community. In Dershowitz's account of von Bülow's two trials, which spans the years 1982–5, von Bülow himself is a relatively minor figure; the stage is dominated by Dershowitz himself as the real star of the case, the unflappable lawyer who prepared the successful appeal of the first verdict that won his client the right to a second trial.

Nicholas Kazan turned Dershowitz's sprawling book into a screenplay by retaining his central focus on the appeal but changing almost everything else, dropping figures (mostly other lawyers and jurists) who are vital to Dershowitz's account and replacing them with other characters (mostly law students) who appear only briefly in the book's brief hints about his domestic life. In Kazan's account, Dershowitz's students become a surrogate family whose contrast with the von Bülow family provides a structural fulcrum. Kazan changes the relationship between Dershowitz and von Bülow, emphasizing the social differences between them and making Dershowitz far more noncommittal about his client's innocence. Of all Kazan's changes, however, two stand out as crucial. He jettisons half of Dershowitz's story, focusing only on the appeal, and eliminating virtually every possibility for courtroom scenes. Then, although his decision to elide every phase of the legal process in which Dershowitz was not personally involved would seem to leave Dershowitz as the dominant figure in the story, he recasts the narrative voice of the film, dropping Dershowitz's first-person account not for the third-person presentation the material seems to suggest, but for an unexpected new narrator: Sunny von Bülow, whose voice-over commentary frames and repeatedly interrupts the action even though Sunny spends the entire running time of the film in her second, irreversible coma.

The effect is eerie and electrifying. *Sunset Blvd.* (1950) had been narrated by a dead character, but largely for shock and surprise; no film had ever made such a grating issue of giving a voice to a narrator beyond all human speech. The change in voice from the brash, practical Dershowitz to the ethereal, pill-popping Sunny, combined with the flashbacks Kazan strategically interpolates showing glimpses of the von Bülows' strangely dispassionate marriage before the two episodes that left Sunny comatose, elevates her role to star status; Glenn Close, who played Sunny, received top billing. Having the story narrated from a physical limbo, by a woman who is neither dead nor alive, gives the film a formal disengagement that parallels its visual detachment. Nor is this disengagement merely formal, since the spoiled hypochondriac's placidly self-absorbed narration, which presents the facts of the case against her husband but is silent on the film's larger questions, never makes it clear whether she believes, or even cares, whether her husband is guilty of trying to murder her. At the same time, casting the victim as the narrator succeeds in doing something murder trials always strive and fail to do, giving voice to the silenced victim, even though, as Sunny coolly notes, "It's hard to remember that all this is about me." Using Sunny's voice to frame the narrative, even as Dershowitz is framing the action, subtly pits her interests against his, even though their antagonism is never made explicit.

In the role of Sunny's oblique antagonist, the man bent on proving that she injected herself with insulin, the filmmakers cast Jewish Everyman Ron Silver, whose strong physical resemblance to Dershowitz made him an obvious choice for the role. The real casting coup, however, was Jeremy Irons in the role of Claus von Bülow. The patrician Irons, most often cast in cerebral or obsessive romantic roles (*The French Lieutenant's Woman*, 1981; *Betrayal*, 1983; *Swann in Love*, 1984; *Dead Ringers*, 1988), scored a triumph as von Bülow, sweeping all the year's major acting awards.

Organizing the film around these three characters allows Schroeder and Kazan to make Dershowitz a heroic figure while assuming that their audience holds lawyers in low esteem. The film addresses viewers' distaste for lawyers head on. "I'm not a hired gun," Dershowitz tells von Bülow during their first meeting, anticipating the presumption that that is exactly what he is. "I've got to feel that there's some moral or constitutional issue at stake." The conflation of moral and constitutional issues is completed by Dershowitz's pro bono labors on behalf of the Johnson brothers, two black teenagers whose assistance in breaking their father out of jail put them on death row after he shot two guards in the escape. In some cases, at least, Dershowitz is presented as knowing what the truth is, and he is interested in questions of morality as in points of law.

At other times the film is more candid about Dershowitz's personal interest in the case. Dershowitz opens the initial meeting in which he invites his old students to work on the case by telling them, "I take cases because I am pissed off." But the students reveal quite different attitudes. When one of them, Minnie (Felicity Huffman), refuses point blank to work for the defense of a man who is obviously guilty, another, Raj (Mano Singh), replies, "I agree von Bülow is guilty, but that's the fun! I mean, that's the challenge!" Posing before a painting of a family at dinner in order to confirm his legal team's status as surrogate family, Dershowitz responds approvingly: "Now there's a lawyer." The following debate is aimed at persuading Minnie, as the audience's skeptical surrogate, that handling von Bülow's appeal is more ethical than declining to defend him. The legal principle on which Dershowitz bases his moral position is that Sunny's family, by hiring a private prosecutor to gather evidence against her husband, not only violated his rights but established a precedent that, if adopted widely by the wealthy, would undermine the principle of equal justice for all.

As Dershowitz is making his case directly to his former students and the skeptical audience, the film is indirectly making a second case for his moral authority by contrasting him visually to his client. Von Bülow moves slowly and stiffly, even when he is summoning medical assistance for the comatose wife he has sat beside in bed for hours. Von Bülow's throaty voice, varying in volume but never in inflection, is frustratingly inexpressive, and the film shows how cold-blooded are his attempts at moral outrage ("Innocence has always been my position," he tells Dershowitz when invited to give an account of his actions) and humor (when Sunny asks in a flashback whether her first husband, Alfie von Auersperg, should have treated her as if he were her lord and master, von Bülow replies, "Of course not. I am your lord and master," then, after a two-beat pause, adds, "Just kidding") [Fig.

64. *Reversal of Fortune:* A flashback shows the brittle charm of the von Bülows' courtship. (Glenn Close, Jeremy Irons)

64]. When Dershowitz taxes him with his indifference to Sunny's fate, he replies, "Of course I care, Alan, I just don't wear my heart on my sleeve." At von Bülow's Manhattan apartment, painterly, symmetrical shots of von Bülow and his mistress, Andrea Reynolds (Christine Baranski), are intercut with even more severely symmetrical shots of Dershowitz perched uncomfortably alone in a chair in the center of the frame.

Instead of dressing like Hollywood's idea of a lawyer (oxford-gray suits, subdued ties, black wing tips), Dershowitz dresses like Hollywood's idea of an academic (a rumpled tweed jacket and chinos for his first meeting with von Bülow, a flannel shirt and khakis for his working sessions at home). Since von Bülow is always faultlessly attired, the audience is encouraged to project their resistance to Dershowitz's profession onto his client. As a Harvard professor and a successful litigator, Dershowitz may be well off, but his modest home and his scruffy appearance and fondness for takeout pizza give no hint of his financial status; nor does his frenetic activity level [Fig. 65]. After fifteen minutes of oppressively tasteful scenes at Clarendon Court, in which the waxwork characters rarely show enough energy to walk

65. *Reversal of Fortune:* The intense physicality of the lawyer hero. (Ron Silver, with Mano Singh, Felicity Huffman, Alan Pottinger, Annabella Sciorra)

across the room, the cut from a hand swabbing the inside of Sunny's slackly unresponsive mouth to the basketball game that introduces Dershowitz as a scrappy fighter in T-shirt and shorts who relaxes through physical activity is downright refreshing. After the students who have finished a meal von Bülow ordered clamor for an explanation of his behavior, Schroeder shows them falling silent and frozen in a long-held group shot, then cuts to von Bülow placidly stirring his tea. The contrast between the eager, enthusiastic, curious, conflicted yet committed students and the enigmatic, unresponsive man they are working to free could not be greater.

The film is even more emphatic about the class differences between Dershowitz and his client, who begins their relationship by saying, "I should tell you that I have the greatest respect for the intelligence and integrity of the Jewish people." Andrea Reynolds later tells Dershowitz that she had advised von Bülow to seek him out: "Get the Jew, I said." Dershowitz's reply – "The Jew is here" – reveals a self-deprecating Jewish humor that seems to mark von Bülow and Reynolds, by contrast, as members of an alien species. Against the grotesquely dysfunctional von Bülow family, whose members seem to make common cause only for the purpose of gathering evidence against each other, the film sets the reassuringly normal loner Dershowitz, whose absent

66. *Reversal of Fortune:* Dershowitz's patrician client looks more like a lawyer than he does. (Jeremy Irons, Ron Silver)

wife is replaced by his devoted son Elon (Stephen Mailer), his ex-lover Sarah (Annabella Sciorra), and his rowdy team of students-turned-colleagues, herded, in one of the few details borrowed from Dershowitz's book, into different rooms of his house according to their specific assignments.[2] When Dershowitz is on the telephone making still another argument on behalf of the Johnson brothers, Sarah's comment to Elon – "It's great when he's like this, huh? I only wish he had something left for the people around him" – simply confirms Dershowitz's own comfortable self-assessment: "My clients are the people I care about."

These cultural conflicts between Dershowitz and the client who serves as lightning rod for resentment viewers might normally direct against lawyers [Fig. 66] consistently upstage what would be the big moments in other lawyer films. When Dershowitz's team realizes that the crusted insulin on the tip of the hypodermic needle the prosecution offered in evidence as von Bülow's weapon cannot have been produced by injecting it but only by dipping it in insulin, perhaps in an attempt to manufacture evidence against von Bülow, this startling new discovery is less important than the success of Dershowitz's appeal. Even the appeal – which Dershowitz, attired in a rumpled, ill-fitting black suit, is shown arguing before the court – occupies one of the film's briefest scenes. Though Dershowitz's arguments in court ought logically to put the original trial judge on the defensive, the film never even shows this judge, and the Harvard lawyer's defense strategy casts von Bülow in the role instead. Dershowitz succeeds in turning the very qualities that make von Bülow powerful, remote, and dislikable into arguments for his underdog status and his ultimate reversal of fortune. For all his impenetrable sang-froid, the wealthy, powerful, jet-setting socialite becomes, in Dershowitz's narrative, a victim of a system co-opted by greedy, vindictive relatives and a private prosecutor hired to circumvent the system's proper procedures.

How could von Bülow, who looked so transparently guilty at the end of his first trial, be so rehabilitated by the appeal that a second trial could find him innocent? That is the central question of Dershowitz's book, and one the book proposes to answer by "present[ing] the facts, first as the prosecution successfully presented them at the initial trial. Then it will introduce the dramatic new evidence that came to light only after the verdict – new facts that cast an entirely different light both on the prosecution's version and on the dramatis personae in the case. Finally, it will tell the story as it came out in the second trial."[3] In weighing the different versions of this story, Dershowitz, although he has clearly come to believe in his client's innocence, is at his most lawyerly:

> In this book I leave it to the readers to decide what they believe the truth to be. I will not try to tell *the* story of what happened. I don't know for sure what happened, though I have my strong suspicions based on a thorough review of all the evidence and a close association with, and observation of, most of the central characters. So I can only tell the *stories* that each side claims are the truth. My own biases and hunches will surely filter through any veneer of objectivity. Every reader will have to decide which truth seems more compelling. This attitude may seem unduly nihilistic, but it is simply the product of many years of experience with the adversary system of justice.[4]

In fact, Dershowitz's attitude seems anything but nihilistic. Nobody but the von Bülows is ever likely to know the truth of Sunny's comas for certain, but the different stories told about those events can be variously persuasive. In the absence of any absolutely authoritative story, weighing the merits of different stories allows the closest reasonable approach to the truth.

Because the question of how Dershowitz was able to rehabilitate Bülow on appeal is far less central to the film, it comes to a more vertiginous conclusion. As Sarah says in explaining the verdict to Elon: "All we had to do was prove that the State made a lousy case. We didn't prove that Claus was innocent. We couldn't. We didn't have to. And – he probably isn't." In his final meeting with von Bülow, Dershowitz shows the extent to which the two men's fortunes have becomes intertwined in the unusually subdued white shirt and gray patterned tie he is wearing with his tweed jacket. Yet he keeps his distance from his client in his final conclusion: "Legally, this was an important victory. Morally, you're on your own." Instead of a cathartic courtroom sequence that establishes the truth once and for all, the film offers three alternative flashbacks over Isham's eerie music showing how Sunny might have fallen into her second, irreversible coma. In the first alternative, she combines barbiturates and insulin in a suicide attempt, then collapses in her bathroom at Clarendon Court. In the second, the hiked-up position of her nightgown is explained by her attempt to use the toilet just as a fatal spasm wracks her body. In the third, her husband finds her in bed after she has injected herself, but instead of helping her or calling a doctor, he opens the window to the freezing December air in order to ensure that she does not recover and drags her into the bathroom, hiking up her gown in the process, to ensure that she is not found until she is dead. Though the second and third flashbacks seem to explain physical evidence the first leaves mysterious, the film offers no guarantee that any of them shows the truth.[5]

By arguing that von Bülow deserved a new trial but stopping short of showing that trial or endorsing its verdict of not guilty, the film leaves loose ends that are largely, and paradoxically, the privilege of movies announcing their basis in a true story. Although the end titles announcing von Bülow's continued marriage to Sunny, the Johnson brothers' continued tenancy on death row, and Sunny's continued death-in-life bring a certain degree of closure to the film, it remains teasingly, flagrantly open-ended in ways Dershowitz's hard-headed book never is. Sunny's voice-over, despite its formally privileged status, repeatedly declines to settle important questions, not only about her coma, but about her whole life with her husband. Instead of throwing any further light on his personality, she keeps asking unanswerable questions. Gradually, it becomes clear that Sunny's voice-over is holding out the promise of revelations from beyond (or just this side of) the grave for the express purpose of frustrating them. "Time moves in only one direction – forward," she muses as Dershowitz prepares to argue the appeal. "It's stupid and boring, and results in a lot of silliness. Example: the legal process. In this particular case, a great deal of time, effort, and money was spent trying to determine precisely what happened on those two nights so close to Christmas. . . . If you could just go back in time and take a peek, you'd know, and all this would be unnecessary." After the verdict, she adds a metaphysical postlude – "This is all you can know. This is all you can be told. When you get where I am, you will know the rest" – even though there is no way of telling whether Sunny, who is only comatose, not dead, even knows what happened to cause her second coma, especially since it is never clear that she knows what caused the first coma, which her husband was also convicted of inducing. The cumulative effect of all these intimations of a harrowingly secular (and premature) afterlife is at once to invoke and to deny any possibility of transcendental truth or justice, sharpening audiences' appetites for the last word on the von Bülow case in order to dash them more completely.

Von Bülow himself remains a closed book to his lawyer to the end. When Dershowitz lashes out at him in frustration, "It's very hard to trust someone you don't understand. You're a very strange man," von Bülow replies oracularly, "You have no idea." The film's determination to rehabilitate the lawyer hero as a salt-of-the-earth defender of the rule of law while declining to rehabilitate his client or present him definitively as a moneyed monster utterly undeserving of his appeals team's heroic efforts suggests not only that audiences will not and cannot ever penetrate beyond the film's elegant opening shots to the truth of the von Bülow case, but that it is not the law's business to know the truth: Lawyers, like police officers, are finally concerned with power rather than knowledge. The dead-end indeterminacy of the film, which makes Dershowitz into a proletarian hero by showing the ways he protects his clients from the law's power without ever identifying him with that power himself, is brilliantly encapsulated by its insouciant epilogue, a brief scene in which von Bülow, whose legal ordeal has made him a more widely known celebrity than ever, stops in a convenience store to buy a pack of cigarettes. When the wary clerk (Connie Shulman) asks if he'd like anything else, he adds, in a deliberate echo of his earlier joke to his now-comatose wife, "Yes. A vial of insulin." And then, after two beats: "Just kidding."

12

Fargo and the Crime Comedy

Despite their popularity, very little has been written on crime comedies. Crime comedies are more often classified as comedies (films people laugh at) that happen to be about crime than as crime films (films about crime) that happen to be comical because comedy is a stronger, more broadly recognized genre than the crime film. This is despite the fact that comedy has been notoriously difficult to define without circularity (comedies are movies that make people laugh; movies make people laugh because they're funny; people feel free to laugh at things that might not otherwise seem funny because they know they're watching a comedy) ever since Aristotle's theory of comedy, a companion piece to his *Poetics,* was lost.[1]

No one complains that *Hamlet* is not a tragedy if it does not produce tears, but most audiences define comedy in terms of their own laughter, and not every audience laughs at the same things. Philosophies of humor dating back to Aristotle have been dominated by three models proposing variously that people laugh because they appreciate some incongruity in a joke, or because of their sense of superiority to the butts of comedy, or because they enjoy a sense of relief after being wound up by the tension that is released by a punch line.[2] But none of these models – incongruity, superiority, release – has succeeded in explaining all comedy. Literary and dramatic theorists have attempted to circumvent this problem by proposing theories of comedy based on structural models, but the arguments of comedy they propose, to use Northrop Frye's phrase, do little to explain why audiences laugh at comedies.[3] Hence comic theory continues to be divided between two groups of analysts – literary theorists, who focus on what comedy is, and philosophers of humor, who focus on why people laugh – who often resemble blind men talking about elephants.

Although crime comedy is more widely considered a subgenre of comedy than of the crime film, it depends on the conventions of the crime film in one inescapable way. Comedy lacks its own distinctive subject matter because there is no subject that is intrinsically funny. So comedies of any sort are parasitic on the conventions of other genres like the action film, the romance, and the crime film. Crime comedies in particular tend to recycle the plots and characters of apparently straightforward crime films, not only in parodies like *High Anxiety* (1977), *Dead Men Don't Wear Plaid* (1982), and *Jane Austen's Mafia!* (1998), but in films like *Throw Momma from the Train* (1987), a virtual remake of *Strangers on a Train* (1951) turned into a comedy largely by casting Danny DeVito as the importunate killer, Billy Crystal as the man he begs to murder his overbearing mother, and Anne Ramsey as the imperishable victim. Innumerable crime comedies begin with potentially dramatic situations and then add one element that turns them comical: the crooks' need to steal an entire bank in *Bank Shot* (1974), the ineffectuality of both the embattled Mafia widow's suitors in *Married to the Mob* (1988) [Fig. 67], the choice of a hit man's high-school reunion as the place for a murderous showdown in *Grosse Pointe Blank* (1997).

However different their primary impulses might seem, comedies and crime films both depend on outraging the establishment within the film and viewers' expectations about the film. Assuming that viewers wish to laugh at criminal outrages that fulfill their own dark fantasies, and will do so if they can be released from the moral decorum that demands they condemn criminal behavior, many crime films work to establish a decorum of acceptable outrage, just as noncomic crime films might rely on a decorum that accepts mob killings or vigilante cops as normal.[4]

The obvious way to establish a decorum of acceptable comic outrage is to present victims who are comical because they are inconsequential, despicable, or incapable of suffering serious harm, like the eight murdered relatives all played by Alec Guinness in the Ealing comedy *Kind Hearts and Coronets* (1949) and the blustering criminals who end up dying instead of their innocent intended victims in *The Ladykillers* (1955) and *Charade* (1963). Audiences will laugh even at serious crimes, however, if they are investigated by comical detectives like Buster Keaton's daydreaming amateur sleuth in *Sherlock Jr.* (1924),

67. *Married to the Mob:* The embattled Mafia widow (Michelle Pfeiffer) and her ineffectual police suitor (Matthew Modine).

the incompetent detectives played by W. C. Fields in *The Bank Dick* (1940) and Groucho Marx in *The Big Store* (1941) and *Love Happy* (1950), Inspector Jacques Clouseau of the *Pink Panther* movies (1964–93), and Axel Foley in the *Beverly Hills Cop* franchise (1984–94). Finally, criminal threats can be defused and rendered comical if the criminals themselves are played for laughs, like the maiden-aunt killers of *Arsenic and Old Lace* (1944); the oblivious couple who commit the murders in *Eating Raoul* (1982) in hopes of financing a restaurant; the aspiring standup comic of *The King of Comedy* (1982) who kidnaps a talk-show host in order to break into show biz; and the mob boss in *Analyze This* (1999) who consults an unwilling psychiatrist when he unaccountably loses his appetite for killing [Fig. 68].

Although it might therefore seem that crime comedies are simply crime films with comic relief added, like whipped cream on a sundae, it would be a mistake to conclude that comical victims, avengers, and villains are simply extraneous to the plots whose melodramatic force they deflect. Instead, comic caper films, mysteries, and parodies display the same thematic contradictions as their allegedly more serious counterparts but use these contradictions to provoke laughter rather than perturbation. In *The Pilgrim* (1923), Charlie Chaplin, as an escaped convict masquerading as a country parson, plays not only a comic villain whose plans to fleece his new congregation keep going astray, but also a comic victim and a comic avenger. The opening scenes explore the relation between apparent innocence and criminal guilt by dramatizing how uncomfortable Chaplin is in his assumed role as he keeps reverting to criminal habits, holding onto the grate at a ticket window as if it were the bars of his prison cell and stowing away on the train even though he has bought a ticket. But when he meets an old lag (Charles Riesner) who worms his way into the same household, Chaplin's imposter is forced to find increasingly ingenious ways to thwart Riesner's plan to steal the mortgage money from their kindly hostess (Kitty Bradbury) and the daughter (Edna Purviance) for whom Chaplin has fallen. From beginning to end, the film is organized around a series of provocative jokes about the contradiction between the title character's criminal habits and his ever more noble instincts. It is not sufficient, therefore, to say that films like *The Pilgrim* take what would normally be a straightforward dramatic problem typical of crime films and present it with a twist that makes it comical – the victims are eminently dispensable, the detective clumsy and incompetent, the criminals a pair of harmless maiden aunts – because comedy itself is a mode of dramatizing these problems, not an escape from them. The peculiar paradox of crime comedy is that the decorum its twists undermine prescribes a normal, predictable round of violent lawbreaking and summary justice. Crime comedies, which present a world whose decorum is broken both by crime and by laughter, therefore interrogate in a particularly pointed way the very possibility of social and perceptual normality. Just as gangster films and private-eye films present not so much a breakdown of social logic as its displacement onto a world in which criminal behavior is a given, comedy interrogates the fallacies of normality through a logic of its own.

This logic operates at its simplest in animated films, many of which would be readily classified as crime films if they were not classified as cartoons. The submerged generic affiliation of Walt Disney's first animated feature, *Snow White and the Seven Dwarfs* (1937), for instance, as a period crime film with musical interludes emerges clearly in Howard Hawks's two updated, nonanimated retellings of the Snow White story, *Ball of Fire* (1941) and *A Song Is Born* (1948).

A still more straightforward model of the crime cartoon comedy is provided by Warner Bros.' Road Runner animated shorts. The seven-minute stories, each of them presenting several of Wile E. Coyote's

68. *Analyze This:* The iconic mob boss (Robert De Niro) and his unwilling psychiatrist (Billy Crystal).

unsuccessful traps for Road Runner, are so repetitious, both individually and as a series, and feature such a small cast of characters and so few possibilities for motivation and incident that their violent plots become reassuringly ritualized. Audiences who know that the coyote will never catch his innocent prey can relax and enjoy the complexity of his traps and the certainty that he will be caught in them himself, usually in ways unique to the drawn universe of cartoons. When the coyote steps over the edge of a cliff in his enthusiastic pursuit of Road Runner, for instance, he will never fall until he notices that he is in danger; he will have plenty of time for a farewell to the audience; and he will never suffer lasting damage from his well-deserved misadventures. The violence of the series, as the cliché "cartoon violence" suggests, is inconsequential. The ritual repetitions of highly predictable plots, spiced by the playful physical inventions, transformations, and impossibilities proper to the logic of the cartoon universe, at the hands of a villainous agent who will never grow out of his obsession or develop anything but a drolly ad hoc self-consciousness, all work in the service of a comically selective imitation of the real life of criminals, natural predators, and physical reality.

Who Framed Roger Rabbit (1988) extends and complicates this cartoon logic by crossing it with the logic of a carefully calibrated homage to 1947 film noir. The combination of live-action and animated characters in the same scenes produces a universe that combines features of both genres. In physical terms, Roger casts cartoon shadows that look drawn, but can have apparently photographed shadows cast over him; he drinks real liquor and reacts to it by bouncing around the room in antic cartoon fashion or spitting a live-action stream; yet he can be knocked unconscious with a frying pan, and threatened with total annihilation by the evil green "dip" of Judge Doom (Christopher Lloyd). In moral terms, Roger is an irrepressibly madcap hero, the only rabbit among the protagonists, but also a devoted husband distracted and depressed by jealousy of his wife, Jessica, who is playing pat-a-cake (literally, as it turns out) with live-action entrepreneur Marvin Acme (Stubby Kaye). The film repeatedly plays for laughs the conflicts between the mock-noir logic of its live-action world, from its moody lighting to its period costumes, and its cartoon world, jammed with puns, pratfalls, and cameos of Disney and Warners cartoon characters – as when Jessica (voiced by Kathleen Turner), in the film's most famous line, tells private eye Eddie Valiant (Bob Hoskins), "I'm not bad. I'm just drawn that way." The implication is not only that cartoon logic can be adapted to live-action situations, but that live-action logic itself is less monolithic, more multifarious, and in its different versions more parochial and generic and subject to transformation than it might appear.

The logic developed for cartoons can be readily be projected onto live-action comedies like Blake Edwards's five *Pink Panther* films. The animated credit sequence for *A Shot in the Dark* (1964), for example, shows a fireplug Clouseau, shining a flashlight on a succession of dark screens and disclosing, along with the cast and production credits, a series of guns and bombs that shoot him or blow up in his face, leaving him annihilated until the next shot, when he returns intact. This cartoon logic governs the film's live action as well. No matter how often Clouseau (Peter Sellers) is threatened with similar dangers, he survives unharmed, leaving his audience free to enjoy his inventively geometric pratfalls, his ritualistic incompetence, his failure to notice the effects of his clumsiness on himself or others, and his laughable non sequiturs.

Cartoons provide only the most obvious model for the logic of crime comedies. The leading characters in *A Fish Called Wanda* (1988) are each assigned a different place in the film's more capacious comic logic. Otto (Kevin Kline) is a cartoon villain, precise and mechanical in his movements, implacable in his enmity, comical in his obsession with Nietzsche and his two refrains, "Asshole!" (to the drivers he repeatedly sideswipes) and "Don't call me stupid" (to the romantic trysters he interrupts in more and more incongruous ways). Ken (Michael Palin) is a cartoon hero, the bemused innocent whose love for both Wanda the woman (Jamie Lee Curtis) and Wanda the fish is so pure that when he tries to kill Mrs. Coady (Patricia Hayes), the imperious witness to the robbery (another quasi-cartoon figure) and succeeds in his first two attempts only in killing her dogs, viewers can readily sympathize with his frustration and heartbreak at the animals' deaths instead of condemning him as a killer. Wanda is the film's object of universal desire, the bringer of fertility and sexual healing who promises a comic resolution to whoever is lucky enough to possess her at the fade-out. The barrister Archie (John Cleese), whom Wanda tries to seduce in the hope of extracting information about where her accomplice George (Tom Georgeson) stashed the crucial safe-deposit key, is the unlikely romantic hero most in need of Wanda if he is to escape the stultifying life represented by his legal profession and his killjoy wife Wendy (Maria Aitkin) and survive Otto's jealous death threats to blossom in the light of Wanda's sexual promise. Once these characters establish the comic tone of the film, the noncomical George emerges as the straight man whose function in hiding the key from the other gang members is to set up their schemes, remind them by example of how much they have to lose, and attack Wanda in court when she declines to testify on his behalf. Because George has been set up as a straight man who never does anything funny, his rage when he trashes the courtroom (in an inversion of *Witness for the Prosecution*) becomes a comic release, undercutting both his dignity and the majesty of the law. *A Fish Called Wanda* suspends Archie between two staples of comedy: the improbable cartoon threats represented by Otto (and ultimately visited on Ken) and the improbable romantic rewards represented by Wanda, in order to supplant the potentially pathetic story of the criminal gang's breakdown with the comical story of the virtuous hero's rescue from his life and inhibitions.

As the core cast of *A Fish Called Wanda* attest, there are as many ways of integrating comic and criminal conflicts as there are crime comedies. Woody Allen, for example, has returned to the genre repeatedly in films united only by their affection for the crime melodramas they parody. In *Take the Money and Run* (1969) and *Small Time Crooks* (2000), he casts himself as an robber. In the earlier film, a parody of crime films from *I Am a Fugitive from a Chain Gang* (1932) to *Bonnie and Clyde* (1967) that marked Allen's directorial debut, he is fated to fail at even the simplest robberies; in the later film, he is rescued from a life of equally inept crime by the runaway success of the cookies his wife is baking as a cover for his criminal activities. In *Manhattan Murder Mystery* (1993), a valentine to *The Thin Man* (1934), the crime he and his wife are nominally investigating is little more than a backdrop to their trademark connubial bickering. In *Bullets over Broadway* (1994), he casts John Cusack as a younger version of himself, a naïve playwright whose first Broadway production is invaded and rewritten by a gangster with an unexpectedly literary bent. Most recently, *The Curse of the Jade Scorpion* (2001) internalizes the conflict between cops and robbers in a farcical version of Wilkie Collins's Victorian whodunit *The Moonstone* (1868) by casting Allen as a private eye who is hypnotized into carrying out a series of robberies.

Despite their different strategies, all these films work by defusing the intractable problems crime films tackle through laughter. Billy Wilder's Prohibition transvestite comedy *Some Like It Hot* (1959) shows the range of ways strategic displacements can make crime comical. Although the film's comic tone is established early on by numerous dialogue jokes and the banter between its two heroes, sax player Joe (Tony Curtis) and bass player Jerry (Jack Lemmon), they begin the film by losing their jobs, their coats, and their safety when they witness the St. Valentine's Day Massacre and are pursued by the killer, Spats Columbo (George Raft), and every gangster in Chicago. The film displaces this serious threat at the hands of murderous criminals onto a series of increasingly comical threats that will maintain the energy of the initial conflict while defusing its consequences. Joe's and Jerry's exhilaratingly unlikely masquerade as female musicians Josephine and Daphne does not so much decrease the story's tensions as turn them comic, especially when Joe, on their band's arrival at the Seminole–Ritz in Palm Beach, takes the nubile Sugar Kane (Marilyn Monroe) away from Jerry by dressing as Sugar's beau ideal, a bespectacled oil heir who talks just like Cary Grant. The melodramatic threat of Spats Columbo is eclipsed by the friends' comic threats against each other and by Jerry's danger from another quarter: Osgood Fielding (Joe E. Brown), the much-married old roué who has taken a fancy to Daphne.

Just when the film seems to have wandered furthest from the criminal threat that got it started, Spats and his gang, arriving at the Seminole–Ritz for a gangsters' convention, reaffirm the death threats that had been displaced onto successively more innocuous threats. Although the criminals take themselves as seriously as ever, the film's prevailing comic mode sweeps them up in a series of visual parodies of *Scarface* (1932), *The Public Enemy* (1931), and *Citizen Kane* (1941) before killing off Spats and delivering Joe and Jerry and their lovers from the surviving gangsters. As Joe protests that he is not worthy of Sugar, and she rapturously responds, "Go ahead, talk me out of it," Jerry brings up one obstacle after another to his marriage to Fielding, all to no avail. When he finally tells reveals himself as a man, the unflappable suitor replies, "Nobody's perfect."

Some Like It Hot displaces its criminal threats so completely that many viewers do not consider it a crime comedy at all. Yet the film consistently uses comedy to explore problems its criminal plot first raises – problems of power, social role-playing, injustice, and victimization – by projecting the conventions of crime melodrama onto the comical but far more volatile territory of gender politics. Joe's unlikely romance gradually transforms him from a user of women, a sexual criminal, to a suitably empathetic mate for Sugar, and Jerry turns into a victim of the same sort of predatory male he and Joe have been. Just as the decorum of criminal outrage in crime films reminds viewers how naïve they are if they assume that the normal world is noncriminal, or that criminals, victims, and avengers represent mutually exclusive categories, the decorum of comic outrage in crime comedies like *Some Like It Hot* represents not a swerve from the authentically serious tone proper to the crime film but a dramatic mode that shows the fallacies of assuming that the normal world is not comical.

The intimacy between criminal outrage and comical outrage is even clearer in films like *Heathers* (1989) that reverse *Some Like It Hot*'s trajectory by beginning as comedies and gradually darkening to melodrama. Veronica Sawyer (Winona Ryder), a student who aspires to membership in the coveted clique of Westerburg High's three Heathers (Shannen Doherty, Lisanne Falk, Kim Walker), nonetheless believes that since they are responsible for setting the school's bitchy, cruel, remorselessly competitive tone, "killing Heather would be like killing the Wicked Witch of the West." Veronica's dark but nonserious fantasies come true when her friend J. D. (Christian Slater) encourages her to play a prank on the lead Heather that turns lethal when he secretly spikes Heather's hangover remedy with drain cleaner. From that moment on, Veronica struggles to reconcile her continuing hatred of that Heather, who becomes more iconically powerful than ever in death, with her remorse for killing her and her implication in the murders of two football players that follow. At the players' joint funeral, where they are laid to rest in their football helmets, Veronica's giggles at the mourners' vacuity and hypocrisy are cut short by her look at one of the dead boys' little sisters, quietly weeping in his team jacket. The rest of the film makes Veronica pay for her comically murderous fantasies by forcing her to recognize her kinship with the genuinely sociopathic J. D. so that she can withdraw not only from his plot to murder the entire population of Westerburg High (in an eerie prefiguration of the massacre at Columbine High) but from her own flippancy. Instead of moving toward comedy in order to explore the broader implications of social aggression, like *Some Like It Hot, Heathers* begins by taking the universality of that aggression, and the comic response to it, as a given and then gradually retreats from its implications by confronting its heroine with consequences that are more authentic than her comic attitudinizing. Comedy is presented as one more antisocial response the heroine needs to outgrow if she is to distinguish herself from a criminal.

Heathers's drift away from comedy might suggest that crime comedies must decide in the end between comic outrage and criminal outrage, laughing at crimes or putting aside the impulse to laugh in order to take them seriously. In a world in which purportedly serious action is ineffectual, however, laughter may be the most serious response of all, as war comedies from *To Be or Not to Be* (1942) to *Love and Death* (1975) suggest. Stanley Kubrick, the director and cowriter of the blackest of all war comedies, *Dr. Strangelove; or, How I Learned to Stop Worrying and Love the Bomb* (1964), told film critic Joseph Gelmis that he had bought Peter George's 1958 thriller *Red Alert* intending to make a serious film of it, presumably along the lines of the contemporaneous *Fail-Safe* (1964), but that after a month of discarding ideas "because they were so ludicrous," he realized that "all the things I was throwing out were the things which were the most truthful,"[5] and brought ribald comic novelist Terry Southern onto the project to heighten the comic elements he had been downplaying.

Why would a film about nuclear annihilation keep veering toward comedy? An early scene suggests why by showing the pained response of Group Captain Lionel Mandrake (Peter Sellers) to the news of Brigadier General Jack D. Ripper (Sterling Hayden) that the country is now in a shooting war: "Oh, hell." For not only is Mandrake's response comically inadequate to the threat of nuclear annihilation; the scene suggests that *any* conceivable response would be inadequate, however heroically films like *Fail-Safe* might struggle to dignify the alternatives. Because it threatens not merely particular people or nations or cultures or ideologies but the whole future of humankind, all-out nuclear war, which in Kubrick's nihilistic account spares no one from utter defeat, makes every possible reaction into the stuff of black comedy. Kubrick's audience ends up laughing, not at the enemy or the service or war itself, but at the ironic denial of human power and freedom by the magnitude of the dehumanizing, but all-too-human, drive toward self-destruction. Kubrick's comedy emerges as the engine of horror and perception. As Pauline Kael has remarked in opposing Brian De Palma's telekinetic thriller *The Fury* (1978) to Steven Spielberg's *Close Encounters of the Third Kind* (1977): "With Spielberg, what happens is so much better than you dared hope that you have to laugh; with De Palma, it's so much worse than you feared that you have to laugh."[6]

Of course, you don't really have to laugh, and not everyone does. Few viewers laugh out loud at *Dr. Strangelove,* and even fewer at *The Fury.* But Kubrick and Kael help explain why so many viewers have laughed uproariously at the most unlikely moments in *Pulp Fiction* (1994): when Mia Wallace (Uma Thurman) literally springs back to life after her terrified date Vincent Vega (John Travolta) injects a shot of adrenaline into her heart; when prizefighter Butch Coolidge (Bruce Willis) returns with a samurai sword to the pawnshop basement to rescue his enemy, Marsellus Wallace (Ving Rhames), from the redneck rapists who had taken them both prisoner; and when Vincent, turning around in his car seat to ask Marsellus's underling Marvin (Phil LaMarr) whether he believes it was a divine miracle that protected Vincent and Jules Winnfield (Samuel L. Jackson) from a hail of bullets, accidentally shoots Marvin in the face. They laugh because they are witnessing a miracle of resurrection, because Butch's nightmarish ordeal has won him a heady dose of freedom and power they are eager to share, because Marvin's gratuitous death is the perfect punch line to a discussion of the role of miracles in the modern world, and because they realize that the violent, unpredictable world around them is always potentially, explosively funny.

The leading practitioners of this mode of crime comedy – whose comic elements do not follow *Arsenic and Old Lace* and *Some Like It Hot* in displacing the threatening aspects of the criminal plot but, rather, intensify them – are Joel and Ethan Coen. No two of their eight films to date are quite alike, but virtually all of them are crime comedies ranging from light gray to pitch black. The Coen brothers borrow a central paradox from animated cartoons: The banality of criminal impulses as inescapable as Wile E. Coyote's is recorded by a spectacularly baroque audiovisual style and an equally baroque use of crime-genre conventions.

The Coens established their trademark sensibility with their first film, *Blood Simple* (1984), a noir update tracing the murderous double-crosses that ensue when suspicious Texas husband Julian Marty (Dan Hedaya) hires shady private eye Loren Visser (M. Emmet Walsh) to kill his wife, Abby (Frances McDormand), and her lover, Ray (John Getz). The cross-plotting gains a darkly comic edge from the lovers' ignorance of Visser's existence, and their panicked belief, right up to the film's last line, that the husband they thought they had killed and buried is still dogging them. *Raising Arizona* (1987), a knockabout comedy about the efforts of inept bank robber H. I. "Hi" McDonnough (Nicolas Cage) and his childless cop wife Ed (Holly Hunter) to kidnap one of the quintuplets of furniture magnate Nathan Arizona (Trey Wilson) [Fig. 69], covers similar material in a more humorous tone established by Hi's deadpan narration and the film's frantic camera work. The Coens' third film, *Miller's Crossing* (1990) is a bleak fantasia on themes from Dashiell Hammett's 1931 novel *The Glass Key*, and one of only two of their films to date with no important comic elements (the other being *The Man Who Wasn't There* [2001]).[7] These films established not only the Coens' fondness for convoluted crime plots, ironic reversals, and a wildly inventive visual style, but also their working methods. All three were produced by Ethan Coen, directed by Joel Coen, and cowritten by both brothers. All three were photographed by Barry Sonnenfeld and scored by Carter Burwell with an emphasis on systematically distancing effects. After *Miller's Crossing,* Sonnenfeld left the Coens to direct his own series of loopy dark comedies, from *The Addams Family* (1991) to *Men in Black* (1997) and *Men in Black 2* (2002), and the brothers replaced him with Roger Deakins, who has shot all their films since. Given the stability of the Coens' core personnel – their works have been written, photographed, scored, produced, and directed by a total of five technicians, and they have returned repeatedly to cast such favorite actors as John Goodman, Steve Buscemi, John Turturro, and Joel Coen's wife, Frances McDormand – it is no wonder that their films have been so distinctive.

69. *Raising Arizona:* The inept kidnappers (Holly Hunter, Nicolas Cage) welcome home the baby (T. J. Kuhn) they have snatched.

Barton Fink (1991) marked the brothers' critical breakthrough [Fig. 70]. The film, reportedly begun when the Coens were stuck on the screenplay of *Miller's Crossing,* is a horrifying comedy about politically committed Broadway playwright Barton Fink (John Turturro), who, bound for Hollywood "to make a difference" by writing films about the little people nobody notices, checks into a nightmarish art-deco hotel that is the center of a net of mediocrity, depravity, and homicide at the hands of one of the little people he has presumed to patronize. The film's hallucinatory intensity won it an unprecedented three prizes at the 1991 Cannes Film Festival for best film, best director, and best actor. Buoyed by their success at home and abroad, the Coens turned to a big-budget project, *The Hudsucker Proxy* (1993), which larded the rise-of-company-mailboy story recycled in models from Horatio Alger to *How to Succeed in Business Without Really Trying* (1967) with hundreds of allusions to earlier movies and an all-star cast (Tim Robbins, Jennifer Jason Leigh, Paul Newman, Charles Durning) that edged out all their regulars except for Buscemi, and disappointed both their core audience and the wider audience they had aimed for.

It was at this point that the Coens began work on *Fargo* (1996), their signature black comedy about hapless car dealer Jerry Lundegaard (William H. Macy), who, desperate to cover the money he has embez-

70. *Barton Fink:* The writer hero (John Turturro) is blocked, but not the Coen brothers, in their breakthrough film.

zled from his father-in-law's dealership, hatches the idea of hiring two thugs to kidnap his wife, Jean (Kristin Rudrüd), so that her father, Wade Gustafson (Harve Presnell), can pay a ransom Jerry will split with the kidnappers. So far, the story could easily have served as the basis for a madcap crime comedy worthy of Wilder or Preston Sturges, but Jerry's plot spins rapidly out of control when the kidnappers, with

71. *Fargo:* Indoors, the emotional temperature of the opening scene between Jerry and the thugs (Steve Buscemi, Peter Stormare) he wants to hire is no warmer.

their victim tied up in the back seat, are pulled over for driving with an expired registration, and taciturn Gaear Grimsrud (Peter Stormare) brutally kills the police officer, then chases down two witnesses who saw the corpse as they were driving past and murders them as well. Four more victims will follow, dispatched in increasingly hair-raising ways, until Brainerd police chief Marge Gunderson (Frances McDormand, in her Oscar-winning role), investigating the murders, surprises Gaear as he is feeding the leg of his late partner, Carl Showalter (Steve Buscemi), into a wood chipper, producing instead of chips a haze of bright blood.

What could possibly make such a festival of carnage funny? Far more than the *Pink Panther* movies or *Some Like It Hot, Fargo* depends for its humor on its ruthlessly stylized visuals. The film's opening sequence, which picks up Jerry's car as it is heading down a snowy road to the Fargo bar where he is meeting the kidnappers, sets up the conventional expectation that the film will move from generally expository shots of an inhospitable outdoor environment to warmer, more intimate and comforting interiors; but this expectation is repeatedly undermined [Fig. 71]. Except for the home of Marge and her husband,

Norm (John Carroll Lynch), none of the film's interiors is warmly lit. Its bars are dim but not monochromatic, its other public spaces – hotel lobbies, restaurants, Wade's office, Jerry's car dealership – neutrally blue-gray with prominent picture windows showing the snowscaped outdoors. When the characters do roost indoors, the object most likely to capture their attention is the blue-white light of a television set. Moreover, a surprising number of the film's key scenes – a fatal roadside stop after the kidnapping, Marge's initial investigation of the resulting three murders, the parking lot where Wade brings the payoff money to Carl and the two of them trade shots, the cabin exterior when Gaear shoots Carl and is feeding his body into a wood chipper when Marge captures him – take place outdoors. Most of these exterior scenes are extravagantly bleak, showing cars' headlights approaching from a seamless whiteout or their taillights threatening to vanish into undifferentiated darkness. Even in its interiors, however, the film persistently withholds facial close-ups that would encourage intimacy with the characters. It is as if the Coens had sat repeatedly through *Basic Instinct* and determined to make a film whose visual style was precisely antithetical, since the film gives off exactly the opposite aura – chilly, detached, and composed within an inch of its life – in order to root its characters more fully in a self-enclosed physical world and abstract them from an audience free to laugh heartlessly at their misfortunes.

Many viewers, of course, declined to laugh anyway. The film polarized citizens of the North Dakota locations where parts of it were shot. Many of them complained that the Coens were casting their birthplace as a Grand Guignol house of horrors and the natives as yahoos whose laconic response to almost every utterance – the flat midwestern "Yah" – made them look like idiots. But many other viewers, whether or not they lived in North Dakota, found the film's exaggerated regionalism a hilariously matter-of-fact counterpoint to its tale of kidnapping, fraud, and homicide. Certainly the innocuousness of so much of the dialogue, in which repetition is so persistent that the speeches gravitate toward the condition of music, emphasizes the ironic contrast of the gruesome plot even as it increases both suspense and comedy by forcing impatient audiences to wait for the placid witnesses to come to the point. In one of the film's best-known sequences, Marge questions a pair of teenaged hookers (Larissa Kokernot, Melissa Peterman) who spent the night before the kidnapping with Carl and Gaear, hoping to get descriptions of the pair. After establishing that

72. *Fargo:* The incorrigible shark (Harve Presnell) and the hopeless loser (William H. Macy).

one of them is a graduate of White Bear Lake High School ("Go Bears," she helpfully volunteers), Marge asks what the two suspects looked like, provoking the following exchange:

HOOKER: Well, the little guy, he was kinda funny-lookin'.
MARGE: In what way?
HOOKER: I don't know. Just funny-lookin'.
MARGE: Can you be any more specific?
HOOKER: I couldn't really say. He wasn't circumcised.
MARGE: Was he funny-lookin' apart from that?
HOOKER: Yah. . . .
MARGE: Is there anything else you can tell me about him?
HOOKER: No. Like I say, he was funny-lookin' – more 'n most people, even.

Still another effect of the heavy overlay of regional dialect is to emphasize the static nature of the characters, locked into unchanging humors as completely as Road Runner and Wile E. Coyote. Jerry never realizes that his early hope of averting the kidnapping by persuading Wade to put up the money for a land investment is doomed to failure because Wade is such an incorrigible shark and Jerry such a hopeless loser [Fig. 72]. Having offered an Olds Cutlass Ciera as the down pay-

ment to his wife's kidnappers, Jerry, the eternal car salesman, natu-
rally begins their first conversation, just after they have abducted his
wife and killed three people, "How's that Ciera working out for you?
. . . How's Jean?" Much later, during Wade and Carl's confrontation
over the ransom drop at a snowy parking lot, they shout at each other
with no hope of changing each other's minds; only shooting each other can make much of an impression on either one, and Carl, who kicks
Wade's supine body after he has killed him and been wounded himself, clearly believes in some way that their discussion is just warming
up. En route to the Lundegaard house in Minneapolis, the exasperated
Carl begs Gaear, who has said nothing but "Nope" all the way from
Brainerd, to make some conversation, and when Gaear does not reply,
says, "I don't have to talk to you either, man. See how you like it. Just
total fuckin' silence. Two can play at that game, smart guy. We'll just
see how you like it. Total silence." Carl is no more capable of shutting
up than Gaear is of making small talk.

All these scenes are carried off in the same deadpan style by characters obsessed with the Coyotean question of how to carry out their
individual plans yet trapped in a universe utterly indifferent to their
cares. Because they are so oblivious to their own limitations or the
plans of others, both the violence and the comedy of the film erupt
with shocking suddenness. When Jean fights the menacing Gaear by
biting his hand, the hitherto inarticulate Gaear abandons his pursuit
of her to look in the bathroom cabinet for "unguent," leaving viewers
wondering where he learned the word. Moments before Gaear attacks
and kills him with an axe, Carl, who has hidden away practically all
the unexpectedly large ransom from his unsuspecting partner, cannot
resist haggling with him over the Ciera (unwittingly echoing Jerry's
earlier decision to ask Wade for a much larger ransom than he intends
to pay the kidnappers), climaxing his diatribe with the incredible announcement: "I've been listening to your fuckin' bullshit all week!"

In the most gratuitous and ambiguous of the film's many comically obsessive tangents, the hugely pregnant Marge, in Minneapolis to
interview Jerry, has dinner with her old school friend Mike Yanagita
(Steve Park), a Japanese-American midwesterner whose "yahs" are as
broad as hers. After she briskly turns away his attempt to sit on her
side of the dinner table, he suddenly breaks down in tears and pours
out the heartrending tale of his wife's death from leukemia as Marge
stares stricken at him. Not until a later phone conversation in which
a friend tells Marge that Mike's wife is alive and well does the film raise
the question of why the episode was ever included, and the corre-

sponding suspicion that perhaps Marge consoled Mike with sex and is now finding out why she shouldn't have; but this can be only a theory, for the film never returns to resolve the question.

In fact, ambiguity and irresolution are at the heart of *Fargo*'s comedy, which, unlike that of cartoons like Road Runner or comedies of displacement like *Some Like It Hot,* works by systematically depriving viewers of any single privileged perspective from which to interpret its outrageous events. Hence the film's wide-open spaces and motivic long shots provide a theater that imposes no particular meaning on any action except to reduce it to insignificance. The statue of the legendary logger Paul Bunyan that welcomes visitors to Brainerd, Minnesota, is shown three times, in different lighting conditions that make it look by turns comical, menacing, and familiar, though always grotesque. The statue is a representation of a mythic figure, an attempt to visualize someone who exists only as a point on which to project iconic significances that can shift with each new context. When Carl and Gaear arrive in Brainerd, they resolve their disagreement about the evening's entertainment by going out for pancakes, then picking up the hookers with whom they are shown coupling, with a placid unconcern for privacy, in a single hilariously disengaged long shot of adjacent double beds. A fade to black is followed by a straight cut to the same camera setup showing them snuggled down like a pair of suburban married couples to watch Johnny Carson, with only the flickering light from the television indicating that the tableau of four stationary bodies is not a freeze-frame.

Later, Marge, examining the starkly dramatic scene of Gaear's third murder, bends over in the snow, and Lou, an officer at the scene, asks if she sees something. "No, I just think I'm going to barf," answers Marge, then, after straightening up: "Well, that passed." The gesture whose meaning is so obvious from the generic context could mean something completely different, like Mike's fictional tale of love and loss. It could be simply a black-comic confession of inadequacy, like Carl's *Strangelove*-like underreaction to the tableau of his partner blowing a hole in a police officer's head only inches from Carl's face: "Oh . . . whoa, daddy . . . oh, daddy." In fact, it could mean anything at all, like the statue of Paul Bunyan or the hooker's description of her "funny-lookin'" client, or nothing at all, like Gaear's silences or the film's ubiquitous "yahs." Nonetheless, the interlocked genres of crime film and comedy the film invokes encourage the audience to mine its hardscrabble surface for meaning, though it does not always reward them for doing so.

Burwell's otherworldly music, plaintive and balladic, suggests an epic, legendary dimension to what the film's opening credits insist is a true story, and the film's outrageous bursts of violence and comedy together indicate how arbitrary and fragile is the zone of normalcy they take as their point of departure. The criminals and their victims are destroyed by their comical, yet thoroughly logical, inability to surrender their grasp of normalcy in the interests of what must seem to most viewers blindingly obvious generic cues. Jean, watching a man in a black ski mask who stands outside her sliding window with a crowbar, does not react to the menace he patently represents until he releases her from her assumption that the moment will pass by smashing the glass. The long moment of suspension between her apprehension and her reaction to the threat is an echo of the corresponding moment in *Pulp Fiction* when the Pop-Tart that Butch Coolidge has put in his toaster pops up, jolting him out of his stasis by giving him permission to shoot Vincent Vega.[8] In both cases, the percussive sound gives viewers permission as well to expel their breath and react, as many of them do by laughing. The scene continues to wobble between terror and slapstick comedy, as Jean's eminently sensible reactions to the intruders – she locks herself in an upstairs bathroom, attempts to phone the police, then hides in the bathtub after opening a window to make them think she has climbed out – are repeatedly undermined by Gaear's ferocity and her own realistic panic, which sends her hurtling out of the tub tangled in the shower curtain to fall down the stairs.

Even after Carl and Gaear bring her to the isolated house where she will die off-camera for no particular reason, Jean cannot bring herself to give up hope: bound and hooded, she darts around the snowy yard aimlessly, even though she cannot see where she is going and has no chance of escape. Is the hope to which she clings a sign of her unquenchable spirit, or of her witlessly mechanical behavior? Or does it simply attest – like Carl's comically futile attempt to mark the burial spot of the ransom money alongside a fence that stretches for mile upon identical mile by sticking a tiny snow scraper into the snow above it – to the universal impetus, however vain, to set one's activities apart from the bleakly uncaring world figured by the film's elemental mise-en-scène of blandly anonymous interiors surrounded by acres of trackless snow?

Fargo might be read as the *Dr. Strangelove* of crime comedy, a film that mocks its witless characters' banal responses to their peril as hopelessly inadequate while darkly suggesting that their peril is so irrational and extreme that any response whatever would be equally, comically inadequate. The film's deepest outrage is neither its outbursts of violence nor its cruel laughter but the air of normalcy it establishes, for example, by the casting of affable William H. Macy as Jerry Lundegaard, the casual extortionist who seems to think that none of the problems arising from the disastrous kidnapping he has masterminded is proof against a really nice smile. It is not the snowballing errors, comic or melodramatic, that represent a deflection from the normal state of affairs, but Jerry's own laboriously composed facade of normalcy, which hides the monstrous egoism that allows him to announce wearily to his shocked, grief-stricken son, "I'm goin' ta bed now," instead of returning the call from Wade's office that would tell him Wade has been shot dead. The film's eruptions of crime and comedy mark a return to the normal state of chaos vain human attempts at social normalcy have simply obscured.

Against this reading of the film stands the good-natured normalcy of Marge herself, the earth mother whose loving marriage to unglamorous Norm offers such a reproach to Jerry Lundegaard. Returning to interview the desperate Jerry a second time, Marge cuts through his doubletalk by calmly repeating her questions about a missing vehicle until his voice rises, and then telling him, "You have no call to get snippy with me. I'm just doin' my job here," her gravity so unnerving Jerry that he announces his intent to check the inventory immediately, then drives off as Marge murmurs to herself, "For Pete's sake. He's fleein' the interview. He's fleein' the interview." Jerry's smiling hypocrisy, Carl's snakelike scheming, and Gaear's dull brutality are no match for Marge's adherence to police routine, her impervious good humor, and the moral certitude she displays in her climactic lecture to Gaear after she arrests him and takes him to task over the matter of "your accomplice in the wood chipper": "There's more to life than a little money, ya know. Doncha know that? And here you are. And it's a beautiful day. Well. . . . I just don't understand it" [Fig. 73]. But Marge is literally correct: Having far too little imagination to understand Gaear or Carl or Jerry, she can only cuff the survivors and lay down the law to them, then retreat to her own connubial bed. There, before the ubiquitous television, she congratulates her husband on having had his painting chosen to illustrate the three-cent duck-hunting stamp, and echoes his incantatory closing reference to her pregnancy: "Two more months."

Marge represents *Fargo*'s moral center, but the film refuses to put her and the unexceptionable moral values she stands for at its formal center. Instead it merely suggests that the normal world Marge repre-

73. *Fargo:* Marge Gunderson (Frances McDormand) – good-humored earth-mother or unimaginative dolt?

sents poses as direct an affront to the criminal outrages perpetrated by the kidnappers as their outrages do to the ideas of normalcy represented by Jerry's smile, Paul Bunyan's statue, and the film's endless wastes of snow. Nor does the film show either side able to comprehend the other, either in individual collisions or at the fadeout; it mere-

74. *The Big Lebowski:* A naïf sucked into a world of kidnapping, bowling, and impossible dreams come true. (Jeff Bridges, John Goodman)

ly shows that each exists in the other, like yin and yang, so that the criminal world is as comically normal as the normal world is comically outrageous.

In the end, *Fargo,* however differently than *Some Like It Hot,* works by consistently displacing viewers' expectations. Despite its title, only its opening scene takes place in Fargo, even though the exterior shooting, originally planned for Minnesota, had to be moved to North Dakota when Minnesota was struck by its most snow-free winter in a hundred years. The assurance with which the film begins – "THIS IS A TRUE STORY" – is even more misleading than its title, since the Coens later admitted that it was false.[9] The most subversive aspect of the film, however, and the one that links its crime most closely to its comedy, is its refusal to establish the sort of unmarked governing tone that makes *Arsenic and Old Lace* so reassuring, *A Shot in the Dark* so antic, *Trouble in Paradise* (1932) so cynically sentimental about its world of thieves and their equally corrupt victims, the Coens' succeeding films *The Big Lebowski* (1998), *O Brother, Where Art Thou?* (2000), and *The Man Who Wasn't There* so surrealistically laid back in presenting the adventures (respectively) of a naïf sucked into a world of kidnapping, bowling, and impossible dreams come true [Fig. 74], or of a trio of escaped convicts unwittingly reenacting the *Odyssey,* or of a small-town barber observing, as if from another planet, the nightmarish impact of the murder that has come to define his life. Instead of establishing a leading tone from which the film's episodes can diverge in order to shock the audience into laughter or pathos or fear, *Fargo* is nothing but a collection of tangents. Everything in the film, especially its most banal details, is off kilter – a reminder that the outrageousness of crime comedy, as of comedy and crime films themselves, is as normal as any alternative genres and the ways of seeing they provoke.

13

Conclusion: What Good Are Crime Films?

Now that this survey of crime subgenres has ended, it is time to return to the question that haunted its opening chapter: What is illuminated by considering a given film like *The Godfather* (1972) or *Murder on the Orient Express* (1974) or *Fargo* (1996) as a crime film rather than a gangster film or a detective story or a black comedy? More generally, what is gained by defining the crime film as a strong genre that not only incorporates but logically underpins such better-known genres as the gangster film, the private-eye film, the film noir, and the police film? Discussing crime comedies like *Fargo* as crime films that happen to be humorous rather than comedies that happen to involve crime seeks to expand the range and resonance of the crime genre at the risk of choosing examples many viewers might dismiss – and indeed of diluting the genre as a whole. Many viewers, perhaps most, do experience *The Thin Man* (1934) or *Charade* (1963) or *Fargo* as crime films with comic relief, but how many viewers, after all, would categorize *Arsenic and Old Lace* (1944) or *The Trouble with Harry* (1955) or *Some Like It Hot* (1959) as crime films rather than comedies?

The point of discussing such films as crime films is not to inflate the importance of one genre at the expense of another but to indicate the ways in which previous definitions of crime films may have been unwisely parochial. No extant definition of crime films prescribes solemnity as a criterion of the genre, yet historians of crime films regularly ignore crime comedies, presumably on the grounds that they are not really crime films.[1] Such distinctions between more and less real members of a given genre, however, are as futile as they are inevitable, not

289

because genre films cannot be consensually categorized, but because these distinctions ignore the nature and purpose of generic classification in the first place.

Whatever grounds they take as their basis, all attempts to distinguish real crime films from the less real, like all attempts to distinguish crime films categorically from members of other genres, assume that genres are essential and logical, parallel and mutually exclusive, like Platonic norms. But because generic categories are as culturally constructed as the works they are intended to categorize, they are always historically situated, ad hoc, subjective, and inflected by (indeed rooted in) a particular agenda. This is the real point of Rick Altman's distinction between semantic and syntactic genre markers, as he notes in proposing that "the relationship between the semantic and the syntactic constitutes the very site of negotiation between Hollywood and its audience, and thus between ritual and ideological uses of genre."[2] Although Steve Neale aptly notes that many accounts of Hollywood genres "have been driven by critical and theoretical agendas rather than by a commitment to detailed empirical analysis and thorough industrial and historical research,"[3] the whole project of genre theory, from the construction of films as members of a genre to the attempt to synthesize genres or their rationales in the service of a more general theory of communications, remains by its very nature agenda-driven.

It seems clear, then, that the question of what good is the conceptual category of crime films is really another, and more illuminating, way of posing an apparently simpler question: What good are crime films? The business of this final chapter is to indicate briefly what sort of cultural work crime films as a genre do for the corporations that produce them, the viewers that consume them, and the society that authorizes their currency, and how the answers to those questions are connected to the questions of what counts as a crime film and why – why the category might be useful in revealing some of the films' leading family connections and motives, which depend on what Altman has called "the uses to which members of the family are put."[4]

The most obvious features crime films of different subgenres share are a grammar of typological situations and a cast of stock characters. Whatever their subgenre, most crime films present events, twists, and revelations that are so formulaic not only in themselves but in their interrelations that they can truly be called a grammar (or, in Altman's terms, a syntax). Part of this consistency, of course, stems from Hollywood's injunction that crime does not pay. Thus gangsters rise only to fall; an ambitious, well-planned robbery involving a gang of thieves working closely together will invariably go wrong sooner or later; the most mysterious crime, whether or not it is presented as a mystery to the audience, will always be resolved by a close examination of the evidence, even when that evidence is inconclusive, as in the Claus von Bülow case; and crooked policemen are inevitably brought down by the institutional power of the police force, even though that same force, once it is corrupted, is no match for a single crusading officer. Crime films are equally consistent in the opportunities they offer criminals: Unstealable jewels like the Pink Panther, protected by state-of-the-art security systems, are nothing more than a trope, an invitation to theft; informers and undercover police officers are sure to have their lives threatened, even if they elude these threats; and nervous, secretive characters who beg for official protection are marked for death whatever their subgenre.

None of this is surprising or especially illuminating; it is merely an indication of the extent to which the subject of crime, bracketed by Hollywood's official morality and its imperative to sensationalism, generates a formula that transcends specific subgenres. What is more revealing is the changing role the stock characters of crime films play in different subgenres. The no-nonsense cop who plays by the book, for example, is a staple of the crime film; but he (or, very occasionally, she) has radically different roles in different subgenres. In private-eye films like *Lady in the Lake* (1947) and *Chinatown* (1974) he is the hero's antagonist; in victim films like *Fury* (1936) and *Suspicion* (1941) he is either a menace or a failed protector to the beleaguered hero. In some police films, like *Touch of Evil* (1958) and *The Untouchables* (1987), he is the hero; in erotic thrillers whose heroes happen to be police officers, like *Basic Instinct* (1992), he is the loose-cannon hero's conscience or his nemesis. Lawyers are the heroes as well as the villains of lawyer films, but in police films and private-eye films their penchant for legalism always makes them untrustworthy. *A Perfect World* (1993) even manages to create an evil victim who is much more dangerous than the good-hearted fellow-convict who kills him [Fig. 75]. To a remarkable extent, the subgenres of the crime film are distinguished from each other not by the stories they tell but by the attitudes they adopt toward those stories.

A stock question gangster films raise, for example, is why people become criminals. These films suggest that the reasons are specifically sociopathic: an alienation from a remote or uncaring society combined with an overreaching vanity or megalomania. But just as different westerns adopt very different attitudes to the conflict they all share between the frontier and the coming of civilization (so that, for instance, the civilizing rancher heroes of *Red River* [1948], become the anticivilizing outlaws of *Shane* [1953]), police films and lawyer films tend to peg criminal behavior much more narrowly to greed, films noirs to sexual victimization by a predatory woman, erotic thrillers to masculine hysteria. Hence police heroes pursue criminals who deserve to be caught or killed because they have chosen to be criminals, but films noirs and erotic thrillers present criminals who cannot help but kill. Caper films like *The Asphalt Jungle* (1950) and nihilist neo-noirs like *The Grifters* (1990) bring the question full circle by suggesting that the question is beside the point, since there is no reason to look for an explanation for any particular criminal behavior when society itself is necessarily criminal.[5]

Criminal behavior, then, is the fault of a cruelly alienating society, or of ethnic self-identification, or vaulting personal ambition, conscious avarice, sexual beguilement, male hysteria, the fatal need for the company of others – not just a warped society, but the social impulse as such. In every case, the subject of criminality is used to focus the problematic relationship between individual and social power and justice, but each adopts a different point of view that restricts it to telling only part of the story. To tell the full story, even if it were possible, would far exceed Hollywood's recipe for mass entertainment.

The full story, however, continues to haunt the partial story each subgenre presents, for every film in every crime subgenre is marked by numberless traces of the alternative crime story it could have been. A crime comedy like *Arsenic and Old Lace,* which sets its batty maiden aunts against their dangerously sociopathic nephew, is filled with intimations of the serious crime film it could have been, and may still (but probably will not) turn into. *Fargo,* going still further, is a crime comedy whose every sequence toys with the possibility of consequential terror, even at its most disturbingly amusing. The kidnappers' trip to Brainerd is filled with jokes that break the tension but do not prevent them from kidnapping and eventually killing Jean Lundegaard. What's more, if every crime comedy is potentially a crime melodrama, the reverse is equally true. *The Godfather,* for all its tragic pretensions, could have been a comedy – a possibility explored intermittently by *GoodFellas* (1990) and released full throttle by *Jane*

75. *A Perfect World:* Escaped convict Butch Haynes (Kevin Costner), a killer whose rapport with lonely Phillip Perry (T. J. Lowther) brings out his gentler side.

Austen's Mafia! (1998). Indeed, if parodies in general, from *Dead Men Don't Wear Plaid* (1982) to the three *Naked Gun* films (1988–94) are considered to release the comedy repressed by their progenitor texts' self-seriousness, then it is no wonder that crime films have so often been parodied, since cultural repression is as central to their agenda as cultural analysis.

In the same way, crime films are haunted by the visual traces and tones of other crime subgenres. Just as the gold lighting used to invoke the nostalgic past in *The Godfather* and *The Godfather, Part II* (1974) is invoked by the ubiquitous wood-paneled train interiors in *Murder on the Orient Express,* the low-key lighting characteristic of films noirs haunts private-eye films and police films as well, sometimes by its presence (*Experiment in Terror,* 1962), sometimes by its absence (*Chinatown*), and the expressionistically cluttered spaces of Fritz Lang are echoed by *Double Indemnity* (1944), modulated by *Kiss Me Deadly* (1955), or resolutely refused by *Fargo.* Moreover, *Fargo's* vertiginous comedy serves as a reminder that every crime film is shadowed by the farce it might have been if the criminals' petty obsessions had been considered from a different angle. Every crime film is informed by an enriching awareness of the alternative subgenres it invokes, if only by contrast. The crucial importance of the crime-film genre is that it foregrounds the ambivalence that makes these alternative ways of seeing bad cops or the past or petty obsession essential to each subgenre's and each individual film's presentation of its stock elements.

Although each crime subgenre is haunted by implicit possibilities explicitly realized by other subgenres, these possibilities, helpful as they are for ad hoc classification, cannot be used to distinguish different crime subgenres categorically from each other. Even within a given subgenre, typological figures will assume ambiguities based on their affinities to other subgenres. In *L.A. Confidential* (1997) it is obvious that Ed Exley (Guy Pearce) is the loner cop familiar from hundreds of earlier movies; but will he turn out to be a vigilante cop like Frank Bullitt, a crooked cop like Capt. McCluskey in *The Godfather,* or a suspicious cop like Det. Williams in *Blue Velvet?* For most of the film's running time, the answer is ambiguous. Even after *L.A. Confidential* has run its course, its police hero remains indelibly marked, as each of his progenitor heroes is marked, by the possibilities of what he might have been.

Grouping well-established crime genres like the gangster film and the film noir together under the more comprehensive, albeit synthetic, genre of the crime film illuminates many of their formulaic family resemblances; but reversing the procedure and defining these genres as subsets of a more global crime genre goes further to explain the abiding source of their power. It is only the crime genre itself, and not any single subgenre, that accounts for the enabling ambiguity at the heart of all crime subgenres and every film within them: the easy recognition of the genre's formulas coupled with a lingering uncertainty about their import.

Even films that are not normally considered crime films can benefit from this enrichment if they are considered hypothetically as crime films. It is clear from the beginning of *Unforgiven* (1992) that the retired gunslinger William Munny (Clint Eastwood) will overcome his reservations about returning to violent ways and ride out to Big Whiskey to claim the bounty the local whores have offered for killing the two cowboys who disfigured one of their number and were let off by Sheriff Little Bill Daggett (Gene Hackman) with a fine payable to the saloonkeeper whose place was disturbed. It is equally obvious that the film will end with a confrontation between Munny and Little Bill that Little Bill can hardly survive. What remains in doubt until the film's unsettling ending, and perhaps beyond, is how viewers will feel about the climax they have been awaiting for two hours, when an eerily self-contained ex-killer who insists that all that is behind him goes up against a genially crooked sheriff who represents, along with Munny's dead wife and the whores' thirst for vengeance, the closest thing to moral authority in the film. *Unforgiven* has rightly been considered a meditation on the Hollywood western; but like *Rancho Notorious* (1952) and *The Naked Spur* (1953), it is also haunted by its affinities with contract-killer films like *Murder, Inc.* (1960), avenger films like *D.O.A.* (1950), and vigilante police films like those featuring Clint Eastwood's most recognizable hero, Dirty Harry Callahan.

Such exercises reveal not only the elastic boundaries of the crime film but the ways in which the genre's cultural work is linked to the recognition of individual gangster films and police films and crime comedies as first and foremost crime films; and they help to explain the rise and fall of the different subgenres within the constant popularity of the crime genre. Crime films are always likely to be popular in liberal democracies because such cultures place the debate between individual liberty and institutional power at the heart of their constitutional agenda. Indeed, the very idea of a constitution is already a privileged site for such a debate. Unlike utopian cultures, which would have no need of crime films, or repressive regimes, which would not tolerate the antisocial fantasies they license, liberal democracies renegotiate the relations between individual liberty and institutional power ceaselessly, in every new political campaign and election, every law and trial and arrest. Most of these actions, of course, involve competing institutions – corporations, aspiring beneficiaries of government funding, ethnic and racial groups, governments – rather than individuals; but crime films, like elections, personalize this process by focusing it on a small number of individuals, even (or especially) if they are set against faceless groups like the police, the law, or the Mob. The constant ferment liberal democracies prescribe over private rights and the public weal explains the success of crime stories in such cultures as England, whose abiding fascination with crime-story heroes from Richard III to Magwitch, from Sherlock Holmes to Jack the Ripper, far outpaces the occurrence of actual crimes.

Within this context, however, different crime subgenres flourish or recede depending on a multitude of factors: studios' economic imper-

atives; institutional censorship; the power of their nonfictional for-
bears (the decline of the Hollywood gangster is mandated by a mora-
torium that corresponds to both the enforcement of the Production
Code and the repeal of Prohibition); viewers' changing attitudes toward the government and their own majoritarian culture (as the social
conformism of *The Desperate Hours* [1955] gives way to the antiauthor-
itarianism of *Bonnie and Clyde* [1967] and the brooding nostalgia of
the *Godfather* films); the shifting attraction to or revulsion from the
power of the law (from the righteous social engineering of *To Kill a
Mockingbird* [1962] to the cynical distrust of lawyers and all their
works in films based on John Grisham novels); the will to social be-
longing or estrangement (from the yearning for trust and acceptance
by the hero of *"G" Men* [1935] to the impatience with the system in
The French Connection [1971] and the disillusionment with the system
in *Serpico* [1973]); and disruptions in the social order too deep for government to cure (the wartime threat of working women in films noirs,
the backlash against women's broader claims to empowerment in
erotic thrillers). It is no mystery why so many of the staple crime subgenres often flourish at the same time, as they have during the 1990s,
since their partial, apparently inconsistent views of the conflict are as
logically compatible as the assumption in individual films like *Reversal of Fortune* (1990) and *A Few Good Men* (1992) that lawyers are both
crusading heroes and the scum of the earth.

Still, the crime genre, like all popular genres, is not simply parasitic
on political or social history; it has a history of its own that acts as
another engine of change. Each genre has a logic of its own that is constantly subject to retrospective change by three closely related kinds
of development. The arrival of a new work, if it is accepted as part of
the genre, encourages viewers to reconsider previous members of the
genre in its light, as *The Godfather* and *Chinatown* not only extended
the gangster and private-eye genres but spearheaded a critical re-
assessment of them, and *Psycho* (1960) inaugurated a revival of the
horror film by setting a new standard for onscreen violence that was
in turn rapidly outmoded. New developments in contemporary social
history may awaken viewers to a new sense of the parallels or contrasts between their time and that represented in earlier films, as *Bonnie and Clyde*'s use of the Depression as a mirror to the social and institutional estrangement of America's youth in the sixties provoked
debates about both the sixties and the thirties, even to a new interest
in the heroes' Depression chic fashions. In addition, contemporary

arguments by film theorists and analysts can function, as effectively as new additions to a film genre, as intertexts that cast new light on old genres, often in unintended ways. Laura Mulvey's influential "Visual Pleasure and Narrative Cinema," for example, ends its argument about the exclusion of female viewers from the movies by expressing the wish that demystifying this exclusion will lead to a decline in such sexist commercial cinema that female viewers will greet with no more than "sentimental regret."[6] In the twenty-five years since Mulvey wrote, commercial cinema has certainly not changed in the directions she hoped; but critics seeking to theorize a place for female viewers and to liberate the repressed female voices of older films have revolutionized the ways contemporary viewers watch films noirs, reordering the genre and making it central to an understanding of American film.

One result of this constant change from different sources is that although genres like the crime film look stable both from a distance and at any given moment, they are constantly subject to revisionist debate, and one viewer's revisionist update (e.g., *Reservoir Dogs,* 1992; *Pulp Fiction,* 1994) is another viewer's rejected offense against the genre, and a third viewer's classic against which to measure even more contemporary updates like *2 Days in the Valley* (1996) and *Suicide Kings* (1998). So it might seem that the crime-film genre is nothing but a mirage that dissolves on close examination. What all this historical jostling really indicates, however, is simply that the crime genre, though as real as each viewer's opinion and as predictable as viewers' broad consensus, cannot be defined categorically or ahistorically. It is whatever studios, filmmakers, and viewers think it is, and over the years they have felt free to think it was many different things – usually several things at once.

Such a broad critical category might well be further expanded to include all movies in which crime plays however minor a role. On the other hand, if crime films are those that use crimes to figure problems of social justice or institutional power or moral guilt in specifically legal terms, the crime genre might become more illuminating, as it would certainly become more powerful, if it were reconfigured as the injustice genre, the social-disorder genre, the power genre, even the action genre. Although to do so would risk stretching it to its breaking point, there would be gains as well as losses in such a procedure.

Alternatively, the crime film could well be organized around different subgenres this book has neglected. The most obvious of these, the

76. *Wall Street:* Michael Douglas as the king of white-collar crime.

man-on-the-run story, has been analyzed at length not only by Charles Derry and Martin Rubin[7] but by forty years' work of commentary on Alfred Hitchcock. To emphasize the importance of such films from *The 39 Steps* (1935) to *The Fugitive* (1993) to the crime genre would foreground questions not only about the fugitive's and the pursuing system's moral complicity but about the range of tactics fugitives employ to keep one step ahead of the law. To emphasize films about white-

collar criminals, which invert the world of *The Asphalt Jungle,* would raise questions about the relation between normal business practices and criminal practices, and ultimately about the fetishizing of work-space and the work ethic, whether the heroes are innocents caught in unethical situations that skirt illegality to a greater or lesser extent (*All My Sons,* 1948; *Executive Suite,* 1954; *Patterns,* 1956; *The Apartment,* 1960; *Wall Street,* 1987 [Fig. 76]; *The Hudsucker Proxy,* 1993; *Disclosure,*

77. *Cape Fear* (1991): Robert De Niro's downscale sociopathology. (De Niro, Nick Nolte)

1994) or businesspeople whose turn toward literal criminality indicts their professional milieu metaphorically (*The Lavender Hill Mob,* 1951; *The Bad Sleep Well,* 1960; *A Shock to the System,* 1990; *Glengarry Glen Ross,* 1992; *American Psycho,* 2000). Films about outlaws – sympathetic lawbreakers like Robin Hood, Jesse James, and the protagonists of *Thelma & Louise* (1991) – provoke debates about the morality of the established order. Films about prisons like those in *The Big House* (1930), *20,000 Years in Sing Sing* (1932), and *Brute Force* (1947) present them as social microcosms from which escape, the convicts' one obsession, is no more possible than from life itself; even when Tom Connors (Spencer Tracy) does escape from Sing Sing, he is obviously fated to return. The doomed capers in *The Asphalt Jungle* and *The Killing* (1956), whose gangs are assembled, like pickup ball teams, for the purpose of pulling off one big job, exchange the romantic fatalism of the gangster film's promethean, system-defying individual hero for a cynical fatalism about social organizations themselves.

All these subgenres focus on contradictions within the social order the heroes are constrained to serve, imitate, or flee. Linking *M* (1931), *Gun Crazy* (1949), *Psycho, Cape Fear* (1962/1991) [Fig. 77], *Repulsion*

78. *To Die For:* Nicole Kidman's upscale psychopathology. (Kidman, Joaquin Phoenix, Casey Affleck, Alison Folland)

(1965), *Badlands* (1973), *The Killer Inside Me* (1976), *The Shining* (1980), *Henry: Portrait of a Serial Killer* (1990), *The Silence of the Lambs* (1991), *Single White Female* (1992), *Natural Born Killers* (1994), *Speed* (1994), and *To Die For* (1995) [Fig. 78] – customarily parceled out among diverse subgenres – as films about sociopathic or psychopathic criminals would raise questions about the psychopathology of crime, its status as a mark of social alienation or of internalized conflicts typical of an alienating society itself. Finally, giving pride of place to the subgenre of superheroes and supercriminals from Dr. Mabuse to Superman, Batman, and Darkman would recast what have most often been considered action fantasies as allegories that examine the relations between institutional and physical laws and the limits of the humanity constructed by earthly powers.

One could go still further by exploring the complementary genres of espionage and international intrigue, which are clearly related to crime films.[8] Most of the early James Bond films, for instance, involve some form of international blackmail by terrorists who have stolen something dangerous or irreplaceably valuable, and much of Bond's time in *Goldfinger* (1964), *Thunderball* (1965), and *Diamonds Are Forever* (1971) is spent in detective work as he tries to figure out just what SPECTRE or its allies are up to this time. These affinities become even more pronounced in films like *The Parallax View* (1974) and *Betrayed* (1988), which meld domestic terrorism with undercover detective work.

Alternative theories of the crime film, then, could readily be constructed by postulating the primacy of any of these genres. Any film in which a crime occurs can fairly be considered a crime film; the test of the classification, as of the resulting definition of the genre, depends on its usefulness in illuminating individual examples and the relations among them. More generally, crime films could certainly, as noted earlier, be redefined as injustice films or social-disorder films or power films or action films. The best reason to resist any of these labels is suggested by the last one: Action films all involve the attempt to right some perceived wrong through physical action, and therefore have a great deal in common with crime films; but assimilating one category to the other would achieve only a single purpose – underlining these similarities, in order, for example, to explore the morality of power exchanges in mass culture – at the cost of putting one of two enormously popular genre labels out of business. Studies of the relations between the two genres, perhaps overlaying one of them hypothetically on the other, are therefore far more likely, because more useful, than a consensual redefinition of either one in terms of the other.

In the same way, redefining the crime genre as the injustice genre, the social-disorder genre, or the power genre would make it virtually coextensive with what David Bordwell, Janet Staiger, and Kristin Thompson have called "classical Hollywood cinema" – fictional narratives in which an individual or group of people struggle to overcome obstacles toward a clearly defined goal whose decisive success or failure marks the end of the story. Hence Bordwell, Staiger, and Thompson argue that the narrative and stylistic deviance of film noir, which "no more subverts the classical film than crime fiction undercuts the orthodox novel," can readily be recuperated within the Hollywood paradigm.[9] Several years earlier, Steve Neale had already argued that the leading Hollywood genres are all "modes of . . . [a] narrative system" that "mainstream cinema produces as its commodity."[10] Broadening the crime genre to the extent of identifying it with this entire narrative system would indicate the degree to which Hollywood narrative is rooted in social problems that have specifically illegal manifestations, but at the cost of erasing the crime film's distinctiveness from other Hollywood narratives.

What is the point in maintaining this distinctiveness if the crime film's frontiers are so ragged? The answer is that the genre is not defined by its borders but by its center, its core appeal to different viewers. Not everyone laughs at the same things, but nearly everyone recognizes the importance of laughter in defining comedy.[11] In the same way, though not everyone will agree what counts as a crime film, this volume's survey of crime subgenres suggests that most viewers for any popular genre are responding to an appeal most economically encapsulated by Poe's representation of the criminal and the detective as mirror images of each other: to turn cultural anxiety into mass entertainment. Although this imperative may sound peculiar, it is behind all the great Hollywood genres, which gain their power not by ignoring or escaping from viewers' problems but by exploring, and usually attempting to resolve, social and psychological problems that are far more intransigent outside the movies. The western and the war movie romanticize problems of masculinity, violence, and national identity by transplanting them to a mythic past or projecting them onto a geopolitical canvas that makes them necessary for survival. The domestic melodrama, like its television cousin, the soap opera, heroically inflates the problems of family life and the domestic sphere in order to make the corresponding problems of its homebound target audience more palatable, even glamorous. Romantic comedies mine the uncertainties of courtship for laughs; musical comedies show the triumph of self-created performers over their doubts and inhibitions.

In each case the basic recipe for manufacturing entertainment is the same. First, anxieties about violence or personal identity or the dignity of home life are projected onto a typological, and thus reassuringly familiar, generic canvas, preferably one whose mise-en-scène is comfortably remote from the audience's own – as in the western, which takes place long ago and (for many) far away; or the animated cartoon, in which unendingly homicidal conflicts are played out against a drawn background whose two-dimensional unreality and promise of magical transformations render it doubly reassuring; or the film noir, which follows the mean streets of a stylishly seedy modern city.

Next, the anxieties that give the genre its cultural currency are simplified from multifaceted dilemmas into conflictual dualities. Having transported Dorothy Gale from the intractable problems of the Depression to the magical land of Oz, her film transforms the sorts of questions that bedeviled her at home (How can she keep Miss Gulch from taking Toto away? How can she get the adults in her world to take her seriously? Where can she find her heart's desire?) into simpler choices she can use to define her direction and her goal under the guidance of the good witch Glinda and the yellow brick road that leads her to adult surrogates who do take her seriously because she has rescued them of her own accord. More generally, popular genres reduce the anxieties they engage by redefining them in terms of dualities that can be more simply resolved. The passengers in *Stagecoach* (1939) cannot defeat the Indians, but the cavalry can; the problems of how to domesticate romance without killing it are resolved in Hollywood romantic comedies either by treating marriage as a conclusion that resolves all problems, preferably by rescuing one of the lovers from an unsuitable alternative match (*It Happened One Night,* 1934) or by giving married couples a chance at a second courtship (*The Awful Truth*, 1937; *The Palm Beach Story*, 1942). Musicals from *Top Hat* (1935) to *The Band Wagon* (1953) allow their singing and dancing principals to overcome their inhibitions and express the emotions that would otherwise leave them painfully vulnerable through performance. Action films reduce the complexities of geopolitics to a series of showdowns between Us and Them.[12]

The genius of these dualities is that they not only give viewers a strong rooting interest in a radically simplified moral conflict but also can easily vindicate either party to the conflict by demonizing the other, and present an unqualified triumph through decisive action. The hero's triumph or heroic defeat is a vindication not only of the social order but also of the audience's psychic health, a wish-fulfillment fantasy that manages to celebrate both individualism and social action even as it valorizes the movies' tendency to convert social or psychological stalemates, like Frank Bullitt's conflicts with politician Walter Chalmers, into Bullitt's more thrilling, visually arresting, and easily resolved car chase through the streets of San Francisco.

All the genres of popular entertainment are celebrations of individual heroic action as a way of cutting through the complexities of moral dilemmas; but all genres also acknowledge the limits of this heroic stance by somehow criticizing or undermining their enabling dualities as simplistic and individual heroism as an all-purpose recipe for problem solving. Since, as American classics from *The Gold Rush* (1925) to

Citizen Kane (1941) to *Do the Right Thing* (1989) show, the dialectic between the celebration and the critique of heroism is Hollywood's most enduring subject, it is hardly surprising that this dialectic animates so many Hollywood genres and provides the impetus behind their historical evolution.

In the case of the crime film, this complication is joined by another one constitutive of the genre. Although all crime films focus on a heroic individual, they vary widely not only in their attitudes toward that individual (as in the criminal heroes of gangster films or the antiheroes of film noir) but in the character positions they choose to anoint as heroes. It is rare to see self-professed enemies of love as the heroes of romantic comedies, or Native Americans cast as the heroes of westerns like *Cheyenne Autumn* (1964) or *Dances with Wolves* (1990) that question the heroism of ethnic European settlers; yet criminals are as likely to be the heroes of crime films as detectives or avengers, and far more likely than victims. The active heroic role is more important than the nature of the character who fills that role.

This point is driven home with particular emphasis by *Traffic* (2000), Steven Soderbergh's film about the Mexican–American drug trade, which dramatizes the costs of heroin addiction by following three separate stories whose characters, though unaware of each other, repeatedly act out the slippery relationship among the roles of criminal, victim, and avenger. The Mexican cop (Benicio del Toro) who goes undercover in the attempt to exploit the rivalry between two drug cartels relies on his criminal-looking behavior to preserve his life, and sees his best friend killed when his criminal mask slips; the California druglord's wife (Catherine Zeta-Jones) whose husband is arrested turns into a criminal herself in order to survive [Fig. 79]; and the American judge (Michael Douglas) who is named to head the Drug Enforcement Agency has to confront his own daughter's drug use, which ends up turning the nation's top drug cop into a victim and a would-be avenger himself. Once it has established the importance of each of these leading characters, the film is able to maintain considerable sympathy for them through several truly distorting transformations.

In both its synoptic view of the drug trade and its awareness of the ways the trade changes the behavior and even the moral role of everyone it touches, *Traffic* might be nominated as the complete crime film. But although its view of the heroin trade is more comprehensive than that of most crime films – though considerably less nuanced than that

of *Traffik* (1989), Alistair Reid's BBC miniseries on which it is based –
it is no more complete than that of *Scarface* (1932) or *Fury* or *The Godfather.* Crime films of every stripe present what might seem to be pat
social conflicts, moral questions sharpened by their parties' alliance
with legal right and wrong; but their attitude toward that conflict is
sharply ambivalent, if only because they function on behalf of both the
socially repressive agendas of their capitalist distributors and the es-
capist fantasies of the mass audience whose patronage they seek. In
their quest to make entertainment out of taboo behavior, they treat
crime as both realistic and ritualistic, a shocking aberration and business as usual, a vehicle of social idealism and of social critique. But
although the nature of the character who embodies the heroic role the
genre prescribes can vary from one crime film to the next even in the
same multiplex, the genre itself is best defined in terms of a single constitutive theme: the romance of criminal behavior. This behavior is
most often incarnated in a criminal, of course, whether that criminal
is an outsized gangster like Tony Camonte in *Scarface,* an unwilling
killer like Al Roberts (Tom Neal) in *Detour* (1945), or a tragically ailing
paterfamilias like Michael Corleone in *The Godfather, Part III* (1990).
Even when the crime film focuses on a victim or detective or avenger, however, those heroes become interesting, admirable, and heroic
precisely to the extent that they begin to act like criminals – unlike
the criminals themselves, who may well end up acting like victims or
moral avengers but who need only act like criminals to hold viewers'
interest. Hence the criminal, more than the victim or the avenger, illustrates the central function of the crime film: to allow viewers to experience the vicarious thrills of criminal behavior while leaving them
free to condemn this behavior, whoever is practicing it, as immoral.
The continued fascination of the genre is not that it tirelessly incul-
cates either or both of these positions for viewers that already understand them to a fault, but that it encourages them to experience the
contradictions among these positions and their corollaries in a way
no analysis can capture.

The crime film is therefore well named, because of its three leading
figures – the victim, the criminal, and the avenger – it is the criminal
and the kind of behavior he or she represents that are primary, and
it is only to the extent that other characters are tempted by the criminal's example that their films become crime films: films whose specific cultural task is to examine the price of social repression as im-
posed by the institutions of the justice system. Joe Wilson struggles

79. *Traffic:* Catherine Zeta-Jones as one more victim who turns criminal to survive.

with himself over whether he should emulate the mob that tried to kill him in *Fury. Double Indemnity*'s Walter Neff and *Basic Instinct*'s Det. Nick Curran are drawn into criminal behavior through their involvement in forbidden romance. J. J. Gittes confronts his own pettiness and greed in *Chinatown,* and Jeffrey Beaumont his outlaw sexuality in *Blue Velvet,* through their battles with monstrous antagonists; Det. Lt. Frank Bullitt and Alan Dershowitz confront endless criticisms of their work; Marge Gunderson restores law and order to Fargo by her failure to understand the dark humor her story embodies; even Hercule Poirot, in *Murder on the Orient Express,* ends by covering up a crime committed by a group of vigilantes whose cause he feels is just. Each of these films, like the subgenres they represent, appeals to the audience's own antisocial tendencies by cloaking them in the glamour and mystery of the criminal, reassuring the audience that this fantasy is only a waking dream, and leaving behind a lingering suggestion that the duality of right and wrong that supported it may be due for a closer look next week.

Notes

1. The Problem of the Crime Film

1. Carlos Clarens, *Crime Movies* (New York: W. W. Norton, 1980); rev. ed., with an afterword by Foster Hirsch (New York: Da Capo Press, 1997), pp. 12–13. See Robert Warshow, "The Gangster as Tragic Hero," *Partisan Review 15,* no. 2 (February 1948): 240–4; rpt. in *The Immediate Experience: Movies, Comics, Theatre and Other Aspects of Popular Culture* (Garden City, N.Y.: Doubleday, 1962; rpt. New York: Atheneum, 1975), pp. 127–33.

2. Larry Langman and Daniel Finn, *A Guide to American Crime Films of the Forties and Fifties* [Bibliographies and Indexes in the Performing Arts, no. 19] (Westport, Conn.: Greenwood, 1995), p. ix.

3. Raymond Bellour, "Segmenting/Analyzing" *Quarterly Review of Film Studies 1,* no. 3 (August 1976): 331–53, rpt. in Philip Rosen, ed., *Narrative, Apparatus, Ideology: A Film Theory Reader* (New York: Columbia University Press, 1986), pp. 66–92, at p. 75.

4. For more on the generic conventions of studio melodrama and the well-made Hollywood film, see David Bordwell, Janet Staiger, and Kristin Thompson, *The Classical Hollywood Cinema: Film Style and Mode of Production to 1960* (New York: Columbia University Press, 1985), pp. 3–41; and Michael Wood, *America in the Movies* (New York: Basic, 1975), pp. 3–23. Bordwell et al. use the term "classical Hollywood cinema" to talk about the well-made Hollywood film prominent during the studio era; Wood, more tendentiously, identifies studio melodrama of the 1940s with "the movies" (p. 4).

5. This question has been raised most influentially in Andrew Tudor, *Theories of Film* (New York: Viking, 1974), pp. 135–8.

6. *Jacobellis* v. *Ohio,* 378 U.S. 184, 197 (1964), quoted in Linda Williams, *Hard Core: Power, Pleasure, and the "Frenzy of the Visible"* (Berkeley: University of California Press, 1989), p. 283.

7. For a useful summary of the ways film viewers commonly use genres, see Rick Altman, *Film/Genre* (London: British Film Institute, 1999), p. 165.

8. See Altman, *The American Film Musical* (Bloomington: Indiana University Press, 1987), p. 92.
9. Altman, *Film/Genre,* p. 214.
10. Martin Rubin begins his study *Thrillers* (Cambridge: Cambridge University Press, 1999) with an account of *TV Guide*'s amusingly arbitrary classifications of closely related films as Crime Dramas, Thrillers, Comedies, Mysteries, or Science Fiction (p. 3).
11. Barry K. Grant, ed., *Film Genre: Theory and Criticism* (Metuchen, N.J.: Scarecrow, 1977), p. 215. Grant makes the same distinction between crime films and gangster films in the bibliographies to both volumes of *Film Genre Reader* (Austin: University of Texas Press, 1986, 1995).
12. Janet Staiger, "Hybrid or Inbred: The Purity Hypothesis and Hollywood Genre History," *Film Criticism* 22 (Fall 1997): 5–20, at p. 6.
13. Altman has analyzed at length Hollywood studios' motives and techniques for initiating, transforming, combining, and abandoning specific genres. See *Film/Genre,* pp. 54–62, 128–39.
14. See Brian Henderson, "*The Searchers:* An American Dilemma," *Film Quarterly 34,* no. 2 (Winter 1980–1): 9–23; rpt. in Bill Nichols, ed., *Movies and Methods,* 2 vols. (Berkeley: University of California Press, 1976–85), 2: 429–49.
15. Cf. Rubin's argument that the thriller "emphasizes visceral, gut-level feelings rather than more sensitive, cerebral, or emotionally heavy feelings" (*Thrillers,* p. 5).
16. John G. Cawelti, *Adventure, Mystery, and Romance: Formula Stories as Art and Popular Culture* (Chicago: University of Chicago Press, 1976), p. 16. Charles Derry extends this analysis by borrowing Michael Balint's distinction in *Thrills and Regressions* (London: Hogarth, 1959), p. 36, between "philobatic" (thrilling or sensationalistic) and "ocnophilic" (reassuring) elements in each thriller. See Derry, *The Suspense Thriller: Films in the Shadow of Alfred Hitchcock* (Jefferson, N.C.: McFarland, 1988), p. 23.
17. Clarens, *Crime Movies,* p. 13.
18. See Eric Rohmer and Claude Chabrol, *Hitchcock: The First Forty-Four Films,* trans. Stanley Hochman (New York: Frederick Ungar, 1979); and Robert J. Corber, *In the Name of National Security: Hitchcock, Homophobia, and the Political Construction of Gender in Postwar America* (Durham, N.C.: Duke University Press, 1993). Rubin characterizes Hitchcock films like *Strangers on a Train* (1951) as "psychological crime thrillers" whose generic interest focuses on "the psychological motivations and emotional relationships of characters affected by a crime" (*Thrillers,* p. 203).
19. See Derry, *Suspense Thriller,* p. iii. The definition proposed by Derry's subtitle, however problematic, is far superior to his definition of thrillers as "films whose content consists essentially of thrills" (p. 7). Derry's most elaborate definition – "*The suspense thriller can be defined as a crime work which presents a violent and generally murderous antagonism in which the protagonist becomes either an innocent victim or a nonprofessional criminal within a narrative structure that is significantly unmediated by a traditional figure of detection in a central position*" (p. 62; italics in original)

– shows both how closely he keeps to the Hitchcock model and how clearly he casts thrillers as victim films, as against films about detectives and professional criminals. Elizabeth Cowie recasts this distinction in phenomenological terms when she differentiates "the detective or mystery thriller," which is an "unraveling of the enigma through clues and deduction" whose significance is typically withheld from the audience, from "the suspense thriller," which is marked by three features: "a continuous holding back, interruptions in the pursuit of the resolution of the enigma by the characters," and dramatic irony that emphasizes the audience's superior knowledge. See Cowie, "The Popular Film as a Progressive Text – A Discussion of *Coma,*" in Constance Penley, ed., *Feminism and Film Theory* (New York and London: Routledge, 1988), pp. 104–40, at p. 126. Though Rubin weighs several different accounts that define thrillers in terms of typological characters, questions, or symbolic topographies, his remarks about the importance of viewers' "ambivalent desires" to surrender to "a series of sharp sensations" while "remain[ing] within the uneasy security of our . . . world" incline toward an affective definition of the thriller (*Thrillers,* pp. 8, 268).

20. François Truffaut, *Hitchcock*, trans. Helen G. Scott, rev. ed. (New York: Simon & Schuster, 1984 [1st ed. 1967]), p. 191.
21. See Staiger, "Hybrid or Inbred," 7–14, and Altman, *Film/Genre,* pp. 179–94.

2. Historical and Cultural Overview

1. See Alvin B. Kernan, "The Henriad: Shakespeare's Major History Plays," *Yale Review 59,* no. 1 (October 1969): 3–32, rpt. (revised and expanded) in Kernan, ed., *Modern Shakespearean Criticism: Essays on Style, Dramaturgy, and the Major Plays* (New York: Harcourt, Brace & World, 1970), pp. 245–75, for an analysis of this order's breakdown in Shakespeare's histories.
2. Lionel Trilling, *Sincerity and Authenticity* (Cambridge: Harvard University Press, 1972), p. 16.
3. Larry Langman and Daniel Finn, *A Guide to American Silent Crime Films* [Bibliographies and Indexes in the Performing Arts, no. 15.] (Westport, Conn.: Greenwood, 1994).
4. Charles Musser has noted that the success of the film created a vogue not for westerns but for other crime movies like *The Bold Bank Robbery* (1904). See Musser, "The Travel Genre: Moving towards Narrative," *Iris 2,* no. 1 (1984): 47–60; rpt. as "The Travel Genre in 1903–1904: Moving towards Fictional Narrative" in Thomas Elsaesser with Adam Barker, eds., *Early Cinema: Space, Frame, Narrative* (London: British Film Institute, 1990), pp. 123–32, at p. 131.
5. Scott Simmon, *The Films of D. W. Griffith* (New York: Cambridge University Press, 1993), p. 5.
6. Benjamin B. Hampton, *A History of the Movies* (New York: Covici–Friede Publishers, 1931; rpt. New York: Arno, 1970), p. 313.

7. Eugene Rosow, *Born to Lose: The Gangster Film in America* (New York: Oxford University Press, 1978), p. 151.

8. Rosow points out that Hollywood gangsters, originally holed up in "dark and dingy" hideouts, moved to "increasingly well-decorated offices, usually in the back of a nightclub" like *Underworld*'s Dreamland Cafe, and that these nightclubs themselves became more and more elaborate as the 1920s came to a close (*Born to Lose,* p. 124).

9. For a more detailed history of the pulps, see William F. Nolan, *The Black Mask Boys: Masters in the Hard-Boiled School of Detective Fiction* (New York: Morrow, 1985).

10. Jonathan Munby, *Public Enemies, Public Heroes: Screening the Gangster Film from Little Caesar to Touch of Evil* (Chicago: University of Chicago Press, 1999), p. 44.

11. Carlos Clarens, *Crime Movies* (New York: W. W. Norton, 1980); rev. ed., with an afterword by Foster Hirsch (New York: Da Capo Press, 1997), p. 78.

12. For more on the relationship between the Legion of Decency and the Production Code, see Leonard J. Leff and Jerold L. Simmons, *The Dame in the Kimono: Hollywood, Censorship, and the Production Code from the 1920s to the 1960s* (New York: Grove Weidenfeld, 1990), pp. 47–54. Leff and Simmons reprint the complete 1930 Production Code on pp. 283–92.

13. See Jon Tuska, *The Detective in Hollywood* (Garden City, N.Y.: Doubleday, 1978), p. 278.

14. This pattern of colorful villains upstaging heroes whose popularity eventually outlasted their own continues in the four Tracy serials for Republic (1937–41), the four RKO features starring Tracy (1945–7), and Warren Beatty's Touchstone extravaganza *Dick Tracy* (1990), as well as the comic strips and films featuring Batman (who first appeared in *Detective Comics* in 1937) and his equally picturesque antagonists.

15. The character began as a mysterious voice on a radio show featuring tales from *Detective Story* magazine. His popularity led to his own magazine, written by Walter Gibson. It was Gibson who added the Shadow's alias. The Shadow finally got his own short-lived radio show in 1932, followed years later by the more successful program starring Orson Welles (1937). Anthony Tollin, *The Shadow: The Making of a Legend* (New York: Advance Magazine Publishers/Conde Nast, 1996), pp. 7–19.

16. Hence *The Thin Man* (1934) and *The Postman Always Rings Twice* (1946) flaunted their literary credentials by displaying the jackets of their source books, the novels by Dashiell Hammett and James M. Cain, behind their opening credits.

17. Raymond Chandler, *Stories and Early Novels,* ed. Frank MacShane (New York: Library of America, 1995), p. 589.

18. This same determination to master the terrors of technology was at the same time reinventing the science-fiction genre, a thriving literary phenomenon that had never had much impact in Hollywood, by channeling paranoid fantasies of nuclear annihilation into heroic fantasies of space exploration in *Destination Moon* (1950), with such later entries as *The Thing from Another World* (1951), *The Day the Earth Stood Still* (1951), and

Invasion of the Body Snatchers (1956), combining heroic and paranoid fantasy in different proportions.

19. Walter Metz, "'Keep the Coffee Hot, Hugo': Nuclear Trauma in Lang's *The Big Heat*," *Film Criticism 21* (Spring 1997): 43–65, at p. 63.

20. Fredric Wertham, M.D., *Seduction of the Innocent* (New York: Rinehart, 1954), p. 118.

21. R. Barton Palmer points out that this shift coincides with the economic decline of the major Hollywood studios beginning with the Paramount decree of 1946. See Palmer, *Hollywood's Dark Cinema: The American Film Noir* (New York: Twayne, 1994), p. 167.

22. A few years after *Psycho*'s release, Hitchcock told François Truffaut that "people will say, 'It was a terrible film to make. The subject was horrible, the people were small, there were no characters in it.' I know all of this. . . . I didn't start off to make an important movie." See Truffaut, *Hitchcock*, trans. Helen G. Scott, rev. ed. (New York: Simon & Schuster, 1984 [1st ed. 1967]), p. 283.

23. The four ratings originally proposed were G (general audiences), M (mature audiences), R (restricted to audiences over 17 and children accompanied by an adult), and X. The M rating was replaced by PG (parental guidance suggested) in 1972; a new rating, PG-13 (parents strongly cautioned), was created in 1984; and the X rating was changed to NC-17 (no one under 17 admitted) in 1990 to distinguish serious adult films like *Henry and June* (1990) from the hardcore ("XXX") pornography the X label had seemed to promise.

24. Writing at the end of the decade, John G. Cawelti attributes the current spate of genre transformations to the antiestablishment belief that "not only the traditional genres but the cultural myths they once embodied are no longer fully adequate to the imaginative needs of our time." See Cawelti, "*Chinatown* and Generic Transformation in Recent American Films," in Gerald Mast and Marshall Cohen, eds., *Film Theory and Criticism, Introductory Readings,* 2d ed. (New York: Oxford University Press, 1979), pp. 559–79; rpt. in Barry Keith Grant, ed., *Film Genre Reader* (Austin: University of Texas Press, 1986), pp. 183–201, at p. 200.

25. For more on blaxploitation films, see Donald Bogle, *Toms, Coons, Mulattoes, Mammies, & Bucks,* 3rd ed. (New York: Continuum, 1994), pp. 232–42; Daniel J. Leab, *From Sambo to Superspade: The Black Experience in Motion Pictures* (Boston: Houghton Mifflin, 1975), pp. 233–59; and Ed Guerrero, *Framing Blackness: The African American Image in Film* (Philadelphia: Temple University Press, 1993), pp. 69–111.

26. See Timothy J. Flanagan, "Public Opinion and Public Policy in Criminal Justice," in Flanagan and Dennis R. Longmire, eds., *Americans View Crime and Justice: A National Public Opinion Survey* (Thousand Oaks, Calif.: Sage, 1996), pp. 151–8, at p. 157.

27. See Michael Medved, *Hollywood vs. America* (New York: HarperCollins, 1992), pp. 161–3.

28. Munby points out that gangsta films, which revive the gangster "as a seditious site in the struggle for representation against iniquitous and prej-

udicial forces" (*Public Enemies, Public Heroes,* p. 225), have a heritage as old as Tony "Scarface" Camonte and Cesare "Rico" Bandello.

3. Critical Overview

1. G. K. Chesterton, "A Defence of Detective Stories," in Chesterton, *The Defendant* (London: R. B. Johnson, 1901), pp. 157–62; rpt. in Howard Haycraft, ed., *The Art of the Mystery Story* (New York: Grosset & Dunlap, 1946), pp. 3–6, at p. 4.
2. G. K. Chesterton, "How to Write a Detective Story," *GK's Weekly* 17 (October 1925), rpt. Chesterton, *The Spice of Life and Other Essays,* ed. Dorothy Collins (Philadelphia: Dufour, 1966), pp. 15–21, at p. 17.
3. John Dickson Carr, "The Grandest Game in the World" (1946), first published in *Ellery Queen's Mystery Mix . . . #18* (New York: Random House, 1963), pp. 148–67, at p. 150.
4. John Strachey, "The Golden Age of English Detection," *Saturday Review of Literature* 19 (7 January 1939): 12–14.
5. Haycraft's anthology includes both the leading historical surveys that introduced E. M. Wrong's *Crime and Detection* (London: Oxford University Press, 1926; Haycraft pp. 18–32), Willard Huntington Wright's *The Great Detective Stories* (New York: Charles Scribner's Sons, 1927; pp. 33–70), and Dorothy L. Sayers's *Great Short Stories of Detection, Mystery, and Horror* (1st series, 1928; pp. 71–109), and the more striking "Twenty Rules for Writing Detective Stories" by S. S. Van Dine [Wright's pseudonym] (*American Magazine 106* [September 1928]: 129–31; Haycraft pp. 189–93); "Detective Story Decalogue," by Ronald A. Knox (Introduction to Knox, ed., *The Best Detective Stories of 1928* [London: Faber & Faber], 1929; pp. 194–6); and [Anthony Berkeley's?] Detection Club Oath (1928; pp. 197–9).
6. Nicholas Blake, "The Detective Story – Why?" Introduction to Howard Haycraft, *Murder for Pleasure: The Life and Times of the Detective Story* (London: Peter Davies, 1942), rpt. in Haycraft, *Art of the Mystery Story,* pp. 398–405, at p. 400.
7. W. H. Auden, "The Guilty Vicarage," *Harper's* (May 1948): 406–12, rpt. in Auden, *The Dyer's Hand and Other Essays* (London: Faber & Faber /New York: Random House, 1962; rpt. New York: Vintage, 1968), pp. 146–58, at pp. 157, 158.
8. Raymond Chandler, "The Simple Art of Murder," *Atlantic Monthly 174,* no. 6 (December 1944): 53–9, rev. and rpt. Chandler, *Later Novels and Other Writings,* ed. Frank MacShane (New York: Library of America, 1995), pp. 977–92, at pp. 977, 990, 989.
9. Carr ("Grandest Game," pp. 160–3) had criticized the lack of realism in the hard-boiled formula as early as 1946. For a more even-handed analysis of Chandler's claims to realism, see Edward A. Nickerson, "'Realistic' Crime Fiction: An Anatomy of Evil People," *Centennial Review 25* (Spring 1981): 101–32. The equally formulaic rhythms of Chandler's prose have been the subject of parodies from S. J. Perelman's "Farewell, My Lovely Appetizer," *New Yorker 20,* no. 44 (16 December 1944): 19–21, rpt. in *The Most of S. J.*

Perelman (New York: Simon & Schuster, 1958), pp. 191–6, to Woody Allen's "Mr. Big," in *Getting Even* (New York: Random House, 1971), pp. 139–51.

10. Parker Tyler, *Magic and Myth of the Movies* (New York: Simon & Schuster, 1947; rpt. New York: Garland, 1985), p. xxiii.

11. Parker Tyler, *The Hollywood Hallucination* (New York: Simon & Schuster, 1944; rpt. New York: Garland, 1985), p. 237.

12. Tyler, *Magic and Myth of the Movies,* pp. 177, 178, 188, 187, 189; emphasis in original.

13. Ibid., pp. 212, 218, 227.

14. Compare Tyler's analysis of *Citizen Kane* in *The Hollywood Hallucination*, pp. 190–207. Tyler returns to this argument in the similar terms twenty-five years later in his analysis of *Blowup* (1966) in *The Shadow of an Airplane Climbs the Empire State Building: A World Theory of Film* (Garden City, N.Y.: Doubleday, 1972), pp. 67–86.

15. Robert Warshow, "The Gangster as Tragic Hero," in *The Immediate Experience: Movies, Comics, Theatre and Other Aspects of Popular Culture* (Garden City, N.Y.: Doubleday, 1962; rpt. New York: Atheneum, 1975), pp. 127–33, at pp. 128, 129, 131, 130, 132, 133.

16. Andrew Sarris, *The American Cinema: Directors and Directions, 1929–1968* (New York: Dutton, 1968); François Truffaut, *Hitchcock*, trans. Helen G. Scott, rev. ed. (New York: Simon & Schuster, 1984 [1st ed. 1967]).

17. See Charles Derry, *The Suspense Thriller: Films in the Shadow of Alfred Hitchcock* (Jefferson, N.C.: McFarland, 1988), p. 4.

18. Colin McArthur, *Underworld U.S.A.* (London: Secker & Warburg, 1972), p. 8.

19. Ibid., p. 149.

20. Raymond Borde and Étienne Chaumeton, "Towards a Definition of *Film Noir*" (excerpted from *Panorama du film noir américain* [Paris: Éditions du Minuit, 1955]), trans. Alain Silver, in Silver and James Ursini, eds., *Film Noir Reader* (New York: Limelight, 1996), pp. 17–26, at p. 25; emphasis in original.

21. The matrix of early French criticism of film noir behind Borde and Chaumeton's work, much of it translated in R. Barton Palmer's *Perspectives on Film Noir* (New York: G. K. Hall, 1996), indicates that their assessment of the genre is by no means unanimous. See especially Palmer's translation (pp. 25–7) of Jean-Pierre Chartier's dour response, "The Americans Are Making Dark Films Too" ("Les Americains aussi font des films 'noirs,'" *Revue du cinéma 2* [November 1946]: 67–70): "It would be difficult to imagine going further into pessimism and a disgust for humanity" (p. 25). The heroes of *Double Indemnity*, *The Lost Weekend* (1945), and *Murder, My Sweet* (1944), unlike their French counterparts in *Quai des brumes* (U.S. title: *Port of Shadows*) and *Hôtel du nord* (both 1938), "are monsters, criminal, or victims of illness; nothing excuses them, and they act as they do simply because of a fatal, inner evil" (p. 27).

22. Raymond Durgnat, "Paint It Black: The Family Tree of *Film Noir,*" *Cinema* [UK] *6–7* (August 1970): 49–56; rpt. in Silver and Ursini, eds., *Film Noir Reader,* pp. 37–52, at p. 38.

23. See Robert Porfirio, "No Way Out: Existential Motifs in the *Film Noir,*" *Sight and Sound 45,* no. 4 (Autumn 1976): 212–17; rpt. in Silver and Ursini, eds., *Film Noir Reader,* pp. 77–93. See also Glenn Erickson, "Expressionist Doom in *Night and the City,*" in ibid., pp. 203–7.

24. Charles Higham and Joel Greenberg, "Black Cinema," from *Hollywood in the Forties* (New York: A. S. Barnes/London: Tantivy, 1968), pp. 19–36; rpt. as "*Noir* Cinema" in Silver and Ursini, eds., *Film Noir Reader,* pp. 27–35, at p. 27.

25. Paul Schrader, "Notes on *Film Noir,*" *Film Comment 8,* no. 1 (Spring 1972): 8–13; rpt. in Silver and Ursini, eds., *Film Noir Reader,* pp. 53–64, at pp. 53, 58, 59, 61.

26. Ibid., pp. 57, 58.

27. Janey Place and Lowell Peterson, "Some Visual Motifs of *Film Noir,*" *Film Comment 10,* no. 1 (January–February 1974): 30–5; rpt. in Silver and Ursini, eds., *Film Noir Reader,* pp. 65–75, at pp. 66, 68.

28. In *The Classical Hollywood Cinema: Film Style and Mode of Production to 1960* (New York: Columbia University Press, 1985), David Bordwell, Janet Staiger, and Kristin Thompson argue on the contrary that film noir cannot be defined in terms of a coherent style but merely as a marker of "particular patterns of nonconformity within Hollywood" (p. 75).

29. Stuart M. Kaminsky, *American Film Genres,* 2d ed. (Chicago: Nelson-Hall, 1985), p. 3.

30. Warshow, "Gangster as Tragic Hero," p. 130.

31. Northrop Frye, *Anatomy of Criticism: Four Essays* (Princeton: Princeton University Press, 1957). See John G. Cawelti, *Adventure, Mystery, and Romance: Formula Stories as Art and Popular Culture* (Chicago: University of Chicago Press, 1976), p. 319.

32. James Damico, "*Film Noir:* A Modest Proposal." *Film Reader* no. 3 (1978): 48–57; rpt. in Silver and Ursini, eds., *Film Noir Reader,* pp. 95–105, at p. 103.

33. Tzvetan Todorov, "The Typology of Detective Fiction" ("Typologie du roman policier," 1966), in *The Poetics of Prose,* trans. Richard Howard (Ithaca: Cornell University Press, 1971; rpt., with a new Introduction by Jonathan Culler, 1977), pp. 42–52, at pp. 50, 51.

34. For a summary of more recent attempts to define the thriller, see Martin Rubin, *Thrillers* (Cambridge: Cambridge University Press, 1999), pp. 22–36.

35. See George Grella, "Murder and Manners: The Formal Detective Novel," *Novel 4,* no. 1 (Fall 1970): 30–48, and "Murder and the Mean Streets: The Hard-Boiled Detective Novel," *Contempora 1* (March 1970): 6–15. The two essays are reprinted as "The Formal Detective Novel" and "The Hard-Boiled Detective Novel" in Robin W. Winks, *Detective Fiction: A Collection of Critical Essays* (Englewood Cliffs, N.J.: Prentice–Hall, 1980), pp. 84–102, 103–20.

36. Cawelti, "Notes toward a Typology of Literary Formulas," *Adventure, Mystery, and Romance,* pp. 37–50.

37. See Gary C. Hoppenstand, *In Search of the Paper Tiger: A Sociological Perspective of Myth, Formula and the Mystery Genre in the Entertainment Print*

Mass Medium. Bowling Green, Ohio: Bowling Green University Popular Press, 1987), pp. 23–4.

38. Derry, *The Suspense Thriller*, pp. 55–62.

39. William K. Everson, *The Bad Guys: A Pictorial History of the Movie Villain* (New York: Cadillac, 1964), p. xiii; Everson, *The Detective in Film* (Secaucus, N.J.: Citadel, 1972), p. 3. More recent books applying a similar approach – stills illustrating the movies, text glossing the stills – include Lawrence Hammond, *Thriller Movies: Classic Films of Suspense and Mystery* (London: Octopus, 1974); and John McCarty, *Thrillers: Seven Decades of Classic Film Suspense* (New York: Carol Publishing/Citadel, 1992).

40. See Jon Tuska, *The Detective in Hollywood* (Garden City, N.Y.: Doubleday, 1978), revised as *In Manors and Alleys: A Casebook on the American Detective Film* [Contributions to the Study of Popular Culture, no. 17] (Westport, Conn.: Greenwood, 1988). His *Dark Cinema: American Film Noir in Cultural Perspective* [Contributions to the Study of Popular Culture, no. 9] (Westport, Conn.: Greenwood, 1984), continues this approach in its expansion of chap. 10 of *Detective in Hollywood.*

41. Jack Shadoian, *Dreams and Dead Ends: The American Gangster/Crime Film* (Cambridge: MIT Press, 1977), p. x.

42. John Baxter, *The Gangster Film* (New York: A. S. Barnes/London: Zwemmer, 1970), p. 7.

43. Shadoian, *Dreams and Dead Ends*, pp. ix–x, 2, 11, 173.

44. Eugene Rosow, *Born to Lose: The Gangster Film in America* (New York: Oxford University Press, 1978), pp. 134, 135.

45. Carlos Clarens, *Crime Movies* (New York: W. W. Norton, 1980); rev. ed., with an afterword by Foster Hirsch (New York: Da Capo Press, 1997), pp. 12, 13. Hirsch updates Clarens's analysis to the period of *The Godfather: Part III*, *GoodFellas*, and *Pulp Fiction.*

46. Foster Hirsch, *The Dark Side of the Screen: Film Noir* (San Diego/New York/London: A. S. Barnes, 1981), p. 21. Bruce Crowther's later volume *Film Noir: Reflections in a Dark Mirror* (New York: Frederick Ungar/Continuum, 1988) follows Hirsch's synthetic approach, imitating its sequence of topics with amusing fidelity, but keeps much more closely to appreciation than analysis.

47. Molly Haskell, *From Reverence to Rape: The Treatment of Women in the Movies* (1974), 2d ed. (Chicago: University of Chicago Press, 1987), p. 189.

48. Christine Gledhill, "*Klute* 1: A Contemporary *Film Noir* and Feminist Criticism," in E. Ann Kaplan, ed., *Women in Film Noir*, rev. ed. (London: British Film Institute, 1980 [1st ed. 1978]), pp. 6–21, at pp. 8, 7, 13; emphasis in original.

49. Laura Mulvey, "Visual Pleasure and Narrative Cinema," *Screen 16,* no. 3 (Autumn 1975): 6–18; rpt. in *Visual and Other Pleasures* (Bloomington: Indiana University Press, 1989), pp. 14–26, at pp. 14, 19.

50. Claire Johnston, "*Double Indemnity*," in Kaplan, ed., *Women in Film Noir*, pp. 100–11, at p. 102.

51. Sylvia Harvey, "Woman's Place: The Absent Family of *Film Noir,*" in Kaplan, ed., *Women in Film Noir*, pp. 22–34, at pp. 25, 33.

52. Pam Cook, "Duplicity in *Mildred Pierce*," in Kaplan, ed., *Women in Film Noir*, pp. 68–82, at p. 69.
53. Elizabeth Cowie, "*Film Noir* and Women," in Joan Copjec, ed., *Shades of Noir: A Reader* (London: Verso, 1993), pp. 121–65, at p. 135.
54. Mary Ann Doane, *Femmes Fatales: Feminism, Film Theory, Psychoanalysis* (New York: Routledge, 1991), p. 2.
55. James F. Maxfield, *The Fatal Woman: Sources of Male Anxiety in American Film Noir, 1941–1991* (Madison, N.J.: Fairleigh Dickinson University Press, 1996), pp. 12, 13.
56. Richard Dyer, "Resistance through Charisma: Rita Hayworth and *Gilda*," in Kaplan, ed., *Women in Film Noir*, pp 91–9, at p. 91.
57. Frank Krutnik, *In a Lonely Street: Film Noir, Genre, Masculinity* (London: Routledge, 1991), pp. xiii, 42, 97.
58. Annette Kuhn, *Women's Pictures: Feminism and Cinema* (London: Routledge & Kegan Paul, 1982), p. 73.
59. Carl Richardson, *Autopsy: An Element of Realism in Film Noir* (Metuchen, N.J.: Scarecrow, 1992), pp. 152, 5, 33, 146.
60. J. P. Telotte, *Voices in the Dark: The Narrative Patterns of Film Noir* (Urbana: University of Illinois Press, 1989), pp. 14, 15, 30.
61. Ibid., p. 34.
62. Joan Copjec, "The Phenomenal Nonphenomenal: Private Space in *Film Noir*," in Copjec, ed., *Shades of Noir*, pp. 167–97, at pp. 186, 183, 182. See Pascal Bonitzer, "Les silences de la voix," *Cahiers du cinéma* no. 256 (February–March 1975): 22–33; rpt. as "The Silences of the Voice," trans. Philip Rosen and Marcia Butzel, in Rosen, ed., *Narrative, Apparatus, Ideology: A Film Theory Reader* (New York: Columbia University Press, 1986), pp. 319–34, at p. 323.
63. Marc Vernet, "*Film Noir* on the Edge of Doom," in Copjec, ed., *Shades of Noir*, pp. 1–31, at pp. 4, 26.
64. James Naremore, *More Than Night: Film Noir in Its Contexts* (Berkeley: University of California Press, 1998), pp. 22, 39.
65. See Douglas Brode, *Money, Women, and Guns: Crime Movies from Bonnie and Clyde to the Present* (New York: Citadel, 1995); and Marilyn Yaquinto, *Pump 'Em Full of Lead: A Look at Gangsters on Film* (New York: Twayne, 1998).
66. Naremore, *More Than Night*, p. 255, 117, 120. Cf. Paul Kerr, "Out of What Past? Notes on the B *Film Noir*," *Screen Education* nos. 32–3 (1979–80): 45–65; rpt. in Alain Silver and James Ursini, eds., *Film Noir Reader* (New York: Limelight, 1996), pp. 107–27.
67. Jonathan Munby, *Public Enemies, Public Heroes: Screening the Gangster Film from Little Caesar to Touch of Evil* (Chicago: University of Chicago Press, 1999), pp. 8, 233.
68. Chris Steinbrunner and Otto Penzler, eds., *Encyclopedia of Mystery and Detection* (New York: McGraw-Hill, 1976); William L. DeAndrea, *Encyclopedia Mysteriosa: A Comprehensive Guide to the Art of Detection in Print, Film, Radio and Television* (New York: Macmillan, 1994).
69. Ed Gorman, Lee Server, and Martin H. Greenberg, eds., *The Big Book of Noir* (New York: Carroll & Graf, 1998).

70. Barry Gifford, *The Devil Thumbs a Ride and Other Unforgettable Films* (New York: Grove, 1988), p. ix.
71. Nicholas Christopher, *Somewhere in the Night: Film Noir and the American City* (New York: Free Press, 1997).
72. Eddie Muller, *Dark City: The Lost World of Film Noir* (New York: St. Martin's, 1998), p. 13.
73. Phil Hardy, ed., *The BFI Companion to Crime* (Berkeley: University of California Press, 1997); and Alain Silver and Elizabeth Ward, eds., *Film Noir: An Encyclopedic Reference to the American Style* (Woodstock, N.Y.: Overlook, 1978; rev. and expanded, 1988). James Ursini, a contributor to the first two editions of Silver and Ward, is a coeditor of the third (Woodstock, N.Y.: Overlook, 1992).
74. Spencer Selby, *Dark City: The Film Noir* (Jefferson, N.C.: McFarland, 1984); Joseph J. Cocchiarelli, *Screen Sleuths: A Filmography* (New York: Garland, 1992); and Robert Ottoson, *A Reference Guide to the American Film Noir: 1940–1958* (Metuchen, N.J.: Scarecrow, 1981).
75. James Robert Parish and Michael R. Pitts, *The Great Gangster Pictures,* 2 vols. (Metuchen, N.J.: Scarecrow, 1976, 1987) and *The Great Detective Pictures* (Metuchen, N.J.: Scarecrow, 1990); Michael R. Pitts, *Famous Movie Detectives,* 2 vols. (Metuchen, N.J.: Scarecrow, 1979, 1991); Karen Burroughs Hannsbery, *Femme Noir: Bad Girls of Film* (Jefferson, N.C.: McFarland, 1998).
76. Larry Langman and Daniel Finn, *A Guide to American Silent Crime Films* (Westport, Conn.: Greenwood, 1994), *A Guide to American Crime Films of the Forties and Fifties* (idem, 1995), and *A Guide to American Crime Films of the Thirties* (idem, 1995) (numbers 15, 19, and 18, respectively, in the series Bibliographies and Indexes in the Performing Arts).

4. *Fury* and the Victim Film

1. Charles Derry, *The Suspense Thriller: Films in the Shadow of Alfred Hitchcock* (Jefferson, N.C.: McFarland, 1988), pp. 18, 62.
2. Robert Ottoson, *A Reference Guide to the American Film Noir: 1940–1958* (Metuchen, N.J.: Scarecrow, 1981), p. 7.
3. Chapter 11 of the *Poetics* links the *peripety* that marks a reversal of fortune with a discovery and suffering. See Aristotle, *The Basic Works of Aristotle,* ed. Richard McKeon (New York: Random House, 1941), pp. 1465–6.
4. James Naremore, *More Than Night: Film Noir in Its Contexts* (Berkeley: University of California Press, 1998), p. 120.
5. In an earlier version of the screenplay cowritten by Boris Ingster, the director of the proto-noir *Stranger on the Third Floor* (1940), and Nathanael West, author of *Miss Lonelyhearts* (1933) and *The Day of the Locust* (1939), the heroine dramatizes this problematic position by turning against the husband who has just offered her a poisoned glass and shooting him dead. See West, *Novels and Other Writings* (New York: Library of America, 1997), pp. 621–744.
6. In *Narration in Light: Studies in Cinematic Point of View* (Baltimore: Johns Hopkins University Press, 1986), George M. Wilson notes that this ambi-

guity is essential to "the problem of what Eddie has done and who he really is" (p. 19).

7. Despite describing *Fury* as "the only film I know to which I have wanted to attach the epithet of 'great,'" Graham Greene dismissed the final scenes as leading to "a neatly contrived happy ending." See Greene, *Graham Greene on Film: Selected Film Criticism, 1935–1939* (New York: Simon & Schuster, 1972), p. 84.

8. Siegfried Kracauer suggests that often Lang's German films, in which "the law triumphs and the lawless glitters," undermine their plea for rational authority by glamorizing anarchy and chaos. See *From Caligari to Hitler: A Psychological History of the German Film* (Princeton: Princeton University Press, 1947), p. 250.

9. The newsreel is valorized in Lotte Eisner, *Fritz Lang* (London: Secker & Warburg, 1976), p. 162, and its representational strategies (and hence the strategies of the film that incorporates them) attacked in Reynold Humphries, *Fritz Lang: Genre and Representation in His American Films* (Baltimore: Johns Hopkins University Press, 1989), pp. 54–9.

5. *The Godfather* and the Gangster Film

1. In "Paint It Black: The Family Tree of *Film Noir*," Raymond Durgnat points out that *The Public Enemy* combines moral, sociological, and psychological explanations for Tom Powers's criminality while insisting at the same time that his own conscious choices have made him "a mad dog who must die." *Cinema* [UK] *6–7* (August 1970): 49–56; rpt. in Alain Silver and James Ursini, eds., *Film Noir Reader* (New York: Limelight, 1996), pp. 37–52, at p. 49. In the same year, John Baxter suggests in *The Gangster Film* (New York: A. S. Barnes/London: Zwemmer, 1970), that "the urban wolf" is "the product of his harsh environment . . . but his involvement in crime seems a matter of chance rather than choice" (p. 7).

2. Quoted by John Hess in "*Godfather II:* A Deal Coppola Couldn't Refuse," *Jump Cut* no. 7 (May–July 1975): 1, 10–11; rpt. in Bill Nichols, ed., *Movies and Methods,* 2 vols. (Berkeley: University of California Press, 1976–85), 1: 81–90, at p. 81.

6. *Double Indemnity* and the Film Noir

1. See Nino Frank, "Un nouveau genre 'policier': L'aventure criminelle," *L'Écran français 61* (28 August 1946): 8–14, at p. 14; rpt. as "The Crime Adventure Story: A New Kind of Detective Film," trans. R. Barton Palmer, in Palmer, ed. *Perspectives on Film Noir* (New York: G. K. Hall, 1996), pp. 21–4, at p. 24.

2. As David Reid and Jayne L. Walker note in "Strange Pursuit: Cornell Woolrich and the Abandoned City of the Forties," noir's expressionistic paranoia was rooted in an attitude of romantic and philosophical fatalism rather than any widespread economic hardship, since "there was no

post-war depression." In Joan Copjec, ed., *Shades of Noir: A Reader* (London: Verso, 1993), pp. 57–96, at p. 61.

3. Steve Neale, *Genre and Hollywood* (London: Routledge, 2000), p. 173.

4. In *Hollywood's Wartime Women: Representation and Ideology* (Ann Arbor: UMI Research Press, 1988), Michael Renov points out that as early as 1944, "the internal memoranda of government agencies show that the female work force was being termed 'excess labor' and efforts were being made to induce voluntary withdrawal" (p. 33).

5. Lucy Fischer, *Cinematernity: Film, Motherhood, Genre* (Princeton: Princeton University Press, 1996), p. 101.

6. Frank Krutnik, *In a Lonely Street: Film Noir, Genre, Masculinity* (London: Routledge, 1991), p. 29.

7. Paul Kerr, "Out of What Past? Notes on the B *Film Noir,*" *Screen Education* nos. 32–3 (1979–80): 45–65; rpt. in Alain Silver and James Ursini, eds., *Film Noir Reader* (New York: Limelight, 1996), pp. 107–27, at p. 125. Compare Colin MacCabe, "Theory and Film: Principles of Realism and Pleasure," *Screen 17,* no. 3 (Autumn 1976): 7–29; rpt. in Philip Rosen, ed., *Narrative, Apparatus, Ideology: A Film Theory Reader* (New York: Columbia University Press, 1986), pp. 179–97, at p. 183.

8. Thom Andersen, "Red Hollywood," in Suzanne Ferguson and Barbara Groseclose, eds., *Literature and the Visual Arts in Contemporary Society* (Columbus: Ohio State University Press, 1985), pp. 141–96, at p. 183. Compare Carl Richardson, *Autopsy: An Element of Realism in Film Noir* (Metuchen, N.J.: Scarecrow, 1992), p. 198.

9. Mike Davis, *City of Quartz* (London: Verso, 1990), p. 18; Dean MacCannell, "Democracy's Turn: On Homeless *Noir,*" in Copjec, ed., *Shades of Noir,* pp. 279–97, at p. 284; Copjec, Introduction to *Shades of Noir,* p. ix.

10. Janey Place and Lowell Peterson, "Some Visual Motifs of *Film Noir,*" *Film Comment 10,* no. 1 (January–February 1974): 30–5; rpt. in Silver and Ursini, eds., *Film Noir Reader,* pp. 65–76, at pp. 66, 68; David Bordwell, Janet Staiger, and Kristin Thompson, *The Classical Hollywood Cinema: Film Style and Mode of Production to 1960* (New York: Columbia University Press, 1985), p. 76.

11. Paul Schrader, "Notes on *Film Noir,*" *Film Comment 8,* no. 1 (Spring 1972): 8–13; rpt. in Silver and Ursini, eds., *Film Noir Reader,* pp. 53–64, at p. 57. Compare Frank, "Crime Adventure Story": "Because [noirs] are purely psychological stories, action, either violent or exciting, matters less than faces, behavior, words" (p. 23).

12. Dana Polan, *Power and Paranoia: History, Narrative, and the American Cinema, 1940–1950* (New York: Columbia University Press, 1986), p. 210.

13. Cf. Foster Hirsch, who writes in *The Dark Side of the Screen: Film Noir* (San Diego/New York/London: A. S. Barnes, 1981) that "perhaps [*Citizen Kane*], rather than Huston's thriller, should be considered the primal American *film noir*" (p. 122).

14. Hence Barry Gifford observes in *The Devil Thumbs a Ride and Other Unforgettable Films* (New York: Grove, 1988) that "*noir* is handy as a catchall but useless as a definition" (p. 1), and Jon Tuska suggests in *Dark Cin-*

ema: American Film Noir in Cultural Perspective [Contributions to the Study of Popular Culture, no. 9] (Westport, Conn.: Greenwood, 1984) that the term be understood as referring to "both a style and a kind of narrative structure" (p. 151).

15. James Naremore points out in *More Than Night: Film Noir in Its Contexts* (Berkeley: University of California Press, 1998) that Wilder and Pereira based their designs for the Pacific All-Risk office closely on Paramount's home office in New York (p. 86).

16. For a more extended discussion of the importance of the flashback and voiceover in *Double Indemnity* and film noir generally, see J. P. Telotte, *Voices in the Dark: The Narrative Patterns of Film Noir* (Urbana: University of Illinois Press, 1989), pp. 40–56.

17. As R. Barton Palmer notes in *Hollywood's Dark Cinema: The American Film Noir* (New York: Twayne, 1994), *Double Indemnity* "domesticates crime, makes it an element of family life and its discontents" (p. 51), since the film's stifling domestic sphere provides an intensification of, rather than an escape from, the principals' sordid self-entrapment.

18. Raymond Chandler, Introduction to *The Simple Art of Murder* (Boston: Houghton Mifflin, 1950); rpt. in Chandler, *Later Novels and Other Writings,* ed. Frank MacShane (New York: Library of America, 1995), pp. 1016–19, at p. 1017.

19. Wilder described the film to John Allyn as "a love story between the two men and a sexual involvement with the woman." See Allyn, "*Double Indemnity:* A Policy That Paid Off," *Literature/Film Quarterly 6,* no. 2 (1978): 116–24, at p. 120.

20. In "Tales of Sound and Fury: Observations on the Family Melodrama," *Monogram 4* (1972): 2–15, Thomas Elsaesser extends the pattern of institutional repressions that encourage the excessive, overemphatic visuals of Vincente Minnelli and Douglas Sirk in "a conscious use of style-as-meaning, the mark of a modernist sensibility working in popular culture" to the contemporaneous domestic melodrama as well. Rpt. in Barry Keith Grant, ed., *Film Genre Reader* (Austin: University of Texas Press, 1986), pp. 278–308, at p. 290.

21. Raymond Chandler, *Double Indemnity,* in *Later Novels and Other Writings,* pp. 875–972, at p. 882.

22. Most of Phyllis's costume changes, of course, differ from those specified in Cain's novel. More surprisingly, Phyllis herself is far more treacherous in the film than in the novel, which ends with her and the still-smitten Walter escaping from California aboard a cruise ship to Mexico and planning to commit suicide together, before the ship's captain puts them under guard.

7. *Basic Instinct* and the Erotic Thriller

1. James Naremore points out in *More Than Night: Film Noir in Its Contexts* (Berkeley: University of California Press, 1998) that, by the mid-1990s, direct-to-television video had become "a seventeen-billion-dollar-a-year

industry, involving more money than all the major studios combined"
(p. 161).

2. It is this emphasis on the female body that distinguishes the new crop
of neo-noirs from such earlier neo-noir candidates as *The Kremlin Letter*
(1970), *The French Connection* (1971), and *Night Moves* (1975) – all cited
in the first edition of Alain Silver and Elizabeth Ward, eds., *Film Noir: An
Encyclopedic Reference to the American Style* (Woodstock, N.Y.: Overlook,
1979) – as well as from female-psycho movies like *Play Misty for Me* (1971).

3. Hence Fredric Jameson's observation in "Postmodernism and Consumer
Society" that the film seems to take place in "an eternal '30s." In Hal Fos-
ter, ed., *The Anti-Aesthetic: Essays on Postmodern Culture* (Port Townsend,
Wash.: Bay Press, 1983), pp. 111–25, at p. 117.

4. Several erotic thrillers do recycle the once-fashionable noir conventions
of flashback and voice-over (and they are among the few contemporary
films that do). But the frames of films like *Romeo Is Bleeding* (1993) and
Traces of Red (1992) are more likely to be tricky or teasing than fatalistic.

5. Silver and Ward, eds., *Film Noir,* rev. and expanded ed. (Woodstock, N.Y.:
Overlook, 1988), p. 372.

6. Hence the erotic thriller perfectly illustrates Laura Mulvey's suggestion,
in "Visual Pleasure and Narrative Cinema," *Screen 16,* no. 3 (Autumn
1975): 6–18, that Hollywood cinema protects its investment in voyeurism
by reducing the female to a spectacle, alternatively fetishizing her body
or treating her as a dangerous riddle to be resolved, while going further
than any other genre to justify the breathtaking logical leap with which
Mulvey opens her analysis: "The cinema offers a number of possible pleasures. One is scopophilia." Rpt. in Mulvey, *Visual and Other Pleasures*
(Bloomington: Indiana University Press, 1989), pp. 14–26, at p. 6.

7. In *A Lure of Knowledge: Lesbian Sexuality and Theory* (New York: Columbia University Press, 1991), Judith Roof uses Hollywood representations
of lesbian sexuality and experiences of lesbian audiences "to question
the genderment and heterosexism of film theory" (p. 17).

8. The film's original ending, available on some videotape prints, shows Alex
killing herself in a way that is certain to throw suspicion on Dan for her
murder – an ending borrowed from *Leave Her to Heaven* (1945). When
test audiences pronounced this ending anticlimactic, Paramount substituted the horror-film climax that exorcises the femme fatale while letting
the hero off the hook – framed, in the film's final shot, with Beth and Ellen
in a family portrait atop a shelf in their new home.

9. According to Naremore, "Glenn Close has said that she regards *Fatal Attraction* as a film noir" (*More Than Night,* p. 263).

10. The convention, which is shared by other erotic thrillers like *Body of Evidence* (1993) and *Color of Night* (1994), goes back at least to the bank
robbery in *You Only Live Once* (1937), which misleadingly suggests that
Eddie Taylor is the robber, and the shooting of Miles Archer by an offscreen killer in *The Maltese Falcon* (1941).

11. R. Barton Palmer, *Hollywood's Dark Cinema: The American Film Noir* (New
York: Twayne, 1994), p. 186.

12. Even in *Wild Things* (1998), in which men and women join in endless conspiracies and double-crosses, a lone woman predictably emerges on top.

8. *Murder on the Orient Express, Blue Velvet,* and the Unofficial-Detective Film

1. For more on the whodunit, see Colin Watson, *Snobbery with Violence: Crime Stories and Their Audience* (London: Eyre & Spottiswoode,1971), which emphasizes the dependence of the English country-house mystery on class distinctions. George Grella economically summarizes the con-trasting features of the whodunit and the private-eye formulas in "Mur-der and Manners: The Formal Detective Novel," *Novel 4,* no. 1 (1970): 30–48, and "Murder and the Mean Streets: The Hard-Boiled Detective Novel," *Contempora 1* (March 1970): 6–15; rpt. as "The Formal Detective Novel" and "The Hard-Boiled Detective Novel," respectively, in Robin W. Winks, *Detective Fiction: A Collection of Critical Essays* (Englewood Cliffs, N.J.: Prentice–Hall, 1980), pp. 84–102, 103–20.
2. To these series can be added the later British films starring Margaret Rutherford in her salty, active portrayals of Agatha Christie's spinster-sleuth Miss Jane Marple, beginning with *Murder She Said* (1961). Miss Marple's lineal descendant, Jessica Fletcher of CBS Television's *Murder, She Wrote* (1984–96), suggests that the natural home of whodunits whose detectives are continuing characters is television. The British Broadcast-ing System has brought to life many stories by Christie, Conan Doyle, Dorothy L. Sayers, P. D. James, Ruth Rendell, and Colin Dexter. Although police detectives and private eyes have predominated on American tele-vision from the time of *Dragnet* (1952–9) and *Peter Gunn* (1958–61), the long history of television whodunits inaugurated by Ellery Queen (e.g., *The Adventures of Ellery Queen,* 1950–2, 1954–7), already a long-running success on radio, has continued with series like *The Snoop Sisters* (1973–4), *Nero Wolfe* (1981), and *Murder, She Wrote.*
3. François Truffaut, *Hitchcock,* trans. Helen G. Scott, rev. ed. (New York: Si-mon & Schuster, 1984 [1st ed. 1967]), p. 74.
4. This statement, though apparently tautological, is not really true, because many detectives who have all the generic marks of unofficial detectives actually have close ties to the system whose rules they so often flout. Her-cule Poirot has retired from the Belgian police; Nero Wolfe is a licensed private investigator whose clients pay him to solve crimes; Philo Vance is a close friend of the New York District Attorney; Ellery Queen is the son of a New York police detective. Even Sherlock Holmes begins his career as a consulting detective – that is, a detective whose clients are them-selves detectives who cannot solve their cases. Holmes soon gives up this pretense but continues throughout his career to accept paying clients. Perhaps the ultimate cases of confusion are the Twentieth Century–Fox series of films featuring Charlie Chan, who, despite having all the manner-isms of an amateur detective, works for the Honolulu Police Department; the MGM series of *Thin Man* films featuring Nick Charles, a licensed pri-

vate detective who always gets into cases backward, by happenstance or as a favor to some friend, and whose knockabout domestic establishment is obviously rooted in the rituals of the unofficial detective; and *Devil in a Blue Dress* (1995), whose hero Easy Rawlins, a generally unwilling amateur, is given many of the trappings of the hard-boiled dick. These rituals and trappings are just as important as the detective's professional status in establishing a given film's generic ties.

5. Although the film was distributed in the United States by Paramount, it was produced, appropriately enough, at England's Elstree Studios, where Hitchcock had shot a dozen films in the twenties and thirties for British International.

6. Herbert Ross achieves a similar effect in *The Last of Sheila* (1973), whose screenplay by Anthony Perkins and Stephen Sondheim is filled with in-jokes that invite the audience to guess which real-life Hollywood stars are represented by the films' characters, whose scandalous secret pasts give them motives for murder.

7. This is particularly true of George Sluizer's 1993 English-language *The Vanishing,* which adds a rather unconvincing happy ending to Sluizer's own 1988 Dutch film of the same title.

8. James F. Maxfield, *The Fatal Woman: Sources of Male Anxiety in American Film Noir, 1941–1991* (Madison, N.J.: Fairleigh Dickinson University Press, 1996), p. 147.

9. *Chinatown* and the Private-Eye Film

1. Raymond Chandler, "The Simple Art of Murder," *Atlantic Monthly 174,* no. 6 (December 1944): 53–9, rev. and rpt. Chandler, *Later Novels and Other Writings,* ed. Frank MacShane (New York: Library of America, 1995), pp. 977–92, at p. 984.

2. Ibid., pp. 991–2.

3. Frank Krutnik, *In a Lonely Street: Film Noir, Genre, Masculinity* (London: Routledge, 1991), p. 95.

4. The private eye's homophobia is not an isolated fact in Hollywood history, for the Production Code's suppression of all reference to "sex perversion" changed the motive for murder in *Crossfire* (1947) from homophobia to anti-Semitism and made the hero of *The Lost Weekend* (1945) struggle with alcoholism instead of homosexuality. See Foster Hirsch, *The Dark Side of the Screen: Film Noir* (San Diego/New York/London: A. S. Barnes, 1981), p. 190. Robert J. Corber's *In the Name of National Security: Hitchcock, Homophobia, and the Political Construction of Gender in Postwar America* (Durham, N.C.: Duke University Press, 1993) argues for a systematic nexus in Hitchcock's 1950s films between homosexuality and anti-Americanism. By the time of *The Usual Suspects,* Nicholas Christopher explains the virtual absence of women by noting that "the femme fatale has been internalized by the male seducer, who then employs both masculine and feminine wiles." Christopher, *Somewhere in the Night: Film Noir and the American City* (New York: Free Press, 1997), p. 254.

5. See R. Barton Palmer, *Hollywood's Dark Cinema: The American Film Noir* (New York: Twayne, 1994), p. 96; and Robert Lang, "Looking for the 'Great Whatzit': *Kiss Me Deadly* and *Film Noir*," *Cinema Journal 27*, no. 3 (Spring 1988): 32–44; rpt. in Palmer, ed., *Perspectives on Film Noir* (New York: G. K. Hall, 1996), pp. 171–84, at p. 174.

6. See John G. Cawelti, "*Chinatown* and Generic Transformation in Recent American Films," in Gerald Mast and Marshall Cohen, eds., *Film Theory and Criticism, Introductory Readings,* 2d ed. (New York: Oxford University Press: 1979), pp. 559–79; rpt. in Barry Keith Grant, ed., *Film Genre Reader* (Austin: University of Texas Press, 1986), pp. 183–201.

7. Laura Mulvey, "Visual Pleasure and Narrative Cinema," *Screen 16,* no. 3 (Autumn 1975): 6–18; rpt. in *Visual and Other Pleasures* (Bloomington: Indiana University Press, 1989), pp. 14–26, at pp. 23–4. In "*Chinatown* and the Detective Story," *Literature/Film Quarterly 5,* no. 2 (1977): 112–17, R. Barton Palmer roots Gittes's ultimate failure in the film's obsessive emphasis on images of distorted vision, from Noah Cross's broken eyeglasses to the taillight Gittes smashes on Evelyn's car to the flaw in Evelyn's eye (p. 117) – a list to which James F. Maxfield, in *The Fatal Woman: Sources of Male Anxiety in American Film Noir, 1941–1991* (Madison, N.J.: Fairleigh Dickinson University Press, 1996), adds the black eye Curly ends up giving his cheating wife (p. 130).

8. John Alonzo suggests that Polanski continually kept his camera so close to Dunaway that "it made her nervous" and deepened her performance. See Dennis Schaefer and Larry Salvato, *Masters of Light: Conversations with Contemporary Cinematographers* (Berkeley: University of California Press, 1984), p. 32.

9. Polanski notes in his autobiography that Towne originally "wanted the evil tycoon to die and his daughter, Evelyn, to live"; it was Polanski who insisted on the film's incomparably bleak ending. See Roman Polanski, *Roman by Polanski* (New York: Morrow, 1984), p. 348.

10. As Maxfield notes in *Fatal Woman* (p. 124), Mulwray's movements precisely anticipate Gittes's. Like Mulwray, Gittes sits waiting in the spillway for hours, nearly drowns in the process, and ends up, like the dead Mulwray, losing a shoe before consummating his affair with Mulwray's widow in Mulwray's bed.

11. Maxfield concludes, after examining the evidence for rape in Robert Towne's screenplay and the completed film, that *Chinatown* remains stubbornly ambiguous about the extent to which "Evelyn at least half-willingly succumbed" to her father's monstrous advances (*Fatal Woman,* p. 127).

10. *Bullitt* and the Police Film

1. Robert L. Pike, *Mute Witness* (New York: Doubleday [for Crime Club], 1963); rpt. as *Bullitt* (London: Bloomsbury, 1997), p. 1.

2. François Truffaut, *Hitchcock*, trans. Helen G. Scott, rev. ed. (New York: Simon & Schuster, 1984 [1st ed. 1967]), p. 109.

3. George N. Dove, *The Police Procedural* (Bowling Green, Ohio: Bowling Green University Popular Press, 1982), p. 68.

4. For a closer look at the uniquely experimental matrix of the period, see Peter Lev, *American Films of the 70s: Conflicting Visions* (Austin: University of Texas Press, 2000).

5. Martin Rubin, *Thrillers* (Cambridge: Cambridge University Press, 1999), p. 255.

6. Jon Tuska reports that the role of Harry was originally offered to John Wayne, who turned it down because "the character was not right for him." See Tuska, *In Manors and Alleys: A Casebook on the American Detective Film* [Contributions to the Study of Popular Culture, no. 17] (Westport, Conn.: Greenwood, 1988), p. 405. Carlos Clarens notes that the role was refused as well by Paul Newman and Frank Sinatra; Clarens, *Crime Movies* (New York: W. W. Norton, 1980); rev. ed., with an afterword by Foster Hirsch (New York: Da Capo Press, 1997), p. 302.

7. Clarens, *Crime Movies*, calls Scorpio "an amalgam of the major criminals of the sixties, from Charles Manson to Charles Whitman . . . and from San Francisco's own Zodiac Killer to the kidnappers who buried alive a Florida heiress . . . in 1968" (p. 304) and notes that *Dirty Harry* had consequences as well as antecedents in the headlines, since "two real-life murders were traced directly to the film" (p. 303).

8. Pike, *Bullitt*, p. 4.

9. The latter term, coined by the detective story writer Philip MacDonald in his Foreword to *Three for Midnight: The Rasp, Murder Gone Mad, The Rynox Murder* (Garden City, N.Y.: Doubleday, 1963), p. vii, is far more appropriate to the film than to the novel, which preserves its mystery, à la Agatha Christie, to the end of the penultimate chapter before allowing its hero to preside over a climactic explanation.

10. Note by contrast the increasingly complex chases in comedies like *It's a Mad Mad Mad Mad World* (1963) and *What's Up, Doc?* (1972).

11. *Reversal of Fortune* and the Lawyer Film

1. Thomas L. Shaffer, with Mary M. Shaffer, *American Lawyers and Their Communities: Ethics in the Legal Profession* (Notre Dame: University of Notre Dame Press, 1991), p. 1. Shaffer notes (pp. 2–5) that the American Bar Association's statement of legal ethics and the rise of law school courses in the subject date from this period.

2. In Alan M. Dershowitz, *Reversal of Fortune: Inside the von Bülow Case* (New York: Random House, 1986), the author mentions his sons Elon and Jamin but indicates that they were away at college while the appeal was being prepared, although Elon contributed the book's title (pp. ix–x, 117–18). The Elon of the film seems to be several years younger, and is clearly living with his father. In the film, the students' different assignments are indicated not only by the signs outside their rooms, but by the T-shirts they wear ("BLACK BAG," "INSULIN NEEDLE," etc.) for Dershowitz's inveterate basketball games.

3. Ibid., p. xxv.
4. Ibid.
5. Compare the multiple scenarios Dershowitz noncommittally considers in ibid., pp. 250–2.

12. *Fargo* and the Crime Comedy

1. Aristotle's lost treatise on comedy is the MacGuffin in Umberto Eco's medieval detective story *The Name of the Rose,* trans. William Weaver (New York: Harcourt Brace Jovanovich, 1983).
2. Most of the important philosophical discussions of comedy are excerpted in John Morreall, ed., *The Philosophy of Laughter and Humor* (Albany: State University of New York Press, 1987).
3. See Northrop Frye, "The Argument of Comedy," in D. A. Robertson Jr., ed., *English Institute Essays 1948* (New York: Columbia University Press, 1949), pp. 58–73. Frye's structural analysis of comedy is incorporated into his *Anatomy of Criticism: Four Essays* (Princeton: Princeton University Press, 1957), pp. 163–86.
4. Compare Raymond Durgnat, who notes in *The Crazy Mirror: Hollywood Comedy and the American Image* (New York: Horizon, 1970), that "often all that's needed to turn drama (for the characters) into comedy (for the audience) is to present reality absolutely straight. One simply withholds those compassionate emphases and tactful idealizations which lead an audience to sympathize fully with the screen character" (p. 27).
5. Joseph Gelmis, *The Film Director as Superstar* (Garden City, N.Y.: Doubleday, 1970), p. 309.
6. Pauline Kael, *When the Lights Go Down* (New York: Holt, Rinehart & Winston, 1980), p. 420.
7. Douglas Brode would include *Miller's Crossing* as at least a marginal entry in the Coens' list of comedies, since throughout the film, as he argues in *Money, Women, and Guns: Crime Movies from Bonnie and Clyde to the Present* (New York: Citadel, 1995), "it's often difficult to tell whether the Coens are kidding, serious, or trying for a middle ground" (p. 157).
8. Steven Carter suggests that Jean is "too desensitized by [the] television [she has been watching] to react appropriately . . . to a life-threatening situation" until the intruder "breaks through the screen – e.g., *becomes real.*" See Carter, "'Flare to White': *Fargo* and the Postmodern Turn," *Literature/Film Quarterly 27,* no. 4 (1999): 238–44, at p. 241.
9. The preface to the Coen brothers' published screenplay of *Fargo* (London: Faber & Faber, 1996) describes the film as one that "aims to be both homey and exotic, and pretends to be true" (p. x).

13. Conclusion: What Good Are Crime Films?

1. Compare Rick Altman's attempt in *The American Film Musical* (Bloomington: Indiana University Press, 1987), pp. 90–102, to distinguish more

and less "real" Hollywood musicals by invoking a distinction between semantic and syntactic approaches to genre.

2. Ibid., p. 98.
3. Steve Neale, *Genre and Hollywood* (London: Routledge, 2000), p. 1.
4. Rick Altman, *Film/Genre* (London: British Film Institute, 1999), p. 98.
5. Compare *The Silence of the Lambs* (1991), which sets the mystery of Hannibal Lecter's evil against the mystery of Clarice Starling's courage, principle, and selflessness, making goodness as unfathomable as its more celebrated opposite.
6. Laura Mulvey, "Visual Pleasure and Narrative Cinema," *Screen 16,* no. 3 (Autumn 1975): 6–18; rpt. in *Visual and Other Pleasures* (Bloomington: Indiana University Press, 1989), pp. 14–26, at p. 26.
7. See Charles Derry, *The Suspense Thriller: Films in the Shadow of Alfred Hitchcock* (Jefferson, N.C.: McFarland, 1988); and Martin Rubin, *Thrillers* (Cambridge: Cambridge University Press, 1999).
8. This is Rubin's procedure in *Thrillers,* which considers "the spy thriller" typified by Lang's *Man Hunt* (1941) as one of the four leading varieties of thriller otherwise represented by the detective thriller, the psychological crime thriller, and the police thriller (p. 226).
9. David Bordwell, Janet Staiger, and Kristin Thompson, *The Classical Hollywood Cinema: Film Style and Mode of Production to 1960* (New York: Columbia University Press, 1985), p. 77.
10. Stephen Neale, *Genre* (London: British Film Institute, 1980), p. 20. Neale has expanded this argument in his *Genre and Hollywood,* pp. 22–8.
11. Nearly everyone, that is, except for Harry Levin, who begins his discussion of comedy in *Playboys and Killjoys: An Essay on the Theory and Practice of Comedy* (New York: Oxford University Press, 1987), by noting that not "much light has been shed [on the definition of comedy] . . . by isolating the phenomenon of laughter" (pp. 10–11).
12. Many amalgams of these different genres are facilitated by their related dualities. *True Lies* (1994), for example, suggests not only that America's foreign policy can succeed by a campaign against Arab terrorists, but that secret agents suffering marital problems arising from the conflict between professional and domestic spheres can cure them by involving their spouses in their work.

Selected Bibliography

Allen, Woody. *Getting Even.* New York: Random House, 1971.

Allyn, John. "*Double Indemnity:* A Policy That Paid Off." *Literature/Film Quarterly 6,* no. 2 (1978): 116–24.

Altman, Rick. *The American Film Musical.* Bloomington: Indiana University Press, 1987.

    Film/Genre. London: British Film Institute, 1999.

Andersen, Thom. "Red Hollywood." In Suzanne Ferguson and Barbara Groseclose, eds., *Literature and the Visual Arts in Contemporary Society.* Columbus: Ohio State University Press, 1985, pp. 141–96.

Aristotle. *The Basic Works of Aristotle.* Ed. Richard McKeon. New York: Random House, 1941.

Auden, W. H. *The Dyer's Hand and Other Essays.* London: Faber & Faber/New York: Random House, 1962; rpt. New York: Vintage, 1968.

Balint, Michael. *Thrills and Regressions.* London: Hogarth, 1959.

Baxter, John. *The Gangster Film.* New York: Barnes/London: Zwemmer, 1970.

Bellour, Raymond. "Segmenting/Analyzing." *Quarterly Review of Film Studies 1,* no. 3 (August 1976): 331–53. Rpt. in Rosen, *Narrative, Apparatus, Ideology,* pp. 66–92.

[Berkeley, Anthony?] "The Detection Club Oath." 1928. Rpt. in Haycraft, ed., *Art of the Mystery Story,* pp. 197–9.

Blake, Nicholas. "The Detective Story – Why?" Introduction to Howard Haycraft, *Murder for Pleasure: The Life and Times of the Detective Story.* London: Peter Davies, 1942. Rpt. in Haycraft, ed., *Art of the Mystery Story,* pp. 398–405.

Bogle, Donald. *Toms, Coons, Mulattoes, Mammies, & Bucks.* 3d ed. New York: Continuum, 1994.

Bonitzer, Pascal. "Les silences de la voix." *Cahiers du cinéma* no. 256 (February–March 1975): 22–33. Rpt. as "The Silences of the Voice," trans. Philip Rosen and Marcia Butzel, in Rosen, ed., *Narrative, Apparatus, Ideology,* pp. 319–34.

Borde, Raymond, and Étienne Chaumeton. *Panorama du film noir américain.* Paris: Éditions du Minuit, 1955. Excerpt rpt. as "Towards a Definition of

Film Noir," trans. Alain Silver. In Silver and Ursini, eds., *Film Noir Reader,* pp. 17–26.

Bordwell, David, Janet Staiger, and Kristin Thompson. *The Classical Hollywood Cinema: Film Style and Mode of Production to 1960.* New York: Columbia University Press, 1985.

Brode, Douglas. *Women, Money, and Guns: Crime Movies from Bonnie and Clyde to the Present.* New York: Citadel, 1995.

Carr, John Dickson. "The Grandest Game in the World." 1946; first published in Ellery Queen, ed., *Ellery Queen's Mystery Mix . . . #18* (New York: Random House, 1963), pp. 148–67.

Carter, Steven. "'Flare to White': *Fargo* and the Postmodern Turn," *Literature/ Film Quarterly 27,* no. 4 (1999): 238–44.

Cawelti, John G. *Adventure, Mystery, and Romance: Formula Stories as Art and Popular Culture.* Chicago: University of Chicago Press, 1976.

"*Chinatown* and Generic Transformation in Recent American Films." In Gerald Mast and Marshall Cohen, eds., *Film Theory and Criticism, Introductory Readings.* 2d ed. New York: Oxford University Press, 1979, pp. 559–79. Rpt. in Grant, ed., *Film Genre Reader,* pp. 183–201.

Chandler, Raymond. *Later Novels and Other Writings.* Ed. Frank MacShane. New York: Library of America, 1995.

Stories and Early Novels. Ed. Frank MacShane. New York: Library of America, 1995.

Chartier, Jean-Pierre. "Les Americains aussi font des films 'noirs,'" *Revue du cinéma 2* (November 1946): 67–70. Rpt. as "The Americans Are Making Dark Films Too," trans. R. Barton Palmer, in Palmer, ed., *Perspectives on Film Noir,* pp. 25–7.

Chesterton, G. K. "A Defence of Detective Stories." In Chesterton, *The Defendant.* London: R. B. Johnson, 1901, pp. 157–62. Rpt. in Haycraft, ed., *Art of the Mystery Story,* pp. 3–6.

The Spice of Life and Other Essays. Ed. Dorothy Collins. Philadelpia: Dufour, 1966.

Christopher, Nicholas. *Somewhere in the Night: Film Noir and the American City.* New York: Free Press, 1997.

Clarens, Carlos. *Crime Movies.* New York: W. W. Norton, 1980. Rev. ed. Afterword by Foster Hirsch. New York: Da Capo, 1997.

Cocchiarelli, Joseph J. *Screen Sleuths: A Filmography.* New York: Garland, 1992.

Coen, Ethan, and Joel Coen. *Fargo.* London: Faber & Faber, 1996.

Cook, Pam. "Duplicity in *Mildred Pierce.*" In Kaplan, ed., *Women in Film Noir,* pp. 68–82.

Copjec, Joan. "The Phenomenal Nonphenomenal: Private Space in *Film Noir.*" In Copjec, ed., *Shades of Noir,* pp. 167–97.

ed. *Shades of Noir: A Reader.* London: Verso, 1993.

Corber, Robert J. *In the Name of National Security: Hitchcock, Homophobia, and the Political Construction of Gender in Postwar America.* Durham, N.C.: Duke University Press, 1993.

Cowie, Elizabeth. "*Film Noir* and Women." In Copjec, ed., *Shades of Noir,* pp. 121–65.

   "The Popular Film as a Progressive Text – A Discussion of *Coma.*" In Constance Penley, ed., *Feminism and Film Theory* (New York and London: Routledge, 1988), pp. 104–40.

Crowther, Bruce. *Film Noir: Reflections in a Dark Mirror.* New York: Frederick Ungar /Continuum, 1988.

Damico, James. "*Film Noir:* A Modest Proposal." *Film Reader* no. 3 (1978): 48–57. Rpt. in Silver and Ursini, eds., *Film Noir Reader,* pp. 95–105.

Davis, Mike. *City of Quartz.* London: Verso, 1990.

DeAndrea, William L. *Encyclopedia Mysteriosa: A Comprehensive Guide to the Art of Detection in Print, Film, Radio and Television.* New York: Macmillan, 1994.

Derry, Charles. *The Suspense Thriller: Films in the Shadow of Alfred Hitchcock.* Jefferson, N.C.: McFarland, 1988.

Dershowitz, Alan M. *Reversal of Fortune: Inside the von Bülow Case.* New York: Random House, 1986.

Doane, Mary Ann. *Femmes Fatales: Feminism, Film Theory, Psychoanalysis.* New York: Routledge, 1991.

Dove, George N. *The Police Procedural.* Bowling Green, Ohio: Bowling Green University Popular Press, 1982.

Durgnat, Raymond. *The Crazy Mirror: Hollywood Comedy and the American Image.* New York: Horizon, 1970.

   "Paint It Black: The Family Tree of *Film Noir.*" *Cinema* [UK] *6–7* (August 1970): 49–56. Rpt. in Silver and Ursini, eds., *Film Noir Reader,* pp. 37–52.

Dyer, Richard. "Resistance through Charisma: Rita Hayworth and *Gilda.*" In Kaplan, ed., *Women in Film Noir,* pp 91–9.

Eco, Umberto. *The Name of the Rose.* Trans. William Weaver. New York: Harcourt Brace Jovanovich, 1983.

Eisner, Lotte. *Fritz Lang.* London: Secker & Warburg, 1976.

Elsaesser, Thomas. "Tales of Sound and Fury: Observations on the Family Melodrama." *Monogram 4* (1972): 2–15. Rpt. in Grant, ed., *Film Genre Reader,* pp. 278–308.

Erickson, Glenn. "Expressionist Doom in *Night and the City.*" In Silver and Ursini, eds., *Film Noir Reader,* pp. 203–7.

Everson, William K. *The Bad Guys: A Pictorial History of the Movie Villain.* New York: Cadillac, 1964.

   The Detective in Film. Secaucus, N.J.: Citadel, 1972.

Fischer, Lucy. *Cinematernity: Film, Motherhood, Genre.* Princeton: Princeton University Press, 1996.

Flanagan, Timothy J. "Public Opinion and Public Policy in Criminal Justice." In Timothy J. Flanagan and Dennis R. Longmire, eds., *Americans View Crime and Justice: A National Public Opinion Survey.* Thousand Oaks, Calif.: Sage, 1996, pp. 151–8.

Foster, Hal, ed. *The Anti-Aesthetic: Essays on Postmodern Culture.* Port Townsend, Wash.: Bay Press, 1983.

Frank, Nino. "Un nouveau genre 'policier': L'aventure criminelle," *L'Écran français 61* (28 August 1946): 8–14. Rpt. as "The Crime Adventure Story: A New
Kind of Detective Film," trans. R. Barton Palmer, in Palmer, ed., *Perspectives on Film Noir,* pp. 21–4.

Frye, Northrop. *Anatomy of Criticism: Four Essays.* Princeton: Princeton University Press, 1957.

  "The Argument of Comedy." In Robertson, ed., *English Institute Essays 1948,*
  pp. 58–73.

Gelmis, Joseph. *The Film Director as Superstar.* Garden City, N.Y.: Doubleday,
1970.

Gifford, Barry. *The Devil Thumbs a Ride and Other Unforgettable Films.* New
York: Grove, 1988.

Gledhill, Christine. "*Klute* 1: A Contemporary *Film Noir* and Feminist Criticism." In Kaplan, ed., *Women in Film Noir,* pp. 6–21.

Gorman, Ed, Lee Server, and Martin H. Greenberg, eds. *The Big Book of Noir.*
New York: Carroll & Graf, 1998.

Grant, Barry Keith, ed. *Film Genre: Theory and Criticism.* Metuchen, N.J.: Scarecrow, 1977.

  Film Genre Reader. Austin: University of Texas Press, 1986.

  Film Genre Reader II. Austin: University of Texas Press, 1995.

Greene, Graham. *Graham Greene on Film: Selected Film Criticism, 1935–1939.*
New York: Simon & Schuster, 1972.

Grella, George. "Murder and Manners: The Formal Detective Novel." *Novel 4,*
no. 1 (Fall 1970): 30–48. Rpt. as "The Formal Detective Novel" in Winks,
ed., *Detective Fiction,* pp. 84–102.

  "Murder and the Mean Streets: The Hard-Boiled Detective Novel." *Contempora 1* (March 1970): 6–15. Rpt. as "The Hard-Boiled Detective Novel" in
  Winks, ed., *Detective Fiction,* pp. 103–20.

Guerrero, Ed. *Framing Blackness: The African American Image in Film.* Philadelphia: Temple University Press, 1993.

Hammond, Lawrence. *Thriller Movies: Classic Films of Suspense and Mystery.*
London: Octopus, 1974.

Hampton, Benjamin B. *A History of the Movies.* New York: Covici–Friede Publishers, 1931; rpt. New York: Arno, 1970.

Hannsberry, Karen Burroughs. *Femme Noir: Bad Girls of Film.* Jefferson, N.C.:
McFarland, 1998.

Hardy, Phil, ed. *The BFI Companion to Crime.* Berkeley: University of California Press, 1997.

Harvey, Sylvia. "Woman's Place: The Absent Family of *Film Noir.*" In Kaplan,
ed., *Women in Film Noir,* pp. 22–34.

Haskell, Molly. *From Reverence to Rape: The Treatment of Women in the Movies.*
2d ed. Chicago: University of Chicago Press, 1987.

Haycraft, Howard, ed. *The Art of the Mystery Story.* New York: Grosset & Dunlap, 1946.

Henderson, Brian. "*The Searchers:* An American Dilemma." *Film Quarterly 34,*
no. 2 (Winter 1980–1): 9–23. Rpt. in Nichols, ed., *Movies and Methods,* 2:
429–49.

Hess, John. "*Godfather II:* A Deal Coppola Couldn't Refuse." *Jump Cut* no. 7 (May–July 1975): 1, 10–11. Rpt. in Nichols, ed., *Movies and Methods,* 1: 81–90.

Higham, Charles, and Joel Greenberg. *Hollywood in the Forties.* New York: A. S. Barnes /London: Tantivy, 1968.

Hirsch, Foster. *The Dark Side of the Screen: Film Noir.* San Diego /New York / London: A. S. Barnes, 1981.

Hoppenstand, Gary C. *In Search of the Paper Tiger: A Sociological Perspective of Myth, Formula and the Mystery Genre in the Entertainment Print Mass Medium.* Bowling Green, Ohio: Bowling Green University Popular Press, 1987.

Humphries, Reynold. *Fritz Lang: Genre and Representation in His American Films.* Baltimore: Johns Hopkins University Press, 1989.

Jameson, Fredric. "Postmodernism and Consumer Society." In Foster, ed., *Anti-Aesthetic,* pp. 111–25.

Johnston, Claire. "*Double Indemnity*." In Kaplan, ed., *Women in Film Noir*, pp. 100–11.

Kael, Pauline. *When the Lights Go Down.* New York: Holt, Rinehart & Winston, 1980.

Kaminsky, Stuart M. *American Film Genres.* 2d ed. Chicago: Nelson–Hall, 1985.

Kaplan, E. Ann, ed. *Women in Film Noir.* Rev. ed. London: British Film Institute, 1980.

Kernan, Alvin B. "The Henriad: Shakespeare's Major History Plays." *Yale Review 59,* no. 1 (October 1969): 3–32. Rpt. (revised and expanded) in Kernan, ed., *Modern Shakespearean Criticism: Essays on Style, Dramaturgy, and the Major Plays.* New York: Harcourt, Brace & World, 1970, pp. 245–75.

Kerr, Paul. "Out of What Past? Notes on the B *Film Noir.*" *Screen Education* nos. 32–3 (1979–80): 45–65. Rpt. in Silver and Ursini, eds., *Film Noir Reader,* pp. 107–27.

Knox, Ronald A. "Detective Story Decalogue." Introduction to Knox, ed., *The Best Detective Stories of 1928.* London: Faber & Faber, 1929. Rpt. in Haycraft, ed., *Art of the Mystery Story,* pp. 194–6.

Kracauer, Siegfried. *From Caligari to Hitler: A Psychological History of the German Film.* Princeton: Princeton University Press, 1947.

Krutnik, Frank. *In a Lonely Street: Film Noir, Genre, Masculinity.* London: Routledge, 1991.

Kuhn, Annette. *Women's Pictures: Feminism and Cinema.* London: Routledge & Kegan Paul, 1982.

Lang, Robert. "Looking for 'the Great Whatzit': *Kiss Me Deadly* and Film Noir." *Cinema Journal 27,* no. 3 (Spring 1988): 32–44. Rpt. in Palmer, ed., *Perspectives on Film Noir,* pp. 171–84.

Langman, Larry, and Daniel Finn. *A Guide to American Crime Films of the Forties and Fifties.* [Bibliographies and Indexes in the Performing Arts, no. 19.] Westport, Conn.: Greenwood, 1995.

A Guide to American Crime Films of the Thirties. [Bibliographies and Indexes in the Performing Arts, no. 18.] Westport, Conn.: Greenwood, 1995.

A Guide to American Silent Crime Films. [Bibliographies and Indexes in the Performing Arts, no. 15.] Westport, Conn.: Greenwood, 1994.

Leab, Daniel J. *From Sambo to Superspade: The Black Experience in Motion Pictures.* Boston: Houghton Mifflin, 1975.

Leff, Leonard J., and Jerold L. Simmons. *The Dame in the Kimono: Hollywood, Censorship, and the Production Code from the 1920s to the 1960s.* New York: Grove Weidenfeld, 1990.

Lev, Peter. *American Films of the 70s: Conflicting Visions.* Austin: University of Texas Press, 2000.

Levin, Harry. *Playboys and Killjoys: An Essay on the Theory and Practice of Comedy.* New York: Oxford University Press, 1987.

McArthur, Colin. *Underworld U.S.A.* London: Secker & Warburg, 1972.

MacCabe, Colin. "Theory and Film: Principles of Realism and Pleasure." *Screen 17,* no. 3 (Autumn 1976): 7–29. Rpt. in Rosen, ed., *Narrative, Apparatus, Ideology,* pp. 179–97.

MacCannell, Dean. "Democracy's Turn: On Homeless *Noir.*" In Copjec, ed., *Shades of Noir,* pp. 279–97.

McCarty, John. *Thrillers: Seven Decades of Classic Film Suspense.* New York: Carol Publishing/Citadel, 1992.

MacDonald, Philip. *Three for Midnight: The Rasp, Murder Gone Mad, The Rynox Murder.* Garden City, N.Y.: Doubleday, 1963.

Mast, Gerald, and Marshall Cohen, eds. *Film Theory and Criticism: Introductory Readings.* 3d ed. New York: Oxford University Press, 1985.

Maxfield, James F. *The Fatal Woman: Sources of Male Anxiety in American Film Noir, 1941–1991.* Madison, N.J.: Fairleigh Dickinson University Press, 1996.

Medved, Michael. *Hollywood vs. America.* New York: HarperCollins, 1992.

Metz, Walter. "'Keep the Coffee Hot, Hugo': Nuclear Trauma in Lang's *The Big Heat.*'" *Film Criticism 21* (Spring 1997): 43–65.

Morreall, John, ed. *The Philosophy of Laughter and Humor.* Albany: State University of New York Press, 1987.

Muller, Eddie. *Dark City: The Lost World of Film Noir.* New York: St. Martin's, 1998.

Mulvey, Laura. *Visual and Other Pleasures.* Bloomington: Indiana University Press, 1989.

Munby, Jonathan. *Public Enemies, Public Heroes: Screening the Gangster Film from Little Caesar to Touch of Evil.* Chicago: University of Chicago Press, 1999.

Musser, Charles. "The Travel Genre: Moving towards Narrative." *Iris* 2, no. 1 (1984): 47–60. Rpt. as "The Travel Genre in 1903–1904: Moving towards Fictional Narrative." In Thomas Elsaesser with Adam Barker, eds., *Early Cinema: Space, Frame, Narrative.* London: British Film Institute, 1990, pp. 123–32.

Naremore, James. *More Than Night: Film Noir in Its Contexts.* Berkeley: University of California Press, 1998.

Neale, Stephen. *Genre.* London: British Film Institute, 1980.

[as Steve]. *Genre and Hollywood.* London: Routledge, 2000.

Nichols, Bill, ed. *Movies and Methods.* 2 vols. Berkeley: University of California Press, 1976, 1985.

Nickerson, Edward A. "'Realistic' Crime Fiction: An Anatomy of Evil People." *Centennial Review 25* (Spring 1981): 101–32.

Nolan, William F. *The Black Mask Boys: Masters in the Hard-Boiled School of Detective Fiction.* New York: Morrow, 1985.

Ottoson, Robert. *A Reference Guide to the American Film Noir: 1940–1958.* Metuchen, N.J.: Scarecrow, 1981.

Palmer, R. Barton. "*Chinatown* and the Detective Story." *Literature/Film Quarterly 5,* no. 2 (Spring 1977): 112–17.

    Hollywood's Dark Cinema: The American Film Noir. New York: Twayne, 1994.

    ed. *Perspectives on Film Noir.* New York: G. K. Hall, 1996.

Paravisini, Lizabeth, and Carlos Yorio. "Is It Or Isn't It? The Duality of Parodic Detective Fiction." In Earl F. Bargainnier, ed., *Comic Crime.* Bowling Green, Ohio: Bowling Green Popular Press, 1987, pp. 181–93.

Parish, James Robert, and Michael R. Pitts. *The Great Detective Pictures.* Metuchen, N.J.: Scarecrow, 1990.

    The Great Gangster Pictures. 2 vols. Metuchen, N.J.: Scarecrow, 1976, 1987.

Perelman, S. J. *The Most of S. J. Perelman.* New York: Simon & Schuster, 1958.

Pike, Robert L. *Mute Witness.* New York: Doubleday (for Crime Club), 1963. Rpt. as *Bullitt.* London: Bloomsbury, 1997.

Pitts, Michael R. *Famous Movie Detectives.* 3 vols. Metuchen, N.J.: Scarecrow, 1979–2001.

Place, Janey, and Lowell Peterson. "Some Visual Motifs of *Film Noir.*" *Film Comment 10,* no. 1 (January–February 1974): 30–5. Rpt. in Silver and Ursini, eds., *Film Noir Reader,* pp. 65–75.

Polan, Dana. *Power and Paranoia: History, Narrative, and the American Cinema, 1940–1950.* New York: Columbia University Press, 1986.

Polanski, Roman. *Roman by Polanski.* New York: Morrow, 1984.

Porfirio, Robert. "No Way Out: Existential Motifs in the *Film Noir.*" *Sight and Sound 45,* no. 4 (Autumn 1976): 212–17. Rpt. in Silver and Ursini, eds., *Film Noir Reader,* pp. 77–93.

Reid, David, and Jayne L. Walker. "Strange Pursuit: Cornell Woolrich and the Abandoned City of the Forties." In Copjec, ed., *Shades of Noir,* pp. 57–96.

Renov, Michael. *Hollywood's Wartime Women: Representation and Ideology.* Ann Arbor: UMI Research Press, 1988.

Richardson, Carl. *Autopsy: An Element of Realism in Film Noir.* Metuchen, N.J.: Scarecrow, 1992.

Robertson, D. A., Jr., ed. *English Institute Essays 1948.* New York: Columbia University Press, 1949.

Rohmer, Eric, & Claude Chabrol. *Hitchcock: The First Forty-Four Films.* Trans. Stanley Hochman. New York: Frederick Ungar, 1979.

Roof, Judith. *A Lure of Knowledge: Lesbian Sexuality and Theory.* New York: Columbia University Press, 1991.

Rosen, Philip, ed. *Narrative, Apparatus, Ideology: A Film Theory Reader.* New York: Columbia University Press, 1986.

Rosow, Eugene. *Born to Lose: The Gangster Film in America.* New York: Oxford University Press, 1978.

Rubin, Martin. *Thrillers.* New York: Cambridge University Press, 1999.

Sarris, Andrew. *The American Cinema: Directors and Directions, 1929–1968.* New York: Dutton, 1968.

Sayers, Dorothy L. "Introduction" to *Great Short Stories of Detection, Mystery, and Horror.* Ed. Dorothy L. Sayers. London: Victor Gollancz, 1928. Rpt. as "The Omnibus of Crime" in Haycraft, ed., *Art of the Mystery Story,* pp. 71–109.

Schaefer, Dennis, and Larry Salvato. *Masters of Light: Conversations with Contemporary Cinematographers.* Berkeley: University of California Press, 1984.

Schrader, Paul. "Notes on *Film Noir." Film Comment 8,* no. 1 (Spring 1972): 8–13. Rpt. in Silver and Ursini, eds., *Film Noir Reader,* pp. 53–64.

Selby, Spencer. *Dark City: The Film Noir.* Jefferson, N.C.: McFarland, 1984.

Shadoian, Jack. *Dreams and Dead Ends: The American Gangster/Crime Film.* Cambridge: MIT Press, 1977.

Shaffer, Thomas L., with Mary M. Shaffer. *American Lawyers and Their Communities: Ethics in the Legal Profession.* Notre Dame: University of Notre Dame Press, 1991.

Silver, Alain, and James Ursini, eds. *Film Noir Reader.* New York: Limelight, 1996.

Silver, Alain, and Elizabeth Ward, eds. *Film Noir: An Encyclopedic Reference to the American Style.* Woodstock, N.Y.: Overlook, 1979.
   Film Noir: An Encyclopedic Reference to the American Style. Rev. and expanded ed. Woodstock, N.Y.: Overlook, 1988.

Silver, Alain, Elizabeth Ward, and James Ursini, eds. *Film Noir: An Encyclopedic Reference to the American Style.* 3d ed. Woodstock, N.Y.: Overlook, 1992.

Simmon, Scott. *The Films of D. W. Griffith.* New York: Cambridge University Press, 1993.

Staiger, Janet. "Hybrid or Inbred: The Purity Hypothesis and Hollywood Genre History." *Film Criticism 22* (Fall 1997): 5–20.

Steinbrunner, Chris, and Otto Penzler, eds. *Encyclopedia of Mystery and Detection.* New York: McGraw–Hill, 1976.

Strachey, John. "The Golden Age of English Detection." *Saturday Review of Literature 19* (7 January 1939): 12–14.

Telotte, J. P. *Voices in the Dark: The Narrative Patterns of Film Noir.* Urbana: University of Illinois Press, 1989.

Todorov, Tzvetan. *The Poetics of Prose.* Rev. ed. Trans. Richard Howard. Introduction by Jonathan Culler. Ithaca: Cornell University Press, 1977.

Tollin, Anthony. *The Shadow: The Making of a Legend.* New York: Advance Magazine Publishers/Conde Nast, 1996.

Trilling, Lionel. *Sincerity and Authenticity.* Cambridge: Harvard University Press, 1972.

Truffaut, François. *Hitchcock.* Trans. Helen G. Scott. Rev. ed. New York: Simon & Schuster, 1984 (1st ed. 1967).

Tudor, Andrew. *Theories of Film.* New York: Viking, 1974.

Tuska, Jon. *Dark Cinema: American Film Noir in Cultural Perspective.* [Contributions to the Study of Popular Culture, no. 9.] Westport, Conn.: Greenwood, 1984.

The Detective in Hollywood. Garden City, N.Y.: Doubleday, 1978.

In Manors and Alleys: A Casebook on the American Detective Film. [Contributions to the Study of Popular Culture, no. 17.] Westport, Conn.: Greenwood, 1988.

Tyler, Parker. *The Hollywood Hallucination.* New York: Simon & Schuster, 1944. Rpt. New York: Garland, 1985.

Magic and Myth of the Movies. New York: Simon & Schuster, 1947. Rpt. New York: Garland, 1985.

The Shadow of an Airplane Climbs the Empire State Building: A World Theory of Film. Garden City, N.Y.: Doubleday, 1972.

Van Dine, S. S. "Twenty Rules for Writing Detective Stories." *American Magazine 106* (September 1928): 129–31. Rpt. in Haycraft, ed., *Art of the Mystery Story,* pp. 189–93.

Vernet, Marc. "*Film Noir* on the Edge of Doom." In Copjec, ed., *Shades of Noir,* pp. 1–31.

Warshow, Robert. *The Immediate Experience: Movies, Comics, Theatre and Other Aspects of Popular Culture.* Garden City, N.Y.: Doubleday, 1962; rpt. New York: Atheneum, 1975.

Watson, Colin. *Snobbery with Violence: Crime Stories and Their Audience.* London: Eyre & Spottiswoode, 1971.

Wertham, Fredric, M.D. *Seduction of the Innocent.* New York: Rinehart, 1954.

West, Nathanael. *Novels and Other Writings.* New York: Library of America, 1997.

Williams, Linda. *Hard Core: Power, Pleasure, and the "Frenzy of the Visible."* Berkeley: University of California Press, 1989.

Wilson, George M. *Narration in Light: Studies in Cinematic Point of View.* Baltimore: Johns Hopkins University Press, 1986.

Winks, Robin W., ed. *Detective Fiction: A Collection of Critical Essays.* Englewood Cliffs, N.J.: Prentice–Hall, 1980.

Wood, Michael. *America in the Movies.* New York: Basic, 1975.

Wright, Willard Huntington. Preface to Wright, ed., *The Great Detective Stories.* New York: Charles Scribner's Sons, 1927. Rpt. as "The Great Detective Stories" in Haycraft, ed., *Art of the Mystery Story,* pp. 33–70.

Wrong, E. M. Introduction to Wrong, ed., *Crime and Detection.* London: Oxford University Press, 1926. Rpt. as "Crime and Detection" in Haycraft, ed., *Art of the Mystery Story,* pp. 18–32.

Yaquinto, Marilyn. *Pump 'Em Full of Lead: A Look at Gangsters on Film.* New York: Twayne, 1998.

Filmography/Videography

This chronological list of one hundred crime films aims to strike a balance among a greatest-hits list, a list of especially influential crime films, a list of films that exemplify the leading subgenres this book considers, and a list of films analyzed in particular detail in the preceding chapters. Because few film programs and even fewer private viewers now screen films in 16mm prints – still fewer in the 35mm gauge in which all these films were originally shot – the list is restricted to VHS videotape, LaserDisc, and DVD. Since versions in all three of these media can go out of print as quickly as paperback books, and especially since the number and range of films available in DVD has recently exploded as the format has largely replaced LaserDisc as a videophile medium, the accuracy of all information below should be regarded with due skepticism. In particular, dozens of films listed below as n/a (not available) may well be back in print by the time this list is published.

The Great Train Robbery (dir. Edwin S. Porter, 1903) Gangster
VHS: KINO (in "The Movies Begin: Vol. 1")
LaserDisc: IMAGE (in "Landmarks of Early Film")
DVD: n/a

The Musketeers of Pig Alley (dir. D.W. Griffith, 1912) Gangster
VHS: KINO (in *The Musketeers of Pig Alley and Selected Biograph Shorts*)
LaserDisc: n/a
DVD: n/a

Alias Jimmy Valentine (dir. Maurice Tourneur, 1915) Gangster
VHS: LIBRARY OF CONGRESS (in *Origins of the Gangster Film*)
LaserDisc: n/a
DVD: n/a

Little Caesar (dir. Mervyn LeRoy, 1930) Gangster
VHS: CBS, MGM, REPUBLIC
LaserDisc: MGM (with *The Public Enemy*)
DVD: n/a

The Public Enemy (dir. William A. Wellman, 1931) Gangster
VHS: CBS, MGM, REPUBLIC, TURNER
LaserDisc: CBS, MGM (with *Little Caesar*)
DVD: n/a

Scarface (dir. Howard Hawks, 1932) Gangster
VHS: MCA
LaserDisc: MCA
DVD: n/a

I Am a Fugitive from a Chain Gang (dir. Mervyn LeRoy, 1932) Victim
VHS: MGM
LaserDisc: n/a
DVD: n/a

The Case of the Howling Dog (dir. Alan Crosland, 1934) Lawyer
VHS: TEAKWOOD
LaserDisc: n/a
DVD: n/a

The Thin Man (dir. W. S. Van Dyke, 1934) Unofficial Detective; Comedy
VHS: WARNER
LaserDisc: n/a
DVD: n/a

"G" Men (dir. William Keighley, 1935) Police
VHS: MGM
LaserDisc: n/a
DVD: n/a

Fury (dir. Fritz Lang, 1936) Victim
VHS: MGM
LaserDisc: n/a
DVD: n/a

The Hound of the Baskervilles (dir. Sidney Lanfield, 1939) Unofficial Detective
VHS: KEY
LaserDisc: n/a
DVD: n/a

The Maltese Falcon (dir. John Huston, 1941) Private Eye
VHS: CBS, MGM, REPUBLIC, TIME-LIFE
LaserDisc: MGM

DVD: WARNER
> The DVD includes a documentary tracing Bogart's career at Warner Bros. through his trailers and additional supplementary material.

Suspicion (dir. Alfred Hitchcock, 1941) Victim
VHS: TURNER
LaserDisc: n/a
DVD: n/a

Shadow of a Doubt (dir. Alfred Hitchcock, 1943) Victim
VHS: MCA
LaserDisc: MCA
DVD: MCA
> DVD includes a 68-minute feature, *Beyond Doubt: The Making of Hitchcock's Favorite Film,* and additional supplementary material. Advertised as "pan-and-scan," although the film was shot in the Academy ratio.

Arsenic and Old Lace (dir. Frank Capra, 1944) Comedy
VHS: WARNER, TURNER, CBS, MGM
LaserDisc: CRITERION, MGM, CBS
DVD: WARNER
> The MGM VHS release is colorized.

Double Indemnity (dir. Billy Wilder, 1944) Film Noir
VHS: MCA
LaserDisc: MCA
DVD: IMAGE

Gaslight (dir. George Cukor, 1944) Victim
VHS: WARNER
LaserDisc: n/a
DVD: n/a

Laura (dir. Otto Preminger, 1944) Police; Film Noir
VHS: FOX
LaserDisc: n/a
DVD: n/a

Murder, My Sweet (aka *Farewell My Lovely*) (dir. Edward Dmytryk, 1944) Private Eye; Film Noir
VHS: TURNER
LaserDisc: IMAGE
DVD: n/a

Phantom Lady (dir. Robert Siodmak, 1944) Film Noir
VHS: MCA
LaserDisc: n/a
DVD: n/a

The Woman in the Window (dir. Fritz Lang, 1944) Film Noir
VHS: MGM
LaserDisc: n/a
DVD: n/a

Leave Her to Heaven (dir. John M. Stahl, 1945) Film Noir
VHS: FOX
LaserDisc: n/a
DVD: n/a

Mildred Pierce (dir. Michael Curtiz, 1945) Film Noir
VHS: WARNER
LaserDisc: n/a
DVD: n/a

The Big Sleep (dir. Howard Hawks, 1946) Private Eye
VHS: COLUMBIA, MGM, REPUBLIC
LaserDisc: CBS, MGM
DVD: WARNER
    The DVD includes the 1946 release version of the film, an earlier 1945 version, and a documentary comparing the two.

The Killers (aka *A Man Alone*) (dir. Robert Siodmak, 1946) Gangster; Film Noir
VHS: MCA
LaserDisc: n/a
DVD: n/a

Lady in the Lake (dir. Robert Montgomery, 1946) Private Eye; Film Noir
VHS: WARNER, MGM
LaserDisc: n/a
DVD: n/a

The Postman Always Rings Twice (dir. Tay Garnett, 1946) Film Noir
VHS: MGM, REPUBLIC
LaserDisc: MGM
DVD: n/a
    Released both in black-and-white and in colorized versions on MGM VHS.

Out of the Past (aka *Build My Gallows High* [U.K.]) (dir. Jacques Tourneur, 1947) Film Noir; Private Eye
VHS: TURNER
LaserDisc: IMAGE
DVD: n/a

The Lady from Shanghai (dir. Orson Welles, 1948) Film Noir
VHS: COLUMBIA, REPUBLIC
LaserDisc: COLUMBIA
DVD: COLUMBIA
> The DVD version includes a documentary featurette and additional supplementary material.

Adam's Rib (dir. George Cukor, 1949) Lawyer; Comedy
VHS: WARNER, MGM
LaserDisc: MGM, CRITERION
DVD: WARNER
> Released in a colorized version on MGM VHS and Criterion LaserDisc and in black-and-white in MGM and Warner Bros. VHS.

The Set-Up (dir. Robert Wise, 1949) Victim
VHS: CRITICS' CHOICE
LaserDisc: n/a
DVD: n/a

White Heat (dir. Raoul Walsh, 1949) Gangster; Film Noir
VHS: TURNER
LaserDisc: n/a
DVD: n/a

The Asphalt Jungle (dir. John Huston, 1950) Gangster
VHS: MGM, WARNER
LaserDisc: CRITERION, MGM
DVD: n/a

D.O.A. (dir. Rudolph Maté, 1950) Victim
VHS: MADACY, IMAGE, TROMA, VCI, ALLIED ARTISTS, ANCHOR BAY
LaserDisc: n/a
DVD: IMAGE
> The Anchor Bay VHS release is colorized.

The Big Heat (dir. Fritz Lang, 1953) Police; Gangster; Film Noir
VHS: COLUMBIA
LaserDisc: IMAGE
DVD: COLUMBIA

Rear Window (dir. Alfred Hitchcock, 1954) Unofficial Detective
VHS: MCA, TIME-LIFE
LaserDisc: MCA
DVD: MCA
> Although the film was shot in the Academy ratio, the DVD release, which includes a documentary on the film's production, an interview with the screenwriter, and other supplementary material, is labeled "widescreen."

The Desperate Hours (dir. William Wyler, 1955) Victim; Gangster
VHS: PARAMOUNT
LaserDisc: PARAMOUNT
DVD: n/a

Kiss Me Deadly (dir. Robert Aldrich, 1955) Private Eye; Film Noir
VHS: MGM, REPUBLIC
LaserDisc: MGM
DVD: MGM
> Released in pan-and-scan on VHS and letterboxed on LaserDisc and DVD; the DVD version includes an alternative ending and additional supplementary material.

The Killing (aka *Clean Break* [U.S.]) (dir. Stanley Kubrick, 1956) Gangster; Film Noir
VHS: MGM
LaserDisc: CRITERION, MGM (with *Killer's Kiss*)
DVD: MGM

Witness for the Prosecution (dir. Billy Wilder, 1957) Lawyer
VHS: MGM
LaserDisc: n/a
DVD: MGM

Touch of Evil (dir. Orson Welles, 1958) Film Noir; Police; Gangster
VHS: MCA
LaserDisc: PIONEER, MCA
DVD: MCA
> The 1998 restoration, following the director's detailed notes, is timed at 111 minutes (vs. earlier 93- and 108-minute versions). The Pioneer Laser-Disc pans and scans the 108-minute version; the MCA videotape includes a production documentary; the letterboxed DVD release includes the 1998 restoration and the full text of Welles's editorial notes.

Some Like It Hot (dir. Billy Wilder, 1959) Comedy; Gangster
VHS: MGM
LaserDisc: MGM, CRITERION
DVD: MGM
> Released in pan-and-scan on VHS; all other versions are letterboxed. The DVD includes an interview with Tony Curtis and additional supplementary material.

Inherit the Wind (dir. Stanley Kramer, 1960) Lawyer
VHS: MGM
LaserDisc: n/a
DVD: MGM

Sergeant Rutledge (dir. John Ford, 1960) Lawyer
VHS: WARNER
LaserDisc: n/a
DVD: n/a

To Kill a Mockingbird (dir. Robert Mulligan, 1962) Lawyer
VHS: MCA
LaserDisc: MCA, MCA SIGNATURE COLLECTION
DVD: MCA
> Released in a letterboxed version on both VHS and DVD. The MCA Laser-Disc is pan-and-scan; the letterboxed MCA Signature Collection LaserDisc includes audio commentary by the producer and director and interviews with both of them and with Gregory Peck and Robert Duvall.

The Killers (dir. Don Siegel, 1964) Gangster; Victim; Unofficial Detective
VHS: MCA
LaserDisc: n/a
DVD: n/a

A Shot in the Dark (dir. Blake Edwards, 1964) Comedy; Police
VHS: MGM
LaserDisc: CBS, MGM
DVD: MGM
> Released on pan-and-scan on VHS and CBS LaserDisc, and letterboxed on MGM LaserDisc and DVD.

Bonnie and Clyde (dir. Arthur Penn, 1967) Gangster
VHS: WARNER
LaserDisc: WARNER
DVD: WARNER
> Released in pan-and-scan on both VHS and DVD and in either pan-and-scan or letterboxed versions on LaserDisc.

Bullitt (dir. Peter Yates, 1968) Police
VHS: MOVIES, WARNER
LaserDisc: WARNER
DVD: WARNER
> Released in pan-and-scan on VHS and LaserDisc. The DVD includes both pan-and-scan and letterboxed versions.

Dirty Harry (dir. Don Siegel, 1971) Police
VHS: TIME-LIFE, WARNER
LaserDisc: CRITERION, WARNER
DVD: WARNER
> Released in alternative pan-and-scan and letterboxed versions on both VHS and LaserDisc. The DVD includes both versions.

The French Connection (dir. William Friedkin, 1971) Police
VHS: FOX
LaserDisc: FOX
DVD: FOX
> Released in pan-and-scan on VHS and in alternative pan-and-scan and letterbox versions on LaserDisc. The letterboxed Fox Five Star DVD includes two documentaries, seven deleted scenes, and additional supplementary material.

Klute (dir. Alan J. Pakula, 1971) Unofficial Detective; Victim
VHS: WARNER
LaserDisc: WARNER
DVD: WARNER
> Released in alternative pan-and-scan and letterboxed editions on both VHS and LaserDisc. The letterboxed DVD includes a documentary.

Shaft (dir. Gordon Parks, 1971) Private Eye
VHS: WARNER
LaserDisc: n/a
DVD: WARNER
> Released in pan-and-scan on VHS and letterboxed on DVD.

The Godfather (dir. Francis Ford Coppola, 1972) Gangster
VHS: PARAMOUNT
LaserDisc: PIONEER
DVD: PARAMOUNT
> Released in alternative pan-and-scan and letterboxed versions on VHS and letterboxed on LaserDisc. A letterboxed "*Godfather* DVD Collection" includes a production documentary, voice-over commentary by the director, and additional supplementary material.

The Long Goodbye (dir. Robert Altman, 1973) Private Eye
VHS: MGM
LaserDisc: MGM
DVD: n/a
> Released in pan-and-scan on VHS and letterboxed on LaserDisc.

Serpico (dir. Sidney Lumet, 1973) Police
VHS: PARAMOUNT
LaserDisc: n/a
DVD: n/a

Chinatown (dir. Roman Polanski, 1974) Private Eye
VHS: PARAMOUNT
LaserDisc: PARAMOUNT
DVD: PARAMOUNT

Released in alternative pan-and-scan and letterboxed versions on both VHS and LaserDisc, and letterboxed on DVD.

Conversation (dir. Francis Ford Coppola, 1974) Private Eye
VHS: PARAMOUNT
LaserDisc: PARAMOUNT
DVD: PARAMOUNT
Released in pan-and-scan on VHS and LaserDisc and letterboxed on DVD.

The Godfather, Part II (dir. Francis Ford Coppola, 1974) Gangster
VHS: PARAMOUNT
LaserDisc: PARAMOUNT
DVD: PARAMOUNT
Released in alternative pan-and-scan and letterboxed versions on both VHS and LaserDisc. A letterboxed "*Godfather* DVD Collection" includes a production documentary, voice-over commentary by the director, and additional supplementary material.

Murder on the Orient Express (dir. Sidney Lumet, 1974) Unofficial Detective
VHS: PARAMOUNT
LaserDisc: n/a
DVD: n/a

The Parallax View (dir. Alan J. Pakula, 1974) Unofficial Detective
VHS: PARAMOUNT
LaserDisc: n/a
DVD: PARAMOUNT
Released in pan-and-scan on VHS and letterboxed on DVD.

Night Moves (dir. Arthur Penn, 1975) Private Eye
VHS: WARNER
LaserDisc: n/a
DVD: n/a

Looking for Mr. Goodbar (dir. Richard Brooks, 1977) Victim
VHS: PARAMOUNT
LaserDisc: n/a
DVD: n/a

Blow Out (dir. Brian De Palma, 1981) Unofficial Detective
VHS: GOODTIMES
LaserDisc: IMAGE
DVD: MGM
Released in alternative pan-and-scan and letterboxed versions on LaserDisc and letterboxed on DVD.

Body Heat (dir. Lawrence Kasdan, 1981) Erotic Thriller
VHS: WARNER
LaserDisc: WARNER
DVD: WARNER
> Released in alternative pan-and-scan and letterboxed versions on Laser-Disc and letterboxed on DVD.

The Postman Always Rings Twice (dir. Bob Rafelson, 1981) Erotic Thriller
VHS: WARNER
LaserDisc: WARNER
DVD: WARNER
> All versions are pan-and-scan. The DVD includes the theatrical trailer and other supplementary material.

The Verdict (dir. Sidney Lumet, 1982) Lawyer
VHS: FOX
LaserDisc: FOX
DVD: n/a
> Released in pan-and-scan on VHS and in alternative pan-and-scan and letterboxed version on LaserDisc.

Blood Simple (dir. Joel Coen, 1984) Film Noir
VHS: MCA
LaserDisc: n/a
DVD: MCA
> The letterboxed DVD follows the director's 2000 rerelease cut in trimming several minutes.

Blue Velvet (dir. David Lynch, 1986) Unofficial Detective; Erotic Thriller
VHS: MGM
LaserDisc: LORIMAR, WARNER
DVD: MGM
> Released in pan-and-scan on VHS and Lorimar LaserDisc and letterboxed on Warner LaserDisc and DVD.

Angel Heart (dir. Alan Parker, 1987) Private Eye
VHS: ARTISAN
LaserDisc: IMAGE, ARTISAN
DVD: ARTISAN
> The Artisan LaserDisc is letterboxed; all other versions are pan-and-scan.

Fatal Attraction (dir. Adrian Lyne, 1987) Erotic Thriller
VHS: PARAMOUNT
LaserDisc: PARAMOUNT
DVD: PARAMOUNT

Released on LaserDisc in both pan-and-scan and letterboxed versions. The letterboxed version includes an alternative ending, as do some videotape prints and the letterboxed DVD, which also adds an audio commentary by the director and three documentary featurettes.

RoboCop (dir. Paul Verhoeven, 1987) Police
VHS: MGM
LaserDisc: IMAGE, CRITERION
DVD: IMAGE
Released in alternative pan-and-scan (Image) and letterboxed (Criterion) versions on both VHS and LaserDisc and letterboxed on DVD.

The Untouchables (dir. Brian De Palma, 1987) Police; Gangster
VHS: PARAMOUNT
LaserDisc: PARAMOUNT
DVD: PARAMOUNT
Released in alternative pan-and-scan and letterboxed versions on both VHS and LaserDisc and letterboxed on DVD.

The Accused (dir. Jonathan Kaplan, 1988) Victim
VHS: PARAMOUNT
LaserDisc: PARAMOUNT
DVD: PARAMOUNT
Both videotape and LaserDisc are pan-and-scan; the DVD is letterboxed.

A Fish Called Wanda (dir. Charles Crichton, 1988) Comedy
VHS: MGM, FOX
LaserDisc: MGM, FOX
DVD: MGM
The DVD includes both pan-and-scan and letterboxed versions. All other versions are pan-and-scan.

GoodFellas (dir. Martin Scorsese, 1990) Gangster
VHS: WARNER
LaserDisc: WARNER
DVD: WARNER
Released in alternative pan-and-scan and letterboxed versions on VHS and letterboxed on LaserDisc and DVD.

Presumed Innocent (dir. Alan J. Pakula, 1990) Lawyer
VHS: WARNER
LaserDisc: WARNER
DVD: WARNER
Released in pan-and-scan on VHS and letterboxed on LaserDisc. The DVD includes both versions.

Reversal of Fortune (dir. Barbet Schroeder, 1990) Lawyer
VHS: WARNER
LaserDisc: n/a
DVD: WARNER
> Released in pan-and-scan on VHS and letterboxed on DVD.

Boyz N the Hood (dir. John Singleton, 1991) Gangster
VHS: COLUMBIA
LaserDisc: COLUMBIA, CRITERION
DVD: COLUMBIA
> Released in alternative pan-and-scan and letterboxed versions on VHS and Columbia LaserDisc, and letterboxed on Criterion LaserDisc. The DVD includes both versions.

One False Move (dir. Carl Franklin, 1991) Police; Gangster
VHS: COLUMBIA
LaserDisc: COLUMBIA
DVD: COLUMBIA
> Released in pan-and-scan on VHS and letterboxed on LaserDisc and DVD.

The Silence of the Lambs (dir. Jonathan Demme, 1991) Police
VHS: MGM
LaserDisc: COLUMBIA, CRITERION
DVD: MGM
> Released in pan-and-scan on VHS and Columbia LaserDisc, letterboxed on Criterion LaserDisc, and in alternative pan-and-scan and letterboxed versions on DVD.

Basic Instinct (dir. Paul Verhoeven, 1992) Erotic Thriller
VHS: ARTISAN
LaserDisc: ARTISAN
DVD: ARTISAN
> Released in pan-and-scan on VHS, letterboxed on DVD, and in alternative pan-and-scan and letterboxed versions on LaserDisc.

A Few Good Men (dir. Rob Reiner, 1992) Lawyer
VHS: COLUMBIA
LaserDisc: COLUMBIA
DVD: COLUMBIA
> Released in alternative pan-and-scan and letterboxed versions on VHS and letterboxed on LaserDisc and DVD.

The Firm (dir. Sydney Pollack, 1992) Lawyer
VHS: PARAMOUNT
LaserDisc: PARAMOUNT
DVD: PARAMOUNT

Released in pan-and-scan on VHS, letterboxed on DVD, and in alternative pan-and-scan and letterboxed versions on LaserDisc.

Reservoir Dogs (dir. Quentin Tarantino, 1992) Gangster
VHS: ARTISAN
LaserDisc: ARTISAN, PIONEER
DVD: ARTISAN
Released in alternative pan-and-scan and letterboxed versions on VHS and on Live LaserDisc, and letterboxed on Pioneer LaserDisc. The DVD includes both versions.

The Fugitive (dir. Andrew Davis, 1993) Victim
VHS: WARNER
LaserDisc: WARNER
DVD: WARNER
Released in alternative pan-and-scan and letterboxed versions on VHS and letterboxed on LaserDisc and DVD.

Menace II Society (dir. Albert and Allen Hughes, 1993) Gangster
VHS: COLUMBIA, IMAGE, NEW LINE
LaserDisc: IMAGE, CRITERION
DVD: NEW LINE
Released in pan-and-scan on VHS and letterboxed on LaserDisc and DVD. The Criterion LaserDisc includes an audio commentary by the directors and additional supplementary material.

The Last Seduction (dir. John Dahl, 1994) Erotic Thriller
VHS: POLYGRAM
LaserDisc: IMAGE
DVD: POLYGRAM
Originally intended for theatrical release, but shown first on HBO in the Academy ratio, which all versions reproduce; the DVD adds a letterboxed alternative.

Pulp Fiction (dir. Quentin Tarantino, 1994) Gangster
VHS: BUENA VISTA
LaserDisc: MIRAMAX, CRITERION
DVD: BUENA VISTA
Released on VHS and LaserDisc in alternative pan-and-scan and letterboxed versions and letterboxed on DVD. The Criterion LaserDisc includes two deleted scenes, an interview with the director, and additional supplementary material.

Devil in a Blue Dress (dir. Carl Franklin, 1995) Unofficial Detective; Private Eye
VHS: COLUMBIA

LaserDisc: COLUMBIA
DVD: COLUMBIA
> Released in pan-and-scan on VHS and letterboxed on LaserDisc and DVD.

Heat (dir. Michael Mann, 1995) Gangster; Police
VHS: WARNER
LaserDisc: WARNER
DVD: WARNER
> Released in alternative pan-and-scan and letterboxed versions on VHS and letterboxed on LaserDisc and DVD.

Se7en (*aka Seven*) (dir. David Fincher, 1995) Police
VHS: NEW LINE
LaserDisc: IMAGE, CRITERION
DVD: NEW LINE
> Released in pan-and-scan on VHS and letterboxed on LaserDisc and DVD. The Criterion LaserDisc includes audio commentary by several members of the cast and crew and additional supplementary material.

The Usual Suspects (dir. Bryan Singer, 1995) Gangster; Police
VHS: MGM
LaserDisc: IMAGE, POLYGRAM
DVD: MGM
> Released in alternative pan-and-scan and letterboxed versions on VHS; the DVD includes both versions. Both LaserDisc pressings are letterboxed; the Polygram release includes audio commentary by the writer and director.

Bound (dir. Andy and Larry Wachowski, 1996) Erotic Thriller
VHS: REPUBLIC
LaserDisc: REPUBLIC
DVD: REPUBLIC
> Released in pan-and-scan on VHS and letterboxed on LaserDisc and DVD. The LaserDisc includes audio commentary by the directors, the stars, and others.

Fargo (dir. Joel Coen, 1996) Comedy; Police
VHS: MGM
LaserDisc: POLYGRAM
DVD: MGM
> Released in pan-and-scan on VHS and letterboxed on LaserDisc and DVD.

Set It Off (dir. F. Gary Gray, 1996) Gangster
VHS: NEW LINE
LaserDisc: IMAGE
DVD: NEW LINE
> Released in pan-and-scan on VHS and letterboxed on LaserDisc and DVD.

L.A. Confidential (dir. Curtis Hanson, 1997). Police
VHS: WARNER
LaserDisc: WARNER
DVD: WARNER
> Released in both pan-and-scan and letterboxed versions on VHS and letterboxed on LaserDisc and DVD.

Memento (dir. Christopher Nolan, 2000) Film Noir
VHS: COLUMBIA
LaserDisc: n/a
DVD: COLUMBIA
> Released in pan-and-scan on VHS and letterboxed on DVD.

Traffic (dir. Steven Soderbergh, 2000) Police; Gangster; Victim
VHS: POLYGRAM
LaserDisc: n/a
DVD: POLYGRAM
> Released in pan-and-scan on VHS and letterboxed on DVD.

Producers

The following studios do not sell directly to the public the films they release:

Artisan Entertainment
  15400 Sherman Way, Suite 500, P.O. Box 10124, Van Nuys, CA 91406

CBS/Fox Video
  P.O. Box 900, Beverly Hills, CA 90213

Columbia Tristar Home Video
  Sony Pictures Plaza, 10202 W. Washington Blvd., Culver City, CA 90232

MCA/Universal Home Video
  70 Universal City Plaza, Universal City, CA 91608-9955

MGM/UA Home Entertainment
  2500 Broadway, Santa Monica, CA 90404-6061

Paramount Home Video
  Bludhorn Building, 5555 Melrose Ave., Los Angeles, CA 90038

Polygram Filmed Entertainment
  Doornveld 1 Box 42, Zellic, 1731 Belgium

Republic Pictures Home Video
  5700 Wilshire Blvd., Suite 525, Los Angeles, CA 90036

Turner Home Entertainment
  P.O. Box 105366, Atlanta, GA 35366

Warner Home Video
  4000 Warner Blvd., Burbank, CA 91522

Distributors

The following video producers do sell directly to the public:

Allied Artists Entertainment Group
3415 Sepulveda Blvd., Los Angeles, CA 90034

Anchor Bay Entertainment/Video Treasures
1699 Stutz Ave., Troy, MI 48084

Buena Vista Home Video
350 S. Buena Vista St., Burbank, CA 91521-7145

The Criterion Collection
578 Broadway, Suite 1106, New York, NY 10012

Goodtimes Entertainment
www.goodtimes.com

Image Entertainment
9333 Oso Ave., Chatsworth, CA 91311

Key Video
2334 W. North Ave., Chicago, IL 60647

Kino on Video
333 W. 39th St., Suite 503, New York, NY 10018

Library of Congress Video Collection,c/o Smithsonian Video
955 L'Enfant Plaza, Suite 7100, Washington, DC 20560

Lumivision
877 Federal Blvd., Denver, CO 80204

MPI Home Video
16101 S. 108th Ave., Orland Park, IL 60467

Madacy Video
31304 Via Colinas, #103, Westlake Village, CA 91362
www.madacyvideo.com

Miramax Pictures Home Video
7920 Sunset Blvd., Suite 230, Los Angeles, CA 90046-3353

New Line Home Video
116 N. Robertson Blvd., Los Angeles, CA 90048

Pioneer Laser Entertainment, c/o LDC America
2265 E. 220th St., P.O. Box 22782, Long Beach, CA 90810

Teakwood Video
7954 Transit Rd., Suite 206, Williamsville, NY 14221

Time-Life Video and Television
1450 E. Parham Rd., Richmond, VA 23280

Trimark Pictures
   4553 Glencoe Ave., Marina Del Rey, CA 90292

Troma Entertainment
   733 Ninth Ave., New York, NY 10019

20th Century–Fox Home Entertainment
   2121 Avenue of the Stars, 25th floor, Los Angeles, CA 90067

VCI Home Video
   11333 E. 60th Pl., Tulsa, OK 74146-6828

Winstar Home Video
   685 Third Ave., New York, N.Y. 10017

The following distributors handle video software from many producers:

amazon.com
   www.amazon.com

Barnes and Noble
   www.bn.com

BigStar
   www.bigstar.com

Critics' Choice Video
   900 N. Rohlwing Rd., Itasca, IL 60067
   ccvideo.com

Digital Eyes
   www.digitaleyes.net

Express.com
   www.dvdexpress.com

Facets Multimedia
   1517 W. Fullerton Ave., Chicago, IL 60614; 1-800-331-6197
   www.facets.org

Ken Crane's DVD/LaserDisc
   www.kencranes.com

Movies Unlimited
   3015 Darnell Rd., Philadelphia, PA 19154-3295; 1-800-668-4344
   www.moviesunlimited.com

Timeless Video
   10010 Canoga Ave., #B-2, Chatsworth, CA 91311
   www.timeless-video.com

Video Yesteryear
   Box C, Sandy Hook, CT 06482

yahoo.com
   www.shopping.yahoo.com

Index

Note: All titles not otherwise marked refer to films, which are followed by their release date and director. When books, radio and television programs, films, and remakes bear the same title, they are listed as separate chronological entries. Fictional characters are indexed only when their life extends beyond one book or film. The titles of books and essays are indexed only when they are mentioned in the text, and names in the endnotes are indexed only when there is no direct reference to the corresponding passage in the text. Boldface numbers refer to illustrations.